Chicago

GENERAL MAP OF THE CITY SHOWING SEVERAL IMPORTANT NEIGHBORHOODS. (DENNIS MCCLENDON.)

A Biography

CHICAGO

DOMINIC A. PACYGA

THE UNIVERSITY OF CHICAGO PRESS Chicago & London

The University of Chicago Press, Chicago 60637
The University of Chicago Press, Ltd., London
© 2009 by The University of Chicago
All rights reserved. Published 2009.
Paperback edition 2011
Printed in the United States of America

20 19 18 17 16 15 14 13 12   5 6 7 8

ISBN-13: 978-0-226-64431-8 (cloth)
ISBN-13: 978-0-226-64428-8 (paper)
ISBN-10: 0-226-64431-6 (cloth)
ISBN-10: 0-226-64428-6 (paper)

Library of Congress Cataloging-in-Publication Data

Pacyga, Dominic A.
  Chicago: a biography / Dominic A. Pacyga.
    p. cm.
  Includes index.
  ISBN-13: 978-0-226-64431-8 (cloth: alk. paper)
  ISBN-10: 0-226-64431-6 (cloth: alk. paper)
  1. Chicago (Ill.)—History. I. Title.
  F548.3.P339 2009
  977.3'11—dc22
                                        2009001192

♾ This paper meets the requirements of ANSI/NISO Z39.48-1992
(Permanence of Paper).

To Kathy, for everything

Contents

Writing an Urban Biography

Chicago has been called by many different names. New York journalists gave it the sobriquet "Windy City," referring to the city's boastful politicians. Some have called it the "City That Works." Many have referred to it as "the most American city." Other observers have said Chicago is a "real" city, "City of the Big Shoulders," or even "The Jungle." Chicagoans boasted of their home as the "Paris of the Midwest," a place of beauty and culture, while some have seen it as a cold, capitalist, soulless place, a "City on the Make," in the words of one of its greatest writers, Nelson Algren.

Whatever Chicago has been called, it certainly has made an impression from the very beginning. Poets, artists, kings, emperors, presidents, and everyday people have tried to capture the city's essence. Some have left memorable impressions, but none have captured it fully. Given the history of the place, it would be folly to try. There seems to be a different Chicago around every street corner, behind every bar, and within every apartment, two-flat, cottage, or bungalow. City of immigrants or city of heartless plutocrats, say what you will, Chicago almost defies interpretation. In many ways Chicago is like a snake that sheds its skin every thirty years or so and puts on a new coat to conform to a new reality.

Writing the history of such a place obviously presents its problems. What approach should the historian take? I chose to call this an urban biography because I felt that perhaps the art of the biographer might capture at least part of the spirit of this place. A biographer sifts through his subject's life and highlights those people, places, events, and relationships that capture the essence of the individual. This is not a complete history of Chicago—that would take much more space than a single book. Still the city's trends and highlights make for a compelling story, one that I have been telling for some thirty years both in and out of the classroom and on and off of the printed page. Put simply, my goal is to try and tell the story of Chicago through events major and minor that I believe explain its importance to America and the world.

LINSEED OIL
WHEN BUYING
QUALITY Is ALWAYS Important
YOU can't afford to take CHANCES

"THE KING" Is Always THE BEST
THEREFORE ORDER
"THE KING"
MADE ONLY BY
The Chicago White Lead & Oil Co.
Green and Fulton Streets, - CHICAGO, ILLINOIS

Figure 1. Chicago developed a diverse economic base supplying natural resources and finished products across its ever-expanding hinterland. (Advertising, Author's Collection.)

Chicago is already perhaps the most written about city in the world.[1] It has had many suitors. It has always been an immigrant city, a place that others have come to try and make their own. From the arrival of Marquette and Jolliet to the appearance of today's new "settlers," Chicago has presented both challenges and opportunities to those who come to the southwestern shore of Lake Michigan. Cultural clash has long been the name of the game. Native Americans clashed with French, British, and American invaders. The Yankee entrepreneurs who left their stony New England and Upstate New York homes to place their cultural and economic mark on the city and create its future built a Yankee city and tied it to New York and the East Coast only to have it overwhelmed by others. In turn, they took their fortunes and moved to the suburbs and points west, setting the stage for others to do the same. Intruders have always found a home in Chicago, whether they were French fur traders, German "Forty-Eighters," Irish workers, Christians or Jews from the "other" Europe, African Americans from the South, Mexicans, Chinese, Vietnamese, Nigerians, Indians, Palestinians, or any of the myriad groups in search of opportunity. Much of Chicago's history is a result of this constant assault. The city's street names and church cornerstones, its institutions and politics, tell the tale of this constant transformation. It is a story difficult to convey, but one that captures America's history in the telling.

Why did they come? The Lithuanian characters in Upton Sinclair's epic novel *The Jungle* came to make their fortune and a better life among the packinghouses and two-flats of the South Side. They dreamt of returning to their homeland as successes with enough money to buy land and live the life of the gentry. Instead, they found the horrors of American industrial capitalism and a Social Darwinian reality on muddy streets. While Sinclair exaggerated to make his point, it was the same one that Hamlin Garland, Theodore Dreiser, and other writers also made over and over again. Chicago could be a cold and heartless place. As a young Norwegian immigrant would warn his family and friends back home, this was not an easy place to work or live. Yet it presented opportunity, and that managed to attract these colonists, for colonists they were, to this place on a slow-moving river that somehow tied the emerging country together. William Ogden came to town from New York to sell his brother-in-law's land and stayed on to become mayor and make a fortune. Men like Ogden built the railroads that connected the two coasts and made Chicago the nation's economic center. Many followed, but few attained his level of success.

Before the Civil War, Chicago had already become an important lake port and gate to the West. The struggle that ensued made Chicago the Emporium of the West and the driving power source for the expansion of the Republic. By the end of the Civil War, Chicago's success and permanence was ensured— even the devastating fires of 1871 and 1874 could not bring it to its knees. Those events, along with mass industrialization ushered in a new era of cultural, social, and economic turmoil in Chicago and other American cities. The last third of the nineteenth century saw the city as a major center of radical thought and of attempts to change and even destroy the emerging industrial capitalist system.

Figure 2. Chicago's downtown expanded after the fire. The Wells-Monroe Building (formerly the Pancoe Building and the Indian Building) stood just outside the cable car loop in 1889. (Albertype-neg 8-10, Chicago History Museum.)

Chicago struggled with and reflected these changes in different ways, ranging from George Pullman's hope for utopia with a profit, to Jane Addams's settlement house, or to the countless ethnic groups who built communities throughout the city and suburbs. Sometimes their goals clashed and the Great Emporium became a city of violence. The Bloody Summer of 1877, the Haymarket riot, and the Pullman strike haunted America and brought a different image of Chicago than its elite families hoped to portray. Anarchism worried Chicago and the nation's wealthy, from the Haymarket clash through the Democratic Party's convention of 1968, as did the gangsters that always seemed to be part of the city's daily life, contributing their own form of anarchy.

Any city that played such an important role in the development of the American economy was necessarily on the cutting edge of technological change. Indeed, the city grew as a result of a planned canal and then prospered as railroads almost immediately made that canal obsolete. Chicago is the home of vast technological changes resulting both from peace and war. The Loop positioned Chicago as a leader in architecture with its startling skyscrapers heralding a new American approach to the ancient art of building. The downtown, proscribed first by a tight cable car loop and then the Union Elevated, became a forest of buildings reaching for the sky. After the disaster of the fire, Chicago attracted new and young architects who rebuilt it several times, amazing European and American visitors with a vision of a future more realistic than the White City of the Columbian Exposition of 1893.

Chicago also led the way in creating a new economy. In 1848 the Board of Trade established a new way of giving order to the vast wealth of the nation's farms. Seventeen years later the Union Stock Yard opened. These two institutions enhanced Chicago's reputation as the driver of change and also as the forefront of greed as the city's traders controlled the flow of grain, lumber, and livestock across the world. Names such as Armour, Swift, and Wilson became known worldwide. The city's slaughterhouses symbolized the new industrial economy in many different ways, as Chicago's businessmen quickly seized their opportunities and Chicago's workers resisted their power.

But of course a city is more than its economy. Chicago has also been called a "City of Neighborhoods" and a "City of Churches," and its ethnic stores, churches, and ubiquitous saloons helped create the city and its reputation. In many ways, they embodied an alternate core of convictions and apprehensions to those held by the downtown business elite. What is a neighborhood? This is a question that everyday residents of Chicago struggled with in a much more visceral way than any sociologist, social worker, or historian could. Chicagoans have always identified themselves by their neighborhoods and in many cases by their parish, the local manifestation of the Catholic Church. Even Protestant and Jewish children often made reference to the local Catholic Church, echoing European customs in a very immigrant city. What parish are you from? What are you? These two questions often greeted newcomers to the city. An

Figure 3. State Street is pictured here looking north from about Madison Street in 1885. Chicago's Loop developed into a regional powerhouse, as all transportation systems in the area led to this retail center. (Stereopticon, Author's Collection.)

answer to either one often meant an answer to both. For example, in the 1920s or even the 1950s, if someone claimed to be from Sacred Heart Parish on South Lincoln (Wolcott) Street, it could pretty much be guessed that they were not only Polish American, but a *Polski Goral* or mountaineer, and were most certainly working class and probably knew many people who worked in the stockyards. By the end of the twentieth century that ethnic industrial Chicago had largely passed away as new immigrant waves and deindustrialization shifted the landscape. Sacred Heart Parish closed in 1990, and that event and other church closings ushered in a new era in the history of the "City of Neighborhoods."

Today Chicago has seen its way through a tremendous industrial upheaval that resulted from forces unleashed during the long cold war. It is repositioning itself as a global city with worldwide connections. But as we will see, Chicago has *always* been a global city connected to international economic, social, and cultural movements—from the time when Father Jacques Marquette and Louis Jolliet paddled across the Chicago Portage, the area was inexorably caught up in a quickly growing European economy and culture.

Chicago's South Side plays an important role in this story, as it has in my own life, so I hope readers will tolerate whatever slight bias they may find here. Except for a few short years, I have always lived as close as possible to that wonderful place where the White Sox play baseball, and I must admit I yearn for the South Side football Cardinals to return home from their wanderings across the West. But more importantly, many of the big issues Chicago has faced have been played out in a most dramatic fashion in that part of the city south of the river. Massive packinghouses and steel mills, not to mention other vast industrial developments such as Pullman City, thrived on the South Side. Large white ethnic settlements clashed with a large African American ghetto there too. Residents built effective neighborhood organizations to deal with urban problems resulting from industrialization and then what Arnold Hirsch has called the making of the second ghetto. Unions rose and fell and rose and fell again in the shadow of these industrial colossuses, which in turn disappeared under the impact of deindustrialization and globalization. Nearly all of Chicago's mayors in the twentieth century have been from those neighborhoods south of Roosevelt Road. The South Side does not contain the entire history of the city, but it highlights many of the issues that have faced Chicago since the beginning.

Location, Location, Location!

It really wasn't much of a place at all. A swamp on the shore of an enormous lake where a small, sluggish, foul-smelling river wound its way across the flat prairie and through the small forests that marked the area as one of transition, to the east lay vast woodlands, and to the west almost endless grasslands. Buffalo, elk, beavers, and wolves, as well as mosquitoes, called the place home. Native Americans also lived here, at least during part of the year. After the long, hard Illinois winter they would return to the place they called Chicago, which referred to the wild leeks or onions that proliferated in the area and gave off a distinct smell. They came to hunt and to search the river and lake for fish. In the summer, the wetlands to the southwest would dry up, and the various Native American nations that traveled to the place would have to portage their canoes to reach the little river as they made their way from the Illinois River. In the spring and fall, if the snow and rain had been plentiful, they could canoe across Mud Lake. This place at the end of the known world certainly did not hold out a lot of promise to Europeans who had come to stay in what they called North America. The Miami held sway over the area, and later the Pottawatomie replaced them. Other Native Americans such as the Ojibwa and Illinois knew the locale. None stayed year round along the banks of the Chicago River.

The French

The French were the first white men to come to the bog on the southwest shore of Lake Michigan. In 1673, Father Jacques Marquette and the explorer Louis Jolliet made their way from Green Bay to explore the West. They had been sent on their mission by the French governor of New France, Comte de Frontenac, and by Jean Talon, "Intendant of justice, policing and finance in Canada, Acadia, Newfoundland and France's other northern territories," to discover new lands for the burgeoning French Empire and to bring the word of God to those nations they might find along the way. With the voyage dedicated to the Immaculate Conception of the Blessed Virgin Mary, the priest, the explorer, and their small retinue of five men in two bark canoes made their way to the Mississippi, leaving the Mission of St. Ignace at Michilimackinac on May 17, 1673. Like so many other Europeans, Marquette and Jolliet searched for a water route across the North American continent and to China, the fabled Northwest Passage, as well as several legendary kingdoms of gold that reportedly bordered Canada. The two Frenchmen found neither gold nor a water route to China. They instead discovered the closest thing that existed to a Northwest Passage, although it did not lead to the Pacific. Rather, it led to a prosperous future that no Frenchman could have imagined in the seventeenth century.

Marquette and Jolliet visited various Indian nations along the way; each tried to dissuade them from going further west with stories of hostile tribes, wars, monsters, and even a demon that protected the Mississippi River from intruders. Marquette thanked the Indians for their advice but carried on for the greater glory of God and France. On June 10, two Miami joined the group as guides, conducting them across a portage and helping them to reach the Mississippi on June 17. As the explorers descended down the great river, the Illinois Nation welcomed them but also warned the Frenchmen not to proceed to the mouth of the river. At the end of June, the party left the Illinois country and traveled south on the Mississippi eventually reaching the Arkansas River. Here, the local Indians told them of the Spanish further south, and they decided to avoid the dangers of meeting rival Europeans. They then retraced their steps back toward Green Bay, and it was on this return voyage that the French would mark the spot of Chicago.

The expedition visited the Illinois village of Kaskasia, near present day Utica. Here Marquette promised to return to instruct the Indians in the Catholic faith. The Illinois convinced the explorers to take a "short cut" on the way back to Green Bay by entering the Illinois River and heading northeast toward Mud Lake and then Lake Michigan. Marquette and Jolliet had seen nothing like this river before. Bordered by fertile soil, its prairies and woods were filled with live game, and many small lakes and rivers covered the country. Only a short portage of about one league presented itself. The Illinois escorted the French to Lake Michigan. Despite an earlier visit by a French missionary and some fur traders, this was the defining moment in the discovery of the site of Chicago. The Frenchmen marked the portage on the map as a route that future fur traders and missionaries could take.

In 1674, Marquette planned his return to Illinois to establish a mission to the Native Americans. He was not well, but despite health problems he left the Mission of St. Ignace in November with two men, one of whom had made the earlier voyage with him. As the snow began to fall, Marquette and his entourage were forced to camp on the South Branch of the Chicago River near what today would be Damen Avenue. The priest became ill again, and expecting to die at this spot, he spent the early winter praying and preparing for his death. Shortly after Christmas, he and his companions made a special novena asking that they be blessed with the ability to finalize their plans for a permanent mission among the Indians. His health improved, and on March 29, as the ice melted on the river, the Jesuit moved on to the Illinois country farther southwest. After preaching to the Indians Marquette attempted to return to Michilimakinac but died on Friday May 19, 1675, at the age of thirty-eight. His fellow explorers buried him in the wilderness. Two years later a group of Christian Indians exhumed Marquette's body and returned it to the Jesuit Mission at St. Ignace at Michilimakinac.[1]

Marquette and Jolliet's mission to the Mississippi symbolized the two wings of European expansion in North America. Father Marquette personified the cultural expansion of Europe as embodied in Christianity and in this case particularly the Roman Catholic Church. Jolliet, however, represented the secular, political, and economic extension of Europe. Both would be very important in the story of white expansion in North America. Missionaries, explorers, and fur traders might lead the invasion, but others would soon follow in much larger numbers. These two men were but the scouts of what would soon be a massive incursion, one that would reshape the wilderness of the seventeenth century into a world metropolis.

Jolliet proved to be an astute observer. He saw the promise of the Chicago portage and its possible implications for French empire. For Jolliet, Mud Lake seemed crucial. He recommended the French build a canal that would connect the Great Lakes with the Mississippi, thus insuring French control over the interior of the continent. On the return from the 1673 voyage, Jolliet's canoe capsized and two voyageurs as well as the Indian boy who had led the expedition through the Illinois River valley died. In addition Jolliet lost his papers and maps in the catastrophe. His journal apparently survived back in the Jesuit mission, but an Indian attack later that year meant it too was lost to posterity. A map Joliet made from memory shows the importance the explorer put on the Chicago site. Despite Jolliet's reputation and recommendations, the French ignored his proposal. The rival explorer, René-Robert Cavelier Sieur La Salle, dismissed Jolliet's call for a canal. History would validate Jolliet's prophetic remarks about the site and his ambitions for Chicago, however; Chicago eventually tied the continent together and insured domination of the country's interior, but the French would not make this happen.[2]

Events in Europe often impacted those in North America. Louis Jolliet hoped to settle permanently in the Illinois River valley. In 1676, he petitioned Louis XIV, king of France, to allow him to take twenty men into the Illinois country to establish a colony. Jolliet, although a skilled geographer and a fearless explorer, operated poorly in the political realm. While he had excellent relations with the Jesuits, he understood little about the Royal Parisian Court. Jolliet had good dealings with Charles Aubert de la Chesnaye, one of the king's two tax collectors in New France and a leader of the Canadian commercial class. Jean Duchesneau, the provincial administrator, agreed to send Jolliet's request on to Paris. Unfortunately, Duchesneau had little influence in France and spent much of his energy intriguing against Governor Frontenac. The effort resulted in a resounding no to Jolliet's plans. The king and Jean-Baptiste Colbert, his minister of finance, did not want to expand France's colonies, but rather to develop France's holdings more intensely. They dreamt that the French, who had spread out across the North American interior living among and marrying Native Americans, would instead settle in large numbers in a fairly compact area such as their rivals did in New England.[3]

It does seem that La Salle was basically correct in his evaluation of the area and that Jolliet's plans may have been too hopeful given conditions at the time. LaSalle visited the area several times and hoped to expand French influence here. The waters of the Des Plaines River and Mud Lake varied considerably with the seasons, and Jolliet's plans for a short canal proved too optimistic for the technological realities of the time.

Nevertheless, the Chicago Portage attracted French fur traders and missionaries. Jesuits again visited Chicago in 1677 when Father Claude Allouez arrived. La Salle followed the priest as Frontenac's agent. After an initial voyage failed, La Salle took the Chicago Portage route in 1681. La Salle built a cabin and a stockade there, and it provided shelter for both passing missionary and fur trader alike. In 1696, Father Pinet established the Mission of the Guardian Angel at Chicago, but Frontenac ordered it closed. Two years later, however, missionaries reported that the mission was thriving. Shortly thereafter, Chicago's importance dwindled, as Indian wars threatened the French and trade shifted southward. Chicago was mentioned on occasion as a wintering place or a concentration point for military operation. A few baptisms were also listed for the area, but for the first half of the eighteenth century little was heard of Chicago.

From 1756 to 1763 during the French and Indian War (Seven Years War) trade flowed again along the portage. Once again, European affairs resonated in this area far from the centers of power, prestige, and battle. The war ended in a British victory, and while its immediate impact on Illinois and Chicago would be slight, the long-range effect of the Treaty of Paris (1763) would reshape the region. The French had lost their North American empire on the battlefields of Europe and Canada.[4] Of course, nothing much changed on the ground. No British settlements appeared in the areas along the Great Lakes, and although the French flag no longer flew, French-Indian families still carried on trade on both sides of the Mississippi. Given the technology of the time, it would be difficult for the British to wrest trade from the mixed French and Indian populations of the area (this again proved a problem later for the Americans when the territory passed into their hands after the Second Treaty of Paris in 1783). The transfer of land on paper mattered little unless soldiers and settlers alike could enforce it on the ground. In 1774, British authorities reestablished New France as Quebec, and the Chicago area remained part of the new political order that was in effect run under the old local regime. The Quebec Act and the Proclamation Act (1763), which created the Proclamation Line designed to keep British settlers east of the Appalachians, exasperated Americans. Why had the French and Indian War been fought if not to open the West to exploitation? Again, American interests seemed frustrated by a distant parliament and imperial bureaucracy.[5]

Point de Sable and the Coming of the Americans

When war finally broke out between the upstart Americans and the British in 1775, Chicago seemed little effected, even though Britain showed concern that the rebels might use the portage to create havoc in the West. At this moment, Jean Baptiste Point de Sable, a fur trader of mixed West African and French ancestry first appeared in the historical record.[6] By the late 1770s Point de Sable already operated a successful fur trading business in northern Indiana almost certainly near present day Michigan City. In 1779, British authorities arrested him and sent him to Michilimakinac, probably because of his suspected pro-French and pro-American feelings. Satisfied that de Sable was not a traitor, the following year British Lieutenant Governor Sinclair hired Point de Sable to operate the Pinery, his estate, adjoining Fort Sinclair north of Detroit, which he did until 1784, when the governor sold the land. Point de Sable then moved his family to Detroit and became associated with William Burnett, a wealthy trader who had a trading post at Chicago. Not long after, Point de Sable came to Chicago to build a home at the river's mouth.[7] He most likely arrived after the American Revolution; certainly by 1790 he was well established at Chicago, and he is recognized as the first permanent resident of the place. His post marked the beginning of continuous settlement at the mouth of the river. For the first time, Chicago was not simply a place where traders and Indians stopped occasionally—now it had a permanent resident. Point de Sable operated a farm known as the only source of produce in the area. As a British subject, he worked in the district still under de facto British control despite the 1783 treaty granting the area to the Americans. British influence did not wane in Illinois and the West until after the War of 1812.

Point de Sable married a Pottawatomie woman named Catherine and had two children; they lived on the north bank of the Chicago River, near what would later be Michigan Avenue and Pioneer Court. The family had considerable material possessions: several buildings, including a milk house, a chicken house, and a barn that housed thirty head of livestock. Most importantly, de Sable maintained a gathering place for Indian and fur trader alike. He kept up good relations with the Pottawatomie and provided supplies to anyone who could pay on the frontier.[8]

The Treaty of Greenville (1795) between the new American government and the Indians may have had a direct impact on de Sable and caused him to leave the area in 1800, as the arrival of Americans seemed more likely. General "Mad" Anthony Wayne waged war against the Indians in an attempt to break their alliance with the British. At Greenville, Native Americans ceded the area around the mouth of the Chicago River as well as land on Lake Peoria, and the free use of the Chicago harbor and portage as well as the Illinois River, to the American government. The treaty specifically mentioned, "one piece of land six miles square, at the mouth of the Chicago River, emptying into the southwest end of Lake Michigan, where a fort formerly stood." The reference to a fort is probably the old French stockade first established by La Salle in the seventeenth century. Rumors of a new American fort spread quickly.[9]

In 1800, de Sable sold his property to Jean La Lime for six thousand French livres and left for the west bank of the Mississippi, away from American influence. William Burnett financed the deal. The arrival of white Americans on the frontier meant a dim future for Point de Sable, whose black skin marked him as inferior in the white American mind. Also it seems his probable allegiance to Britain might have played a role in his decision to leave. Point de Sable may have had more than a familial and economic relationship with the Pottawatomie. There is some conjecture that he held a political or military office of some kind, but this is largely speculation. Point de Sable had moved further west to maintain his way of life among the Indians and fur traders he knew best, and the first settler on the city would not be the last Chicagoan to move on.[10]

La Lime and Burnett sold the property to John Kinzie, who arrived in 1804 from St. Joseph, Indiana. Kinzie, often called the Father of Chicago in older histories, was rather a latecomer to the area, and the title belongs more squarely with Point de Sable. Kinzie, however, had changed allegiances from Britain to the United States during the War of 1812, throwing in his lot with the young republic. For early Chicagoans and the writers of their history, a white Protestant Scotsman involved in trade and politics would be a fitting symbol for the new settlement that appeared on the banks of the Chicago River.

The U.S. Army preceded Kinzie by a few months, arriving on August 17, 1803, after a thirty-five-day land journey from Detroit. Captain John Whistler, who met the contingent of sixty-nine soldiers by boat just as they approached Chicago, headed the expedition. By the end of 1803, only four civilian homesteads stood on the north bank of the river opposite the site of the proposed fort. In the spring, soldiers completed a log fort surrounded by a double stockade with two blockhouses. Traders and others soon began to make their way to Fort Dearborn, named after Henry Dearborn, Thomas Jefferson's secretary of war. Kinzie quickly became the civilian leader of the small settlement. He served as justice of the peace and performed the first marriage at Chicago that November for James Abbott and Captain Whistler's daughter Sarah. John Kinzie competed with Ebenezer Belknap, who arrived in 1805 as the first government trader. By 1812 about ten cabins huddled near the fort with a population of about forty French Canadians, British traders, Americans, and a mixed European-Indian population living along the river. Small numbers of other settlers lived farther out in what would become Bridgeport and other more distant and sparse agricultural settlements.

Kinzie sent trading expeditions out from Chicago across the Old Northwest and obtained the privilege, in partnership with Captain Whistler's son, of providing supplies to the troops at Fort Dearborn. In addition, the Scotsman furnished local settlers, French engagés, and various travelers with necessary supplies. He also hired his men out to the government factor (trader). Kinzie even played the role of moneylender to the government and acted as a slave trader on at least one occasion.

By 1812, Fort Dearborn attracted several farmers, discharged soldiers, and a cattle dealer to the small settlement. Frontier life proved to be monotonous, and Indians, soldiers, and fur traders entertained themselves by hunting and foot racing, along with frequent drinking and fighting. In 1810, Kinzie and Whistler argued over Kinzie's willingness to trade alcohol to the Indians. The partnership between the younger Whistler and Kinzie was dissolved, and the two families' feud divided the frontier community. John Kinzie had various political connections through the American Fur Company, and in April Captain Whistler and the other principal officers of the fort were removed—the first known use of political clout in Chicago! The following June, Captain Heald took command of Fort Dearborn. Soon Heald also quarreled with Kinzie over the same issue of alcohol and Indians. Tensions in the small community continued: Indians killed two settlers on Lee's farm at Hardscrabble (Bridgeport) in April. In June 1812, John Kinzie argued with Jean La Lime and stabbed him to death just outside the fort. Kinzie fled north to Wisconsin but returned after an investigation by the Fort Dearborn authorities exonerated him. War broke out with Great Britain on June 18. All along the western frontier Indians discussed their options as the two white powers moved against each other.

On July 12, American forces invaded Canada, a campaign that proved to be a catastrophe for the United States. The British took Mackinaw on July 17 and threatened Detroit and the entire West. Captain Heald received instructions to encourage Chicago's Indians to go to a special council at Piqua (Ohio). Kinzie assisted and seventeen chiefs of the Pottawatomie, Ottawa, Chippewa, and Winnebago went to the meeting as Indians all along the frontier waited to see the outcome of the invasion of Canada.

For some time the Shawnee Indian leader Tecumseh's influence had been growing across the West. In 1795, the chief refused to attend the treaty conference at Greenville, which put an end to the Northwest Indian War waged by General "Mad" Anthony Wayne. He and his brother, Tenskwatawa, known as the Prophet, went on to convince many Native Americans that they had a last chance to drive the whites out. Tecumseh attracted militant Native Americans beyond the Shawnees. He hoped to unite the Native Americans in a more structured way than the old tribal alliances had. In 1811, the Battle of Tippeca-noe set off tensions in the West. After the attack on Lee's farm, Captain Heald raised a small militia of white settlers.

On August 8, Winamac, a Pottawatomie messenger, brought word from General Hull, ordering Heald to abandon Fort Dearborn and bring his troops to the defense of Detroit. Hull further instructed Captain Heald to distrib-ute whatever extra supplies he had to the local Indians in an attempt to win their favor. Once again alcohol became an issue. The soldiers destroyed their supply of rum and extra arms. Like a good soldier, Heald obeyed the general's orders despite his misgivings about abandoning the fort and marching across the wilderness. The destruction of liquor and weapons angered the Indians, and the distribution of the remaining goods caused a fatal delay. Meanwhile Tecumseh sent word of Hull's defeat in Canada and advised the local tribes to destroy Fort Dearborn.

On the morning of August 15, 1812, a small band of fifty-five army regulars, twelve militia, nine women, and eighteen children loaded into two wagons and left Chicago for Fort Wayne. Thirty Miami escorted the small retinue. As the procession moved south along the lakefront, other Indians ambushed them. The Miami quickly abandoned the whites, and the column was cut in two. While Heald led an attack, Indian braves quickly cut down the militia and army regulars. Two women and most of the children died in the attack, and Heald was forced to surrender. Meanwhile friendly Indians rescued the Kinzies. That night, some of the captured were ritually killed along the lakefront, their bodies undiscovered until four years later when U.S. Army troops returned. Chicago again lapsed into prairie wilderness.

On July 4, 1816, two companies of troops arrived under the command of Capt. Hezekiah Bradley to erect a new fort. The new Fort Dearborn once again attracted settlers who congregated near its gates. The eventual defeat and death of Tecumseh sealed the Indians' fate—the dream of a Pan-Indian republic died with him. Trade resumed at Chicago and, though the government factors in-creasingly lost their market to private traders, private traders gained advantage by again offering alcohol to Native Americans. The factors' business declined rapidly across the West, and the federal government officially closed all of its trading posts in 1822.

John Jacob Astor's America Fur Company, the young nation's first monop-oly, dominated the local trade. In 1819, Jean Baptiste Beaubien came to Chicago from Milwaukee to head its local interests. Beaubien quickly expanded the company. By 1822, John Craft, the leader among local traders joined the firm. From 1823 until his death Craft headed the company in Chicago eventually setting up headquarters in the old government trading post. In 1828, when the local fur trade went into steep decline, the American Fur Company sold its interests in Illinois to Gurdon S. Hubbard and moved on to other ventures further west.

As the local fur trade declined, the relationship between Native Americans and Washington, D.C., changed as Indians became dependent on the largess of the federal government. In turn, Washington put more pressure on the Indian nations to give up their land and move west. In August 1821, roughly three thousand Pottawatomie, Ottawa, and Chippewa met with federal representatives and agreed to cede 5 million acres of land in Michigan and the right of way of roads from Detroit to Fort Wayne. The government promised $6,000 in annuities to the Indians to be paid at Chicago. A new trade developed as traders arrived in the fall to take advantage of the Indians who gathered yearly for their payment of money.

Geologist William H. Keating visited Fort Dearborn as part of Major Stephen H. Long's expedition for the U.S. Army Corps of Engineers in June 1823 and found the place almost uninhabitable. Keating's work with Long represented one of the first topographic and mineralogical surveys of the Great Lakes. Chicago's appearance disappointed him and contradicted Henry R. School-craft's claim that the site was "the most fertile and beautiful that can be imagined." Keating complained about the "shallowness of the soil, from its humidity, and from its exposure to the cold and damp winds which blow from the lake with great force during most part of the year." Despite Keating's views, settlers continued to arrive at Chicago and put pressure on Native Americans.[11]

In October 1823, as the Indians no longer seemed to present a threat, the U.S. Army abandoned the garrison at Fort Dearborn. French Canadian *voyageurs* and their families quickly occupied the empty barracks. The army would not be gone for long, returning five years later as fears of another Indian attack mounted. The troops left again in May 1831 only to return the following spring as the Blackhawk War erupted. Residents formed a militia in May 1832 and regular army troops soon joined them. The arriving soldiers brought cholera, a hazard more devastating than the Indians. They also sent glowing reports about the Midwest, and Chicago in particular, to their family and friends back home, missives that spurred a wave of immigration. Soon, Yankee migrants outnumbered the old French and Indian inhabitants. The defeat of Blackhawk meant the end to any Indian threat, and the U.S. Army abandoned the fort for good in 1836 with the small community already a town and soon to proclaim itself a city.

In September 1833, the final Indian Conclave met at Chicago to negotiate the cession of land in northeastern Illinois and southwestern Wisconsin and the relocation of Native Americans west of the Mississippi River. More than six thousand Indians arrived at Chicago to meet with federal representatives, who forced the Native Americans to sign two treaties on September 26 and 27, 1833. They agreed to leave the area in three years, and the old hybrid culture that had dominated Chicago and northern Illinois since the arrival of the French soon disappeared.

Even as the Indians passed from the area, the physical shape of the future city appeared as a grid laid out by as the surveyor James Thompson in 1831. Two

Figure 4. Chicago's small frontier settlement centered on the Chicago River, as portrayed in this sketch depicting Wolf Point, now the site of the Merchandise Mart, in the early 1830s. (ICHi-20583, Chicago History Museum.)

Figure 5. This illustration of the mouth of the Chicago River in 1831 taken from a sketch by Mrs. Kinzie illustrates the importance of the army post and its relationship with the river and Chicago's small frontier settlement. The Kinzie House sits on the river directly across from Fort Dearborn. (ICHi-39375, Chicago History Museum.)

years later, residents organized Chicago as a village with a population of under five hundred residents. The years 1835 and 1836 marked the last gathering of the Indians at Chicago. These turned into huge celebrations, in which traders hoped to rid the Indians of their newly acquired federal money. In 1837, Chicago officially became a city with a population of over four thousand. Many believed the site would grow quickly if a proposed canal were built. Jolliet's dream of a canal linking the Great Lakes with the Mississippi River was to be a reality over 150 years later.[12]

The Yankees, the Canal, and the Railroads

The canal proved to be crucial for the future of the city. Residents promoted the idea even before the establishment of Illinois as a state in 1818, but funding was sparse on the frontier and such a large public works undertaking seemed impossible. As late as 1834, a proposal to lay track for an Illinois-Michigan Railroad from the city to the Illinois River looked more likely than a canal. Observers felt that either the waterway or the railroad or both would ensure Chicago's position in the West, yet it was not until 1836 that construction of the canal actually began. Even before the huge project commenced, land speculators bid up property values at an astonishing rate. Prices went up daily, even hourly, as fortunes were made and lost in the feverish speculation. Men and women crowded into taverns or onto street corners to hear of land sales. One rather ostentatious presentation saw a black man dressed in scarlet and bearing a scarlet flag riding on a white horse through the town to announce land sales, gathering crowds wherever he stopped to shout out. Easterners, primarily Yankees from New England and Upstate New York, flocked to the city to trade in land.[13]

The opening of the Erie Canal in 1825 connected New York City via the Hudson River to Buffalo and the Great Lakes. Now a water connection created an east-west trading route that required a good port as far west and south on the Great Lakes as possible. Chicago provided just such a place, with its sluggish river flowing into Lake Michigan. The river held out the promise of a vast inland harbor if only a few obstacles could be overcome. Then, if that river could be connected to the Mississippi as the proposed canal promised, trade would flow directly from the Mississippi Valley to New York without taking dangerous ocean routes. New Orleans sugar would reach the East more easily. More importantly, the new canal and the Great Lakes would push open a giant door to the yet untapped West. An added benefit of the new Erie Canal/Great Lakes/Illinois and Michigan Canal route was that it avoided much of the South at a time when slavery presented a divisive and potentially dangerous issue for Americans. One prescient observer pointed out in 1850 that this inland system could prove very important during wartime.[14]

Such dreams proved advantageous for land speculators along the canal route. Canal commissioners established several towns along the almost one-hundred-mile course of the Illinois and Michigan (I&M) Canal. These included Lemont, Lockport, and Ottawa, among others, but it was Chicago at the head of the canal that benefited the most. Chicago potentially included forty-two miles of protected harbor in its river system. The Chicago River, which was actually the confluence of three rivers that spread across the prairie with its North, South, and Main Branches, provided a wide array of land available for use by ships, docks, and granaries.

The mouth of the river, at the time just north of today's Madison Street, however, proved a problem. A long sandbar blocked direct access to the river and boats had to navigate the obstacle. From the beginning, Chicagoans depended on the federal government to spend money to improve their harbor. The federal government's land grant to the Canal Commissioners in 1827 allowed them to raise funds to build the canal system. Despite the myth of the self-made frontier town, in almost every way possible the federal government played an important role in making Chicago an attractive place for investors to make their fortunes. In 1832, the federal government built a lighthouse, and the Army Corps of Engineers cleared the sandbar and dredged the river in July 1833 to provide easier access to the river harbor from Lake Michigan. Despite various continuing problems and dredging, Chicago was established as a port, and in 1836, over two hundred ships visited Chicago to discharge their cargoes. By 1838, Congress spent over $200,000 to create Chicago's harbor, and by the mid-1840s over one thousand ships arrived annually. This waterborne trade, along with Fort Dearborn and the removal of Indians from the area, proved to be crucial for the small settlement as Chicago eventually developed into the great gateway and emporium to the West.[15]

Trade and settlement pushed the frontier farther and farther west. Americans, set free by the revolution, poured over the Appalachians and put pressure on Native Americans. The I&M Canal was the last major canal to be constructed, ending a period of intense canal building that had made possible the continued white American invasion of the West. The Erie Canal and the I&M Canal changed the whole pattern of trade and settlement in the United States, securing New York's domination of the economy. In many ways Chicago was a child of New York and the East Coast, as the merchants who had become rich on the Atlantic trade reached out to conquer a continent. Chicago provided a point for eastern capital to spread west. From its very beginnings, even as a fur trader, it tied itself to the Atlantic economy. This could be clearly seen in the sources of investment and the city's diverse population.

As Chicago rose haphazardly on the mud flat near the intersection of the river and the lake, it attracted investment from the East. In 1835, William B. Ogden arrived at the height of land fever in Chicago to supervise the sale of land that his New York investor brother-in law, Charles Butler, had purchased on a visit two years earlier. Ogden was not impressed with the muddy land and advised his relative to sell while he could. Ogden turned a good profit on the sale and decided to stay. It was not exactly El Dorado, but the young entrepreneur saw its possibilities. Ogden's arrival proved to be lucky both for the youthful, energetic, and ambitious New Yorker and for the young settlement. He rose quickly to the forefront of the emerging Yankee community, which elected him the city's first mayor in 1837.[16] Ogden represented a whole new type of western entrepreneur. These men, collectively known as "boosters," proved crucial to the city's development as they came to dominate the social, political, and economic life of the settlement. Advertising the advantages of Chicago over its other western rivals—St. Louis, Cincinnati, Galena, and Milwaukee—they exploited their connections to the Yankee East.

Land speculators rushed to the town to make their fortunes. Newcomers flooded Chicago, and storehouses had to be thrown open to shelter them as they arrived on the frontier. The city's population seemed to grow haphazardly with one estimate in 1835 claiming between 2,500 and 3,000 inhabitants, but without much reliability as to who was a resident, who was just passing through, and who was a speculator hoping to make a quick dollar and move on.[17] In July 1835, the *Chicago American* editorialized: "Old established farmers are disposing of their lands, and quitting the bleak hills of New England, and the more arable lands of New York, and are coming with their families, and all their household effects, to possess the land of higher promise and hope, and which they have long desired to see." The newspaper claimed that whole communities intended to resettle in northern Illinois, including two hundred families from one town in upstate New York.[18]

New Hampshire native John Wentworth arrived on October 25, 1836. Within a month, the six feet eleven, 330-pound giant of a man took charge of the newspaper the *Chicago Democrat* and became a force among local Jacksonians. Walter L. Newberry, formerly of Windsor Connecticut, made a fortune as a land speculator and went on to promote libraries. They joined the legendary booster John Stephen Wright, born in Sheffield, Massachusetts, who took the first census of the city and published a handsome lithographed map of the town's shacks that he termed edifices and buildings. Wright also went into the real estate business and made a fortune in those wild speculative early years. He made $200,000 by the age of twenty-one but due to the economic depression of 1837 went bankrupt at twenty-two. He then founded the *Prairie Farmer* with Vermonter Jerum Atkins and began to manufacture the Atkins Automaton, a device that severed grain from the platform of a reaper, which became a sensation in rural America for some five years. But this venture also failed as Atkins produced machines out of green wood and they broke down on farms across the Midwest. Wright then went back into real estate and attracted more eastern capital to Chicago.

With the Yankees came institutions. The Presbyterians, Methodists, Baptists, and other Protestant congregations soon followed in what had basically been a small unchurched but Roman Catholic community. In 1833, the Catholics formed their first official parish in the city, St. Mary's, to serve a new community of Irish settlers. But while the town's population always attracted a diverse group of people, the Yankees set the standards for the growing settlement.[19]

The town grew chaotically, with wooden buildings appearing at the whim of their owners who sometimes ignored the platted dirt streets. Mud was a perennial problem, especially in the spring and fall, and, of course, if the winter was not cold enough, the endless mud pits did not freeze over. Most houses huddled near the river, and sanitation presented a problem. The corner of State and Madison seemed far from the town center.

Early residents, even Yankees, often dressed in deerskin and at times painted their faces like Native Americans. Gurdon Saltonstall Hubbard, dressed in rough deerskin, traded with the Indians and had an Indian wife. Hubbard drove hogs to Chicago up what would become State Street and began the city's meatpacking business killing hogs in a warehouse at La Salle and South Water Streets. Eventually, as Chicago developed as a Yankee city, Hubbard left his Native American wife, married a white woman, and became part of the local elite, not an unusual story for the frontier.[20]

As the white population grew in Chicago and across northern Illinois, local establishments, such as the Sauganash Hotel built by Mark and Monique Beaubien in 1831 at Wolf Point (today's Wacker Drive and Lake Street), catered to newcomers. The building of the new hotel next to the owners' small cabin proved to be a wise investment as the local population boomed. While an impressive structure in the town, it was more of a frontier tavern with rooms above it than the eastern image of a hotel.

In a most precapitalist un-Chicago way of land distribution, Mark Beaubien, who had arrived in 1826, gave valuable plots of land away to friends and family. The new Yankee settlers scorned Beaubien's son, Mador, despite his Clark College education, because of his Indian heritage. He left with the Pottawatomie in 1835 donning "mourning" clothing and taking part in a funeral dance around the new Yankee city. Mador Beaubien would not be the last "real" Chicagoan to complain about "neighborhood change" and leave the town. Like many Chicagoans after them, the Beaubiens moved on, and in 1843 they exchanged the Sauganash for a tavern close to Naperville on the Southwest Plank Road in what is today west suburban Lisle. Beuabien said he "didn't expect no town."[21]

By the end of 1833, a new Chicago appeared, as more Yankees arrived, changing the town's culture. Those who settled in the city created Chicago's first building boom. Between 1834 and 1837, as the population surged, Chicagoans built over three hundred buildings. Others settled on the outskirts of the settlement. Proximity to Fort Dearborn was no longer seen as a necessity as the Pottawatomie left the region. Outlying regions also witnessed construction and growth. In 1835, Methodists had a regular preaching circuit that included Yorkville, Oswego, Aurora, St. Charles, Winfield, Elk Grove, Wheeling, Plum Grove, Libertyville, Deer Grove, Crystal Lake, and Dundee. By 1840, Chicago with a population of 4,470 competed with Lemont, Thornton, Naperville, Lockport, Waukegan, and Blue Island and other small settlements.[22]

William Bross first came to the city in 1846 and later recalled that most homes stood between Randolph and Madison Streets, although some scattered residences stood as far south as Van Buren Street and some four or five blocks north of the river with a scattering of homes on the West Side. A few wholesale houses stood on Water Street, while most of the retail stores operated on Lake Street. The so-called balloon frame building, although probably not invented in Chicago by Augustine Taylor as traditionally believed, came to dominate construction. Steam-powered saws providing mass-produced two-by-four lumber and the mass production of nails made quick, light frame production possible and supplied most of the construction in the frontier city and across the area.

Streets remained unpaved, and the problem of mud made travel difficult throughout much of the year. Chicagoans had to wade knee deep in mud to get around the town. Wagons got stuck in the mud. City people could not get about in the sea of mud, and farmers could not get into the city to sell their produce. The streets were simply country lanes hastily planked over. As Chicago-

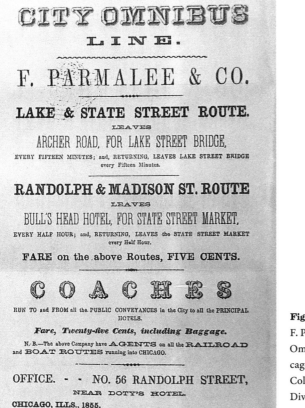

Figure 6. Advertisement for F. Parmalee and Company Omnibus Line, 1855. (Chicago Public Library, Special Collections and Preservation Divisions.)

ans tried to find humor in the situation they often decorated holes left behind after the drays were dug out with signs that read "No Bottom Here" or "The Shortest Road to China." Sometimes an old hat and coat would be nailed to a sign that said "On His Way to the Lower Regions." One of the first attempts to deal with the mud was the planking of Lake Street, which was intended to allow sewage to flow through the gutters to the river, but the experiment failed and the stench under the planked street became unbearable.[23]

In many ways Chicago remained a frontier settlement. No public transportation existed, so many Chicagoans lived near or in the same building in which they worked. This "walking-city" meant congestion and the unintended integration of Chicago by race, ethnicity, and social class. Until the 1850s, Chicago remained very much a male city. Few institutions for the young, such as schools, existed. A more equitable gender balance grew in the 1850s as the city acquired the characteristics of a nonfrontier settlement. But the city first developed as a fast growing merchant city with few niceties populated by young men seeking their fortunes.

The omnibus, little more than an extended stagecoach, provided the first public transportation system in the city. In 1852, M. Laflin established an omnibus line that ran from the State Street Market to the Bull's Head Hotel

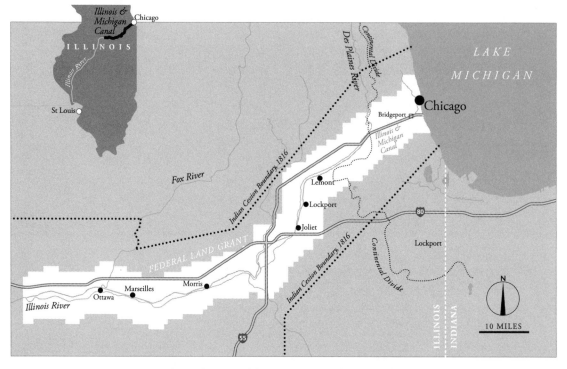

Map 1. This maps shows the route of the Illinois and Michigan Canal as it connects Chicago first to the Illinois and then to the Mississippi River, greatly expanding the city's hinterland and creating an east-west trade pattern. (Dennis McClendon.)

along Randolph Street. Peck and Company followed with a route from the Lake Street Bridge to Twelfth Street along State Street every hour with the line eventually being extended to the city limits at Twenty-second Street. J. Frink and Company ran an omnibus from the Lake House on the North Side down Clark Street to the Michigan Southern Railroad Depot that same year. The *Daily Democrat* pointed to the new omnibus lines as both a convenience and as evidence of the city's growing prosperity.[24]

The I&M Canal remained central to the city's future. Most businesses gathered along the riverfront. Construction began in 1836 but soon hit a glitch with the 1837 economic panic and subsequent depression. In 1843, the canal board suspended construction of the huge public works project. Work resumed in 1845, and the canal finally opened in 1848, tying the Great Lakes with the Mississippi. In its first year of existence the sixty-foot-wide six-foot-deep canal was open 224 days, and the canal commission collected $87,890 in tolls.[25]

In the beginning, traffic on the canal included passengers as well as all types of freight. Sugar and molasses from New Orleans, as well as corn, wheat, sugar, and coal, made their way into the port of Chicago. Out of the city came lumber, salt, and manufactured merchandise supplying the farmers and smaller cities of the West. The I&M Canal proved an instant success and a much quicker way to move across the mud-filled prairies. In 1850, which the *Tribune* considered to be a rather ordinary year in trade without either an economic collapse nor extraordinary prosperity, the canal carried a great deal of the city's commerce despite competition from the expanding railroad system. St. Louis, Chicago's principal rival for the Mississippi trade, saw itself embarrassed by a lack of grain from its usual suppliers, and the shortage drove up the price. Looking to Chicago for help, the city shipped 34,439 barrels of flour and 95,193 bushels of wheat down the canal to St. Louis from March 15 until July 10. Over seventeen thousand passengers used the canal in 1850. In its first nine years the I&M Canal collected $1,606,000 in tolls.

Together the canal and the harbor ensured Chicago's role as a great port. By 1854, the *Cleveland Herald* pronounced Chicago the busiest of the Great Lakes' ports. In May 1856, the *Tribune* listed the ships that had arrived and departed in just two days. The list included cargoes that consisted primarily of lumber but also iron, horses, apples, salt, and other goods. Traffic clogged the docks of the city and kept the bridges open, blocking street traffic to the North and West sides. One observer pointed to the crowds that gathered on both banks of the river when the Clark Street Bridge opened to let ships and barges pass.[26] It was no wonder that residential and commercial development on the North and West sides were slowed by river traffic. The canal, river, and lake provided the basis for the city's early growth as a leading mercantile city in the West. The *New York Tribune* stated that Chicago prospered despite its disadvantages (especially the constant mud) because it provided the natural merging point for the produce of the West. Chicago serviced a huge territory that was not "blighted by Slavery."[27]

The lake trade had its problems. Storms caused wrecks, and ships cluttered the bottom of the Great Lakes. Lake sailors worked very long hours under difficult conditions. One sailor, in answer to a published complaint in the *Tribune* in 1852 pointed to the harsh conditions of the lumber trade on the Great Lakes. He wrote about sheer exhaustion and chided "Mr. Sleep" for not recognizing the sailors' humanity, arguing that sailors were not simply "tools to get rich." Sailors found their way to Chicago neighborhoods that took on all the characteristics of ports anywhere with cheap hotels, taverns, and brothels operating along streets leading to the river. In the southern part of downtown and the nearby Lower West Side (Pilsen) ships' masts towered over the docks and vied with church steeples as the tallest structures of the city. Masts could be seen from across the prairie. The lake trade made Chicago, but it would soon have competition as technology again changed the American economy.[28]

Before a rail connection was built, the trip to Chicago from Detroit was a long one. In 1848, two routes existed either via the lakes or by the Michigan Central Railroad and stagecoach. During the summer season, lake travelers leaving Detroit reached Chicago on Sunday at sunrise after a 1,500-mile five-day water journey on Lakes Huron and Michigan at a cost of $21.00 ($462.41

Figure 7. The Sisters of Mercy, a Catholic order from Ireland, converted the Lake House on the river near the Rush Street bridge into Mercy Hospital, the first chartered hospital in Chicago, in 1852. In 1859, Mercy Hospital became the first Catholic hospital to affiliate with a medical school, Lind Medical School. (Sisters of Mercy Chicago Regional Community Archives.)

in 2007). Rail travelers took the Michigan Central daily at Detroit at 8:00 a.m. and arrived at Kalamazoo at 6:00 p.m. Stagecoaches then left Kalamazoo at 7:00 p.m. (or after the arrival of a late train) and arrived at St. Joseph's on Lake Michigan at 7:00 a.m., a trip of fifty-five miles. A steamboat left daily after the arrival of the stage and made the sixty-nine-mile trip to Chicago, arriving at about 2:00 p.m. The fare, paid at Detroit, was $6.50 ($143.13). All of this changed within a matter of years as rail lines spread across the American West making the trip safer, faster, and more comfortable.[29]

William B. Ogden, who had been a driving force behind the I&M Canal, also provided the energy for the Galena Railroad. In 1847, finding it difficult to attract eastern capital as he had for the canal, Ogden scoured the countryside along the planned route of the Galena and Chicago Union (G&CU) Railroad and raised stock subscriptions from farmers and others interested in the success of the new transportation form. Six months after the canal opened, the G&CU Railroad made its way west from Chicago to Oak Park. The railroad proved an unqualified success. In its first full year (January 1, 1849, to December 1, 1849) the railroad made a profit of $23,763. The following year the main branch, with its three locomotives going west from the city, earned $104,359.62. Two other branches also opened: the St. Charles Branch in December 1849 and the Aurora Branch in September 1850. The *Tribune* stated in 1850, "The business of the Road and its branches has thus far exceeded the expectations of the most sanguine of its friends." Within seven years, Chicago became the center of the nation's railroad industry. In 1855, seventeen railroad lines made their way to and from the city, including the new vital rail connection to the East Coast. The federal government gave out massive land grants to the railroads as they soon fulfilled their promise to unite the country with a national market as rail lines reached out from Chicago in every direction.

Nothing succeeds like success, and soon other railroads radiated from the city. Investors planned a new railroad to southern Illinois as the city searched out a wider and wider hinterland for its markets and those of the East. The *Tribune* predicted a prosperous future for the city and Illinois, proclaiming that "Chicago will be the commercial centre of a numerous, wealthy and prosperous people." Meanwhile Great Lakes shipping brought the iron to lay the new vast railroad system. In September 1852, the brig *Andes* brought 312 tons of railroad iron for the Illinois Central Railroad, while the brig *Preble* unloaded 234 more tons for the building of the Illinois and Wisconsin Railroad. The *Daily Democrat* proclaimed that Chicago's "Manifest Destiny" was to tie the center of the country together with an "iron band" of railroads from the Gulf of Mexico to Lake Superior.[30]

New rail lines changed the market dynamic across Illinois and the Midwest in the last half of the nineteenth century. Now, marginal farms located an impractical distance from the canal could take part in Chicago's new market system. Farms a day's journey from the Chicago market might now just be a few hours from Market Square. Subsistence farming soon gave way to market farming and even specialization. Soon farmers concentrated on dairying, truck farming, or haying. Others raised grain and livestock. Horse breeding took precedence for others as the city provided a great market for the animals. In 1855 4,513,202 bushels of wheat and over 3,760,000 bushels of corn came into the city on the G&CU Railroad alone. The Rock Island Railroad, which competed directly with the I&M Canal, brought in over nine hundred thousand bushels of wheat that same year. One railroad alone shipped over ten thousand head of cattle from Chicago to New York in 1855.

Whereas older market towns had arisen near crossroads and waterways, market centers appeared near railroad stops throughout the region. Milk stops and cheese and condensed milk factories appeared across Illinois and Wisconsin. Lisle, Geneva, and other such rural communities supplied Chicago with milk. Specific ethnic groups often dominated these various settlements—the Irish in Lemont, the Dutch in South Holland, the Germans in Niles Center, and the Swedes in many northwestern Indiana communities.[31]

The city developed into a vast marketplace for lumber, grain, livestock, and produce even as it became a distribution point for eastern goods such as stoves, clothing, and hardware. The vast western hinterland needed lumber to build

CHICAGO FROM THE LAKE.

Figure 8. The mouth of the Chicago River pictured in 1850. By this time the full impact of the canal and lake trade could be seen as the city developed into a busy harbor employing immigrants and native born alike. (ICHi-39370, Chicago History Museum.)

farmhouses, silos, barns, and towns. Chicago, located within reach of the vast forests of Michigan and Wisconsin, was the obvious gathering and shipping point for the industry. Water traffic was crucial to this movement of pine toward its natural market in the West. Lake Michigan funneled lumber to the Port of Chicago, which could then send it on its way. The city "lay not only on the border between forest and grassland, but also on the happy margin between supply and demand."[32] Chicago's vast lumberyards were famous the world over. In 1850, over 100 million feet of lumber arrived in the city by Great Lakes shipping. Of this amount, 1,500,000 feet planked Chicago's streets. In turn, 38 million feet of lumber was shipped on the canal while over 8 million feet of lumber moved on the Galena Railroad. Fifty lumber dealers traded on the Chicago market. In 1852, lumberyards stretched on both sides of the South Branch of the river for nearly two miles. By the 1870s the lumberyards along the South Branch stood as the largest in the world. Lumber companies also dominated a considerable part of the North Branch as the business expanded.[33]

Grain also made its way into the city, and although the first grain elevator appeared in Buffalo in 1842, they soon became symbols of Chicago's might. In the 1840s the process of moving grain to market was a long, chaotic, and clumsy one as sellers attempted to find buyers and vice versa. Commission men, representing producers, transported grain to the larger costal markets for a price. Sacks of grain remained the key to the whole process. The traditional way of shipping grain in sacks entailed workers loading and unloading grain on wagons, barges, and ships. By the 1850s railroads provided the key to changes in the grain trade, as a stream of golden grain found Chicago as its ready market. Chicagoans transformed the system that collected and distributed the West's most important product. In 1855, Chicago surpassed St. Louis as the West's granary as the city took advantage of the new grain elevators and took grain out of sacks and put it into machinery that moved it quickly and efficiently. The elevator used technology, rather than human labor, to move the grain. Captain Robert C. Bristol built Chicago's first elevator with a capacity for eighty thousand bushels in 1848. Within ten years the largest grain elevators dwarfed Bristol's, as in 1856 the Chicago and Rock Island's largest elevator had a capacity of seven hundred thousand bushels. Chicago newspapers pointed out that two or three hundred men unloaded a one-hundred-thousand-bushel shipment in St. Louis, while at Chicago this could be done with a handful of men, giving the city a tremendous cost-saving advantage. The Illinois Central Railroad's elevator could simultaneously empty twelve railroad cars and load two ships at a rate of twenty-four thousand bushels per hour.

Figure 9. Various types of transportation from ox carts to rail and lake boats served the lumber market at the mouth of the Chicago River. Looming overhead is the massive Grain Elevator "A" in 1872. (ICHi-13999, Chicago History Museum.)

The new system, however, mixed the grain of many different farmers in elevators, confusing the quality and making the farmer's profit harder to calculate. It was difficult to keep grain separate in the massive elevators. Technology demanded a better system. Eventually the Chicago Board of Trade (1848) fashioned such a scheme. When the Crimean War (1853–56) resulted in an increased demand for grain, exports doubled in volume and tripled in value, and the Board of Trade grew in influence and began to regulate the city's grain trade. In 1856 it proposed a system of regulations that transformed the Chicago and world grain market. The Board of Trade designated three categories of wheat and set standards for quality, thus solving the elevator operators' problems about mixing the grain of several owners in the same bins. Farmers and shippers brought grain to a warehouse where it was graded and mixed with others of the same grade. They then received a receipt for their grain which could be redeemed by the holder in the future. The receipt could also be sold to speculators. Other problems with standards developed, but the Board of Trade devised means to deal with them and further expanded the grading system. In 1859 the Illinois legislature granted a special charter to the Board of Trade that gave it the right to impose standardized grades and inspection rules. Eventually, out of this system evolved the Chicago futures market. Chicago traders no longer had to deal with the physical grain itself, but only contracts for grain as an abstract commodity. The confusing vocabulary of the new market strained relations between farmers and buyers, but shaped the new system making the city even a more important player in the world capitalist system.[34]

Ethnic Diversity

After the opening of the Erie Canal, immigrants moved westward on ships and the Port of Chicago became an obvious destination for these travelers going west. The mercantile fame of Chicago spread and attracted individuals to its shore. In 1856, the *Tribune* stated that Chicago contained a larger percentage of the foreign born than any other major city except Milwaukee. The new arrivals in turn spurred the housing market that attracted more workers in what seemed to be an endless cycle of development. The *Tribune* wrote:

> The demand for raw labor is consequently without limit. Every able-bodied man, who has talent enough to guide a wheelbarrow on a plank, or capacity enough to drive a dray, or mount a ladder with a hod of brick or mortar on his shoulder, or sense enough to heave coal upon our wharves, or shovel grain from a car or canal boat, or pile lumber, can find employment and high wages. In no other city on the American continent does the number of laborers bear so large a ratio to the whole population as in our city, and for that reason above noticed that in no city is there so large a demand for services of unskilled laborers.[35]

The Irish, many of whom arrived to dig the I&M Canal and then lay track for the railroads, first dominated the immigrant population although the Germans soon outnumbered them to hold the title of the city's largest immigrant/ethnic group into the twentieth century.

While many Irish arrived in the 1830s, it was in the 1840s with the Great Famine that the Irish began to flood into Chicago and the United States. In 1850, 6,096 Irish lived in the city. Over the next twenty years the Irish numbers exploded with almost forty thousand Irish natives living within Chicago. Afterward the Irish foreign-stock population grew more slowly, reaching 73,912 by the end of the century.[36] Many Irish lived along the canal, especially in Bridgeport where they founded St. Bridget's parish in 1850. Earlier the West Side Irish had founded St. Patrick's. Irish squatters lived on the Lower West Side and out in Brighton Park and beyond along Archer Avenue, which had been the supply road for the canal builders. The Catholic parish became an important building block for the Irish community. It would prove to be crucial for later arriving immigrant groups as well.[37]

In the 1840s the Irish became identified with the Democratic Party. The party of Jackson defended immigrants and Catholics against the prejudice of the American Protestant majority. The Irish had some knowledge of political participation before they arrived and took full advantage of the ability of immigrants in early Illinois to vote in local and state elections. They exercised a good deal of clout in the city and dominated some suburbs such as Bridgeport. The large number of Irish immigrants in the Chicago area guaranteed the ascendancy of the Democrats over their rivals the Whigs and later the Know Nothings. They continued to be a problem for the Republicans once that party emerged after the chaos resulting from the Kansas-Nebraska Act in the 1850s.[38]

On March 17, 1856, the Irish community celebrated St. Patrick's Day with a parade showing their ethnic pride and their importance in the city's political equation. That morning, the Montgomery, Emmett, and Shields Guards marched with the Hibernian Benevolent Society down the city's principal streets, followed in the afternoon by a celebration in the West Market Hall. The Hibernian Benevolent Society's stated purpose was to help sick members, bury the dead, and encourage brotherhood among the Irish without regard to the parts of Ireland they came from or their political or religious preferences. Such fraternal organizations played a crucial part in the creation of community in immigrant neighborhoods, second only to the founding of parishes.[39]

The Germans as well as the Irish were victims of the potato blight, but the Germans also emigrated after 1848 as a result of the unsuccessful European revolutions that gave birth to Marxism. Political exiles flooded into Chicago's "Deutschdom," planting the radical seeds that would flower after 1871. In 1850, Germans made up about one-sixth of the city's population. In that census they surpassed the Irish, and by the end of the century 470,000 Chicagoans (25 percent of the city's population) had either been born in Germany or were born to a German immigrant. Since German immigration was now in its third or fourth generation, the number of Chicagoans who identified as German American was even larger.[40]

Only forty Swedes lived in Chicago in 1848. Some worked on the construction of the canal. The Swedish community remained small but proved to be the largest cluster of Swedes in the United States. On the eve of the Civil War, 816 called the city home, but by 1870, 6,154 lived in the city. The following decade saw the Swedish population double in size, and after 1880 the Swedish population exploded. In the early twentieth century some sixty thousand Swedes and their more than 140,000 children lived in the city. Although the Swedes lived throughout the city, concentrating in various neighborhoods, the largest neighborhoods were along the North Branch of the river.[41]

Other Scandinavians also came to Chicago, including Norwegians, Danes, and a small community of Finns. Already in the 1840s Chicagoans asked newcomers, "What are you?" Early immigrants did not see this as an ethnic insult but as a celebration of American liberty. Norwegians writing home proclaimed, "Here it is not asked, what or who was your father, but the question is what are you?" The Voss Correspondence Society of Chicago, a Norwegian immigrant society, wrote: "Freedom is drawn in with mother's milk." Some six hundred to seven hundred Norwegians lived in the city in 1848.[42]

English, Welsh, Scottish, and Protestant Irish also came to the city. Many of these immigrants arrived as part of the first "brain drain" from the British Isles. These British immigrants often had industrial experience and helped bring about the city's swift transformation into an industrial center. They also quickly intermarried with their American cousins and assimilated into Yankee and American society. In 1847, English immigrants formed the St. George Society, an ethnic mutual aid organization, which celebrated the culture of the homeland. The St. George Society was very active and much celebrated in the city as Chicagoans held British immigrants and their descendants in esteem.[43]

While the Welsh arrived early in Chicago's history, only about 1,800 Welsh immigrants lived in the city in 1900. Their fraternal organization, the St. David Society, often went on excursions to Waukegan organized with the English St. George Society and the Scottish St. Andrew's Society. More Welsh settled in Wisconsin, but the Chicago community maintained at least two churches: the Welsh Presbyterian Church, located on the Near West Side with a mission in Bridgeport, and after 1871 the Welsh Congregational Church joined them. In 1876, Chicago's Welsh gathered at the St. David's Hotel on Lake Street to rally for the Hayes and Wheeler Republican presidential ticket. Immigrants organized the Cambrian Benevolent Society in time for the Columbian Exposition in 1893.[44]

The Scots founded the Illinois St. Andrew Society in 1846 and maintained their ethnic identity well into the twentieth century. They played a crucial role in various industries including meatpacking and steelmaking. The Scottish St.

Figure 10. Clark Street is seen here probably in the 1860s. Notice the dirt street and wooden side-walk. (Chicago Public Library, Special Collections and Preservation Division.)

Andrew Society annual meetings on or near St. Andrew's Day (November 30) were gala affairs. In 1852, George Anderson, president of the society, stated that love of one's homeland allowed for love of America and greeted Scots, Englishmen, Irishmen, Welsh, and Americans to the meeting, toasting the entire group, he then praised the poets of Scotland. The Matteson House was gaily decorated in American and Scottish national symbols. Musicians played traditional Highland songs, and the dinner lasted well into the night. Often the Highland Guards appeared at the meetings dressed in their traditional attire.[45]

Despite the call of Know Nothings, a nativist political movement that spread across the United States including Chicago in the 1850s, and others for an end to immigration, the city depended on the foreigners who had settled within its borders. In 1856, the *Tribune* told again of the important role immigrants played. The newspaper reminded its readers that they took jobs that Americans would not take and provided the muscle to build the new city. Despite the American fear that immigrants would soon dominate the politics of the city, they remained indispensable to its progress. Chicago would remain an immigrant city.[46]

Lake Street That Great Street

Chicago's clogged docks and mast-filled sky presented a picture of prosperity to visitor and resident alike. By the early 1850s the city had become the wholesale center of the region, peddling its wares north and west to within miles of the Mississippi River and as far south as Peoria and Fulton Counties. Its jobbing houses, filled with more goods than ever before, had expanded greatly after the opening of the canal and railroad in 1848.[47] The city centered on Lake Street, paralleling the Main Branch of the river. This was the original "great" street as merchants opened shops along the busy street lined with prosperous cast-iron storefronts. In the 1850s Monsieur Marechal taught voice and piano there, while L. D. Olmsted and Company sold children's goods and T. B Carter announced a new stock of winter goods including kid gloves, shawls, cloth clothing, scarfs, and boots, as well as rich embroidered lace, hosiery, and other such dry goods. R. D. Jones and Sons also offered imported fancy dress goods and trimmings. Beecher, Hollister, and Wilkins offered carpets, oil cloths, curtain goods, bedding, and other items in their store at 135 and 138 Lake Street. L. Anderson sold cooking stoves at 203 Lake Street, while S. C. Griggs offered books, stationary, and school books that it published at both wholesale and retail prices. Chicagoans could buy guns, including dueling pistols, at D. Eaton and Company. At Hollister's Fancy Bazaar, customers could purchase holiday and birthday presents, as well as toys and combs. Especially important for the city's retail and real estate future Potter Palmer opened his dry goods store in 1852 at 137 Lake Street, which, after the Civil War, developed into Chicago's legendary Marshall Field and Company Department Store. Palmer offered a wide range of goods including dress silks, shawls, French mantillas, carpetings, bonnets, ribbons, and all manner of fine dry goods. One could even find an undertaker on Lake Street if needed.[48]

The busy thoroughfare brought all kinds of Chicagoans together in the 1850s. Lake Street was an "Exposition of the Industry of All Nations, a World's Fair" as the people and products of the globe gathered in Chicago. French and English visitors mixed with New England and southern gentlemen as well as Ohioans and Chinese immigrants. All walked past the stores filled with goods from around the globe. American Indian women sold blankets and tobacco on the street. Omnibuses moved through the street as passengers hurried to catch the "bus." Newsboys shouted out headlines to the crowd. Where Father Marquette and Louis Jolliet came to a wilderness in 1673 and soldiers fought Indians for control of the West in 1812, there now stood a city making its mark in the world economy. Chicago had arrived as the merchant city of the West.[49]

Figure 11. Lake Street developed as the original retail center for Chicago in the 1850s. (Lithographer—Jevne and Almini; ICHi-06852, Chicago History Museum.)

E WAR IN THE WEST—BIRD'S-EYE VIEW OF CAMP DOUGLAS, CHICAGO, ILL., NOW USED

Emporium
of the West

At the end of the 1850s, with the nation on the verge of the Civil War, Chicago already ranked as a great merchant city, joining the ranks of Manchester and other "shock" cities that had grown up almost overnight. One observer from Cincinnati referred to the city as "a marvel to the ancient men of the New World, and an inexplicable mystery to the men of the old." He lauded the port and its ability to trade directly with Liverpool via the lakes and the St. Lawrence River and spoke highly of the railroads that connected New York, Philadelphia, and Baltimore with Chicago and the West. The visitor also pointed out that the city provided a natural gathering place for immigrants. All of those who came to settle in the West somehow contributed to Chicago's wealth.[1]

Early Industry

In 1848, Chicago had gone through several important changes, including the opening of the Illinois and Michigan Canal and the Galena and Chicago Union Railroad. Businessmen organized the Board of Trade, the first telegraph message was sent to Detroit, and other "firsts" abounded. That year Cyrus Hall McCormick opened his reaper works, and the progress of his business exemplifies how Chicago grew as an industrial center. McCormick had originally invented a horse-drawn reaper in 1831 on his farm in Rockbridge County in western Virginia and took a patent in 1834. After an unsuccessful attempt at iron smelting, McCormick began to work on the reaper again in 1839. McCormick, his father, and his brother built several reapers on his farm and licensed various machine shops to manufacture others. McCormick moved west because he felt that the natural market for the new machines would be on the prairie. Arriving first in Cincinnati, he decided to move on to Chicago as a more logical place to produce the machines. McCormick first employed about twenty men in his plant. In 1849, McCormick's workforce grew to 123 men turning out 1,500 reapers per year.[2]

Figure 12. This artist's depiction of Chicago in 1853 shows the growth of the South Side as it spreads from the busy river. (ICHi-39369, Chicago History Museum.)

In 1859, the McCormick Reaper Works occupied five buildings of two to five stories each providing 110,000 square feet of space on the north bank of the Chicago River's Main Branch with a huge yard and dock on the river. The offices housed clerks who used maps marked with the chief grain-growing regions of the United States and tracked the offices and agents of the company as well as their sales over the last five years. As visitors passed from the office they entered the mechanical department where 100 carpenters, 115 iron finishers, 40 blacksmiths, and 25 laborers worked making the machines that had transformed the technology of prairie agriculture. The McCormick Works employed about one hundred pieces of machinery. The huge Thurston, Gardiner and Company engine powered the factory. The plant made everything needed to manufacture the reaper, except a small iron finger, from bars of Sheffield steel and rough ash, whitewood, and pine timber. The company kept a year's supplies of lumber, pig iron, and steel bars on hand. In the repair room stood duplicates of every model reaper produced at McCormick's. Each year the company produced new sturdier models with increased efficiency. Pattern men could easily reproduce parts for even the oldest reapers. A new way of doing business had appeared in Chicago.[3]

Steam power proved crucial for the city's large-scale manufacturing. The burning of large amounts of wood and later coal to power the Industrial Revolution had its downside. Already in 1854, Chicagoans began to worry about the "smoke" problem. How could the city deal with the pollution emanating from the factories, railroads, and steamboats as well as that from heating homes and businesses? Pittsburgh already had such a problem with a dark cloud of industrial smoke blocking the sunlight, and the same future awaited Chicago if it followed what seemed to be its natural path toward economic development. Indeed the pollution issue haunted the city throughout the nineteenth and twentieth centuries.[4]

The rapidly expanding economy promised great fortune, and the city lunged into the industrial future. In the 1840s and 1850s, with the exception of the McCormick works and a few other industrial concerns, what Chicagoans called manufacturing was still pretty much done by hand and on a small scale. Edward Hall produced saddles, harnesses, and whips, while C. Morgan made furniture at his downtown shop. H. A. Bromley, manufacturer and dresser of furs, worked at his trade at Griswold and Jackson. These early manufacturers tended to serve a local or, like McCormick, a regional market. They ushered in the third phase of the city's economic development after 1848, as a manufacturer of regional goods.[5]

As the year 1857 began the *Chicago Tribune* looked at the city's manufacturers and anticipated a "brilliant future for the city," stating that Chicago could claim the character of a manufacturing as well as a commercial city. Chicago was beginning to move earnestly toward its industrial future. In 1851, the brick industry, a crucial one in a city growing as fast as Chicago, produced some 15 million bricks. Five years later local manufacturers produced almost 100 million bricks. The agricultural implement industry remained the most important. McCormick's firm saw various rivals rise during this period, including John Wright's plant manufacturing the Atkins Self-Raking Reaper and Mower, which produced 1,860 reapers and mowers in 1856. The *Tribune* listed the major industries in the city as brass foundries, breweries, vinegar distillers, brooms, building materials, lime, carriages, omnibuses and wagons, chemicals, flock, furniture, furs, gloves, glue, iron works, steam boilers and engines, railroad cars, bridges, leather tanners, stoves, trunks, planning mills, pumps, saddles, ship building, and many others. Most were small concerns, but some industries approached or passed one hundred employees. Roughly 150 men labored in brewing alone, as all of these workers were thirsty.[6]

Chicago's problem in the years before the Civil War was a lack of investment capital and a shortage of skilled workers. The *Tribune* in 1859 pointed to the lack of capital, a result of the incredible lure of trade. The newspaper argued that such great fortunes could be made in commerce that it stunted investment in manufacturing. Also artisans could make more money outside of the workshop than in it because of the need for workers in the commercial sector. For years the high cost of land and the high cost of living further weakened industry in Chicago. The economic downturn of the late 1850s somewhat changed the situation. Land on both the North and South branches became cheaper as did living expenses. Chicago now looked east again for capital to expand its economy.[7]

The use of machinery to cut costs would provide a key element of the Industrial Revolution. On July 1, 1858, the Chicago Mechanical Bakery opened on the West Side on Clinton Street off of Lake Street. The Mechanical Bakery's five-level 60-by-75-foot building contained a long covered dock so that delivery wagons could be loaded. A large door opened on the opposite end of the structure with a hoisting machine to lift large bales of flour. In this way flour could be received on one side of the building with shipments sent out on the other, streamlining a process that could be chaotic with only one entrance. Furnaces and a steam engine occupied part of the basement, while the yeast department took up the basement's east end. Large ovens rested on the furnaces. The "Automaton Bakery's" kneading machine consisted of a double-headed wooden cylinder, ten feet long by six feet in diameter, fixed in a horizontal frame. The inner heads were connected by two strong bars situated on opposite sides, and these bars made it possible to mix the flour, water, and sponge. One of these bars even cleaned the machine as it turned. A shaft connecting the two inner heads suspended a plank-shaped hopper that at every revolution descended and cut into the mass of dough and lifted one-half and conveyed it to the top where it fell to the bottom, "thus performing, by machinery, the same process which French bakers perform by hand." The machine kneaded ten barrels of flour in about twenty-five minutes.

All along the way, the "Automaton Bakery" did with machinery what had previously been done by hand. The oven machinery mainly took up the first and second stories of the building. The oven itself stood fifty feet high, twenty-four feet long, and ten feet wide. Two endless chains moved within the oven. The only work done by hand was to round the loaves of dough upon the bread cars outside the oven and then let the machinery carry on the job. As quickly as the dough was received at one end the machinery discharged bread at the other. Workers kept the oven continuously heated and the machinery constantly in motion. The cost was far below that of the traditional way of making bread, and the company claimed that it could produce double the amount baked daily in Chicago and sharply reduce the cost of a loaf.

E. C. Larned, the president of the company's stockholders, spoke proudly of the new bakery and its delivery of the "staff of life." Supposedly, the Automaton Bakery had its origin in an attempt to feed the poor in Brooklyn. It also operated in Baltimore and Philadelphia. Addressing the question of how the bakery would impact bakers across the city, Larned said that they would make more money selling the Chicago Mechanical Bakery's bread than baking their own. He likened his company to various other new industrial enterprises. The inventor, Hiram Berdon, also addressed the concerns of local bakers, claiming that this "revolution" in bread production would relieve Chicago's bakers of endless toil. Berdon said, "No man—ought to spend all of his time working with his hands." The inventor claimed that this would allow the manual laborer to "cultivate his moral and intellectual powers." It would not be the last time such claims would be made in industrialized America.[8]

Growth Problems

Throughout history, American cities, especially western cities, constantly looked toward the federal government for assistance. In 1847, Chicago became the site of the River and Harbor Convention, the city's first major national meeting. The convention was called largely to protest President Polk's 1846 veto of the River and Harbor bill. Western Democrats were furious with Polk, who defended his position by invoking states' rights and the specter of heavy federal debts. The president talked about the disreputable scramble for public money that he felt the bill entailed. President Polk resisted the redistribution of national wealth to use federal money to build projects across the vast territory of the West and asserted that federal funds should be used only in projects that crossed state boundaries. River and harbor improvements, on the other hand, he argued were by their nature local in character and therefore within the purview of local and state governments.

Western Democrats perceived the move as one by the southern Democrats to expand their power as they and Polk supported the Mexican War, which was fought largely for southern interests. Democrats like Chicago's John Wentworth saw southern treachery behind the veto. Wentworth began to turn on the southern Democrats and took his first steps toward eventually breaking with the party and later in the 1850s joining the new Republican Party. Both western Democrats and Whigs demanded that the federal government meet the needs of the West. Despite the argument for the spending of the federal largess on behalf of their interests, Chicagoans ironically refused to use local government money to support the River and Harbor Convention. In fact Chicagoans began to remake their city government in Polk's terms, establishing a segmented ward-based system for local improvements funded by assessments of local landowners as opposed to citywide spending. The irony was lost on many Chicagoans.[9]

In spite of Polk's vetoes the federal government continued to play a major role in the city's life. In September 1849, it began construction of a new Marine Hospital near the former site of Fort Dearborn. Designed for sick and disabled lake sailors the building stood 128.5 feet long, 90.5 feet wide, and three stories tall with a basement. Each floor contained twelve wards. Congress appropriated $45,000 for its construction, and it would be finished in 1851. The sandbar at the mouth of the river, originally removed in 1821, kept reappearing and needed constant dredging. Congress gave its blessing to the building of a new iron lighthouse in 1850, which was also expected to be completed in 1851.

Despite, or perhaps because of its lightning growth, Chicago faced various obstacles to becoming a truly great city. The location was poorly drained and disease ridden. Meanwhile the city constructed plank roads and made improvements so that citizen and visitor could do business along the city's busy streets. The city council began to plank the principal streets in 1849. Drainage continued to be a problem, and several attempts to deal with the dilemma by the city ended in failure. At the end of 1850, only 9.59 miles of the city's streets were planked with some minimal sewers put in place. Lakeshore erosion also presented a quandary for the young city, as did a need to widen the harbor and create more docks and wharfs.[10]

Even Mother Nature sometimes created problems. On March 12, 1849, between nine and ten o'clock in the morning, Chicago's twenty thousand residents heard a thunderous noise that sounded like cannon fire. As Chicagoans came out of their homes and businesses to see what was going on, ice floes breaking up down the river and canal system were heading their way bringing with them a surge of water reaching two stories in height that washed away bridges, crushed canal boats, and lifted some of the largest lake vessels out of the water and deposited them far from their moorings. As the deluge continued, some Chicagoans took to the city's bridges to see the flood with tragic consequences. The wave washed away a boy standing on the Madison Street Bridge, and the rushing water crushed another child. Miraculously, these were the only fatalities suffered during the flood. All of the bridges had been washed away, and the flood caused $108,000 in damages, of which 80 percent were suffered by ships in the "protected" harbor provided by the branches of the river. Afterward a bridge of tangled and destroyed ships provided the only way across the river.

The young city, situated on a marshy flood plain suffering from poor drainage and quick unplanned growth, faced an uncertain future of natural disasters. In the case of the 1849 flood, the poorly drained land on the banks of the river and canal lay frozen after a difficult winter. A spring thaw and fast melting snow, combined with a record March rainfall, resulted in a tremendous ice jam on the Des Plaines River ten miles to the southwest. The ice jam forced water across Mud Lake and into the South Branch of the river. The enormous amount of water raised the level of the river and its top sheet of ice. All of this came crashing down the South Branch. Chicago, to its own dismay, had ignored the power of nature as it created itself on the banks of the river that now rose to crush it.

Eight years later an early thaw and steady rainfall again created a similar problem. Another massive wave washed away railroad bridges on the rivers surrounding Chicago, again with loss of life. Meanwhile the river rose and again threatened the city, flooding lumberyards and storehouses as the city braced for a repeat of the 1849 flood. Nearly two feet of water covered Bridgeport. Homes flooded, and the river swept away docks loaded with lumber and beef. Just below the packinghouses on the river, the ice smashed canal boats. Further ice jams grew at the various bridges. Mud Lake again proved to be much of the source of the flood. Poorly drained, it spilled into the South Branch, providing a constant threat to the city. Fortunately the weather changed again, and the groundwater froze, preventing a greater disaster.[11]

In 1849, cholera arrived from New Orleans on a canal boat. The epidemic raged across the city and, like the flood, focused Chicago's attention on the river and the city's water supply. Chicagoans pressed for the municipal ownership of the water supply. The state had chartered the Chicago Hydraulic Company in 1836 to provide the city's water supply. The company built its waterworks in 1842, but the water pumped directly from the lake was filthy, and in 1850 the firm only supplied about 20 percent of the city's households. Most Chicagoans purchased water from vendors who filled barrels with lake water and went down city streets selling the precious commodity. In 1851, Chicagoans decided to create a Chicago Board of Water Commissioners as a reaction to the cholera threat. Residents clearly wanted a public water system and voted enthusiastically to support it as most saw it as a matter of life or death. Board of Water commissioners brought in an expert engineer, William J. McAlpine, who proposed the construction of a larger pump house at the northeast corner of Chicago Avenue and Pine Street. In addition McAlpine recommended hydrants and free drinking fountains that would immediately present a more democratic answer to the drinking problem.

The wooden city needed water for more than drinking and washing: it also needed fire protection. A fire in 1857 took twenty-two lives and destroyed $700,000 worth of property in the central business district. McAlpine's original three-hundred-horsepower steam engine did not prove adequate to fight the conflagration. After the fire a second bigger engine and pump were installed. Within five years 80 percent of Chicagoans drew water from the new municipal system. By 1861, despite the huge growth in population, nearly the entire city had running water funded by municipal bonds.[12]

But more was needed. In 1864, workers began to dig a tunnel two miles long under the lake to a new water intake beyond what Chief Engineer Ellis Chesbrough believed to be the reach of the polluting river. The tunnel opened in 1866 and supplied water to a new Chicago Avenue pumping station and water tower. Eight years later, the city dug a second tunnel off of the South Side. Chesbrough's original tunnel, however, still had to deal with the pollution-spewing Chicago River. The Army Corps of Engineers extended the pier used to keep the mouth of the river open another one thousand feet in the direction of the two-mile intake crib. The extended pier rerouted the natural path of the river's flow directly toward the intake pipes. The two governments, city and federal, worked unknowingly at cross-purposes, and the pollution problem remained despite the famous tunnel. Something had to be done about the stinking river and its polluted water.[13]

Chicago had obviously neglected its natural setting, and it struck back with ferocity. The original plat maps of the city ignored the environment and placed

Figure 13. Chicago Water Tower, ca. 1870. (Stereopticon, Author's Collection.)

a grid designed to make land sales easy. The city was simply built on a marsh without much thought. Twelve miles to the west the continental divide presented another issue and a possible solution. Not only the city but also the region needed a better drainage system. Somehow the watery ground had to be drained and water sent away from the land just barely above Lake Michigan.

Like the water system, the drainage system originated as a result of the cholera epidemic that had attacked the city for six straight years. The first epidemic claimed 314 lives in 1849. The next year at least 450 victims fell to the disease. In 1854 alone cholera killed 1,500 residents. Most saw a fresh water supply and an effective system of sewers as an answer. The fouled river presented more than an odor problem for the city as it filled with urban waste including the dumping of packinghouse and brewery waste products. At times the dark inky river turned crimson as the meat plant sewers spewed blood into it. Horse and other animal carcasses dumped into the water joined the awful mix of human and industrial waste. In turn the river flowed out into the lake and dangerously impacted on the city's drinking water. It was obvious that the city's health problems were interconnected.

The Illinois legislature empowered Chicago's sewage commissioners to build sewers and ditches in order to drain waste and water runoff from the city. By 1855, Chicago was on the verge of becoming the first American city to create a comprehensive sewer system. Ellis Chesbrough designed a system that drained waste from both private residences and streets into the Chicago River. Drainage was to be carried by gravity, and city streets had to be raised to accomplish this. Sewers were laid on the ground, and then soil from the deepening of the river laid on top. The city then constructed paved streets on top of the new public works system. Owners had buildings jacked up to meet the new streets and laid basements. In some residential areas they ignored the new streets and built elevated walkways from the front door to reach the street. The Chicago River became the city's giant sewer.

Various proposals were made to deal with the increasingly polluted river. The winning proposal was Chesbrough's deep-cut plan. He would reverse the flow of the river by deepening the Illinois and Michigan Canal and using gravity to make the river flow away from the lake. The huge public works project allowed Chicago's polluters to continue using the river as a huge sink while the state government gave taxpayers a virtual free ride by issuing municipal bonds backed by a lien on traffic tolls on the canal. The actual permanent reversal of the river would await the building of a new sanitation and ship canal to open in 1900, but engineering plans began to take precedence in dealing with the city's problems.[14]

The Threat of War

While the Industrial Revolution and its allies, the agricultural, transportation, and communications revolutions, remade the nation, another type of revolt appeared on the horizon. Chicago played a key part in these other revolutions, and it also carried out a central task in the Civil War that would engulf the United States. This struggle played a fundamental role in the eventual complete victory of capitalism in the American economy and in making Chicago one of the premier actors in the victory.

Illinois Senator Stephen A. Douglas, the "Little Giant," supported the traditional Jacksonian view of the economy and of slavery. Looking for a middle way that might avoid a civil war, he supported the Compromise of 1850 concerning the territories won after the Mexican War. His principal of "popular sovereignty" hoped to settle the issue of slavery in the West. In 1854, Douglas supported the settlement of Kansas as part of an attempt to gather southern support for a proposed transcontinental railroad emanating from Chicago. Slave owners from Missouri flooded into Kansas and voted for slavery as a local option. Northerners complained that this repealed the Missouri Compromise

Figure 14. Chicago Tribune Building, late 1850s. The *Tribune* evolved as an early supporter of the Republican Party. Notice the McVickers Theater to the left of the building. (Chicago Public Library, Special Collections and Preservation.)

of 1820 and meant the spread of the "Slaveocracy." The Little Giant lost much of his previous support, and his position cost him the Democratic presidential nomination in 1856. Douglas became increasingly isolated in the late 1850s. As the country teetered toward its most dangerous conflict, Douglas continued to believe in a nationalist political model that viewed slavery not as a political or moral question or, indeed, a constitutional one, but as a local question to be decided by each state.

In 1858, Abraham Lincoln challenged Douglas for the U.S. Senate. This proved to be a trial by fire for the young lawyer representing the new Republican Party. These two men symbolized both the frustrations and hopes of the era and their region as they met at the Tremont Hotel in the heart of Chicago on the evening of July 9, 1858. Lincoln was Douglas's guest, as the Little Giant made his first speech of the senatorial campaign. A torchlight parade lit the streets and fireworks the night sky while Democrats rallied behind their candidate.

Senator Douglas had played a key role in the young city's success. He convinced the Illinois Central Railroad to make its terminus in the young city and brought other investments to Chicago. His South Side real estate developments Groveland and Woodland Parks attracted suburban settlers to the south lakefront, and his colleague Paul Cornell had begun the suburban settlement of Hyde Park on Douglas's advice. Douglas, both as politician and businessman, fit well into Chicago's Yankee booster mentality in the years before the Civil War. He now faced a crucial election that could revive his national standing. Douglas proclaimed that Lincoln advocated war over slavery. Lincoln sat quietly listening to Douglas but did not answer him until the next night on the same Tremont House balcony by taking the high moral ground on slavery. This was the unofficial beginning of the Lincoln-Douglas debates.[15]

Douglas won the 1858 election and returned to the Senate. The seven debates between Lincoln and Douglas have become legends of American political history. They achieved national status for both candidates, laying out the basic debate between Democrats and Republicans across the country. Despite his loss Lincoln gained in national stature among the members of his party. Douglas emerged as the Democratic front-runner for the 1860 presidential election.[16]

Lincoln surfaced as a dark horse candidate for the 1860 Republican presidential nomination. Most Republicans favored William H. Seward of New York. The decision to hold the Republican National Convention in Chicago helped Lincoln's chances but by no means guaranteed the outcome. Seward had built the Republican Party's common philosophy. The party opposed slavery but did not propose its abolition as it met in Chicago's Wigwam on Lake Street in May 16, 1860.

The Wigwam, which boasted the largest gathering space in the Union, had not even existed on April 1. Carpenters erected the structure with a capacity for twelve thousand visitors in just five weeks, using balloon framing. It resembled a huge warehouse, and detractors stuck it with a name that implied a cheaply made structure that could fall down at any time. But despite its nickname, the Wigwam was impressive for the time. Built at a cost of $5,000, it stood two stories tall and 180 feet by 100 feet. One side of the construction was the brick wall of a neighboring building. Convention delegates gathered on the main floor while spectators packed the balconies. Large windows encircled the edifice and allowed for the circulation of air, especially important for the packed, smoke-filled, sweaty convention. Eventually 466 delegates arrived from throughout the North and the Border States to meet in Chicago; and with Lincoln as a contender, thousands of local supporters filled the balconies and rallied outside.[17]

Thurlow Weed of New York arrived in Chicago determined to gain the nomination of the party for Seward. Known as "Lucifer of the Lobby" and both "the Wizard" and "the Dictator," Weed was a powerful force to be reckoned with in party politics. Entrenched at the Richmond House, one of the city's finest hotels, the New Yorker planned his campaign. He had imported thousands of Seward supporters including hundreds of toughs from New York City, anticipating Chicago's legendary election style, as insurance against local Lincoln supporters taking over the convention.

The streets around the Wigwam became a mob scene as supporters of the various candidates arrived. Organizers set aside part of the balcony for ladies, space for about three thousand women and their escorts. Men in search of a place at the convention offered unattached women and even school girls as much as twenty-five cents to escort them into the gallery. Apparently at least one enterprising girl brought six men into the convention. A washerwoman entered the Wigwam with both her wash and a man in hand. When this worked, another would-be attendee arrived with an Indian woman who was selling moccasins to tourists but was told that a "squaw" could not possibly be a lady and was turned away. Chicago's entrepreneurial spirit was not limited to its famous male industrialists.

Republican women decorated the Wigwam with banners, bunting, and evergreen. State banners hung over a huge stage that ran the length of the building. Allegorical paintings of Liberty, Justice, and Plenty adorned the back wall of the stage wall along with other patriotic symbols while busts of Washington and other heroes decorated the front. Gaslights and skylights lit the Wigwam as Governor Edwin D. Morgan opened the convention at 12:15 p.m. with a roll call of the states. The convention adjourned after the roll, the introduction of various committees and a few speeches as a schooner waited to take delegates on an excursion on Lake Michigan. The real politicking took place that evening as delegates gathered at the various hotels.

In what would become a long-standing Chicago tradition of political maneuvering, Judge David Davis, Lincoln's campaign manager, gathered his forces at the Tremont Hotel and moved to stop any momentum that Seward's forces might have shown at the Wigwam. The judge understood that Seward's advantage could not be overcome in the first two ballots. Lincoln would have to give the impression of growing strength. Davis hoped to fill the Wigwam the next day with Lincoln supporters, some of whom arrived by train from southern Illinois on free passes. He employed a Chicago doctor named Ames, who legend credits with a famously loud voice, to shout Lincoln's name above the crowd. On the other side of the Wigwam Davis placed another legendary shouter from Ottawa to serenade the delegates. Meanwhile Lincoln's delegates gathered support for their candidate with pledges of votes for the third and fourth ballots if Seward could be stopped. The Tremont Hotel remained the center of anti-Seward intrigue as Lincoln's delegates continued to make headway. Davis offered political favors for votes while he garnered more votes for his candidate. In the end Davis outmaneuvered Thurlow Weed, and Lincoln won the Republican nomination on the third ballot.

The Republican Platform adopted at the Chicago Convention was more conservative than many Republicans wished. Seward stood at the forefront of the "abolitionist" Republicans. Lincoln and his allies fashioned a document that they hoped would not push the South toward secession. The slavery plank simply stated that slavery could not be established in the territories and condemned the opening of the slave trade. It vowed to preserve the Union. Furthermore Republicans called for a protective tariff, a free homestead policy for the West, river and harbor improvements, and government aid for a railroad to the Pacific. The document also seemed to protect immigrants. This position rallied support across the West, and particularly in Illinois. Wide Awake Clubs, made up of young Republican men, marched through Chicago's streets rallying the faithful and convincing many more of the righteousness of the Republican cause.[18]

Meanwhile Democrats met in Charleston, South Carolina, the center of southern secessionist feeling. Douglas's supporters were in a majority, but when they rejected a party platform supporting the expansion of slavery into all territories southerners walked out of the convention. Douglas had failed to unite his party. The Democrats held another convention in Baltimore, which finally nominated the Little Giant, but without healing the breach in the party. Southerners supported their own candidate, John C. Breckinridge, in 1860 and ensured Lincoln's election. John Bell's campaign on a Constitutional-Union Ticket further divided the nation.[19]

The Chicago Wigwam proved to be a model for other such gathering places across the nation, but its use in Chicago was rather limited. Religious leaders held services in the building throughout the summer of 1860. In November the Wide Awakes held a march ending at the structure. It accommodated the Mechanic's Fair, a Zouave demonstration that featured elegantly dressed troops who marched in formations reminiscent of European, particularly French units, a three-day-long Catholic festival held by the Sisters of the Holy Cross and various other events. What to do with the massive structure became an issue after the presidential campaign of 1860. For a while it lodged troops during the Civil War. In 1862, carpenters transformed the building into a commercial market by dividing it into ten stores that joined other Lake Street businesses. Finally it burned to the ground during the evening of November 13, 1869.[20]

The Civil War

On November 6, 1860, the nation went to the polls. The Republicans captured the White House, and secession immediately became the talk of the nation. Some advised on "a bloodless separation," but few in the Republican Party's leadership wanted to hear about breaking up the Union. On December 20, 1860, South Carolina announced that it was seceding from the Union. Many politicians offered conciliation as a time-honored means of preserving the Union. Others spoke openly about further regional secession, including a northwestern republic as a possible way of avoiding having the Old Northwest dragged into a war many believed only the Northeast truly wanted. Some Chicagoans saw the possibility that the war would benefit the young commercial and industrial center. The *Chicago Record* even predicted that the city would become the capital of a new republic born out of the crisis.

Many Democrats continued to push for compromise with the South. On January 14, 1861, Cyrus H. McCormick and other Democrats called for resolutions of compromise. Senator Douglas worked urgently to draft a compromise plan. He offered new amendments to the Constitution that would guarantee slavery but would also impose limitations on its growth. But Republican senators saw little need for compromises that might limit the new administration's power. Southern politicians talked compromise in Congress but offered little hope for a solution. Republican leaders such as Senator Seward feared that the inauguration might end in disaster, and Chicago's Allan Pinkerton investigated a Lincoln assassination plot in Baltimore.

Long John Wentworth, mayor of Chicago, now an avowed Republican, declared that January 8, the anniversary of the Battle of New Orleans, should be a day when Chicago stores should close their doors and flags should be flown in honor of the Union as well as for Andrew Jackson, the hero of the 1833 Nullification Crises that had avoided an earlier move toward South Carolina's secession, and Major Robert Anderson, the commander at Fort Sumter in South Carolina. On March 4, Lincoln took the oath as president. His speech put an end to all questions of compromise. According to the new president, states had no constitutional right of secession; federal laws must be adhered to in all the states. On April 12, secessionists opened fire on Fort Sumter, and two days later Major Anderson surrendered. The next day Lincoln called for seventy-five thousand troops to protect the Union, and Chicago and the North responded with enthusiasm.

On the evening of April 18, a massive demonstration took place in Chicago when as many as twenty thousand residents packed courthouse square. The city's political leaders appealed to the citizens' patriotism. Young men rushed to join militia units as war fever spread across the North. Most expected a quick northern victory. (southerners also expected to win their independence quickly.) Meanwhile Senator Douglas met with Lincoln the day Fort Sumter fell and pledged his support to fight the secessionists. He advised Lincoln that at least two hundred thousand troops would be needed to defeat the South. Douglas then returned to Illinois where in a Springfield speech he spoke of his "sadness and grief" over the condition of the Union. He called for Illinois to resist secession. Men of both parties hailed the Douglas speech. On May 1, the Little Giant came to Chicago and spoke at the Republican Wigwam proclaiming, "There can be no neutrals in this war: only patriots—or traitors." But the senator fell ill and died on June 3 at the age of forty-eight. He would see neither the Union preserved nor the vast calamity that the nation faced.[21]

Elmer Ellsworth, a friend of Lincoln's and a militia officer from Chicago, was the first Union officer to die in combat as the city quickly shared in the pouring out of blood for the cause. On May 24, 1861, Ellsworth, who had organized a Zouave unit in Chicago and later in New York, died in Alexandria, Virginia. That day he led his New York Fire Zouaves into the city that Confederate troops had already abandoned. He noticed a Confederate flag flying from the Marshall Hotel and moved to take it down. After storming the hotel he cut down the flag and headed back to the street. James W. Jackson, the hotel's proprietor, confronted him on the stairs and killed him with a shotgun blast. Another Zouave instantly shot Jackson and then bayoneted him. On June 2, Chicagoans held a memorial for Ellsworth, who was buried in his native New York.[22]

Chicago responded eagerly to the war. In May, the city reported thirteen companies in service, with twenty-five reserve companies ready and waiting for the call. By June, Chicagoans raised over $36,000 to equip companies and to aid military families. When Lincoln called for three hundred thousand more men in the summer of 1862, they also responded enthusiastically. Native and foreign born alike rallied to the Union cause. Women too joined in providing garments for uniforms as well as other supplies. Illinois troops initially served in the Mississippi Valley, and in February 1862 the battle of Fort Donelson presented the first test for Chicago. Ulysses S. Grant's victory on February 17 resulted in roughly thirteen thousand Confederate prisoners of war. The city sent food, medicine, bibles, and other reading materials to the troops. At midnight, March 1, 1862, the first prisoners of war arrived in Chicago to be interned at the newly organized Camp Douglas on the city's South Side.

This early Union victory did not lead to a quick defeat of the Confederacy but instead stiffened its resolve. Even after the Union gained control of Missouri in May 1862, the rebels remained a determined and formidable foe. From the firing on Fort Sumter in April 1861 to the Battle of Shiloh the following April, Chicago had supported the war. But the vision of a quick and easy victory had passed. Many Chicagoans took a harsher approach toward the conflict. Soldiers reported rebel atrocities, both rumored and substantive. Mass slaughter and closed caskets made the results of war very real for Chicago and the nation.[23]

Nonetheless Chicagoans eagerly took part in the work of the U.S. Sanitary Commission, which had been organized early in the war and emerged as the major coordinating body for war relief agencies in support of the troops. The Chicago Branch (later the Northwestern Sanitary Commission) proved to be an important outlet for women during the war. Despite male figureheads, their daughters and wives did most of the hard work. Eliza C. Porter, the wife of a clergyman, at first directed operations. Jane C. Hoge and Mary Livermore replaced her when she moved on after five months to join the Army of the West with a team of nurses. In December 1861, they held a bazaar, which raised $675.17. The commission invited them to become agents, and they toured hospitals packed with war casualties. After a little less than three weeks, they returned to Chicago and organized the local effort to aid northern soldiers.

The months ahead proved difficult, as the city witnessed antiblack riots, and some Democrats called for peace without victory. Large rallies shook the city, raising patriotic fervor time and time again. During all of this tumult the Northwestern Sanitary Commission almost became a casualty of discouragement and political divisiveness, but Hoge and Livermore kept the institution going. In the spring of 1863, the Sanitary Commission was well organized, and Hoge launched a drive to get fresh fruits and vegetables to the soldiers. By July the commission shipped 18,468 bushels of vegetables and over sixty-one thousand pounds of dried fruit out of Chicago.

The commission also had an impressive system of services for wounded soldiers back in Chicago. On the Fourth of July, 1863, the Northwestern Commission opened the Soldier's Home in the city. The work of the commission severely taxed its resources. Jane Hoge and Mary Livermore proposed a fair to augment funds. Despite the doubts of male commissioners the two women proceeded with their plan to raise at least $25,000. They held a mass meeting at Bryan Hall and appointed an executive committee that included women from every major religion in the city. The committee planned a convention of midwestern women on September 1 and 2, 1863. Hoge and Livermore traveled east to gain support for the proposed fair. The response was overwhelming, and the fair opened on October 27, 1863. It took on the proportions of a world's fair as donated products filled the various halls needed for the exposition of the goods. Crowds filled the halls day and night, and by the time it closed on November 7 with a dinner for Chicago's wounded soldiers, the Northwestern Sanitary Commission Fair had raised $86,000 ($1,766,581.68 in 2007 dollars). After the soldiers left two hundred men entered the dining hall to serve the women who had organized the fair.[24]

When Senator Douglas died, various interests divided the land he owned south of the city. They set part of it aside to train Union troops. The camp lay south of Thirty-first Street and west of Cottage Grove Avenue, an ideal location with the lake and the Illinois Central Railroad and various other railroads nearby. Construction began about six months after the attack on Fort Sumter, and by November Camp Douglas was up and running as a training base for troops. After Grant's victory at Fort Donelson, the Union Army turned Camp Douglas into a prisoner of war camp. Some seven thousand Confederate prisoners soon arrived in Chicago to be housed at the camp.

Authorities at Camp Douglas were ill prepared for the arrival of prisoners, and with few available troops they pressed Chicago police into guarding the southerners. Sixty Chicago police stood as the only barrier between the prisoners and the city. This did not promote confidence among Chicago's worried citizens, especially South Siders. Fortunately the prisoners were in no shape to organize a rebellion, and the city's cold February weather did as much to cool any attempt on the rebels' part to escape. Colonel James Mulligan and the Irish Brigade soon took over guarding Camp Douglas.

Chicagoans came to Camp Douglas to get a close look at their new enemy.

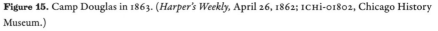

THE WAR IN THE WEST—BIRD'S-EYE VIEW OF CAMP DOUGLAS, CHICAGO, ILL., NOW USED FOR THE DETENTION OF REBEL PRISONERS.—FROM A SKETCH BY MR. F. MUNSON, OF CHICAGO

APRIL 26, 1862.]

Figure 15. Camp Douglas in 1863. (*Harper's Weekly,* April 26, 1862; ICHi-01802, Chicago History Museum.)

Mulligan gave out passes, and Chicagoans from all backgrounds argued politics with the captives. Conditions quickly degenerated as more and more Confederates arrived. Eventually Camp Douglas held about nine thousand men. Many were in very poor health and suffered not only from their wounds but also from the cold. Within a week, twenty-nine Confederates died at Camp Douglas, beginning its notorious reputation among southern soldiers. Organizers raised money at Bryan Hall to aid the stricken rebels, and Chicago doctors worked side by side with Confederate surgeons to help the men. Chicago's women prepared food, and a clothing drive brought coats, blankets, and bedding to the camp. In the first year of operation Chicagoans donated nearly $100,000 worth of clothing. Nevertheless, more than six thousand men died at Camp Douglas as a result of poor conditions in the camp and camp hospitals. Many of these lay buried at the Confederate Memorial Mount in the South Side's Oak Woods Cemetery.[25]

Prisoners plotted various escapes, some successful, some not. One plan had Confederates seizing the camp and finding coconspirators among Chicago's considerable Copperhead population who believed the war was a folly perpetrated by Lincoln and his radical Republican allies. Southern agents had arrived in Chicago to attempt to coordinate a massive breakout from Camp Douglas. The "brigadier general" of the Chicago Copperheads was Charles Walsh, a rather unskilled conspirator with visions of grandeur. Captain Thomas Hines,

Figure 16. Confederate prisoners of war at Camp Douglas, ca. 1863. (ICHi-01800 Chicago History Museum.)

a Confederate soldier and agent, attempted to coordinate a failed breakout before the 1864 presidential election.[26]

A serious challenge to civil rights raised its head in the city during the Civil War. Wilbur F. Storey, editor of the *Chicago Times* and a firm opponent of Abraham Lincoln and the Republican Party, had taken his cue from Douglas, "Forget party—remember your country." Storey, however, let his opinions be known, and soon his support for Lincoln began to cool. After the president issued the Emancipation Proclamation, Storey called the announcement "an act of national suicide." Once he was convinced that the abolitionists influenced Lincoln, the editor attacked the president with all of his vehemence, calling him "an old joker." After emancipation became law, Storey's newspaper proclaimed, "The Awful Calamity of Abraham Lincoln." The *Chicago Times* provided an outlet for a bitter partisan attack on Lincoln during the height of the Civil War. Democrats rallied to Storey and attacked Lincoln on the grounds of states' rights and white supremacy, claiming that Republicans would turn the country over to the newly freed slaves. According to Storey and his supporters, Lincoln accumulated too much power and had become a dictator. Resistance became "a case of life and death" for the white race.

Storey relentlessly attacked Chicago's small African American community. The *Chicago Times* claimed that blacks were incompetent to obey the laws of society. One story's title screamed out, "Shall Illinois Be Africanized?" He wrote accounts of blacks lusting after white women or insulting Union soldiers. His racism seemed to know no bounds as he portrayed a white America on the verge of collapse as a result of Lincoln and the abolitionists. The *Times* editor found himself at the center of controversy, which brought an unwanted response from Lincoln and the federal government.

Storey enjoyed a good deal of influence, and Democrats began to openly call for an end to the fighting. In August 1862, Governor Richard Yates urged that the newspaper be closed down. Indiana's Governor Oliver P. Morton agreed that the *Times* had an evil influence on his state. The *Chicago Tribune* also called for the rival paper's suppression. The federal government at first ignored these appeals, but soon they influenced Lincoln's approach to the war. Democratic-controlled state legislatures in Illinois and Indiana both called for an immediate end to the fighting. Storey then raised again the specter of the Midwest leaving the Union if the war did not quickly come to an end. After General Ambrose E. Burnside arrested Clement L. Valandigham, a former Ohio congressman and antiwar Democrat with eyes on the governorship, Storey jumped to his defense and attacked Burnside, calling the arrest the "funeral of civil liberty." On June 1, 1863, Burnside telegraphed the commander of Camp Douglas and ordered the suppression of the *Chicago Times*. Storey was ordered to cease publication. He defiantly put another issue to press while a horseman waited at the gates of Camp Douglas to warn the editor when troops left. At 4:00 a.m. two companies arrived at the newspapers offices and stopped the presses. That morning the *Times* appeared on the city's streets along with a handbill announcing Burnside's order. Crowds of supporters gathered outside the newspaper's office, calling for Storey to make a speech. Democratic ward bosses worked their districts. One estimate had twenty thousand people demonstrating that night. The threat of mob violence hung in the air. Several Republicans felt the wrath of the crowd as hordes attacked them. Prominent Republican leaders came to the support of Storey and the *Times*. The offices of the *Chicago Tribune* prepared for an attack by the Democratic mob.

Lincoln, while no friend of Storey or the *Times*, did not approve of Burnside's actions and saw the suppression of the Chicago newspaper as a terrible blunder. Judge David Davis, who had organized Lincoln's successful campaign in 1860, telegraphed the president and asked for him to end the suppression. Lincoln, while not wanting to embarrass Burnside, asked the general to lift the order. By June 4, the *Chicago Times* was again free to go to press. Now Republicans filled the streets in anger. The city's streets again boiled over with partisan crowds. Lincoln sent notice to Burnside to reimpose the suppression of the newspaper, but Burnside wisely ignored Lincoln's order.

Storey relished the Republican attack on him and his newspaper. Death threats only made him bolder as he emerged as the only winner in the affair. Burnside had presented the newspaper with a gold mine, and subscriptions grew. The *Chicago Times* became an even larger force in Illinois and national politics as a symbol of Lincoln's tyranny.[27]

The Wartime Economy

Meanwhile the war dragged on and had a profound effect on Chicago's economy. From the beginning there was little doubt that the conflict between the states would play a role in the city's growth as both a commercial and manufacturing center. Compared to her two major rivals, St. Louis and Cincinnati, Chicago was at a considerable distance from the fighting. Furthermore, given her water and rail connections supplies to the army found a natural path through Chicago. Originally, the South believed that its control over the Mississippi River would cripple the North's economy, but early Yankee victories and Chicago's ability to funnel supplies and men prevented the South from reaching its goals.

The initial threat to both Illinois' and Chicago's economy came from the chaos of the Jacksonian-era banking system, which issued various bank notes across the country. As early as November 1860, the city's wholesale businesses felt the impact of the threat that southern bank currencies would be worthless. The following year witnessed massive bank failures in Illinois because they held millions in now worthless southern currencies.[28] Finally in 1863, the federal government established the National Bank System, and the Chicago Board of Trade led the movement to drive state currencies out of the market and replace them with federal greenbacks. This initial havoc hid the almost immediate positive impact of the wartime economy on Chicago.

Orders to supply northern troops flooded the city. The ready-made clothing industry appeared overnight to supply uniforms to Yankee soldiers and sailors. By 1863, Chicago's clothing companies produced $12 million annually in goods and included eighty-five wholesale businesses.[29] The manufacture of military supplies grew out of necessity. The first troops to leave Chicago for the defense of Cairo, Illinois, were poorly equipped. Almost immediately firms opened that produced much needed supplies for northern armies. Companies quickly made equipment needed by the cavalry and infantry at a value of over $1 million. Condict, Wooley, and Company prepared cavalry equipment for Farnsworth's regiment on the Potomac River. In May 1861, the more than four hundred employees of Turner and Sidway turned from the civilian trade in saddles to supplying the military. Others including Gustave Leverenz on Randolph Street, Ward and King, and the D. Horton Company readied goods for the Union Army. By 1862, Chicago concerns proved they could produce high quality wartime goods as easily and as cheaply as could be done anywhere else in the North.[30]

Other industries also either relocated in Chicago because of its distance from the war zone or came to the city because of its growing transportation advantages. In 1860, the R. H. Stewert and Company, manufacturer of soap and candles, moved to Chicago from Detroit, explaining that the city's advantage in transportation and the abundance of cheap and good tallow made it an excellent place to expand the business. That same year Chicago shipped a great deal of wheat, and the wealth of the West seemed ready to supply the Union in the coming war. Higher wages stimulated growth, and workers, both native and foreign born, continued to come to Chicago in search of a better life. The *Chicago Tribune* pointed to the fact of the amazing growth of the country's cities in the twenty years before the Civil War. The brightest and most ambitious people of the republic seemed to be flocking to cities as they provided the natural outlet for the vast American commercial and agricultural empire. It was obvious that despite the initial economic shock of southern secession, the West in general and Chicago in particular were thriving and busily supplying the Union with grain, beef, pork, and other materials.[31]

The *City Directory* recorded the phenomenal growth of manufacturing in Chicago. From 1857 to 1863, the number of agricultural implement manufacturers grew from two to seven, while grain elevators expanded from seven to eighteen and iron foundries from eight to fifteen. By 1863, extensive railroad and machine shops employed several thousand workers. Meanwhile 101 hacks and 99 omnibuses moved Chicagoans around their quickly expanding city—not to mention the street railways, which continued to expand. In between producing and shipping goods Chicagoans could stop at over six hundred saloons and grocers for their daily needs.[32]

Railroad and water traffic combined to give the city an immense advantage over her rivals. The South Branch Dock Company began its colossal project in 1859. That year it unveiled plans to build a massive system of docks that would include over five miles of water frontage and would be connected to all the railroads coming in and out of the city. The project promised the best dockage in the city and superior connections to all parts of the West. The site chosen lay on the West Side just across the river from Bridgeport, taking in the entire north bank from Halsted to Ruben Street. Seven 100-foot wide and 12-foot-deep ship canals with an average length of 1,700 feet were cut at right angles to the river. Streets ran through the project connecting it with every part of the city. Company planners also laid railroad tracks that connected to a Chicago, Burlington and Quincy (CB&Q) track just south of Twenty-second Street. The CB&Q agreed to assist all the other railroads serving the city. The site sat at the head of the Illinois and Michigan Canal and connected directly with the waterway and all the railroads. Railroads could make up lumber trains directly from the yards and send them off to their natural market in the West. Operators purchased land for new mills adjacent to the lumberyards. Chicago at the head of a great transportation system took advantage of wartime and waited for peace to reach its full potential.[33]

Figure 17. This view of the lumberyards along Clark Street between Twelfth and Fourteenth Streets about 1870 shows the vastness of their operation along the South Branch of the river. (ICHi-03740, Chicago History Museum.)

After the Civil War the *Chicago Tribune* lectured Chicago, stating that "it is not enough that our merchants should be the middle men of Eastern manufacturers, but we should begin to make a large percentage of the wares we sell." Chicago seemed at a particular advantage to supply the goods for a rebuilding South and an expanding West as it looked to the postwar world. By September 1865, manufacturing accounted for about one-eighth of Chicago's wealth. The city had both the raw material and the market to further develop its industrial strength.[34]

Indeed while few saw the extent of change at the time, Chicago once again entered into a new age as the Civil War came to an end. The city had developed from a fur trading community to a great commercial district in the first twenty years of its existence. The arrival of the McCormick Reaper Works and other manufacturers between 1848 and 1860 had ushered in a new industrial era. These firms produced largely for local and regional markets. With the wartime expansion and the development of the railroads the city's industries began to seek out a larger national market. After the Civil War this market continued to grow and Chicago's industrial base expanded, making the city a great center of manufacturing with its products being sold throughout the world.

The Industrial New Age

On Christmas Day 1865, investors, cattlemen, farmers, and railroad operators gathered to celebrate the opening of the Union Stock Yard located just south-west of the city in the newly formed Town of Lake. Earlier in January 1865, before the fighting had ended and Lincoln had been assassinated, the Chicago Pork Packers Association, several railroads, and the *Chicago Tribune* proposed and supported the creation of a giant stockyard that would combine all the livestock trading businesses of the city into one huge market.

Four stockyards operated in the city in 1865, the Pittsburgh and Fort Wayne, the Michigan Southern, the Cottage Grove, and the Sherman Stockyards. This resulted in near chaos, and, as in the lumber business, traders looked for a centralized market where prices could be consistent with demand. The proposed yard promised to bring order to the process where only chaos had reigned before. Proponents advised that "the arrangement will be better to the seller, the buyer, and the public, to say nothing of the improvement in the condition of the stock, which will be much better provided for in one yard than where several minor ones are devoted to its reception." The promised location also seemed more than adequate with connections to the three eastern railroads for shipment to coastal markets. Railroad tracks would connect all the roads leading in and out of Chicago.[35]

The three eastern railroads united to purchase 320 acres of land outside of the city's limits for $100,000. They planned to fence and plank the area and construct hotels for shippers and other necessary buildings at a cost of over $1 million. On January 15, 1865, supporters introduced an incorporation bill in the Illinois state senate. The governor signed the legislation on February 13. While some complained that the new stockyard would impose a railroad and packers monopoly on the trade, others called it an important protection for the stockmen who raised livestock.[36]

The railroads proved central to the new venture. By the end of 1850, a 4,700-mile railroad network centered on Chicago. In 1854, the Chicago and Rock Island Railroad reached the Mississippi River. Two years later it crossed the "Father of Waters" and headed further west. Other railroads reached out toward Milwaukee, and by 1865 the old Galena line, now part of the Chicago and Northwestern Railroad, pressed on to the Mississippi River. The great livestock empire of the West became part of Chicago's ever expanding hinterland. Hogs, cattle, and sheep formerly sent to local markets or to St. Louis and Cincinnati now made their way to Chicago, especially as that city's potential as a market expanded with rail connections to the east. In May 1852, the Michigan Central and the Michigan Southern provided the city's first rail connections to the East. Six years later the Pittsburgh, Fort Wayne, and Chicago Railroad reached Chicago, providing Chicago shippers with yet another route to New York City. By 1860 the railroads' victory was complete. The "iron horse" delivered over two-thirds of Chicago's imports and carried three-quarters of its exports to other markets. Chicago's population grew to over one hundred thousand on the eve of the Civil War. The young metropolis acquired yet more railroads without the expenditure of a single cent of public money as it built upon its reputation as a center of commerce and transportation. Now Chicago could develop into a great manufacturing center and meatpacking would be central to the new economy.[37]

Investors hired Parisian-born and American-raised Octave Chanute to design the new livestock market. No such market had ever been contemplated before. The land, purchased from John Wentworth was, like much of Chicago, a huge swamp. The problem of drainage led Chanute to install thirty miles of drains that ran into two large discharge sewers that flowed into the Chicago River's South Branch and South Fork. Groundbreaking for the box sewer on Halsted Street marked the official beginning of construction on June 1, 1865. First materials for the new stockyard arrived by wagon, but once the railroads laid tracks to the site three trains a day arrived with lumber for the great bovine city being constructed at Thirty-ninth and Halsted. Chanute expected local packers to drive their purchases to locations along the South Branch. He laid out the stockyard in a grid and divided it into four parts or divisions, three for receiving livestock and the fourth for shipping animals to the East. The engineer assigned each of the divisions to the various railroads as the original stockyard was conceived as a shipping point for the West's producers. The Union Stock Yard originally contained pens large enough to hold 21,000 cattle, 75,000 hogs, 22,000 sheep, and 200 horses. The six-story Hough House, the market's hotel, provided a showplace for the stockyards with its 130-foot frontage on Halsted Street. Made of the same brick as the exchange and office building in the center of the pens, the hotel presented a lively public face for the Union Stock Yards.[38]

Chicago's elite celebrated the Christmas Day opening of the new Union Stock Yards with fanfare. A special train brought visitors southwest of the city to see the new marketplace with special guests enjoying a particularly "capitalist" Christmas dinner at Hough House. The next day 761 hogs went on sale in the pens brought over by local commission men. But on December 27 trains arrived with 3,700 hogs and the first loads of cattle and sheep as Chicago finally had its central livestock market. In 1866, the yard's first full year of operation the "livestock hotel" catered to 1,564,293 head of livestock. Its rapid growth mirrored Chicago's as producers and shippers brought more and more livestock to the stockyards. By 1900, the original 320-acre site grew to 475 acres with a pen capacity for 75,000 cattle, 50,000 sheep, 300,000 hogs, and 5,000 horses. In that year 14,622,315 animals filled its vast array of pens and chutes. In the 1920s annual livestock runs at the Chicago market would twice exceed 18 million head.[39]

At first Chicago's meatpackers remained along the South Branch, with their workers driving animals purchased at the stockyards down Halsted

Street and Archer Road to their plants. These seasonal operations stretched from Eighteenth Street to the Illinois and Michigan Canal, also lining both the Ogden Slip and Healy Slough connected to the South Branch. Before the development of refrigeration they closed for the summer, and one newspaper reporter said that so did "the life and activity of Bridgeport, Nothing is doing." This was not quite true, as the more than two thousand men who worked in the various plants also found work on the canal or in other industries close to or in Bridgeport, such as the Union Steel Works on Archer and Ashland Avenue. Eventually the packing plants migrated to the Town of Lake. The Hutchinson plant moved there in 1868. The packer purchased land adjacent to the stockyard that September and built a large packinghouse and other buildings including a boardinghouse for his workers. He purchased several smaller firms and incorporated the Chicago Packing and Provision Company. Others soon joined Hutchinson at the new location.[40]

The emerging collection of meat plants just to the west of the stockyard guaranteed its future as a major market. The yearlong storage of ice and its use to keep meat fresh and later the development of refrigeration did away with the seasonal character of the industry. Chicago's packers, led by Swift and Armour, developed refrigerated railroad cars in the 1870s that helped create a national market for the products of Chicago's "river of blood." This technological development came about after several years of experimentation. Railroads declined to carry the new refrigerated cars, and then East Coast butchers refused to sell the meat. Swift and Company finally made a deal with the Canadian carrier, the Grand Trunk Railroad, to move the cars along their line, eventually forcing the American roads to carry the frozen meat to eastern markets. Swift then opened stores of his own in eastern cities and competed with the local butchers, who rejected Swift's "embalmed" beef. Swift and Company meat markets soon outsold local butchers and forced them to take on the Chicago product. Chicago's new capitalists could be ruthless in their use of technology to gain higher profits.[41]

In 1879, the North Chicago Rolling Mill Company began to look for a larger location than the North Branch site it developed less than twenty years earlier. The firm's production of steel rails continued to grow, and downtown businesses complained of pollution and crowded streets caused by industries still located in or near the heart of the city. The Union Stock Yard had shown the advantages to suburban industrial development, and the iron and steel industry soon followed. In 1879, the North Chicago Rolling Mill Company began to consider a site far to the south on the banks of the Calumet River in the Township of Hyde Park. Four years earlier the Brown Steel Company located just up the river in the same general area. South Chicago had been a sleepy fishing village when in 1869 the Calumet and Chicago Canal Company began developing the land along the river. The federal government deepened the Calumet River and improved the harbor.

EXCHANGE BUILDING, UNION STOCK YARDS, CHICAGO

Figure 18. The Livestock Exchange Building in the Union Stock Yards became the center of the nation's livestock industry as packinghouse buyers and livestock commission men created a national market emanating from Chicago. (Postcard, Author's Collection.)

The North Chicago Rolling Mill Company decided on a strip of lakefront adjacent to the mouth of the Calumet River as the site for their new plant. In 1880, the firm built four blast furnaces. Two years later a Bessemer steel mill and a new rail mill began operation. In 1889, the North Chicago Rolling Mill Company merged with Bridgeport's Union Steel Company and the Joliet Steel Company to form the Illinois Steel Company, and the South Chicago plant became known simply as South Works.

By 1898, the South Works had expanded from its original 74.5-acre site to approximately 260 acres. It dominated South Chicago's lakefront, and the industry soon dominated the entire economy of the region. In 1898, 3,500 men worked at South Works. At this time it was one of the most modern in the country. Thirty-six miles of standard track ran through the giant mill along with 6.5 miles of three-foot gauge track. Ore arrived by ship from the Mesabi Range in Minnesota. The North Slip connected directly with the lake and had a capacity of seven hundred thousand tons. The ore yards served by the South

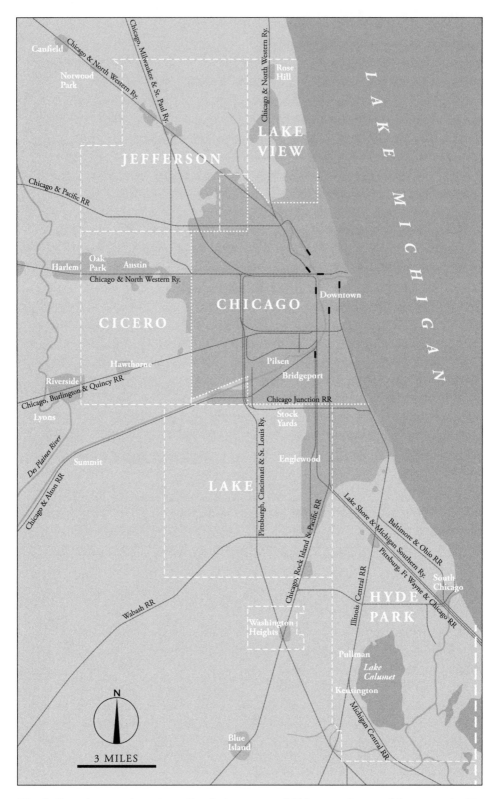

Map 2. Shown here are the various railroads that connected Chicago to the rest of the country in 1880. (Dennis McClendon.)

Slip had a capacity of three hundred thousand tons. In 1897, South Works received a total of 1,629,865 tons of ore during an ice-shortened shipping season that lasted from April 15 to December 15. Other mills soon arrived in South Chicago. In the 1880s Iroquois Steel opened on the south bank of the Calumet River. Later it moved to the mouth of the river just across from the South Works. Three large mills located near 106th Street and the Calumet River: Wisconsin Steel, the successor to Brown Steel and a division of International Harvester, the Federal Furnace Company, and Interstate Iron and Steel Company. The Youngstown Sheet and Tube Company also came to South Chicago. The steel industry expanded down the south lakefront eventually crossing the state line and creating a new city, Gary, after 1900. By this time the South Works was part of a huge new corporation, U.S. Steel. Chicago's industrial economy now served a worldwide market.[42]

The New Relationship between Workers and Owners

Industrial developments in Chicago and across the nation resulted in a new relationship between workers and owners—one that would come to define both labor and management over the next century. Since the beginning of the Industrial Revolution in Britain in the seventeenth century, work and home increasingly developed as distinct places. Men, women, and children traveled away from home to work in the new factories and mills, while their parents and grandparents had worked on family farms or in businesses operated from the family home. This was true for the owners and the growing management class as well as for laborers. This divide had much to do with the alienation of women from the public sphere in postcolonial America and the creation of a private domestic sphere, which was considered the proper place for women to live and work. The accumulation of the large amounts of capital necessary to establish the new factories, such as the packing and steel plants, also changed the basic notion of equality and even the American Dream. Chicago saw the increased separation of domestic and business concerns in the 1850s and 1860s. As factories grew larger, louder, and busier, they no longer operated in homes as traditional shoe cobblers, tanners, grocers, or silver smiths. The rich began to move away from the busy, crowded, polluted, and boisterous riverfront. In Chicago the first neighborhoods defined by wealth appeared along South Michigan Avenue. The poor in the city tried to live as close as they could to work but were often pushed to the edges of urban development. Here they supplemented their meager incomes with gardens or the raising of livestock. Some provided dairy products and vegetables for the growing population. Many immigrants, African Americans, and native-born poor settled near the branches of the Chicago River in districts that were also the sites of the massive industrial concerns.

The growing divide in income and work between laborers and owners meant that class became paramount on the city's streets. Equality of opportunity seemed farther and farther away from reality. The business classes gathered greater and greater power while workers felt more and more like cogs in the great wheel of industry with little power or opportunity to further their interests. Owners met each other in clubs and business associations, and while they could be fierce competitors in the very real game of monopoly, they all agreed that workers should be kept in their place. Workers in turn began to see themselves as a distinct class from the owners, who no longer labored side by side with them as Cyrus McCormick and his brothers did when they first arrived in Chicago. Now McCormick, Gustavus Swift, Potter Palmer, Marshall Field, and others lived in mansions far from the workplace and even greater distances from their workers' experience in the new social world constructed by nineteenth-century capitalism. Workers began in the years after the Civil War to struggle to create unions to give them some leverage in the new industrial city. They attempted to exercise a kind of countervailing power that would return the Republic to some semblance of its long promised goal of equality and democracy.

The rich and the middle class in turn began to seek out neighborhoods farther and farther away from the industrial and commercial concerns they owned. In part this was made possible by the developing mass transit system. At first omnibuses moved the well-to-do from their homes to their places of work. Then after 1860 horse-drawn streetcars began to reach outlying areas. Finally in the 1880s a vast and intricate cable car system would be put in place, to be succeeded by electric trolleys in the 1890s. Commuter railroads also allowed the expansion of residential areas beyond the city's borders to far-flung railroad suburbs.

Emery E. Childs, an eastern investor, formed the Riverside Improvement Company in the 1860s and purchased a 1,600-acre tract of land near the Des Plaines River. It included an oak-hickory forest and was about eleven miles from Chicago's downtown. The well-drained tract was almost mosquito free. Olmsted, Vaux and Associates laid out the town on what had been the Gage Farm. The Chicago, Burlington & Quincy Railroad connected the site with Chicago's downtown. Riverside was different from other suburban towns at the time. It would be a controlled environment. Olmsted rejected Chicago's grid system of streets in favor of curvilinear roads. Lots were generous, and houses were to be set back thirty feet from the street. Park land lay alongside the river, and the original design included essential services more associated with inner city living than suburban homes at the time. Olmsted hoped to combine modern living with the "domestic advantages" of country living.[43]

By 1871, the town attracted a number of Chicago's elite families, but the Chicago Fire of that year in the short run crippled further development. Residential growth of Riverside would not occur until after 1880, and by that time the original development company had gone under. Still, Olmsted's plan remained largely intact into the twentieth century, but complete development did not occur until almost one hundred years after Olmsted and Vaux's plan was drawn up.[44]

To an extent Riverside marked much of future suburban development. Olmsted believed that the "country" residences should be a retreat from the business world of the city with its hurriedness, noise, pollution, and attractions of dubious reputation. Men would go into the city and make a living in the "public" sphere only to retreat afterward to a suburban "domestic" sphere where women provided a gentle and quiet home for them and their children. Riverside then was an early example of the suburban ideal or retreat.

The town may have been born in gentility and attempted to preserve its unique place in the western suburbs, but other suburbs of not so gentle a reputation quickly joined it. Located relatively close to the Illinois and Michigan Canal and its expanding industrial corridor, Riverside attempted to preserve itself as a suburban retreat. The turn of the century saw Riverside surrounded by other suburbs many of a distinctly working-class character as Chicago's industrial base spread across the region. First Samuel E. Gross's development Grossdale (Brookfield) was laid out with more modest lots after 1889. Riverside's oldest neighbor, Lyons, to the south developed as a recreational suburb attracting Chicagoans traveling out to the countryside for picnics and eventually to visit amusement parks such as Cream City. Taverns dotted the small town as thirsty Chicagoans visited Lyons. After 1900, with the construction of the massive Western Electric plant in Cicero, Riverside's immediate neighbor to the east, Berwyn, expanded with working-class housing.[45]

Chicago was a quickly changing city. Charles Cleaver, an early English immigrant, entrepreneur, and South Side real estate promoter who arrived in Chicago in 1833, once counted 160 schooners docked in Chicago from the top of the Bristol and Porter's warehouse on the corner of State and South Water Street. Years later he recalled that all of that soon ended once the railroads arrived from the East in 1852. Grain would be moved all year long by the iron horse as it came to dominate the West. Chicago changed with the new reality, the new technology of transportation. It would not be the first nor the last time that the city shed its skin like a snake and moved on.[46]

The Era of Urban Chaos

On October 8, 1871, a fire broke out in the barn behind the O'Leary house on DeKoven Street. The Near West Side had long lost the rural character it had when real estate magnate and philanthropist Charles Hull built his country retreat there just fifteen years earlier. It now contained a teeming immigrant neighborhood filled with, among others, working-class Irish, German, and newly arrived Czech immigrants. The district symbolized everything that many native whites felt had gone wrong with the country. Young thieves plagued the area as they made their way down the alleys and gangways stealing anything that could be sold to a local junk dealer. The *Chicago Daily News* referred to the West Side as a "nursery for criminals," indicting all working-class neighborhoods across the city.[1] This new post–Civil War immigrant city seemed a chaotic place indeed when compared with a romanticized small town American past. Strange languages and rituals dominated these streets. Catholics chanted in Latin, and men and women with thick brogues or Central European accents filled the tenements and sidewalks. Others with seemingly unpronounceable names spoke what sounded like unintelligible tongues as they made Chicago home. All things seemed to have changed, and not always for the better.

A Wooden Immigrant City on the Prairie

In 1864, a young Norwegian immigrant, Christian H. Jevne, wrote a letter to his parents shortly after his arrival in the city. He complained about the fact that he could not get the "cussed Yankees to speak Norwegian" and that he had to "jabber in English all day long." He grumbled that other ethnic groups mutilated the English tongue. The city's ethnic diversity both impressed and seemed to overwhelm him. Jevne estimated that there were about seventy churches in Chicago and that while Germans, with the largest concentrations on the North Side, seemed to make up about half of the population, all nationalities and all religions made Chicago home. The young Norwegian wrote, "here all people are politicians." The city felt unbearably hot in the summer and colder than

Norway in the winter. He warned that one must work hard in America. Hard work certainly paid off for Jevne. In 1865, the Norwegian opened his own business on East Kinzie Street with a capital investment of $200. Eventually Jevne built the city's largest wholesale and retail grocery business, importing goods from around the world.[2]

As the Civil War ended new problems and difficulties arose, and talk of another civil war could be heard on the city's streets. In early 1871, the Paris Commune, Europe's first communist revolt, portended a terrible future of class warfare. Instead of North and South, the next conflict might be between the rich and the poor, and Chicago had plenty of both. The fire in the barn on DeKoven Street had been waiting to happen for some time. When it burst across the city it seemed to usher in an era of urban chaos.

The economic expansion of the Civil War years increased the city's wealth. Chicago's population continued to explode, growing from 112,172 in 1860 to 298,977 ten years later. Both immigrants and native-born Americans arrived to seek their fortune. Immigrants from the British Isles predominated, with the Irish in the lead, but Germans followed closely behind. Scandinavians also poured into the city. Smaller numbers of Poles, Czechs, and Italians made their way on crowded streets. In 1860 foreign-born residents made up 50 percent of Chicago's population. Ten years later they made up slightly less than half at 48.4 percent, never reaching the fiftieth percentile again. Nevertheless, the foreign born and their American-born children continued to dominate Chicago well into the twentieth century, making up nearly 80 percent of the city's population until World War I.

In 1870, Chicago had about the same average percentage of employment as eastern cities; about 38 percent of the total population worked outside the home, including women and children. Of these workers, Americans made up slightly over one-third while immigrants consisted of 64 percent. Twenty-six percent of the native born worked for someone else. Fifty percent of the foreign born hired themselves out. Manufacturing and mechanical industries employed more than any other part of the economy. The unskilled made up 34 percent of industrial laborers. A larger proportion of immigrants than Americans worked in industry. Germans made up the largest percentage of skilled workers, while 54 percent of the Irish worked in unskilled positions. In the rapidly expanding city, workers in the building trades led the ranks of the skilled.

The wholesale and retail trade, in which Jevne excelled, presented the next largest sector of Chicago's economy. Native-born Americans made up the largest segment, more than 50 percent, of those engaged in trade. The Germans, their nearest competitors, made up 20 percent of those engaged in such pursuits. Scandinavians dominated the numbers of mariners, as many Norwegians took to the Great Lakes as they had to the sea. Scandinavians and Irish women made up the majority of those who worked in domestic service. Native white Americans dominated banking, insurance, and the professions. While Chicago-

Figure 19. Pictured here in the late 1860s, Edward Ely came to Chicago in 1853 at the age of twenty-three from Huntington, Connecticut, and established himself as prominent clothier. By the end of the Civil War, Ely's business had grown, as had its reputation as the finest men's clothing store in the West offering the latest fashions from England, France, and America. Like many businessmen of his generation Ely supported the Republican Party and various charities including the Erring Women's Refuge, to which he left a substantial contribution upon his death in 1891. (Albumen Photo by John Carbutt in Author's Collection.)

ans originally from New England and Upstate New York made up a small percentage of the city's population, they dominated the city's institutions and economic life.

In the decade before the Civil War women found positions beyond domestic service and teaching. In 1870, 3,763 women worked in manufacturing, while earning lower wages than men. Children from ten to fifteen years old made up less than 3 percent of the gainfully employed in 1870, a percentage lower than the national average. Over half of these children labored in industry. Many girls worked as seamstresses, but domestic service attracted more of them.[3]

Less than forty years after its incorporation as a small town in 1833, Chicago grew to be the nation's fifth largest city, just twelve thousand residents behind rival St. Louis, which it surpassed in the 1880s. The city's merchant and industrial leaders created a city that they saw as a mechanism for their own wealth. The quick movement of people, goods, information, and investment not only across Chicago but across the nation and beyond proved crucial to their success. Haphazard growth had to be somewhat controlled, primarily by private agreements, but development would be as uninhibited as possible.

As in other American cities, Chicago's riverfront, filled with docks, ships, granaries, and warehouses, provided the site of the first city center. After the Civil War the waterfronts began to give way to other parts of the city, as a more intricate central city developed along patterns that included the creation of separate areas for different kinds of uses. This segregation by function eventually changed the downtown and gave at least a semblance of logic to the city's growth pattern. Booksellers congregated in one part of the downtown, music stores in another, and theaters on yet another street, while various professionals gathered together at certain street corners. Nevertheless this segregation occurred within an uncontrolled market system and through private agreements among Chicago's emerging economic elite.

In 1867, Potter Palmer began to shift the retail center away from Lake Street near the river to State Street, bringing along his longtime partners and friends, Marshall Field and Levi Leiter. Palmer, long known as the "Merchant Prince" of Chicago, now became a major real estate developer as he bought three quarters of a mile of land along State Street and soon transformed the shoddy narrow road. He persuaded other property owners and the city council to widen State Street as he replaced the shacks at State and Monroe Streets with his elegant hotel. The erection of the fabulous Palmer House and of the six-story building sheathed in Connecticut limestone that housed Field, Leiter and Company in 1868 set the stage for the development of State Street as the retail center of the city.[4]

This migration of the retail heart of the city occurred just after Chicago moved into a new transportation era in 1859. William Bross drove the first spike of the Chicago City Railway Company's tracks at the corner of State and Randolph on April 25, 1859. The North Chicago City Railway also began service in 1859, while the West Side did not see the inauguration of service by the Chicago West Division Railway until 1861 and in 1867 horse car tracks finally reached Thirty-ninth Street, making a faster and more reliable connection to the downtown. Soon an extensive horse streetcar system spanned the growing city.[5] Chicago spread quickly across the muddy prairie. The horse carlines

Figure 20. The Connecticut limestone–clad Field and Leiter Building stood on the corner of State and Washington Streets, ca. 1869. (Chicago Public Library, Special Collections and Preservation Division.)

reached southwest along Archer Avenue to about Ashland Avenue, joining Bridgeport and the expanding canal industrial district to the downtown. Horse cars also ran south on State Street and then over to the Union Stock Yards on Forty-third Street in the suburban Town of Lake. Along the lake riders could go as far north as Irving Park Road and as far south as Fifty-fifth Street. By 1871, West Side residents living near Madison and Harrison could reach Western Avenue by public transit. Although plenty of Chicagoans still walked to work, the days of the "Walking City" were numbered.

The impact of public transportation on these outlying neighborhoods cannot be overestimated. Pre–Civil War Chicago was largely a pedestrian city that saw social classes, ethnic groups, and races living in close proximity to each other and mixing on city streets. The arrival of suburban commuter trains allowed the wealthy to begin creating suburbs just outside the city limits. New horse car lines meant that lower middle class and working-class people might also be able to leave the crowded city center that investors already greedily looked at for business expansion. Outlying districts became available for homes at a more affordable price. After the Civil War, many Chicagoans poured across the prairie, creating various neighborhoods based on social class, race, and ethnicity.[6]

The neighborhoods along the Milwaukee Avenue transportation corridor are good examples of this growth. Milwaukee Avenue is one of the city's few diagonal streets as it makes its way northwest from the downtown. Germans, Swedes, Norwegians, and then Poles and Jews followed the corridor out of the city in the late nineteenth and early twentieth centuries. The earliest settlement in the corridor developed near the North Western Railroad car shops just northwest of the downtown. By 1860, the Milwaukee Avenue horse car line ran northwest from Halsted Street, facilitating residential development. Chicago's burgeoning German population had begun to cross the North Branch of the river, and in 1864 German Catholics petitioned the Archdiocese for a national parish. In 1866, Germans organized St. Boniface Catholic Church on Noble and Cornell (Chestnut) Streets.

As the Germans began to build their community, Polish immigrants from German-occupied western Poland arrived in large numbers. While many Germans welcomed their Catholic coreligionists, others did not, and clashes broke out between the two groups and a group of parishioners forced the German pastor to resign, wanting a strictly German-speaking parish. The new pastor moved quickly against the nationalists, but change continued and Kashubes, a group who spoke a German-Polish dialect, soon predominated at St. Boniface. The Poles meanwhile quickly built their own institutions, erecting two huge Catholic churches within a few blocks of St. Boniface.

The Milwaukee Avenue corridor developed quickly after 1869 with the opening of Humboldt Park on its west end. The Milwaukee Road Railroad soon opened a Humboldt station at Bloomingdale and California Avenues,

Figure 21. This horse car ran down Halsted Street in 1886. Soon after 1859, Chicago's various horse streetcar lines reached outlying areas and ushered in the era of mass transit in the city. (Chicago Public Library, Special Collections and Preservation Division.)

and soon after local real estate advertisements appeared in German as well as English inviting new residents to one of Chicago's "most delightful" suburbs. Many Germans left St. Boniface to move northwest away from the growing Polish community. In turn the Poles would soon follow as transportation lines expanded westward to Jefferson Park.[7]

Transportation improvements were not the only changes coming. The rise of industrial capitalism shifted the economic and cultural landscape. What did equality (for white men) mean in the new capitalist economy? What, if any, controls were there to be on development? What did the large numbers of foreign born mean for American society? What role would the newly freed African American population play in the United States? Perhaps most basic of all, what role would cities have in this traditionally agrarian society? Would cities bring with them all of the problems and unrest that Thomas Jefferson feared, or would they be engines of prosperity as Alexander Hamilton believed? Did the social struggles of Europe portend a similar future for America? Chicago, growing at a shocking pace, provided a laboratory for the new industrial capitalist society. Americans entered an era that made them question their future.

While they did not use terms such as globalization, Chicagoans and other Americans knew this was an international experiment. Europe in particular

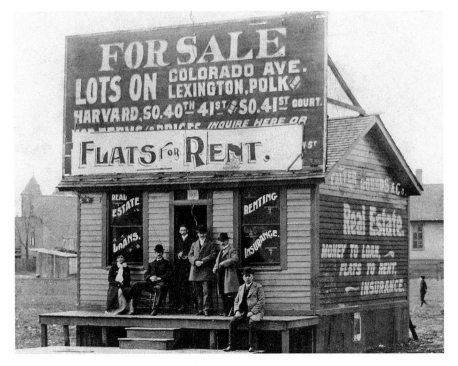

Figure 22. Falter Rounds and Company put up this temporary real estate office about 1890. As traction lines spread investors developed residential properties on the outskirts of the city. (Chicago Public Library, Special Collections and Preservation Divisions.)

seemed to be a bubbling cauldron of change. Immigrants coming to the United States brought new and dangerous ideas and political movements. Catholics, Jews, socialists, anarchists, and others all seemed indistinguishable to many native-born Protestant white Americans. The giant cities resulting from the new economy provided fertile soil for foreign ideas to grow. American farmers rebelled against the new industrial order, creating the Granger and Populist movements. Midwest farmers in particular saw Chicago with its vast industries, its markets for grain and livestock, and its railroads as a major instrument of change and even oppression.

In March 1871, a new generation of French revolutionaries proclaimed the Paris Commune, and for the next seventy-two days Paris and France once again shocked and threatened the status quo. As Paris burned in May of that year, one Frenchmen recalled the times in what might have been prophetic tones for Chicago: "As we stood there silent and still, watching the fire sweep across the city until the break of day, history seemed to unfold before our eyes."[8] The defeat of the Paris Commune did not rid the world of working-class revolt nor of the fear of revolution. Soon Chicago would be the epicenter of change and conflict in the new capitalist world order. Fire, unfortunately, also played a role in the young city's future. In 1871, with a population of over just over three hundred thousand, Chicago embodied the new industrial city.

The Great Chicago Fire

The long, hot, dry summer of 1871 proved to be a dangerous one for the wooden city. Fire constantly threatened, and a conflagration raged across the West Division on Saturday, October 7. It started at the Lull and Holmes planning mill in a district known as the "Red Flash." After causing $1 million in damages and consuming four city blocks, the Chicago Fire Department contained it and saved the city from devastation, extinguishing the blaze on Sunday afternoon. That night, however, the city would not be spared as a fire broke out once again on the West Side, this time in a barn owned by the O'Leary family. Catherine O'Leary ran a small milk business and had just received a new load of hay for her cows. Once the fire started it spread quickly across the city to the northeast of the O'Leary barn. Ironically the fire put out just that afternoon kept the West Side from more damage by creating a buffer against the new and more dangerous blaze.[9]

The fire quickly overwhelmed the 185-member Chicago Fire Department. A wall of flames moving at hurricane speeds spread across the city from the southwest, jumping over the South Branch and devastating the business district before leaping over the river again to attack the North Division. Roughly three and one-half square miles, or over 2,100 acres, of the city lay in ruins. The fire destroyed 17,420 buildings and left nearly one hundred thousand Chicagoans homeless. Although most returned, roughly thirty thousand Chicagoans immediately left the city on free railway passes. Financial losses approached $200 million, about a third of the valuation of the entire city. The "Burnt District" included over twenty-eight miles of streets and over 120 miles of sidewalks. As it swept northeast across Chicago, the conflagration finally died out on the North Side near Fullerton Avenue and the Lake in Lincoln Park. About three hundred people lost their lives, an astonishingly low number given the magnitude of the disaster. That same night over one thousand residents of Peshtigo, Wisconsin, died in a fire that destroyed the lumber town. Ironically, Peshtigo, had supplied much of the raw material for Chicago and its lumber trade. Chicago's William B. Ogden proved to be a major loser in both fires as his Chicago and Peshtigo businesses lay in ruins.[10]

The inferno began in one of Chicago's poorest working-class districts, but it showed no class bias as it roared across the city. It destroyed the Palmer House, the Court House, the Post Office, and the many "fire-proof" buildings. The flames quickly ruined all of the most valuable buildings of the city. The houses of the rich and the poor burned as well as stores, factories, hotels, banks, and newspaper offices.

What the inferno did not destroy proved to be as important as what it incinerated. Two hundred thousand Chicagoans still had their homes. The factories and packinghouses stood intact. While the railroad passenger stations lay destroyed, the web of rail lines leading into Chicago and connecting the city to

Figure 23. The Crosby Theater after the Great Fire of 1871. (Chicago Public Library, Special Collections and Preservation Division.)

both coasts remained in place. Chicago's boosters moved quickly to convince the nation and particularly eastern investors that the city remained a good risk. John Stephen Wright, Chicago's booster king, predicted the city's quick rebirth out of the smoldering ashes of the fire. Chicago's elite advised eastern investors that the fire offered an opportunity. In its first postfire editorial the *Chicago Tribune* told the city to "Cheer Up." The newspaper proclaimed that the worst was over "and we can resume the battle of life with Christian faith and Western grit." The *Tribune* pronounced, "CHICAGO WILL RISE AGAIN." Indeed East Coast investors still considered the city a good place to make a profit.[11]

The story quickly circulated that Mrs. O'Leary's cow had kicked over a lantern while she milked it late at night. She became a symbol of the fire and a permanent feature of the city's popular culture. Chicagoans largely blamed the O'Learys as the city behind their barn lay in ruins while their own home remained intact. Indeed the two Catholic churches that served the West Side Irish community remained unscathed by the blaze, the result perhaps of chance, a miracle, or a papal plot. Catholics were widely hated at the time of the fire, especially Irish Catholics, and a Romanist conspiracy did not seem absurd to many Protestant Chicagoans. Neither did a revolutionary scheme perhaps by a Communard driven from Paris and resettled on the banks of Lake Michigan. The calamity was so immense that natural causes seemed improbable if not impossible. In a world shaken by change and recently witness to a horrific civil war anything seemed possible.

On October 23, the *Chicago Times* published the alleged confession of an exiled Paris Communard who claimed to have set the fire to "humble the men who waxed rich at the expense of the poor." Although certainly a hoax, the confession exposed the fears of a city not only ravaged by fire but also keenly aware of its new class and ethnic structure. Chicagoans widely discussed Paris's tragedy as the *Chicago Tribune* provided intense coverage. Indeed on the same night as the fire, Rev. Robert Collyer of the prestigious Unity Church sermonized about the Parisian misfortune.

Others saw the fire as God's angry punishment for the city's many sins. The greed of its elite, the open prostitution, and the many saloons seemed to call down God's wrath upon this new Sodom or Gomorrah. Certainly for many rural Americans, Chicago symbolized foreignness in America. Some would see the fire as a way of expunging this cancer from the country. Many felt righteous about the disaster. Preachers warned Chicagoans to change their ways before God unleashed his fury.

Figure 24. Burnt District Coffee House after the fire, 1871. Chicago entrepreneurs quickly reacted to establish or reestablish businesses in the fire district. (Chicago Public Library, Special Collections and Preservation Division.)

Social class played an important role in both the perception of and the reaction to the disaster. Chicagoans faced immediate problems of law and order and food and shelter. One hundred thousand citizens needed immediate aid. Fear of the mob permeated the city as false rumors of looting, rape, and murder spread quickly. In fact Chicagoans were surprisingly calm and well behaved during and after the disaster. Nevertheless in the post–Civil War world of 1871 many middle- and upper-class Chicagoans saw the army as the only hope for the maintenance of order on city streets. Mayor Roswell B. Mason turned to Lt. Gen. Philip Henry Sheridan and the U.S. Army to patrol the city's streets for two weeks. Illinois Governor John M. Palmer fiercely opposed the use of troops as a usurpation of local power by the federal government. Working-class aldermen feared that the troops and martial law would be used against their constituencies. The arrival of Sheridan's troops proved that the business elite could take control of the city at a time of crisis, a city some felt they had lost control of before the fire. Relief measures and postfire housing regulations pointed to the assertion of power by the upper classes.

Relief posed an immediate problem, with as many as thirty thousand Chicagoans facing the immediate prospect of starvation. The cold winds and rain of October faced the homeless, as did the certainty of winter. The city turned once again to its elite business class, this time in the guise of the Chicago Relief and Aid Society, an organization founded by the city's wealthy in 1857. Mayor Mason overturned an earlier decision to create a relief committee made up of aldermen and private citizens and gave over all relief activities to that privately run organization on October 13. He saw the private organization as more able to deal with the Herculean task before it than the city government itself. The aldermen could not be trusted; their constituencies too easily influenced politicians.

The class implications of this decision became apparent immediately. The question of who deserved aid emerged. Like most nineteenth-century charitable institutions, the Chicago Relief and Aid Society saw the world as divided between the worthy and unworthy victims of poverty or disaster. Too much help might make the lower classes dependent. They did not see the poor as responsible citizens in a society imbued with frontier ideas of hard work, prosperity, and upward mobility. Social Darwinism and "scientific charity" determined the Chicago Relief and Aid Society's work among the victims of the fire and later during the depression of 1873. Many Chicagoans disagreed with the views of the Relief Society. Even the wives of some leaders spoke out against the policies their husbands enforced. Also, despite Roswell's handing over of relief to the Society, other community groups moved to deal with the fire's victims. At least thirty religious and ethnic based groups worked to aid the afflicted. These, however, paled before the resources of the Chicago Relief and Aid Society.[12]

The city rebounded quickly. Workers pushed much of the rubble into the lake, creating new real estate south of the river's mouth. Within six weeks, work

Figure 25. Rebuilding of Marine Bank Building on northeast corner of Lake and LaSalle Street looking east, 1871. Construction crews quickly erected buildings familiar to prefire Chicagoans. The Marine Bank reconstructed its old building with Italianate windows. (ICHi-02845, Chicago History Museum.)

began on over two hundred stone and brick buildings in the South Division, home of the business district. Within eighteen months new buildings appeared on downtown streets. Chicagoans erected the structures modeled on old plans. John Van Osdel, the city's first professional architect, designed many of the replacement structures. In the first year after the fire, he planned buildings whose frontage equaled one and a half miles. The rebuilding of Chicago created vast opportunities for designers and draftsmen. A Chicago familiar to area residents reappeared in the city's heart. Italianate windows and cast iron fronts faced Lake Street again. Structures, some as tall as eight stories, stood again on the charred lots, though many would be pulled down within twenty years for the skyscrapers of the new Chicago School of Architecture, which would make the city a world-class architectural center.[13]

Social tensions appeared during the reconstruction. City elites proposed the complete ban of wooden structures for all future construction in the city. Politicians from the less wealthy wards immediately protested the move as a form of punishing the poor and working class for the fire. Residents of the German North Side along Pine Street (North Michigan Avenue) and the Irish, Germans, and Czechs of the West Side could not afford to replace their homes with more expensive brick buildings. Furthermore outlying neighborhoods untouched by the flames would also suffer from the new ordinance. The compromise eventually ruled out wooden housing in the Fire District, but even here builders often ignored the law. Many of the "temporary" wooden buildings erected by the Chicago Relief and Aid Society and by residents themselves became permanent homes in Chicago neighborhoods.

City government in general grew in the aftermath of the conflagration, taking on more responsibility for social and economic affairs. The Chicago City Council passed laws regulating the sale of bread and hackney taxi fares and set up a department of building inspection. What had begun with the creation of a municipal water works now continued as Chicago's government expanded its powers. This new attitude toward government evolved out of disaster but also continued to develop out of the more subtle crises implied by the quickly changing free-market industrial economy. Chicago stood at the center of the debate concerning capital and its role in society, labor rights and how they should develop, and government.[14]

The nature of the continuing Industrial Revolution and the world market system shifted regional, national, and even international relationships. New technologies tied the country together. Railroads and telegraph lines allowed information to move quickly across the country. Disputes in one part of the world emerged as factors in another. Chicago workers often marked the anniversary of the Paris Commune. Word of strikes or union organizations and political parties moved along the rail and telegraph lines along with freight, passengers, and market information. The new system united the vast continent with Chicago at its economic center. Livestock prices in Chicago affected cowboys driving cattle to western railheads. Bricklayers in New York or London heard of opportunities in the rebuilding city. The price of Kansas and Iowa wheat on the Chicago market changed the lives of Polish and Ukrainian farmers. Irish, German, and Scandinavian families looked both to Chicago and its expanding frontier hinterland as an opportunity for economic mobility.

Map 3. The 1871 fire made its way from the West Side across the river to downtown and then jumped the river again to scorch the North Side. The 1874 fire, while it destroyed a much smaller area, burned through the area to the south of the 1871 fire zone, burning an area left untouched by the earlier disaster. (Dennis McClendon.)

The Clash between Labor and Capital

After the fire, eastern capital and raw midwestern muscle rebuilt Chicago. Since its foundation, the city had been a magnet for moneyed investors on one hand and men and women willing to do grueling labor on the other. Capitalists and workers clashed even before the Civil War. Working-class strife seemed a constant threat in Chicago as those who worked for the Yankee elite began to demand better wages and rights in their adopted city. Chicago's printers combined in one of the city's first labor organizations in the early 1850s. By 1860, the union had eighty-four members, more than one third of all printers in Cook County. Other workers joined together, but working-class solidarity proved elusive. The realities of the Civil War economy brought a modern union movement. In 1864, Chicago workers created fifteen new unions. Thirteen strikes took place that year, more than the total for the three previous years. Unions promised a chance for workers to improve their lot. As in other industrial centers, skilled workers were the first to organize and a culture of working-class protest emerged that eventually created a vital labor movement.

In the mid-1860s agitation for the eight-hour day grew and made an impact on the 1866 aldermanic elections. Despite election victories, Mayor John B. Rice stymied the movement. The forces of organized labor now turned to state congressional candidates. Chicago labor leader Andrew C. Cameron led workers in demanding eight-hour day legislation. Success came in early 1867 as the Illinois legislature enacted the first eight-hour law in the country. Employers quickly moved to circumvent the law by paying by the hour rather than by the day, claiming that a shorter workday threatened disaster for both workers and employers. Management refused to pay ten hours' wages for eight hours work.

On March 30, 1867, workers held a mass meeting in support of the new law. Some employers made concessions, but others stood steadfast against the eight-hour movement. The General Trades Assembly threatened a general strike. That spring proved to be a volatile one for labor relations. On May 1, 1867, workers held demonstrations cheering the new law. They gathered on Lake Street and started marching toward the lakefront at 10:00 a.m. More than a mile long, the procession included countless banners and flags. Just after noon, the parade reached the lakefront north of the fashionable townhouses of Park Row on Michigan Avenue. Mayor Rice addressed the workers, as did various other speakers.

In the aftermath of Eight Hour May Day celebrations, mass strikes and violence spread, followed by a three-day general strike. Outdoor laborers and unskilled workers roamed the streets in working-class neighborhoods, particularly Bridgeport where many brickyard, lumberyard, and other industrial workers lived, calling out nonstriking workers and clashing with police. Chicago's business leaders called for military action to stop the bands of workers. Mayor

Rice threatened to use force against the strikers. By May 8, the capitalists had defeated the unions, and the eight-hour day remained a dream.

The massive construction that took part in the immediate aftermath of the fire attracted workers from across the country and abroad. The enormous influx of labor depressed wages, drove up rents, and exacerbated class divisions. In January 1872, laborers demonstrated against proposed laws that restricted the use of flammable materials in construction. Workers saw the new laws as detrimental to their communities. They marched to a Common Council meeting at the temporary city hall. Demonstrators carried signs that proclaimed, "Leave a Home for the Laborer" and "Don't Vote Anymore for the Poor Man's Oppressor." On May 15, the city witnessed a massive demonstration of union members. Earlier on May 1, the *Chicago Tribune* reminded workers of the futile 1867 strike and claimed that one editorial calling for replacement workers would flood Chicago with men from across the country. In the early fall carpenters and bricklayers struck construction sites despite the advice of the *Tribune*.[15]

The national economic collapse of 1873 put a temporary halt to Chicago's rebuilding efforts. The decade that began with the fire now entered a dangerous financial slump. Another major fire in 1874 just south of the path of the Great Fire swept across the vice district below Harrison Street. The second great fire consumed forty-seven acres, destroyed 812 structures, and caused $1,067,260 in damages. Approximately twenty people died in the fire that started at about 4:30 p.m. on July 14 near the corner of Taylor Street and Fourth Avenue (Federal Street) just south of the rebuilt commercial district. Fire Marshal Mathias Benner decided to try to contain the fire as it ravaged small wooden buildings that the 1871 fire had missed. He ordered his men to drench a row of brick buildings in the fire's path. The blaze moved on and threatened the new downtown. By about 11:00 p.m., firemen, flame resistant buildings, and open lots retarded the growth of the blaze, which finally spent itself along the lakefront.

This time the poor and those on the edges of respectable society paid most of the price. The area had been home to poor working-class families and brothels that had concentrated in the district. The 1874 fire burned forty-nine of these "houses of ill-repute" on six blocks south of Harrison Street. Many of the working-class poor included African Americans or Russian and Polish Jews. They left the district after the fire. Blacks moved farther south, while the East Europeans made their way to the West Side. Others saw things more optimistically, seeing not a catastrophe but an opportunity from the ashes.

The 1874 fire helped invigorate a political movement among the upper classes aimed at reforming Chicago. Reforms of the immediate post-1871 fire had been compromised and not strictly enforced because of working-class objections to the new fire codes. Now a new consensus emerged among the propertied classes. The *Chicago Tribune* called for reform that would not be influenced by working-class voters. The National Board of Fire Insurance Underwriters demanded, among other reforms, the extension and enforcement of a ban on wooden buildings. Within a year, Chicago's elite forced the reorganization of the city's fire department, improved the water supply to fight fires, and extended the fire district limits to the city's borders. The second fire took a heavy toll among working-class families who now abandoned the downtown for outlying areas. Wealthy families, who still lived along Michigan and Wabash Avenues, left, turning their homes over to business purposes. Many of these families followed Marshall Field to Prairie Avenue, helping to create a new fashionable district on the Near South Side.[16]

Throughout the 1870s, workers across the country faced wage reductions and job losses. On July 16, 1877, in the middle of the worst year of the economic collapse, the Baltimore and Ohio Railroad announced a 10 percent wage cut. Striking workers shut down rail service from Baltimore to St. Louis, and clashes in a dozen cities resulted in hundreds of deaths and injuries. By July 25, the general strike reached as far as the Pacific. Farmers, miners, quarrymen, mill hands, and stevedores, among others, joined the struggle. The United States was in the midst of its first nationwide class conflict. For most Americans the events of 1877 raised the specter of revolution and anarchy and of images of the recent Paris Commune.

Chicago workers were not immune to the strike call. The emergence of the Workingmen's Party provided a source for pro-strike sentiment and agitation. On Saturday, July 21, organizers held a meeting at Sack's Hall on Twentieth Street and Brown Street (Sangamon Street). Albert Parsons, a young socialist printer from Texas, addressed the meeting. Parsons called for the eight-hour day and argued that machinery and the new factory system caused the working class's woes. He advocated a nonviolent approach and asked laborers to vote for the Workingmen's Party to bring about real change.

Albert Parsons stood in the vanguard of the Chicago radicals. Born in 1848 in Montgomery, Alabama, Parsons served in the Confederate Army, but underwent a conversion first to Radical Republicanism and later to socialism and then anarchism. In 1872, he married Lucy Waller, a woman of African American, Creek Indian, and Mexican descent. Mixed marriages were unacceptable in Texas, so the couple came to Chicago. Albert Parsons embodied the fears of the elite at the end of the century. Married to a woman of mixed racial ancestry, he socialized with immigrants and radicals and sought the overthrow of the established order. In many ways Parsons was the worst nightmare of wealthy Americans such as Marshall Field and George Pullman.

On July 22, the party distributed leaflets calling for a mass meeting on Monday the twenty-third at Market Square, the intersection of Madison Street and Market Street (Wacker Drive). In the evening, over ten thousand workers held torchlight processions carrying banners in English, German, and French. Parsons delivered a forceful speech and once again cautioned the crowd against violence. That night forty switchmen struck the Michigan Central Railroad

Figure 26. Workers and troops faced each other in the Battle of the Halsted Street Viaduct in Pilsen on the Lower West Side, 1877. (*Harpers Weekly,* August 18, 1877; ICHi-04893, Chicago History Museum.)

in response to a wage cut. Lumber shovers in the vast lumberyards along the South Branch also decided to walk off the job. These men would prove to be among the most radical of the workers in the city.[17] The national walkout had reached Chicago.

On Tuesday, July 24, when Parsons arrived to work at the *Chicago Times* he found that he had been fired. While at the offices of the German organ of the Workingmen's Party, the *Arbeiter-Zeitung,* two armed men asked Parsons to accompany them to the mayor's office. At city hall they brought him into a room filled with policemen, officials, and leading citizens. After questioning Parsons and insulting him for two hours, Police Superintendent Michael Hickey told him, "those Board of Trade Men would as leave hang you to a lamp-post as not." Mayor Monroe Heath referred to the strikers as "ragged Commune wretches."

Parsons then went to the *Chicago Tribune* office to see if he could find work and talk to the printers, but three men threw him out and threatened his life.

Meanwhile, some three thousand workers gathered again at Market Square. The police attacked the gathering and smashed the speaker's platform. The next day, July 25, the fighting began in earnest. Strikers and police clashed on Blue Island Avenue near the McCormick Reaper Works. On the Lower West Side, crowds attacked the Chicago, Burlington, and Quincy Railroad roundhouse on West Sixteenth Street, destroying two locomotives. The police dispersed the crowds, killing three and wounding seven. Police fought with workers on the Randolph Street Bridge and at the viaduct at Sixteenth and Halsted. For several days the police broke up workers' meetings including a peaceful gathering of Furniture Workers at Vorwarts Turner Hall on West Twelfth Street. In response to the attacks Judge William K. McAllister ruled that workers had the right to free assembly.

As in 1871, businessmen called for the militia to patrol city streets. Leading citizens and "merchant princes" conferred on how to deal with the rioters. On the afternoon of July 25 in the Moody and Sankey Tabernacle near Market Square, Chicago's elites discussed the emergency and how best to arm and organize citizens against the "communists." Rev. Robert Collyer proposed a force of thirty thousand special constables to patrol the streets. Others offered their own schemes. George Pullman, head of the Law and Order League, called for a rigorous response to the strike. Marshall Field and the "Military Committee" of the Citizen's Association raised funds for the militia and the following year donated two Gatling guns for the protection of Chicago.

By July 26 units of the Ninth and Twenty-second U.S. Infantry, two regiments of the Illinois state militia, a battery of artillery, and several companies of cavalry joined the Chicago police, five thousand special deputies, five hundred Civil War veterans, and members of various political organizations in patrolling the streets. The federal government rushed in Indian fighters from the Dakota territories. These men fresh from the frontier and under the command of President Grant's son fought with workers at the Halsted Street viaduct, killing over a dozen civilians and wounding twice as many. By Friday, July 27, the strength of the state had broken the strike. Chicago's hospitals and jails overflowed with workers; perhaps as many as fifty civilians died in the fighting. Not a single policeman or soldier was killed. On Saturday, July 28, the military escorted the first trains to leave the rail yards.[18]

The *Chicago Daily News,* while supporting their demands, had warned workers against violence. The newspaper covered the many clashes between workers and authorities throughout the city. In an editorial on July 27, after the collapse of the strike, the newspaper proclaimed "Tranquility" and lectured the residents, especially of the Near and Lower West Sides where much of the fighting had taken place: "You were whipped, badly whipped, precisely as we predicted, and precisely as you should have been." The newspaper pointed out that the police had no alternative as they had "every possible obligation to enforce order, even though the enforcement cost precious lives."[19]

The chaos of the strike had again raised the ghost of the Paris Commune and frightened the "respectable" citizens of Chicago. Once again they used over-whelming force to end the class conflict. The different social classes learned a great deal from the events of the summer of 1877. The threat of continual con-flict influenced the thinking of many capitalists, but especially George Pullman. For labor leaders, including Albert Parsons and his colleagues, the 1877 strike proved the inability of peaceful democratic change in a society where the forces controlled by the middle and upper classes were overwhelmingly armed and the workers were not.

The Capital of Radicalism

Chicago quickly became known as the center of radicalism in the United States. The ballot box seemed filled with empty promises to many of the veterans of the 1877 strike, and radicals openly debated the use of violence as a tactic. On Saturday evening, March 22, 1879, a crowd of perhaps thirty thousand workers and their families sang the "Marseillaise" and celebrated the Paris Commune of 1871 and the European revolutions of 1848. The day's activities included dem-onstrations by armed working-class ethnic paramilitary organizations. They paraded down the same downtown streets to the Inter-State Exposition Build-ing as the U.S. Army did two years earlier. Militant organizations armed as pri-vate militias, such as the Lehr-und-Wehr Verein, the Bohemian Sharpshooters, and the Irish Labor Guards, frightened middle-class and business leaders.

Parsons addressed the crowd the next day, reminding them of the desire of the French and German revolutionaries to create a working-class republic. He forcefully stated, "We mean to place Labor in Power." Parsons's Socialist Labor Party hoped to use the rally to mobilize workers for the spring elections, but voters abandoned the party in droves that year. The return of prosperity hurt the radical political movement, as did internal ideological divisions. The decline of the Socialist Labor Party further radicalized Parsons who, by 1880, turned to anarchism as an answer for society's problems. Throughout the year labor agi-tation continued, and on July 4, after three days of demonstrations, the Eight-Hour League held a huge parade. The Working Women's Union participated with a pink float supporting the cause. Women, immigrants, and even African Americans seemed to be coming together into a massive radical movement as the 1880s progressed.

The 1880s witnessed yet more demonstrations aimed at unnerving Chicago's elites. On a cold and windy Thanksgiving Day, November 27, 1884, despite rain and sleet, workers joined together in a mass demonstration. About one thou-sand people gathered in Market Square where organizers raised a large black flag, the new anarchist emblem and a symbol of hunger, misery, and death.

Parsons gave a rousing opening address condemning the Thanksgiving dinners of the capitalists. Afterward the crowd marched in line, forming a procession of over three thousand that, led by the black and red flags, moved south toward the wealthy dwellings along Prairie Avenue. As the column passed the Palmer House the band played the "Marseilles." Organizers repeated the demonstration the following year.

In the early 1880s a revolutionary anarchistic movement grew quickly in the United States. In Chicago influential German radical newspapers such as the *Vorbote* and *Arbeiter-Zeitung* placed themselves in the revolutionary fold. The Chicago Social Revolutionary Congress met in the city in October 1881, just three months after a similar meeting in London. Parsons, August Spies, and Justus Schwab, a representative of the Social Revolutionary Club of New York, led the three-day meeting that other radicals called a farce. Mostly German immigrants attended the congress at the North Side Turner Hall. The congress denounced wage slavery and private property and declared itself in union with the "armed organizations of workingmen who stand ready to resist, gun in hand, any encroachments upon their rights."[20]

In 1883, radicals met in Pittsburgh and founded the International Working People's Association (IWPA). This marked the rapid growth of the anarchist movement. The breakout of yet another economic crisis, the depression of 1883–86, brought many laborers back into the ranks of radicalism. The disparity between the rich and poor seemed greater than ever before in American society. Chicago's elite—Fields, Swift, Armour, and Pullman—stood in the first ranks of what revolutionaries called the plutocrats. Conflict broke out across the nation. Strikes, boycotts, and demonstrations abounded. By 1886, the number of strikers nationally tripled and the number of establishments struck quadrupled those of the previous five years. Police brutality once again marked conflicts as local authorities moved to stop strikes by deploying police against workers. In turn radicals, especially among the anarchists, saw dynamite as an answer to the overwhelming power of the capitalist state. Alfred Nobel, a Swedish chemist, had invented dynamite in 1866. The new explosive was safe to transport and relatively easy to use. Anarchists began to see it as the new "equalizer" in their struggle with capital. The *Alarm* advised revolutionaries to "practice the art of throwing bombs."[21]

In April 1885, anarchists led a counterdemonstration during the three-day ceremony marking the opening of the new Board of Trade Building. Having given up on nonviolent demonstrations and the ballot as a means of changing society, Parsons encouraged workers to arm themselves. Police stopped the anarchists from marching to the new building. August Spies, the founder and editor of the *Arbeiter-Zeitung*, spoke of using dynamite to destroy the Board of Trade Building.[22]

The year 1885 set the stage for yet another major conflict between labor and capital. On May 4, 1885, the Illinois Militia fired on strikers at a quarry in Le-

Figure 27. Strikers and their supporters overturn a horse streetcar on the West Side during the 1885 Transit Strike. (*Frank Leslie's Illustrated Newspaper,* July 11, 1885; ICHi-10495, Chicago History Museum.)

mont, killing two. Two months later Chicago found itself paralyzed by a transit strike that brought about a change in the attitude of local government toward organized labor. The election of Mayor Carter Harrison in 1879 had marked a definite adjustment in police actions during labor conflicts. Harrison attracted working-class voters and basically professed neutrality during strikes. Without police action to support business interest, capitalists often had to negotiate with their workers or bring in private guards, especially Pinkertons, to break strikes. The transit strike that year marked yet another change as business elites began to pressure Carter Harrison and the police to act in their interests.

The conflict began when the Chicago West Division Railway Company reduced the number of streetcar trips made by employees. The West Side Streetcarmen's Benevolent Association then asked for a wage increase to compensate for the lost trips. The union also asked that the company shorten the term of service of probationers and dismiss an offensive assistant superintendent. The company agreed, but soon fired fifteen union leaders instead. On June 30, the West Side drivers and conductors went on strike. Strikers first appeared at the car barns on Halsted Street at 4:15 a.m. At that time Bob Hart, the foreman, called out to the crowd for drivers and conductors for the morning runs. The only response was laughter. "We ain't going to run today, Bob," said one of them. Hart replied, "Well, boys you can do as you like. I have nothing to say. I'm sorry to see the strike, but I s'pose you think you're in the right." "You bet your life," said one striker as the crowd gave three cheers for Hart who went back into his office. Saloons in the area remained open to greet the crowds of strikers, but few entered the establishments. The Chicago police and Cook County sheriff's police stood on hand, as did about six Pinkertons mixing in the crowd, but the crowd remained well mannered and in good humor.

Other barns, however, attempted to run cars. As the day continued clashes broke out across the West Side. At 5:05 a.m. at the Western Avenue barn, a car caller summoned conductor number 57 but was met with silence from the crowd of striking conductors and drivers. Superintendent Whitlock attempted to persuade the men to take the morning cars out. Capt. John Bonfield of the Desplaines Street Police Station arrived with a squad of men. A car left the station hounded by strikers and their supporters. Strikers met another cable car as it made its way to the intersection of Western and Madison Avenue. Crowds attacked a Milwaukee Avenue car at Bloomingdale Street. Superintendent Lake of the West Side Company stated, "We cannot yield to the demands of these men, and we will not. They would soon think the company was being run by them." The *Chicago Tribune,* invoking the American ideal of upward mobility, reminded workers that they would one day be employers themselves, and implied they would then see the strike situation from a different perspective.

After a meeting with Superintendent Lake and police officials, Carter Harrison said that it was impossible to protect the forty-five miles of streetcar lines on the West Side. Former Alderman McGrath of the West Side's Fourteenth Ward claimed that the public supported the strike and that they wanted radical changes in management. Mayor Harrison advised the streetcar company to win the public over to their side. Meanwhile management brought in fifty Pinkertons. Chicagoans attempted to go about their business. The E. A. Cummings Company promised that the strike would not delay their July 4 sale of fifty lots near Douglas Park. On the second day of the strike the company advised the "walking was good," suggesting that customers walk the empty streetcar tracks to California Avenue just north of Douglas Park. Commuters tried to make their way from the West Side to the downtown business district by walking or getting rides on a makeshift public transportation system made up of every form of wagon or carriage. The *Tribune* proclaimed that "the streets are so filled that it is almost impossible for a private conveyance to get long." Meanwhile violence continued to break out along the streetcar lines. Cars left the barns filled with deputy sheriffs. Bonfield promised more protection for the next day.[23]

Captain Bonfield took charge of protecting the streetcars and led the attack on strikers. As the strike progressed, police clubbed anyone near the tracks. Determined to restore civil authority, Bonfield told his men to arrest anyone who used the word "scab." The strike had basically collapsed by the Fourth of July. Mayor Harrison, who seemed to change his position of neutrality, rewarded Bonfield after the strike, naming him inspector. The appointment, along with that of a new police superintendent, signified an attempt to placate business interests. The mayor's old labor alliance was a thing of the past. This strike further radicalized labor leaders, especially those leaning toward anarchism. Anarchist numbers jumped in Chicago, reaching roughly 2,800 committed anarchists by 1886, supporting seven newspapers with a circulation of thirty thousand. The events of 1885 set the stage for yet another major conflict between capital and labor.[24]

Meanwhile unionists resurrected the old eight-hour movement. The anarchists at first opposed the movement, seeing it as a panacea and not the final answer to labor's problems. By early 1886, the movement gained momentum, and by April a quarter million workers joined in the demand for the eight-hour day. In November 1885, organizers formed a new Eight-Hour Association in Chicago. It drew together various different groups, including the Knights of Labor, despite the opposition of Grand Master Workman Terrence Powderley. Chicago Mayor Carter Harrison, perhaps in an effort to win back labor backing, also supported the cause. Anarchists in turn began to have second thoughts about the movement, seeing it as a possible revolutionary tool to mobilize the working class. They continued to urge workers to arm themselves for the coming struggle. Parsons, Spies, and Schwab became the most popular speakers at eight-hour rallies and soon assumed the leadership of the local effort. Chicago emerged as the center of the eight-hour movement.

Weekly meetings kept the workers' interest. On April 25, the Central Labor Union held a huge rally on the lakefront, attended by some twenty-five thousand persons. Parsons promised to raise the banner of "liberty, equality, and fraternity." The national leadership marked May 1, 1886, as the beginning of a countrywide action to secure shorter hours for the same amount of pay. Nineteen years earlier Chicago workers had marked the same day to begin their failed eight-hour strike. Gerhard Lizius wrote in the *Alarm* on April 24, "The wage system is the only cause of the world's misery. It is supported by the rich classes, and to destroy it, they must be made either to work or DIE." The city waited nervously for May Day. Once again Chicago businessmen expected the worst, and Albert Parson stood at the center of the agitation.[25]

Haymarket

On Saturday May 1, 1886, about forty thousand Chicagoans walked off their jobs. Nationally the numbers reached three hundred thousand strikers in thirteen thousand businesses on the first day. Nothing like it had been seen since 1877. Chicago seemed quiet, almost as if the city enjoyed a holiday. Spies wrote a rousing editorial and called for Chicago's workers to stand united. Organizers held demonstrations and meetings throughout the city. Albert and Lucy Parsons led some eighty thousand demonstrators up Michigan Avenue in a huge showing of solidarity as May Day passed without any violence. Sunday also remained quiet. Radical leaders feared that the movement might lose momentum. Most unionists, however, felt victorious: after all, even the packinghouses had agreed to the eight-hour day.

On Monday afternoon, violence broke out at the McCormick Reaper Works recalling the clashes there in 1877. The year before strikers had forced McCormick to revoke a 15 percent wage cut. Cyrus H. McCormick, Jr., stood determined to break the union and used various methods to weaken it. In February he declared a lockout and brought in nonunion labor. Management further enraged workers when it brought in three hundred Pinkerton detectives to protect strikebreakers. The Chicago police, under the command of Inspector Bonfield, also cooperated with McCormick. Almost daily clashes occurred between pickets and police on Blue Island Avenue. The struggle continued and then blended into the eight-hour strike of May 1.

On May 3, the Lumber Shovers' Union held a large meeting on Twenty-second Street and Blue Island Avenue, just a few blocks from the McCormick Reaper Works. Spies addressed the crowd on behalf of the Central Labor Union. Speakers made orations in English, German, and Czech before Spies, who then addressed the crowd and called for unity. As Spies finished, the bell rang at McCormick's, signaling the end of the day. About two hundred workers left the rally and went to the Reaper Works to join the pickets. While Spies continued his talk, a clash took place at the McCormick plant, and police fired into a crowd of stone-hurling workers killing two of them and wounding many more. Spies witnessed the carnage and rushed back to the office of the *Arbeiter-Zeitung* where he wrote an angry leaflet in both English and German calling for workers to take up arms. He proclaimed that if the workers had been provided "with good weapons and one single dynamite bomb, not one of the murderers would have escaped his well-deserved fate."[26]

On the night of May 4, 1886, Mayor Carter Harrison ordered police to be on alert and concentrated a large contingent of officers at the Desplaines Street Station near Haymarket Square. Additional reserves stood waiting at the central station and in various other precincts across the city in case of a clash. Harrison planned to attend in order to judge the seriousness of the situation. At about 8:15 p.m., Spies arrived at the Haymarket and noticed the disappoint-

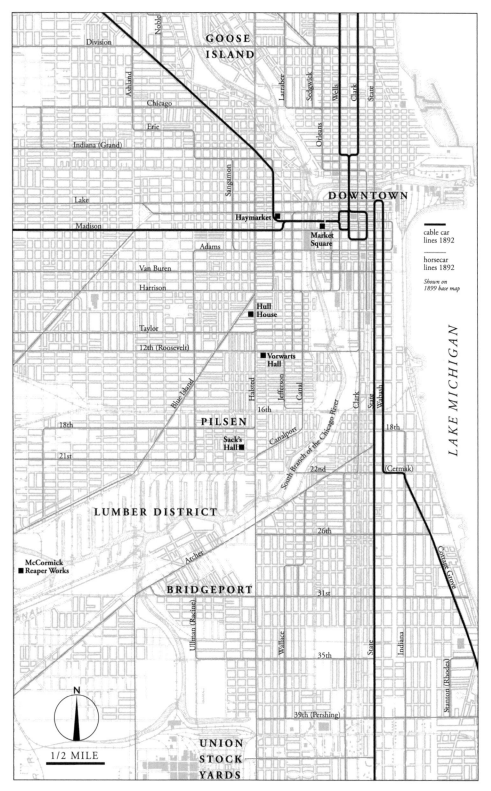

Map 4. Halsted Street provided a radical artery for the city's labor unions, socialists, and anarchists. Many labor organizations and halls stood near the street as it connected various working-class neighborhoods. (Dennis McClendon.)

ing turnout—only about three thousand people attended—and he suggested moving the meeting to Desplaines Avenue behind the Crane Brothers Factory. He chose an empty Crane wagon as a speaker's platform and mounted it, calling out for Parsons. Spies addressed the crowd, denying both the rumors that the meeting had been called to start a riot and Cyrus McCormick, Jr.'s accusation that he had incited the conflict at the reaper plant. When the crowd called out for the hanging of McCormick, Spies warned the crowd not to make idle threats and promised the day of justice would come.

Carter Harrison listened as Spies continued, but thought nothing unusual was occurring at the meeting. He told a friend, "I want the people to know their mayor is here." Albert Parsons arrived while Spies spoke. Spies quickly closed his remarks and introduced him. Parsons called for the workers to arm themselves and concluded that socialism provided the only hope for the working class. Harrison heard nothing that required police action. The crowd remained calm and orderly, and the mayor decided to go to the Desplaines Street Police Station to tell Bonfield to dismiss his reserves, but persistent rumors circulated that the crowd might attack the freight yards of the nearby Milwaukee and St. Paul Railroad. As a result they held reserves at the station. Harrison returned to the rally to hear a little more and then mounted his white horse and rode home to his Ashland Avenue mansion.

Shortly after 10 p.m. Parsons introduced the final speaker, Samuel Fielden, an Englishman, and left. Perhaps three hundred people remained to listen to Fielden. At the end of Fielden's discourse two detectives rushed back to the station to tell Inspector Bonfield that Fielden had used inflammatory language. Bonfield immediately called out his men and marched them to the meeting. Led by Inspector Bonfield and Captain Ward they marched quickly, and as they crossed Randolph Street they pushed the small crowd back up Desplaines and onto the sidewalks. The police stopped a few feet from the speaker's wagon, and Captain Ward shouted out, "I command you in the name of the people of the state of Illinois, immediately and peaceably to disperse." Fielden did not know what to do. He stared at Captain Ward and said, "But we are peaceable." After Ward repeated his statement, Fielden agreed to go and began to step down from the wagon. At that instant a bomb flew over the heads of the workers and into the police line. It exploded, and a number of policemen fell wounded. Then the police opened fire into the crowd, and chaos spread as men, women, and children panicked. The wounded stumbled through the streets. Men trampled each other as they tried to get away from the Haymarket. A bullet hit Fielden in the knee as he fled the site; another felled Spies's brother. Harrison heard the commotion from his bedroom window one mile west on Ashland Avenue and raced back to the Haymarket.

The shooting continued for two or three minutes. Bodies littered the streets. The riot bell summoned police from across the city. Nearly one thousand police cleared a three-block area around the Haymarket. Seven policemen and an

Figure 28. The Haymarket Riot. Police battle workers near Haymarket Square in the aftermath of the bomb explosion. (*Frank Leslie's Illustrated Newspaper,* May 15, 1886; Author's Collection.)

unknown number of civilians were fatally wounded. The police suffered sixty-seven causalities in all. Only one, however, died directly from the bomb, Mathias J. Degan. All others died from bullet wounds or from a combination of bullet and bomb wounds. Nearly all of the policemen wounded by bullets had been victims of their fellow officers' guns.[27]

The bomb shattered more than the lives it took that May evening; it crushed the eight-hour movement and destroyed much of organized labor. Public reaction immediately set in against the workers. Capitalists who had given in to the demand now moved against the unions. In particular the Knights of Labor, the nation's largest labor organization with some seven hundred thousand members, now felt the wrath of public opinion and employers. Immediately the meatpackers began to reassert their control over the situation and do away with the eight-hour guarantees. Meat workers had joined the Knights of Labor, and the backlash of that late spring and early summer meant the end of organized unionism in the stockyards for a generation. Terrence V. Powderley, Grand Master of the Knights of Labor, attempted to forestall the reaction by condemning the anarchists himself. In the public mind all of the organizations that supported the eight-hour movement were of the same ilk, and all were guilty of the riots and mayhem of that evening.

In fact no one knows the identity of the bomb thrower, although an indictment was handed down against Rudolph Schnaubelt, a Bohemian-born machinist whose family played a major role in the International Working People's Association. Police arrested Schnaubelt two days after the Haymarket meeting, but let him go after interrogating him. He quickly left Chicago, making his way first to Canada and then England, eventually fleeing to Argentina. Everyone knew that the seven men immediately picked up by the police—Adolph Fischer, Oscar Neebe, August Spies, Carl Engel, Samuel Fielden, Michael Schwab, and Louis Lingg—did not throw the bomb. Lingg, a known bomb maker and anarchist, in fact did not attend the Haymarket rally and was about two miles from the scene when the bomb exploded. Nor did Albert Parsons, who at first fled to Wisconsin, hurl the explosive. In exile Parsons felt sure that a jury would acquit him, and he made a dramatic entrance into Judge Joseph E. Gary's courtroom on the first day of the trial, June 21, 1886.

The trial proved to be a mockery, with Gary proclaiming to the press the defendants' guilt before it even began. Public opinion raged against the men. Gary allowed the prosecution a good deal of leeway in presenting their case and constantly stifled the defense. The trial lasted until August 20 when the jury proclaimed all eight men guilty as charged. Newspapers across the country applauded the verdict. Judge Gary allowed the convicted men to address the court, which they did for three days. The defendants denounced the court and the system that convicted them. Afterward Judge Gary pronounced the sentence—they were all to hang—and set the date of executions for December 3, 1886.

The appeal process dragged on for over a year, as petitions for clemency arrived from across the nation and the world. On Thanksgiving Day, November 25, Illinois Chief Justice John M. Scott granted a stay of execution. The defense attorney, Captain William P. Black, then moved to appeal the sentence. The Illinois Supreme Court upheld the conviction and death sentence on September 14, 1887. The courts fixed the date of execution for the seven men as November 11. Captain Black now saw an appeal to the U.S. Supreme Court as the only hope for the men. The defense team appeared before the Supreme Court on October 27 and asked for a writ of error. On November 2, the Court gave its unanimous decision not to review the case and sealed the anarchists' fate.

Now only the intervention of Illinois Governor Richard J. Oglesby could stop the executions. Supporters of the defendants established the Amnesty Association to appeal to the Republican governor and Civil War hero. Petitions soon flooded Oglesby's office. Embarrassed by the obvious unfairness of the trial and result, even Potter Palmer sent money to support the work of the Amnesty Association. Lyman J. Gage, executive officer of the First National Bank, and many other business leaders also signed the petition for clemency. Samuel Gompers of the newly formed American Federation of Labor also called for mercy. Sympathizers held meetings in London, Paris, Rome, Madrid, and other European cities. Slowly public opinion shifted toward leniency.

The law required the condemned men to petition for pity, which in effect required the innocent to plead guilty. Supporters came to the jail and tried to convince them to express regret for their actions and ask for compassion. Finally, Fielden, Schwab, and Spies agreed. They wrote a letter to Oglesby on November 3. Engel, Fischer, and Lingg defiantly refused to ask for any consideration. German radicals called Spies a traitor, and three days later he wrote another dispatch withdrawing his request. Parsons refused to sign the letter and maintained his innocence. Despite the fact that Oglesby seemed ready to exercise leniency, the thirty-eight-year-old anarchist refused to bow before the system.

As November 11 approached, Governor Oglesby informed Lyman Gage that, if the business community supported it, he would show mercy to Parson, Spies, Fielden, and Schwab. Gage immediately called a meeting of fifty business leaders and urged them to contact the governor. Julius Grinnell, who prosecuted the case, and Marshall Field spoke against leniency. The other businessmen refused to oppose Field, and the issue was settled. Gage later said, "It was terribly mortifying to me." He recalled how the others could not stand up to Field.

The movement for mercy, however, continued to gain momentum among the public. Then on November 6, four small bombs were found in Lingg's cell. Rumors circulated throughout the city that anarchists planned the destruction of the jail and perhaps the entire city! The detection of the explosives dealt the clemency movement a deadly blow. Despite the discovery, Governor Oglesby announced he would receive petitioners at the State House on November 9. The governor rendered his decision the next day, November 10.

At 10:00 a.m. that morning an explosion ripped through Louis Lingg's cell. Lingg had placed a dynamite cartridge in his mouth and lit it. He clung to life for six hours and then died at 2:50 p.m., cheating the hangman. That late afternoon Oglesby announced the commutation of Fielden's and Schwab's sentences to life imprisonment. Neebe was already serving a lesser fifteen-year sentence. Ogelsby said that the others had not asked for mercy as the law required and would hang the next day.

After eighteen months in jail Albert Parson and the others were executed on November 11, 1887. Spies, Fischer, Engel, and Parsons, covered in baggy white shrouds, were hung shortly after 11:30 a.m. Parsons, the last to speak, yelled out, "Let the voice of the people be heard," just before the hangman released the trap door and sent him and the others to their death.[28]

The Loop: A Dark Vision of the Future

While the various clashes between labor and capital seemed to portend a grim future, the physical city itself often shocked visitors to Chicago as well. The downtown embodied the transformation of America in the late nineteenth century. It did not move after the fire; in fact it expanded both upward and outward.

Documents pertaining to land ownership survived the conflagration, and thus private property remained sacrosanct. Rebuilding could go on without extensive legal conflicts. Here stood massive buildings where crowds of men and women toiled constantly in offices. Streetcars made their way through thoroughfares jammed with vehicles and pedestrians. Sidewalks seemed impassable because of crowds making their way to the vast number of shops and offices.

In many ways the fire hastened the modernization process that had been going on for some time. Segregation by function—business and government centrally located, industry and housing dispersed outward—mirrored developments in other cities, but the fire made the process much quicker. Retail continued to appear along State Street and also on Wabash. Cultural institutions developed south of Randolph on the west side of Michigan Avenue, government offices searched out Clark Street, while financial and legal offices opened on LaSalle Street. Over time a Music Row, occupied by instrument dealers, music instructors, and other such businesses moved to Wabash Avenue at Jackson, while to the north on Wabash, jewelers flourished. Randolph Street between State and Clark saw theaters open for business. This resulted in a more efficient use of land in the downtown area and made the Loop more comprehensible to both Chicagoans and visitors.

To an extent, the 1871 fire resulted in a land grab in downtown Chicago. Residents both rich and poor left the area, and the business district saw considerable expansion, almost doubling in size. Still the downtown remained compact—perhaps the most compact in the country. Despite the threat of fire, land values surged. Prefire building methods left the maximum height of buildings at about five to eight stories, and the rebuilding that took place after the fire followed this general pattern. The new city rising out of the ashes of the old, however, attracted many young architects with new ideas and a grasp of new technologies. Technological advancements such as elevators, steel framing, terracotta fireproofing, pumps that could bring water to upper floors, and interior lighting all made the development of the skyscraper possible. The new buildings that blossomed across the downtown after 1880 gave the business district a new and shocking look.[29]

At the same time that tall buildings turned city streets into caverns, a new form of public transportation appeared. The city's first cable car line ran down State Street from the downtown to Twenty-second Street (Cermak Road) in 1882, tying the expanding South Side residential district to the downtown. Marshall Field saw the promise of the new transportation system, invested in it, and made sure it ran past his store. Soon Chicago operated the largest cable car system in the world. The new cars moving along tracks throughout the business district now increasingly dominated by tall buildings created a modern city with all its benefits and liabilities. Throngs of people made their way through downtown streets now christened "the Loop" because of the cable car loop encircling the business district. To have a business within that transporta-

Figure 29. Blue Island Avenue Cable Car outside cable car barn, 1895. When Chicago's cable system was completed it was the largest in the world. (Chicago Public Library, Special Collections and Preservation Department.)

tion loop meant to be connected to the rest of Chicago. The city's population continued to grow during the period 1880–95 with an annual increase of over fifty thousand people.

Business firms competed for spaces in the roughly nine square blocks (one square kilometer) of the Loop. These massive office structures symbolized the growth of a new white-collar class of office workers in the industrial city. The number of lawyers in Chicago grew from 629 in 1870 to 4,241 thirty years later. By the turn of the century over seven thousand errand and office clerks and nearly ten thousand stenographers worked in Chicago, most in the Loop. Frequently skyscrapers housed three to four thousand workers. In 1896, the *Chicago Tribune* claimed that six thousand people worked in the Monadnock Building alone. Burnham and Root's massive Masonic Temple on the northeast corner of Randolph and State opened in 1893 and soared three hundred feet over the intersection. It dominated a block where the next tallest structure stood at 96 feet.[30]

Visitors stood aghast at the new downtown that emerged in the thirty years after the fire. The *London Times* reported in 1887 that "an overhanging pall of smoke; streets filled with busy, quick-moving people, a vast aggregation of rail-

Figure 30. W. W. Boyington's Columbus Building, built at a cost of $1 million in 1891, soared fourteen stories over the northwest corner of State and Washington Streets. The building replaced a structure that held dental and medical offices, and developers hoped to attract them back to this location by offering a free library for their use. The building was demolished in 1959. (Chicago Public Library, Special Collections and Preservation Department.)

Figure 31. Plymouth Place south of Harrison, ca. 1890. Chicago's skyscrapers created a canyon effect that frightened many visitors in the nineteenth century. (Postcard, Author's Collection.)

ways, vessels, and traffic of all kinds; and a paramount devotion to the Almighty Dollar are the prominent characteristics of Chicago." Rudyard Kipling turned away from the city in disgust, writing, "Having seen it, I urgently desire never to see it again. It is inhabited by savages." Julian Ralph, a New York journalist, remarked on the bustle of the Loop, "It seems as if the men would run over the horses if the drivers were not careful. Everybody is in such a hurry and going at such a pace that if a stranger asks his way, he is apt to have to trot along with his neighbor to gain the information, for the average Chicagoan cannot stop to talk." Chicagoans thrived in the hurried businesslike atmosphere and were

unapologetic about their "rush" to get someplace. One manager of a boot factory met an English visitor and offered to measure his feet and have a new pair
of boots for him in seventeen minutes. Chicagoans bragged about the quick
dispatch of hogs in the stockyards, the swiftness of the cable cars, or the fast
express elevators in the Masonic Temple. They gloried in the details of the city's
speed and efficiency.[31]

From the very beginning of settlement the Chicago River largely defined the
city and provided both a trade route and an open sewer for Chicago. In 1869,
more than thirteen thousand ships entered the river. Chicago became the busiest port in the United States. By the 1890s, $200 million of trade passed yearly
on the Chicago River. (The equivalent of over $4.5 billion in 2007.) Thirty-five
swing bridges crossed the waterway in the 1880s, and in the next decade jack-
knife bridges and vertical lift bridges appeared that allowed for wider boats to
navigate the river harbor. The traffic on the river added to the noise and pollution not only of the downtown area but also in neighborhoods extending along
the North and South Branches.

In 1885, 85 percent of the city's sewage flowed into the river. Attempts to
reverse the river's flow and keep pollution out of Lake Michigan proved only
partially successful. Even the deep canal of 1871, which technically reversed the
river, provided only a partial solution as regular flooding sent the waters flowing
back into Lake Michigan. In 1885, the much heralded water crib system floun-
dered as a stream of sewage over a mile long stretched out and encircled the
two-mile crib, polluting the city's drinking water. This occurred despite the fact
that the Bridgeport pump works had been reopened in 1883 in another attempt

Figure 32. Madison Street Swing Bridge, ca. 1900, connected the busy West Side to the Loop,
crossing the South Branch of the Chicago River. (Postcard, Author's Collection.)

Figure 33. The tugboat *Binghampton* passes the Adams Street swing bridge, ca. 1895. Notice the amount of "smoke" pollution. (Photograph by C.R. Clark; ICHi-31903, Chicago History Museum.)

to permanently reverse the river's flow. Kipling complained that Chicago's river system was "black as ink, and filled with untold abominations."

More than simply an embarrassment or an inconvenience, water pollution posed another serious threat. Citizens suffered from high typhoid rates in 1881, 1885, and 1886. Deaths from cholera, dysentery, and other waterborne diseases that killed an estimated 12 percent of the city's population accompanied the 1885 outbreak of typhoid. The Illinois state legislature passed the Sanitary District Enabling Act of 1889. The bill provided for the construction of the Chicago Sanitary and Ship Canal, but the legislation came too late for the 1,008 Chicagoans who died of typhoid in 1890 or the nearly two thousand who died the following year. These deaths far outnumbered those from either the 1871 or

1874 fires. The death rate for typhoid reached a horrendous 16.64 per ten thousand persons in 1891 or more than 7 percent of all deaths in the city. Chicago became known as "typhoid city," with rates far higher than other major American and European cities. European newspapers warned would-be travelers of the dangers of disease in Chicago. Typhoid death rates dropped in 1893 largely due to the construction of the four-mile crib, but until the opening of the Chicago Sanitary and Ship Canal in 1900, which finally reversed the river's flow, the threat of typhoid continued to hover over the city.[32]

A huge dark cloud of smoke hovered over the city. Chicagoans burned coal to power factories, provide lighting, heat homes, and power the massive railroad and cable car systems. Visitors often spoke about the haze that appeared as their trains came closer to the city. It came into view first as a smudge on the distant horizon, but its full impact could be seen as trains pulled into the various stations surrounding the Loop. Reportedly Chicagoans did not even see the sky on sunny days! Occasionally the cloud disappeared as winds blew it over the lake, or during the summers when coal consumption lessened, but Chicago could seem dark and foreboding even at midday. During the winter, street lights could be on all day and offices, which normally relied on natural light, would have their gas jets, and later electric lights, on constantly. The skyscrapers caused drafts that brought down dirty air that soiled clothes as well as buildings. Many of Chicago's office structures had been built with light-colored materials, only to be turned a dark brown or black by the pollution. In the summer, tug boats on the river and trains kept the cloud hovering over the Loop. Throughout the year the skies over Chicago reminded visitor and city dweller alike about energy choices. In truth the smoke problem, as it was called in the nineteenth century, plagued all industrial cities, but the Chicago problem seemed more intense. Soot appeared everywhere. To foreign visitors Chicago seemed "a true Hell" with its choking bituminous cloud, "the curse of Chicago."[33]

The Levee

To many observers Chicago's hell ran deeper than the polluted sky or the inky foul-smelling river. Just south of the business district stood the Levee, Chicago's infamous red light district. As William T. Stead pointed out in his 1894 expose, *If Christ Came to Chicago,* prostitution could be found throughout the city but especially in the district south of Harrison Street between Clark and Dearborn Streets. Investigators from Hull-House found over fifty brothels lining the streets from Polk Street to Roosevelt Road. Stead told of corruption as madams paid off Chicago policemen and politicians to look the other way as they carried on their illicit activities. Women sat in pairs at bordello windows looking both ways down the street, and when a man walked by, they would rap on the windows to invite him in. One bordello owner, Susan Winslow, installed a mechanical woman who struck the windows and beckoned men to come inside.

Carrie Watson operated one of the most famous of Chicago's brothels out of a brownstone building in the Levee on Clark Street between Polk and Taylor Streets for about twenty-five years. She dealt primarily with the "carriage" trade and operated one of the most expensive houses in the district. Stead estimated that between four hundred and five hundred houses of prostitution operated in Chicago. Lizzie Allen and Vina Fields competed with Watson. In 1890, Allen built a double mansion on South Dearborn Street, called the House of Mirrors, at a cost of $125,000. The three-story building contained fifty rooms. Fields, an African American, had one of the largest houses in the Levee with often more than forty women working the trade. She operated on Customs House Place for fifteen years hiring only black prostitutes and serving only white customers. According to Stead, Fields posted the rules of the house in every room and tried to run a reputable, if illicit, business.

Running an "honest" whorehouse in the Levee was a problem in a district well known for its dangers. The notorious Michael Finn first came to the Levee at the time of the Columbian Exposition to "roll" drunks who made their way on its streets. He then worked as a bartender at Toronto Jim's saloon on Custom House Place but was fired because he was too tough even for that notorious dive. Finn later worked as a pickpocket and a fence for other thieves until he opened the Lone Star Saloon and Palm Garden in 1896, where, two years later, he developed his famous knockout drink known everywhere as the "Mickey Finn." Finn instructed local prostitutes to get their clients to try one of his concoctions. After being drugged Finn dragged the victim into a small room at the rear of the Palm Garden, a hall at the back of the saloon decorated with a single withered palm tree, stripped him and took his money. Finn often kept the man's clothes and substituted old clothing before throwing the target out into the alley. The city finally revoked his saloon license in 1903.

Mickey Finn did not ply his trade alone. Many of the lower class saloons and houses of prostitution worked in the same manner. "Panel houses" proved to be a threat to the unknowing. As the prostitute's customer disrobed, a wall panel opened, and an accomplice took the distracted man's wallet from his pants. In 1896, investigators estimated that victims lost nearly $1.5 million in this manner. Judge James Goggin once said that any man who entered the Levee deserved to be robbed and then acquitted several thieves brought before him.

Shortly before she died Lizzie Allen retired after thirty-eight years and leased the "House of Mirrors" to Effie Hawkins. Hawkins in turn sold the business in 1899 to Ada and Mina Everleigh, successful madams from Omaha. The Everleigh sisters refurbished the old "House of Mirrors" and christened it the Everleigh Club, opening February 1, 1900. For over eleven years the elegant Everleigh Club led the brothel industry in Chicago, employing over six hundred prostitutes during its years of operation. Like Vina Fields, the Everleigh sisters maintained strict house rules and high standards of behavior. They set houses prices very high in order to discourage all but the richest guests. Provid-

Figure 34. The Rose Parlor, Louis Quatorze Rooms in the Everleigh Club, ca. 1900. The Everleigh sisters provided opulent settings for the fantasies of their upper-middle-class and wealthy clients. (ICHi-39382, Chicago History Museum.)

ing a safe haven for upscale customers in the Levee resulted in an outstanding business success. When reformers finally forced the sisters out of Chicago, they retired to New York City with over a million dollars in the bank.

The Levee acted as a semiofficial vice district, part of the spatial segmentation of the city. While various political bosses kept watch on the district, at different times referred to as the Tenderloin, Little Cheyenne, or simply the First Ward, and prevented it from being closed down, the two most infamous of the protectors of the "small people" of the Levee were "Bathhouse" John Coughlin and Michael "Hinky Dink" Kenna, both aldermen of the First Ward. Coughlin, a large boisterous man who dressed nattily, worked hard to protect the gamblers in the First Ward and across the city. Michael Kenna, a short man who dressed quietly and almost never smiled, operated the Workingman's Exchange Saloon on South Clark Street and worked as a precinct captain. As political power began to shift in the ward away from Boss Mike McDonald, who had ruled over vice and politics in the ward for years, Kenna saw a chance to take control and made an alliance with Coughlin. As manager of the First Ward organization, Kenna promised the brothels and gambling houses protection, for a fee. By laying a "tax" payable to Kenna and Coughlin he created a defense fund that kept the police and courts off of the backs of illicit businesses. The duo kept expensive lawyers on retainer to protect their "friends." The idea worked, and soon the streets of the Levee blossomed with all kinds of activities. Freak shows and dime museums, new bordellos and panel houses, concert saloons and dope houses lined the streets while hundreds of strong-arm men, pimps, and others roamed the neighborhood to relieve Levee visitors of their money. The Levee could claim to be the wickedest and wildest district in America.[34]

In 1871, the Chicago Fire seemed to usher in an era of chaos. The city that rose out of the ashes of the Great Fire looked bolder, more prosperous, and more sinful than before and symbolized all that seemed to have gone wrong with America by the end of the nineteenth century. It also presented a model for the new industrial city that would reign supreme in the United States throughout the twentieth century.

Reacting to Chaos

Pullman, the West Side, and the Loop

As society seemed headed toward mayhem, various groups attempted to maintain control. Immigrants and working-class people reacted with a communal response as neighborhoods burst at the seams with churches, synagogues, taverns, fraternal groups, women's clubs, coffeehouses, theaters, and other places that helped create a strong sense of distinctiveness and community identification. To the outsider, these neighborhoods seemed chaotic, but residents perceived them differently. Meanwhile, elite and middle-class Chicagoans attempted to deal with the new urban-industrial order in various ways. Some became part of what proved to be an international response to the new capitalist system: the idea of reform. People all over the industrialized world attempted to rein in the forces that technology and new market systems had unleashed. Intensive academic, ideological, and practical links joined middle-class reform groups on both sides of the Atlantic; Chicago symbolized the problem of the new city and became central to this struggle to find a solution.

Reformers reacted against the chaos. George Pullman attempted to create an ideal industrial town. Jane Addams and Ellen Gates Starr opened Hull-House to help ameliorate the ravages of industrialism in Chicago's immigrant neighborhoods. All of these had connections to the European experience. Pullman looked to the model industrial town of Saltaire in England, London's Toynbee Hall inspired Addams, and immigrant neighborhood residents built on their cultural and historical roots to create viable neighborhoods. For some, the threat of social revolution powered their responses; for others, a sense of justice and perhaps a yearning for an idealized American past; for many, survival motivated their movements.

Meanwhile, market and technological changes remade the Loop. The conception of the skyscraper brought a unique American style of architecture called the Chicago School. The city's architects changed the way that people thought about the city in an attempt to make order out of chaos. Chicago's downtown, rebuilt in the immediate aftermath of the fire, saw itself reshaped again as the

Figure 35. Cable cars share State Street with horse drawn buggies in this view looking south from Randolph Street ca. 1885. (Stereopticon, Author's Collection.)

Chicago School of Architecture not only created a new Loop, but transformed the American city.[1]

The West Side: The Communal Response

Chicago's West Side contained a vast area that stretched in an arc west of the South and North Branches of the Chicago River. It included diverse neighborhoods, as large Irish, Scandinavian, and other immigrant populations met along its busy industrial streets. Immigrant and native born, Jew and Gentile, Protestant and Catholic, rich and poor, mixed on the West Side, along with both sacred and not-so-sacred spaces. In many ways the district, seen in its larger perspective, contained a little bit of everything Chicago had to offer, including West Side Park, the home of the Chicago Cubs baseball team.[2]

Chicago's ward boundaries changed frequently, but the ward at the heart of the Near West Side remained basically the same during the last quarter of the nineteenth century. Called the Ninth Ward in 1870 and the Eighth Ward in 1880, it became most infamous as the Nineteenth Ward under the leadership of Alderman John Powers. It stretched along the South Branch of the river west roughly to Throop Street and from Twelfth Street (Roosevelt Road) north to Van Buren Street. In 1896, the ward embraced a diverse population of over forty-eight thousand residents who spoke twenty-six languages. Residents came from all over Europe, as well as the eastern and western stretches of Asia. Vast changes had occurred in the district over a fifty-year period that would have made the ward unintelligible to someone who had moved away for any period of time. By the 1890s, southern Italians moved in large numbers into the ward, second only to the Irish in numbers. They clustered in the eastern portion between Halsted and Canal and Harrison and Taylor Streets. Polish and Russian Jews settled in large numbers to the south of the Italians. Germans, Czechs, and Irish had begun to leave the ward by the 1890s, moving to the south and west. The history of the Nineteenth Ward, and of the entire West Side, seemed to be one of constant movement. To the outsider, it could be a confusing conglomeration of nationalities and religions living among vast railroad yards and industrial plants that surrounded homes and churches. Within the neighborhoods, social class and nativity mattered most, with the populace sorting itself out by income and the homeland from which they came.[3]

Halsted Street played a major role in connecting the diverse areas of the West Side. In 1889, the *Tribune* declared the stretch of the street north from Harrison to Madison as the "tough" part of Halsted Street. Here the "nightly promenade" of the West Side's most "abandoned" classes could be found. Reputable businesses shared the street with some of the worst "dens" in the city. The intersection of Halsted and Madison, with two theaters, a nearby dime museum, and several clothing stores, as well as many saloons, provided a center of activity between 7 p.m. and midnight. Certainly, to any outsider, the neighborhood symbolized the very era of urban chaos just blocks from the Haymarket, a worldwide symbol of anarchism.[4]

Parts of the West Side did seem without any institutional base. Settled early by squatters, Goose Island, a little piece of land torn away from the West Side by a short canal in 1857 and then claimed to be part of the North Side, developed into an industrial slum identified with petty criminals and street thugs. By the early 1880s, Poles had also come to live on the island officially known as Ogden's Island, but still no churches or other institutions appeared there. In 1891, Capt. Michael Schaak said, "Probably no place in the city has given the police force so much trouble as that muddy strip of territory."[5]

Despite the portrayal of the West Side as both exotic and chaotic, residents carried on a daily life that revealed a complex community structure. Indeed West Siders reacted to the era of urban chaos by creating institutionally rich

Figure 36. Chicago's West Side Ball Park, home of the Cubs World Championship Team in 1908. The park opened in 1893, but the White Stockings (original name) split the season between their new facility and an older South Side Park, located near today's U.S. Cellular Field, probably to attract fans attending the Columbian Exposition. (Postcard, Authors' Collection.)

communities. Outsiders often ignored this communal response, but it had an important impact on the lives of neighborhood people and on the history of the city. This social richness appeared early on, as Irish Catholics opened St. Patrick's Catholic Church at the corner of Randolph and Desplaines in 1846, the second Catholic parish organized in the city and the first west of the river. In 1850, parishioners opened a parochial school. That same year, the pastor Rev. Patrick J. McLaughlin purchased lots at the northwest corner of Adams and Desplaines Streets for a new parish church. The city planned a new public market, eventually known as the Haymarket, and McLaughlin saw a move away from the busy market as advantageous for his congregation. Irish Catholics had moved in large numbers west of the river and they dedicated St. Patrick's new church on Christmas Day 1856. St. Patrick's and other Catholic parishes created a sense of community in opposition to the Protestant majority and other Catholic immigrants. Indeed, just a few months after the opening of the grand new church another Irish parish appeared on the West Side just southwest of St. Patrick's and the Haymarket, Holy Family.[6]

The Jesuit Order organized Holy Family Church on Twelfth Street (Roosevelt Road) in 1857, as the first of three Jesuit churches in the city. Despite a good deal of opposition by the Protestant elite, led by the *Chicago Tribune,* Father Arnold J. Damen raised $30,000 in pledges and laid the cornerstone of a massive Gothic church designed by John Van Osdel at a cost of $200,000 (about $4 million today) on August 23, 1857. Parish building helped to create a sense of community among the Irish in the industrial city. Catholic West Siders held

Figure 37. Union Station pictured here about 1890 and located at Canal and Adams Streets provided one of the gateways to the West Side. Immigrants arrived at this station in large numbers and found their ways to the various ethnic enclaves. (Postcard, Author's Collection.)

large annual fairs to raise money for the quickly growing Parish of the Holy Family. Local politicians such as "Honest John" Comiskey and Patrick Rafferty took part in the drives. The construction of parishes and then parochial schools were central events in the Catholic neighborhood experience. When the Sisters of the Blessed Virgin Mary arrived in 1867 to establish a school, local families rushed to enroll their children. In 1870, the nuns opened St. Aloysius School on Maxwell Street a few blocks south of the parish church. The Jesuit St. Ignatius College opened that same year in a new $230,000 building adjacent to Holy Family Church. Holy Family's spire stood as the city's tallest structure from 1874 until the building of the Masonic Temple in 1892. The Jesuit order had made a permanent impact on the city's West Side.

By 1895, sixty-five Catholic institutions called Holy Family home. Many Irish nationalist organizations also met at Sodality Hall on Blue Island Avenue.[7] By the late 1880s Holy Family's boundaries had been greatly reduced as a result of the creation of more Catholic parishes. Eastern and southern Europeans joined the Irish and Germans of the West Side but built their own institutions. The German Catholic parish of St. Francis Assisi at Twelfth and Newberry (1853) attracted many German Catholics, but German Lutheran and Methodist churches also appeared on the West Side. Immanuel Lutheran Church stood at Taylor and Brown (Sangamon) in 1874, as did Zion Lutheran at Nineteenth near Halsted Street in Pilsen. St. Mathew's German Lutheran Church provided worship for Germans living near Twenty-first and Hoyne on the Lower West Side. The German Maxwell Street Methodist Church offered services just south of St. Francis Assisi.

While Germans were more heavily concentrated on the North Side and in the northern parts of the West Side, the German presence was certainly felt along Twelfth Street. The West Side Turner Hall stood at 251–255 West Twelfth Street and was also known as the Turnverein Vorwart's Hall. The Union Turnverein met at Fifteenth and Halsted. The German Bruederbund met at 376 West Twelfth Street. These Germanic institutions, which mixed class, ethnicity, and physical fitness into their programs, indicated the institutional maturity of these neighborhoods by the 1870s.[8]

Immigrants from the Netherlands also arrived in Chicago, particularly on the West Side. Originally Dutch settlement took place just west of the river near Clinton and Randolph where Haymarket Square would eventually open. Although their relative numbers were small, by 1850 two-thirds of Chicago's Dutch lived west of the river both north and south of Randolph Street. They had come to Chicago for both religious reasons and, like the Irish, as a result of the potato famine. The West Side Dutch developed a neighborhood they called the "Groninger Hoek," where many of the settlers traced themselves back to the Dutch town of Groningen. In 1853, the Dutch Reformed community organized the First Dutch Reformed Church. Three years later the church's first modest sanctuary opened on Foster Street just east of Halsted between Harrison and Polk Streets. In 1868, the First Dutch Reformed Church opened a new place of worship on the southwest corner of Harrison and May. Other Dutch churches appeared, often in conflict with the Reformed Church, such as the True Church and the Christian Reformed Church. Dutch immigrants flocked to the community. By 1860, the West Side contained 53 percent of all Chicago area Hollanders, and most lived between Harrison Street on the north, Twelfth Street to the south, and between the river and Loomis Street. Ten years later, the census revealed an even greater concentration of Dutch in this district where most of the Reformed Dutch lived. A stretch of Fourteenth Place from Ashland Avenue west to Wood Street became known as "Wooden Shoe Boulevard" because of the concentration of Dutch families on the street. The Dutch created local Christian schools and youth groups in an attempt to preserve their religious and ethnic beliefs and traditions. However chaotic these neighborhoods might seem to the outsider, these were hardly rootless immigrants.[9]

Central and eastern Europeans also began to make their way to the West Side. Chicago's Czech community dated back to 1852 when the first Bohemian settlers arrived in the city from New York. These Czechs settled near the North Side German community then making its way along Clark Street. By 1855, they moved from this neighborhood, and a more permanent Czech settlement appeared on the West Side along Canal Street south from Van Buren to Taylor Street. This part of the city became known as "Praha," named after the capital

Figure 38. E. D. Ahlswede Dry Good Store in Humboldt Park, 1886. Ethnic entrepreneurs opened stores to serve their communities throughout Chicago. (Chicago Public Library, Special Collections and Preservation Division.)

of Bohemia. After the 1871 Chicago Fire, which began close to Praha, many Czechs moved farther south to the area around Halsted and Eighteenth Street. In 1881, Matthew Skudera opened the Pilsen Inn at Fisk and McMullen Streets (Carpenter and Nineteenth Place). This new Czech settlement quickly took its name from the inn and from the most famous beer-producing town in Bohemia.

Czech fraternal societies, Sokol gymnastic groups, and the offices of Czech newspapers located their offices and meeting halls in both Praha and Pilsen. Bohemian Catholics founded St. Wenceslaus Church in 1864 on Desplaines Street. A second Czech parish, St. John Nepumocene, opened in 1871 in Bridgeport, just south of the river. In 1875, Pilsen Czechs founded St. Procopius Catholic Church on Eighteenth and Allport. After the emergence of Freethinker or Rationalist societies in Bohemia in the 1870s the movement appeared in Chicago and deeply affected the local community with Freethinkers making up perhaps 50 percent of the Czech population. The new organizations created gymnastic societies, schools, and even their own cemetery, Bohemian National Cemetery on the North Side. Czech Protestant congregations also built churches on the West Side.[10]

Yiddish-speaking East European Jews moved in large numbers to the West Side after the 1874 fire. They tended to be poor and well trained in Hebraic Studies but had little formal secular education. Their neighborhood originally known as the "Poor Jews Quarter," later was referred to as Maxwell Street or "the Ghetto." During the thirty years after 1880, some fifty thousand Jewish immigrants moved into the neighborhood south of Polk Street and north of the railroad tracks at Sixteenth Street from Canal Street to Damen Avenue. Overwhelmingly Orthodox in religion, these immigrants from Russia, Lithuania, and Poland built communities along the narrow streets. Many made a living by peddling or working in the garment factories that called the West Side home. In the 1870s the corner of Maxwell and Halsted Streets became the center of a vast East European–like open market.

Figure 39. Bar Mitzvah Candidate about 1915. Chicago's Jewish population made it the third largest Jewish city in the world before World War II, behind only Warsaw, Poland, and New York City in the number of Jewish residents. (Chicago Jewish Archives, Spertus Institute of Jewish Studies.)

Immigrant Jews often named their synagogues for the East European shtetl that they had left behind. Tradesmen, such as laundrymen and carpenters, founded some synagogues; others were organized according to various religious philosophies. The Jewish ghetto, while seen as chaotic by outsiders, had a complex institutional life, which provided for the social needs of these immigrants. Talmud Torah Hebrew School opened in 1883, and by 1889 the school had moved into a large building at Judd and Clinton Streets and was renamed Moses Montefiore Hebrew Free School. By 1902, it had a daily attendance of over one thousand boys for a program that ran after the public schools let out. The Jewish Training School, a technical school, opened nearby in 1890. In 1903, the Chicago Hebrew Institute was founded at 221 Blue Island Avenue just off of Twelfth Street. Five years later, the Hebrew Institute bought a six-acre tract of land from the Catholic order of sisters, Madams of the Sacred Heart, on Taylor Street and opened its legendary center. The West Side Jews organized *landsmansshaften* or *verein*—these self-help fraternal organizations based on the East European settlements from which immigrants came provided an important connection with traditional Jewish communities and institutions in Europe. Cultural institutions also arose. In 1887, Boris Tomashefsky organized the first Yiddish theater company in a small rented theater on Twelfth Street. The Metropolitan Theater opened in the early 1890s at Twelfth and Jefferson.[11]

Just north of Maxwell Street, Italian immigrants began to replace the Irish. In 1880, Rev. Sostene Moretti, a Servite priest, founded Assumption, BVM Catholic Church to serve the small but growing Chicago Italian community. Italians

Figure 40. Female dance class on Jewish Industrial League Roof ca. 1910. (Chicago Jewish Archives, Spertus Institute of Jewish Studies.)

laid the cornerstone for the parish church in September 1884 and dedicated the completed structure on August 15, 1886. As Italian immigration increased and spread across the city, the Servites celebrated Mass for the growing West Side Taylor Street community at Garibaldi Hall, and in 1899 Holy Guardian Angel parish began to serve West Side Italians. Our Lady of Pompeii Church opened in 1910.

The Italian community, particularly from southern Italy and Sicily, was very poor, but nonetheless developed a remarkable amount of institutional sophistication on the West Side. In 1895, the growing West Side Italian community impressed the city with a massive parade marking Italian unification. A huge crowd met the thirty Italian organizations at the Haymarket. A dozen bands led the parade, playing both Italian and American songs as two hundred carriages gathered to parade through Chicago's streets. The stars and stripes along with the Italian tricolor decorated the carriages and were carried by the members of the immigrant societies. The *Tribune* proclaimed, "No other procession witnessed on the streets of Chicago probably had so large a proportion of participants in carriages. The Italian Political club, the John Powers club, and the First Ward Republican club, near the rear of the column, formed a composite body."[12] The parade symbolized both ethnic identification and assimilation into the American political system.

Beyond ethnic and cultural or religious institutions, West Side streets hosted various working-class organizations. The Social Workingmen's Hall stood at 368 West Twelfth Street, and various organizations used it as a meeting place in 1874. The Stonecutters Union met at the Czech Sokol Hall on Taylor Street. Iron Molders' Union No. 23 met at 376 West Twelfth Street. Local residents were deeply involved in the major labor struggles of the era. In the 1870s and 1880s clashes between police, Pinkertons, and strikers occurred throughout the West Side. While many labor unions met downtown, the Knights of Labor Subordinate assembly No. 852 met at Eighteenth and Blue Island in Pilsen, and the Wood Working Machine Hand Local No. 2 (Bohemian local) also met on Eighteenth Street.

By the late 1880s and early 1890s the West Side Irish had begun to leave the neighborhood. The remaining wealthier Irish lived in the western part of the Nineteenth Ward. Alderman John Powers lived on Macalister Place across from Vernon Park. The *Tribune* reported that it was "a pretty neighborhood, adorned with handsome residences that would confound a person who had heard only of the miseries of the Nineteenth Ward. Indeed there are many wards of much greater pretensions and far less unpleasant notoriety which have no spot as fine to compare with it."[13] The West Side Irish had made it in America. The institutions they built allowed them the social mobility to climb up the class ladder. Others would follow their ascent. What many middle-class observers would see as mere chaos on the West Side was in fact a rich community, with deep layers of institutional development.

The Elite Response: George Pullman

The waves of strikes and riots, along with the squalor of Chicago's slums, shocked both George Pullman and Jane Addams. Both had grown up in small town America. Both remembered the virtues of that earlier time and regarded the industrial city with mixed feelings. Both belonged to a social class that benefited from the vast changes of the Industrial Revolution. Pullman and Addams had left their towns and moved to Chicago looking for a larger stage on which to act.

George Pullman was born in Brocton, New York, in 1831. His father, James Pullman, labored as a farmer turned house builder. The young Pullman grew up in the town of Portland, where his family stressed traditional Protestant virtues such as honesty, hard work, and a disdain for extravagances. At fourteen, George Pullman left his formal education behind and went to work as a clerk in a small general store in Westfield, New York. He also worked as a cabinetmaker, and after his father's death in 1853 he took over family business obligations, especially the moving of houses that stood too near to the Erie Canal. The New York state legislature had decided to widen the canal in the early 1850s. In 1855, after nearly completing the house-moving project, Pullman decided to go to

Chicago. The young entrepreneur put his experience to work, raising Chicago's buildings out of the mud to the new street grade created by the attempt to build a better drainage system in Chicago. Pullman soon turned to other enterprises. In the winter of 1857–58, he entered into a partnership with two brothers, Benjamin and Norman Field, to construct and operate sleeping cars on two Illinois railroad lines. The business was not an immediate success, and Pullman traveled to Colorado and operated a trading post in Central City. He continued to work on the design of a better railroad sleeping car. When he returned to Chicago he perfected his vision and in 1864 created his first sleeper, the "Pioneer." An extraordinary event allowed Pullman to show off his new product. After Abraham Lincoln's assassination, the dead president's body was brought to Illinois by a funeral train that included the Pioneer as it made its way from Chicago to Springfield. The railcar, the first sixteen-wheel car built, attracted national attention, and Pullman was on his way to his fortune. Larger than ordinary coaches, the Pioneer set the standard for future sleeping car development, and the public soon used the new Pullman cars despite the fact that they had to pay more for the privilege. At the end of 1866, Pullman had forty-eight cars in operation and dominated the Midwest's sleeper car business. He then turned his attention to the national market, and the next year, he chartered Pullman's Palace Car Company. A great success, in 1892 the cars traveled 204,453,796 miles carrying 5,673,129 passengers and serving roughly 9,000 meals per day. Over 33 million pieces of Pullman linen were laundered daily! By 1894, 2,573 Pullman cars made their way across the country, including six hundred and fifty buffet cars and fifty-eight dining cars.[14]

The 1877 railroad strike deeply disturbed Pullman; living in Chicago he had witnessed the crowds of striking workers clashing with police and burning railroad cars. Pullman headed the Law and Order League at the time. Seeing Chicago again occupied by federal troops, the sleeping car magnate began to search for an answer to the class conflict that haunted the nation. He found inspiration in Saltaire, England, developed by Sir Titus Salt, and in Essen, Germany, created by the Krupps munitions plant. Pullman took these European ideas and attempted to create a perfect industrial town in the United States. His vision was meant to transform the industrial city and bring peace to the American workplace. In 1880, Pullman announced the location of a new plant to the south of Chicago in the township of Hyde Park.

To Pullman, the new south suburban plant provided an opportunity to not only manufacture railroad cars more efficiently but to reform and uplift workers and avoid the chaos and class conflict of the city. Pullman conceived of a clean and orderly town, pleasant to the eye and rational—much like his palace cars. Like many progressive thinkers, he believed that beauty and cleanliness could change people's lives. An official history published in 1893 stressed that the town was "to surround the workmen in Pullman with such influences as would tend to bring out the highest and best there was in them." In addi-

Figure 41. Arcade Building, ca. 1890. The Arcade Building provided the social center for the Town of Pullman; it included many stores, a library, a post office, and a thousand-seat theater. (Chicago Public Library, Special Collections and Preservation Department.)

tion to making a sizeable profit for himself and his investors, Pullman hoped to save both the American working class and the city by attracting the best laborers and then protecting them from the city's temptations. The planner's sketches and Pullman's wealth and determination would leave the era of urban chaos behind. Pullman thus took his place in a long line of American utopian thinkers—except his ideas also came with a guaranteed profit.[15]

Groundbreaking for the new plant and town took place in May 1880. Pullman hired architect Solon S. Beman and landscape architect Nathan Barrett. The new town, Beman's first major project, featured all the amenities of the modern city: paved streets, brick houses, gas streetlights, indoor plumbing, formal landscaping, and modern public transportation. The population of the town grew to 8,203 residents in September 1884.

The following year, a University of Wisconsin economist, Richard T. Ely, noted that while exact statistics were hard to extract from the Pullman Company, they did claim a capacity of $8 million worth of railcars per year (about $182 million in 2007). While managers expected the plant to manufacture forty freight cars daily, on August 18, 1884, the plant produced one hundred freight cars in ten hours. The Allen Paper-wheel Company claimed a capacity of fifteen thousand railcar wheels per year. Wherever one looked, the numbers astounded. The Pullman brickyard could produce over two hundred thousand bricks daily. Twenty-five thousand tons of ice came from the Pullman ice works annually. In 1885, about four thousand men worked in the town with over three thousand of these working for the Pullman Palace Car Company. Five hundred men worked in the carpenter shops alone.

Observers often portrayed the town as a grand experiment in equality. Ely pointed to the town as one with "no favorable sites" set apart for "drones living on past accumulations of wealth." George Pullman believed that by surrounding laborers, as far as possible, with wealth, he would raise them up to middle-class American standards. The more than 1,500 buildings in Pullman attested to his wishes. Designed in "advanced secular gothic," the homes rented for a wide range of prices from $4.50 to $100.00 per month. According to Ely the usual rent in 1885 ran about $14.00 to $25.00 ($320.00 to $570.00 in 2007). The cheapest flats, designed for the small number of unskilled workers in Pullman, stood hidden away, and yet even these seemed better than traditional urban tenements. Sewers drained the city's waste to a nearby Pullman farm for fertilizer. While the town charmed outsiders with its market, arcade, green spaces, and stately Florence Hotel, residents seemed less touched by its beauty and moral uplift. Many stayed for only a short time. One resident stated that it compared to "living in a grand hotel." She said that residents called it "camping out." All of the Pullman homes belonged to the company, and only those employed by the company could live in the town. House leases could be terminated on ten day's notice, and workers had little or no control over their own homes.[16]

The paternalistic Pullman philosophy demanded a community based on strong families in a rigidly gendered world. The town did not include cafeterias. Men should go home for lunch. No taverns appeared on Pullman street corners, as men should stay home at night with their families. Few jobs existed for women. Women were not to work outside the home but were to reinforce the moral atmosphere called for in the town. Most Americans supported this gender-based ideology. Still conflicts arose. In 1886, one female Pullman resident complained that the company had complete control over workers' homes. Homes could be entered and painted or repaired with no notice to residents. The company then charged for the "service" and deducted costs directly from paychecks with no chance for appeal. Male inspectors might drop in without a moment's notice and sometimes threatened to expel families from their lodgings if they did not live up to Pullman's standards. Eventually the Pullman's Women's Union, made up of wives of the town's more well-to-do citizens and of professional women, took over the task of inspection.[17]

Richard T. Ely criticized the lack of democracy and the overt paternalism of the place. No newspaper existed, and no one seemed willing to speak out against the company. It seemed as if the freedoms expected by most Americans did not exist in the town. In fact the town was not really a town, as far as democratic political processes go. The company made all decisions. The tradition of the New England town meeting, much praised and mythologized in

Figure 42. Industrial neighborhoods developed to the west of Pullman, including the area around 110th and Union Avenue pictured here in 1886. Many Pullman workers were drawn to both Roseland and Kensington as they could develop their own communities and ethnic institutions. (Chicago Public Library, Special Collections and Preservation Division.)

America as the parent of democracy, was nowhere to be seen in Pullman. Even religion seemed to be neglected and stymied in Pullman's utopia. Only one church building existed, and it often went without a congregation, as the company charged high rents for the Greenstone Church. In the end, Ely declared Pullman to be "un-American." Everything in the town, including the lives of the workers, seemed to be "machine-made."[18] It precluded Chicago's chaos, all right, but at what cost?

The Middle-Class Reform Response: Jane Addams

Jane Addams was born in Cedarville, Illinois, near the Wisconsin border on September 6, 1860, and Addams grew up in a small-town atmosphere. The town, however, lay well within the economic grasp of Chicago, as the city's railroads expanded its hinterland, and so Addams's life in Cedarville was not immune from the changes of the nineteenth century. She grew up in the largest house in town—the daughter of its most prosperous citizen, John Addams. In

1864, John Addams opened the Second National Bank in nearby Freeport and three years later founded both the Protection Life Insurance Company and the Buckeye Mutual Fire Insurance Company. John Addams, who had made his first fortune as a miller, also invested in the pioneering Galena and Chicago Union Railroad. Two years after her birth Jane Addams's mother, Sarah, died of complications during a pregnancy. Her eldest sister, Mary, and her stepmother, Anna Haldeman, mothered the child, while her father became a guiding light in the young girl's life as he taught her the obligations of the meritocracy. John Addams dressed the part of the elite in rural Illinois with his shiny silk hat, and Addams learned much from her father, including his devotion to public life as well as a skepticism concerning Christianity. John Addams's encouraged his daughters' education, and in 1877 Jane followed her sister Alice to the Rockford Female Seminary.

During her years at Rockford, Jane Addams firmly established her ideas concerning stewardship that existed outside the formal boundaries of church affiliation. John Addams died just after her graduation in 1881. This calamity changed Jane Addams's plans to go on to Smith College and then to medical school. Over the next three years she moved with her stepmother to Philadelphia and enrolled in the Woman's Medical College of Pennsylvania. As a result of recurring illness she withdrew and went on a grand tour of Europe with her stepmother from the fall of 1883 until the spring of 1885. Later she moved to Baltimore with her family as her stepbrother attended Johns Hopkins University, and slowly her ideas concerning stewardship and her life goals began to come together.

In 1888, she left for another tour of Europe with her Rockford Seminary friend Ellen Gates Starr. During this trip, Addams and Starr visited Toynbee Hall in the East End of London. Run by male graduates of Oxford University and presided over by Samuel and Henrietta Barnett, this new "settlement house" combined various ideas concerning social reform and Christian stewardship to the poor. By the time they returned to the United States in 1888, Addams and Starr had concocted an idea to create a settlement house in Chicago.[19]

Chicago already had a long history of women active in social outreach. Both middle-class and working-class women had been involved in liberal and even radical political action before the arrival of Starr and Addams. Groups such as the Illinois Women's Alliance brought together women from across the city in response to the social issues of the day. Chicago women early confronted the problem of the schools and the poor, as well as labor. Many broke with their husbands regarding the ideas that some of the poor were worthy and some unworthy.[20]

In the fall of 1889, Jane Addams and Ellen Gates Starr rented rooms in the old Hull Mansion on Halsted Street near Polk. The mansion, originally built as a country retreat, had already seen various uses, including as a home for the aged conduct by the little Sisters of the Poor between 1876 and 1880. The two newly dedicated "charity" workers rented the rooms from Helen Culver. Starr and Addams sought to change ideas concerning charity work by using the Toynbee Hall model. Like Pullman they envisioned a new society. Unlike Pullman they attempted a more democratic response; they hoped to be good neighbors to the residents of the West Side, to tame the chaos from within.

In June of 1889, the *Chicago Evening Journal* published an article by Rev. David Swing, a well-known Chicago Protestant preacher, heralding the opening of Hull-House. He immediately displayed the outsider's notion of the West Side as he wrote, "a moral and intellectual home is to be set up in a place where the surrounding people are living without possessing or knowing the highest motives of life." He spoke of Addams and Gates as "fine scholars" and religious in their views and added that they had "enthusiasm and vivacity enough to inspire a neighborhood.[21]

Addams and Starr quickly created a series of social programs and opened Hull-House to their immigrant neighbors. A little more than five years after it opened, Hull-House continued to fascinate the city as a whole. The *Chicago Tribune* likened the settlement house to a theater, claiming that it seemed unreal to the "denizens" of the Nineteenth Ward. The article pointed to the books, paintings, bas-reliefs, busts, and draperies, to the good manners, and to the spaciousness and cleanliness of the place. As in Pullman, beautiful surroundings would provide social uplift for the immigrant working-class slum dwellers. Once again, outsiders did not see or care to comment on the books and art of the churches, synagogues, and religious schools, which already flourished in the neighborhood. Instead the reporter pointed to what he saw as changed habits: "Every man who goes there puts on a clean shirt and combs his hair out of deference, and scrubs his hands because they are certain to be shaken by clean ones. Every woman, after leaving goes home, washes her baby and the floor, puts her bed over the back fence to air, rubs the window panes until they shine and plants a slip of geranium in a tomato can."[22]

Hull-House quickly attracted a large group of talented women who responded to Jane Addams's philosophy of social stewardship. Included in this exceptional group were Florence Kelley, Julia Lathrop, Alzina Parsons Stevens, Eleanor Smith, and Louise DeKoven Bowen, as well as Edith and Grace Abbott.[23] Hull-House provided an opportunity not only for area residents to come together and benefit from the many programs but also an outlet for educated middle-class women and men to serve the larger society, to work for peace between the classes, and to ameliorate the harshness of the industrial city. Hull-House, and other settlements in Chicago and across the nation, offered a chance to be active citizens in a society that more often than not precluded such active public roles for women. Addams bemoaned the state of educated women in an address to the Chicago Women's Club in 1891, speaking of the tremendous social waste of these young women, from whom after years of schooling, "no work is expected." She complained that society restrained young people, especially young women from doing good. Addams stated, "There is nothing, after disease, indigence, and guilt, so fatal to life itself as the want of a proper outlet for active faculties."[24]

Hull-House also soon provided an intellectual home for a new group of social scientists dedicated to understanding the city and its poorer residents. The settlement house attracted many male academics who wanted an "open window" to study the city. Addams, however, clearly did not see Hull-House as primarily a social laboratory. In fact in her preface to *Hull-House Maps and Papers* (1895), a work often regarded as a pioneering sociological study, Addams rejected the view of settlement houses as laboratories and emphasized that the needs of the people loomed more important than that of researchers. In her autobiography, *Twenty Years at Hull-House,* she firmly objected to the phrase "sociological laboratory" in reference to Hull-House or any social settlement. In many ways the argument reflected a gendered approach to the work of the settlement. Yet while Addams, Julia Lathrop, and others rejected the laboratory idea, they still opened the door to research in support of their neighbors. In many ways the work of Jane Addams and her colleagues at Hull-House gave birth not only to modern social work but also to modern sociology. Addams's personal drive led to a fantastic outpouring of articles, books, and public lectures to promote the settlement house movement and made her an international figure.[25]

Jenny Dow ran a kindergarten as the settlement's first project. Changes came quickly to the area as Addams and the other residents began to bring their ideas to fruition. In 1891, Hull-House erected the Butler Art Gallery, which housed a branch of the public library, an art gallery, and space for club and class meetings. Two years later settlement leaders built a building with a coffeehouse and a gymnasium. On May 5, 1894, Hull-House opened the first public playground on Polk Street across from the settlement. Four years later the Jane Club Building opened as a cooperative residence for working girls. Hull-House seemed to be constantly changing and growing.[26] By 1907, Hull-House consisted of a complex of over thirteen buildings covering nearly an entire city block.

Jane Addams and the other residents at Hull-House believed in progress and in the betterment of society and saw their mission as one of outreach to the new immigrant communities of the city. Urbanization, immigration, and industrialization had transformed the commonwealth, and Addams believed that society had not reacted positively toward these changes—hence the crises of the late nineteenth century, with its vast slums and antagonistic class battles. The Hull-House women, influenced by Felix Adler, John Dewey, and William James, hoped to create a new ethical sense and assimilate immigrants into the larger American society. They saw the settlement house as central to this movement. The upper-middle-class reformers and residents who called Hull-House home provided leadership to what they saw as a leaderless community huddled in the city. For Addams and the women of Hull-House, the progressive middle class represented the best chance to both interpret America for the immi-

Figure 43. Hull-House as it looked in the early 1900s. Jane Addams revolutionized social work from this complex of eleven buildings on Halsted and Polk Streets. (Postcard, Author's Collection.)

grants and to interpret the immigrants to America. Addams and her colleagues hoped that cultural and educational programs would change the attitudes of the working class.[27] Her program, to build an ideal society based on respect and democracy, was more ambitious than Pullman's.

While Addams saw Hull-House and other settlements as the ultimate interpreters of the immigrant in society, she believed that ethnic communities had a temporary place in America. Reformers, in the face of obviously vital communities, nonetheless persisted in seeing the immigrants as a helpless mass. The settlement house and the public school provided two tools to integrate and assimilate the immigrant communities into the larger society. In order to do this, Hull-House would have to struggle to "liberate" them from their own native leadership. This task could be accomplished in various ways, including creating alliances with more Americanized ethnic leaders. While granting immigrant cultures a special place in Hull-House through the recognition of their national cultures, these traditions were also seen as bridges to Americanization. Not as outright hostile as those who hoped to ban immigration or forcibly assimilate newcomers, Addams and the residents at Hull-House nevertheless did see these communities as transitory and often under the sway of undemocratic forces. They hoped to liberate them from their "backward"-looking ethnic religious and secular leadership as well as from venal local politicians who used their votes to stay in power. She did not see the creation of local political machines as a way of empowering immigrants but as a means of exploiting them and even enslaving them.[28]

Immigrants and working-class Chicagoans, however, did see these political machines as a way of gaining power in American society. By the Civil War, the Germans and Irish emerged as important factors in Chicago politics. This occurred largely because until 1870 immigrants, once they established residence in Illinois, could vote in local and statewide elections without yet being nationalized citizens. This gave immigrant populations enormous influence. They could get much of their agenda enacted into law, especially with help from the Democrats who garnered much of the ethnic vote. In 1855, American residents of Chicago tried to regain control of the city by passing laws to regulate leisure activities, especially the sale of alcohol. Anti-immigrant reformers such as Mayor Levi Boone passed a law raising the cost of liquor licenses and enforcing laws, which closed saloons and beer gardens on Sunday. This action resulted in the Lager Beer Riots on April 21, 1855. Germans had organized to resist the new $300 license fee ($6,844 in 2007), and a test case of the hundreds of arrests for noncompliance was scheduled for April 21. A major clash occurred at the Clark Street Bridge between police and German protestors marching on City Hall from their North Side enclaves. While the riot ended quickly, it mobilized German and Irish voters for the next municipal elections in March 1856, where they defeated Boone and the nativist Know Nothing Party, and so ethnic politics began in the city. A growing polarization between Democrats and Republicans along ethnic and class lines emerged as well. The signal events of the era of urban chaos—the 1871 fire, the 1877 strike, the events leading up to the 1886 Haymarket Affair, and the reaction to open vice and gambling in the Loop—together made this struggle the key feature of the time period. Ethnic politics came to Chicago and remained an important factor in local politics for generations to come.

Germans grew in importance and influenced the public school system to offer German language classes. Hull-House reformers saw the teaching of ethnic languages in the public schools as a positive force that could wean the ethnic groups from their ethnic religious schools and bring them into the Americanizing influence of the public schools. Ethnic leaders did not often see things in the same way. Even the American-born ethnic middle class was interested in maintaining their identities and communities. They entered politics for reasons other than the social reformers would have hoped for.

Many simply saw politics as a chance to get a job or help during the regularly recurring economic downturns. Ethnic newspapers often advised their conationals to become citizens and vote. In 1888, Northwest Side Poles elected August J. Kowalski as the first Pole to serve on the city council. Originally a Republican, he switched parties and by 1894 served as superintendent of the Water Pipe Extension Department. In a rally that year in South Chicago he proclaimed the Democratic Party as the only party that Polish Americans could depend on. He claimed that over four hundred Poles had found employment with the city and that two hundred and fifty worked in his department alone. In 1897, the Polish newspaper *Zgoda* insisted that Poles had helped make Carter Harrison II's mayoral victory possible and demanded that Polish Americans in the police and fire departments get rewarded with promotions.[29]

Despite the open corruption, immigrants continued to support their ward bosses. In 1898, Jane Addams explained the victory of famously corrupt Nineteenth Ward Alderman John Powers in the municipal election of that year by stating, "Primitive people, such as the South Italian peasants who live in the Nineteenth Ward, deep down in their hearts admire nothing so much as the good man." She explained that the machine politician exhibited the traits of the "good man" in the local culture by not holding a higher morality than his constituents. Despite legal or moral constraints, he must help them in times of need, whether with a job or a favor. Powers once proudly boasted that he had 2,600 people in his ward on the public payroll. The alderman bailed out his neighbors when the police arrested them. He attempted to "fix-up" matters when they appeared before the courts and residents expected him to pay the rent when they could not or to pay for a funeral when a poor man, woman, or child died. Powers gave presents at weddings and christenings. The alderman donated money to the church and used the church bazaar as a stage to show off his philanthropy. As Addams pointed out, he murmured, "Never mind; the money all goes to the poor," or "It is all straight enough, if the church gets it." And of course Powers and others like him did not have the class biases of the rich against the poor. During Christmas 1897, Powers handed out over six tons of turkeys and four more tons of geese and ducks. The alderman did not ask who was worthy and not worthy among the poor. If a family got three or four apiece the alderman did not question it. Addams wrote, "He had none of the nagging rules of the charitable societies, nor was he ready to declare, that just because a man wanted two turkeys for Christmas, he was a scoundrel, who should never be allowed to eat turkey again." The alderman played the role of Robin Hood. No government social safety net existed for poor Chicagoans. The masses of unskilled workers had few places to look for help except to politicians such as Powers. Reformers admonished the poor for supporting these men but did not put in place in the 1890s any practical replacement for them in the political world of the slum. Because of this reality, voters constantly turned back reformers and celebrated men like John Powers.[30]

The Loop: An Architectural Response

The new city rising out of the ashes presented various opportunities to architects such as William Le Baron Jenney. Like many who had served in the Civil War, he now looked to an exciting peacetime future designing America's urban industrial landscape. Visitors to Chicago might see the tall buildings of the Loop as proclaiming a crowded hellish future, but Chicagoans perceived the new buildings as a uniquely American answer to the problems of the American city. Jenney, the son of a successful whaler, was born in Fairhaven, Massachusetts, in 1832. After a brief time at the Lawrence Scientific School, he went to France to study, graduating from the École des Arts et Manufactures in Paris in 1856. In 1861, Jenney enlisted in the Union Army, rising to the rank of major before his discharge five years later. The following year, he came to Chicago and established an architectural business. Jenney became the founder of the Chicago School of Architecture with his creation of the modern architectural office, a collection of draftsmen and architects that dealt with the minute details of a project and the design of the steel frame Home Insurance Building (1885). Many of the architects who came to Chicago after the fire worked, at least for a short time, in Jenney's office, including Louis Sullivan, William Holabird, Martin Roche, and Daniel H. Burnham.

The framing method had been used in several buildings prior to Jenney's Home Insurance Building. As early as 1792, the six-story Calico Mill in Derby, England, used a form of iron framing. By 1844, iron framing had progressed so far in England that it could be used at the exterior of buildings to eliminate the heavy masonry walls. In 1853 the market at Les Halles in Paris was France's first truly freestanding iron structure, and the French took the lead on cast-iron frame construction. James Bogardus built the McCullough Shot and Lead Company tower in 1855 with a cast-iron frame. The following year, Bogardus, who popularized the cast-iron front in New York City, published a description of a modern iron skeleton frame. Even in Chicago, Peter B. Wight and Sanford Loring proposed a fireproof iron-frame-supported column as early as 1874. The following year Gustave Eiffel burst on the international scene with his railroad station in Pest, Hungary, and the Maria-Pia Bridge in Portugal. Back in the United States, James McLaughlin's use of iron framing in 1878 to build the Shillito Department Store in Cincinnati had a marked influence with its simple, no-nonsense exterior. In 1879, Marshall Field and Levi Leiter hired William Le Baron Jenney to design their warehouse, known as the first Leiter Store. This five-story building is usually acknowledged to be the first building of the Chicago School. It is very close in design to the Shillito Store. Jenney brought the skill of an engineer to architecture. Jenney's first Leiter Building at the corner of Wells and Monroe, built in 1879, embodied an intermediate step toward his full steel-framing method of the 1880s. The building anticipated revolutionary ideas such as the "Chicago Window," the steel frame, and the curtain wall, all of which became trademarks of the Chicago School of Architecture.[31]

Like all great thinkers, Jenney synthesized much of the technology that already existed at the time. In 1883, the Home Insurance Company gave the commission for its new Midwest headquarters to Jenny, and construction began in 1884 on the northeast corner of LaSalle and Adams Street. The Home Insurance Building was not a great edifice by any means. It did not live up to its great technical promise. Indeed the second Leiter Building, originally built for Seigel Cooper, and Company between 1889 and 1891 deserved the title of Jenney's best work. Jenney and his various firms developed much of the city's landscape. While Jenney might be the father of the Chicago School, others took the type of buildings being developed in Chicago to their ultimate height.[32]

Figure 44. Central Music Hall (ca. 1890) stood on the southeast corner of Washington and State Streets. In his design, Dankmar Adler experimented with many of the ideas he would later perfect in the Auditorium Building. (Chicago Public Library, Special Collections and Preservation Division.)

In 1861, at the age of seventeen, Dankmar Adler came to Chicago to work for architect Augustus Bauer. The following year, he joined the Union Army, returning to Chicago in 1866. After two attempts at partnerships, he formed his own company in 1878. The Central Music Hall (1879) provided his first independent commission. This building presented the genesis of his later work with Louis Sullivan, the Auditorium Building. Two years after the completion of the Central Music Hall, Sullivan and Adler came together to form one of Chicago's legendary architectural firms.

Louis Sullivan arrived in Chicago in 1873 and was deeply moved by the city. Jenney's Portland Block (1871) impressed him, and he decided to apply to his office for work. The young architect stayed for six months before he left for Paris in 1874 to enroll in the École des Beaux-Arts. As he had in his earlier stay at MIT he found the French school to be sterile and too academic, and he returned to Chicago in 1875. He joined the staff of Johnston and Edelman as a draftsman—a job that provided Sullivan with his first professional opportunity, the interior decoration of Moody's Tabernacle. The intricate floral design would remain a feature of his later work.

Sullivan joined Adler's office in 1879 and became a partner the following year. The third McVicker's Theater (1885) furnished the steppingstone from the Central Music Hall to the Auditorium Building. The architects designed a shell of offices surrounding the theater, much as they had in the Central Music Hall. Here Sullivan began to show some of the talent that would burst forth in the Auditorium Building.[33]

The skyscrapers themselves rose at an unprecedented speed. In 1892, the *Chicago Tribune* reported the fast pace of the construction of the Ashland Block, a new multi-office structure. During a thirteen-day period bricklayers and terra-cotta setters attached the outer walls of four floors to the steel frame of the new building. Steam cranes lifted steel girders high into the air as the workers attached the terra-cotta. In a report to London, the British consul explained that a floor had been completed every three and one-quarter days. Julian Ralph described the "Chicago method" of construction. First, workers erected a steel framework to which they added thin outer walls. He described the buildings as "enclosed bird cages," claiming that the exteriors afforded "mere envelopes" that allowed for large windows that filled the buildings with light and air as they soared above the city.

The new skyscrapers, however, blocked the sunlight and darkened these thoroughfares making the value of the immediate postfire buildings decline. By 1892, John Van Osdel's McCormick Block on the southeast corner of Dearborn and Randolph was dwarfed by architect Clinton J. Warren's Unity Building. The tall buildings dominated and then drove out many of the older structures. There seemed to be no limit to the number of skyscrapers that could be built in the Loop. A Chicago businessman claimed that all of the Loop would soon be made up of "cloud-capped" towers and that only the crowded sidewalks posed a future problem.[34]

The construction of the Auditorium Building was a defining moment for the city. A major example of local cooperation, it came to symbolize the city and the Chicago School of Architecture. Initiated by Ferdinand Peck in 1885, the Auditorium Theater represented another middle-class response to the era of urban chaos. Peck came from a long-standing wealthy family in Chicago. Peck's father, Philip, had come to Chicago in 1831 and opened a store in Fort Dearborn. The following year, he built a two-story structure at LaSalle and South Water Street. One of the original signers of the city's charter, the elder Peck made his money in real estate. The Peck family lived in various places around what would become the Loop, often renting out their property to other developers and moving on. In 1856, Philip Peck invested in Michigan Terrace along the south lakefront between Van Buren and Congress Streets where they lived until the 1871 fire burned their home down.

Figure 45. Burnham and Root designed the Ashland Block on the corner of Clark and Randolph in 1891. (Chicago Public Library, Special Collections and Preservation Division.)

When Philip Peck died shortly after the fire, Ferdinand Peck and his brother Clarence took over their father's estate. The Peck brothers lived in a very different Chicago than the one that their father had known. The Industrial Revolution had transformed the city. Like Pullman and Addams, Ferdinand Peck believed that beauty could lift up the working class and win it over to the middle-class viewpoint. Involved in music and especially opera, Peck supported the Chicago Athenaeum, a kind of workers' college started just after the

Figure 46. Adler and Sullivan's Auditorium Building, ca. 1900, provided an outlet for various social and cultural experiments for the city. (Chicago Public Library, Special Collections and Preservation Division.)

Figure 47. This lithograph of the Auditorium Stage shows the intricate design that marked Sullivan's work. (From *Chicago Album,* Author's Collection.)

fire. The new organization provided workers with a capitalist structured alternative to the radical politics of the time. With the Auditorium Building, Peck saw a chance to bring music to heal the breach in society caused by class warfare. He hoped the Auditorium would build on the earlier successes of Theodore Thomas's orchestra at the Interstate Industrial Exposition Hall on the east side of Michigan Avenue.[35]

On May 29, 1886, less than a month after the Haymarket Affair, Peck presented his ideas for a building to bring all classes together at the Commercial Club. He argued that the new structure could be a permanent home for political conventions, as between 1860 and 1886 the city had hosted seven national conventions and built temporary auditoriums for six of them. The Exposition Building had been refitted several times for concerts. The new Auditorium, to be designed by Adler and Sullivan, would solve these problems. The structure itself was a multiuse building located on the lakefront including the plot of land on which Philip Peck's house had stood just north of Congress Boulevard. Adler had to construct a very complicated structure positioned within one hundred feet of Lake Michigan. His design wove together concrete, heavy timbers, and steel beams to create an enormous platform that allowed the massive building literally to float on the marshy lakefront land. The Auditorium solved the problem of Chicago's muddy ground, but for Ferdinand Peck it also provided an answer to the chaos of Chicago's streets. The Auditorium embodied the idea of social uplift through beauty and practicality.[36]

Daniel H. Burnham started his professional life in 1868 as a business clerk, but he hated the job and joined the office of William Le Baron Jenney. He left shortly thereafter and went to Nevada in search of his fortune. Failing at that, he returned to Chicago and unsuccessfully ran for state senator. He tried architecture again by establishing a firm with Gustave Laureau in 1871. The fire ruined them. Burnham's father then placed him in the office of Carter, Drake, and Wight as a draftsman. Wight became his mentor and inspired Burnham. He met John Root in 1872, and they formed a partnership the following year. In John Root, Burnham found his perfect partner, one whose genius as an architect matched Burnham's business sense. John Root, born in Lumpkin, Georgia, in 1850, became the artistic inspiration for the firm. He had fled the South during the Civil War, attending school in Liverpool. In 1866, he entered New York University where he earned a bachelor of science in civil engineering. The two hired three draftsmen including William Holabird.

While designing a home for the director of the Union Stock Yard, John Sherman, Burnham fell in love with and married Sherman's daughter Margaret in 1874. Besides finding a wife, Burnham fell into a series of commissions at the Union Stock Yards. Burnham and Root now had a firm foundation for their careers. Root married his second wife, Dora Louise Monroe, in 1882. She was the sister of the poet Harriet Monroe, who would also be Root's biographer. Root's architectural philosophy is as important as his body of work. Like

Sullivan, he saw the organic growth of architecture coming out of a peculiarly American experience. The young architect envisioned himself as part of a movement that saw honesty and realism as an expression of this new organic form.[37]

Three important buildings for understanding Root's architecture still stand in Chicago, serving two very different communities. The Rookery (1888) soars eleven stories over the southeast corner of LaSalle and Adams Streets. Despite its heavy facade, the walls have a good deal of glass, and it includes a hollowed square with an interior court that allows all the offices to benefit from natural light. A hybrid of load-carrying wall and steel-frame construction, Burnham and Root built it for Boston's Brooks Brothers as an office structure. It presents a more elaborate style then Burnham and Root's other great building also designed for the brothers. The Monadnock (1891) was unquestionably the Brooks Brothers most profitable building. Unlike the Rookery, they insisted on a simple style that served their business interests. The building itself, at sixteen stories, remains the world's tallest wall-supported structure with seventy-two-inch-thick walls at its base. It follows a slight curve from the second floor upward and ends in an elegant structure at the corner of Jackson and Dearborn. The building is a wonderful expression of the traditional wall-supported building.[38]

While these two buildings served business in the Loop, a third building designed by Burnham and Root built in the years between the two downtown office structures stands in Canaryville to the east of the Union Stock Yards. Root based the Romanesque design of St. Gabriel's Church completed in 1888 on the corner of Forty-fifth and Lowe Streets, loosely on a church in Toulouse, France. Harriet Monroe wrote that the church was "one of the most characteristic designs Root ever put forward, as personal as the clasp of his hand." Root himself felt that St. Gabriel's was one of his finest designs. He especially delighted in the tall masonry bell tower, which Root described as "the breaking of the day." The bell tower stood at 160 feet, the highest all masonry tower in the city at the time.[39]

Chicago's architects took advantage of the opportunities presented by the postfire city to create a uniquely American architecture that had at its heart the goal of building a city that would conquer the chaos of the new industrial era. They would soon attempt to create plans to bring America's cities to the forefront of world architecture and give rise to an American model for city building.

The Columbian Exposition

The city had become involved in the competition to hold a world's fair in 1892 to celebrate the four hundredth anniversary of Columbus's discovery of the New World. In preparation for this, Chicagoans moved to annex the immediate suburbs to the city and increase Chicago's population to over 1 million. An election to determine the fate of these suburbs took place on June 29, 1889. The

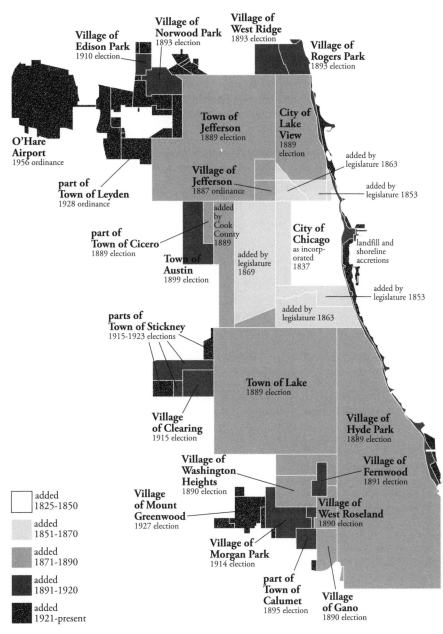

Map 5. In part, Chicago grew because it annexed its inner-ring of suburbs. This map portrays the various annexations in Chicago's history. The 1889 annexation was particularly important as it pushed the city's population passed one million and brought the Columbian Exposition to the city. (Dennis McClendon.)

Town of Lake (with its Union Stock Yard) and Hyde Park (with its prestigious center along the lakefront and heavy industries in South Chicago and Pullman), along with Jefferson Park and Lake View to the northwest and north, all voted to join the city as part of the largest annexation in the city's history. In one day, Chicago gained 125 square miles and 225,000 people. Some suburbs

could not provide adequate services to residents. Many middle-class suburbanites, such as those in Hyde Park proper, however, fought against annexation.
George Pullman opposed his town being dragged into Chicago. The vote however went with the city, and the suburbs gave up their independence, making
Chicago the nations' second largest city overnight.[40]

On Monday, February 24, 1890, Congress selected Chicago as the site of the
World's Fair. It had been a long battle, but the city prevailed against New York,
St. Louis, Washington, D.C., and other smaller rivals. In the end, the battle
had been between Chicago and New York City. New York journalists led the
attack on Chicago, giving it the moniker of "Windy City" not for the wind
that lashed residents but for the hot air emanating from the mouths of its politicians and boosters as they fought to get the exposition. The city now faced a
great challenge: it actually had to raise funds, pick a site, and build a fair.

James W. Ellsworth first suggested that the legendary landscape architect
Frederick Law Olmsted be brought to Chicago to select and then design the
setting for the Chicago exposition. Ellsworth, who had originally opposed the
fair, talked Olmsted into the venture. On August 20, 1890, organizers named
F. L. Olmsted and Company consulting landscape architects and then named
A. Gottlieb as consulting engineer and Burnham and Root consulting architects with Daniel H. Burnham as the chief of construction. The landscape
architect visited various proposed sites and then reluctantly chose Jackson Park
on the South Side for the fair's home. Olmsted and Vaux had designed the park
in 1869, but little of their plan had been executed. Their goal was to bring order
to a largely neglected Jackson Park and construct a grand world's fair in a very
short time.

Daniel Burnham invited a group of East Coast architects, including the
firm of McKim, Mead, and White, to help build the fair. The group decided to
emphasize classical design. Burnham also included five Chicago firms including Adler and Sullivan. The first meeting of the architects took place on January 10, 1891. The next day John Root invited the architects to his house on Astor
Place for tea, and after exposure to the bitter cold while saying good-bye to his
guests Root became ill the next day and later died of pneumonia at the age of
forty-one. The architectural career of John Root was short, but influential beyond its brevity. Daniel Burnham lost his best friend, but stayed on as the chief
of construction of the fair.[41]

Burnham aspired to design a fair that would lead to the reformation of the
American city itself as a place where elites and the middle class could feel comfortable, while largely excluding the city's working class. The decision to use
classical designs for the fair buildings was instrumental in his own development
as an architect and city planner. The Beaux-Arts movement in the United States
owed much to the fair. Many have described this as a reactionary movement,
counteracting the scientific and progressive Chicago School. Certainly, Louis
Sullivan shared this opinion and denounced the Burnham's aesthetic choices.

Figure 48. This prospectus of the Grand Lagoon looking across the Grand Basin presents the classical architecture that predominated in the World's Columbian Exposition of 1893. (*Iliff's Imperial Atlas of the World,* 1892, Author's Collection.)

The fair opened on May 1, 1893, with two distinct areas: one situated along the lakefront south of Fifty-seventh Street; the other along the Midway Plaisance. In the first, Burnham and the eastern architects reigned supreme. The large classically designed buildings and the Court of Honor recalled the imperial past of Rome and foreshadowed the imperial future of the United States just five years before the Spanish-American War. Burnham and the others attempted to put forward a complete vision of the modern American city. The other part of the fair stood on the Midway Plaisance. There popular culture with all of its democratic gaudiness ruled, from the huge Ferris Wheel, which came to symbolize the fair, to the Streets of Cairo and the so-called anthropological exhibits such as the "Amazon and male warriors" of the Dahomey village exhibit. The International Congress of Beauty featuring "Forty Handsome Ladies from Forty Countries in their Native Dress" stood on the Midway. Complaints of lewd behavior by dancers and performers abounded. Just outside of the fair, the Buffalo Bill's Wild West Show operated in a huge tent attracting visitors. Burnham endeavored to portray the American city as both a place of elite and mass culture. He wanted to contain the popular culture of the Midway but not do away with it. The master planner attempted to convince the world of the possi-

Figure 49. A crowd waits for the gates of the Columbian Exposition to open on its first day, 1893. (Stereopticon, Author's Collection.)

Figure 50. World's Columbian Exposition general admission ticket. (Author's collection.)

bility of redefining the American city, not as something wild and out of control, but as a place of beauty that could control its wilder instincts. One again like Pullman, Addams, and Peck, Burnham believed that beauty could overcome the baser instincts of men and women. The World's Columbian Exposition proved a financial and cultural success; about 27.5 million people visited the fair.[42] Soon the great temporary structures stood abandoned on the lakefront, most to be destroyed by fire. The White City disappeared, but its impact would long be felt on urban planning.

On October 28, 1893, the final day of the fair, Mayor Carter Harrison hosted some five thousand mayors and city councilmen, including the mayors of San Francisco, New Orleans, and Philadelphia, at "American Cities Day." Afterward, Harrison headed home to his Ashland Avenue mansion. That evening he was murdered in his home by a disgruntled and deranged office seeker. Chaos reestablished its hold on the city.[43]

Paradise Lost: The Pullman Strike

To the south of the fair, along the Illinois Central Railroad tracks, lay Pullman. It proved to be one of the great attractions of the city during the fair. Over ten thousand foreign visitors alone came to the industrial town during the World's Columbian Exposition. Trains and trolleys connected Pullman with the World's Fair, and at various times George Pullman himself gave tours of the town. He seemed to have answered the two greatest problems facing the new urban America: the formation of permanent social classes and the confusion of manners and mores resulting from shared city space. Pullman offered a controlled environment with a harsher separation of popular culture and high culture than Burnham's fair. The "Sleeping Car King" simply banned from his town what he did not like. Hardly democratic, the Pullman ideal came crashing down shortly after the World's Columbian Exposition.

The nation had already slipped into a depression. Locally the fair held off the worst of the economic downturn, but in the fall of 1893 the economic slowdown hit Chicago. Pullman tried to ban working-class culture and outlaw unions; neither of these approaches worked, however, as workers simply met outside of the town. George Pullman may have tried, but he did not own everything. A working-class community, Kensington, developed to the west of the Pullman city.

The nationwide depression brought reduced wages to Pullman but not reduced rents or utility rates. The company did not cut administrative salaries and continued to pay a profit. Rents remained 20–25 percent higher than in the rest of Chicago. The U.S. Strike Commission, which later investigated the Pullman Strike, said, "The aesthetic features are admired by visitors but have little money value to employees, especially when they lack bread." The whole

Pullman dream seemed to infuriate workers in 1894. The conflict struck a deep chord in Chicago society, dividing it along partisan lines. Even Bertha Palmer, wife of Potter Palmer, condemned George Pullman's actions and urged East Coast supporters of the company to understand how unfairly the firm treated workers.[44]

The Pullman Car Company did try to stave off the effects of the economic downturn and acquired contracts at a loss. It also brought in many of its cars for repairs and closed the Detroit facility, transferring all work to Pullman City. Yet the realities of the economy remained, and from July to November 1893 the number of Pullman employees dropped from 4,500 to 1,100. By bringing in low paying contracts and repairing its sleeper cars, Pullman raised employment to 3,100 men in April 1894. Yet real wages continued to decline. The issue of piecework became important. During normal times, piecework paid better than day wages, but after the cuts the opposite proved true. On December 9, 1893, steamfitters and blacksmiths struck, but the strike ended in defeat after a few days. In the spring of 1894, some Pullman workers joined the American Railway Union (ARU). That winter and spring conditions in the town worsened, and about one-seventh of the Pullman homes stood vacant. Pullman families suffered without adequate food or heat. By early May roughly 35 percent of the men joined the ARU. Negotiations between the workers and Pullman began in earnest.

On May 10, 1894, the company dismissed three members of the workers' grievance committee. That evening in a meeting at nearby Kensington's Turner Hall, the ARU advised against a strike. Eugene V. Debs, the young leader of the industrial railroad union, sent word that a walkout would be ill advised at that time. On May 11, a rumor passed among workers that management had heard about the Kensington meeting and planned to close the plant at noon and lock out the workers. The baseless rumor led workers to strike. By noon some three thousand Pullman employees walked off of their jobs, and by that evening Pullman management placed a sign on the gates of the plant announcing that they had closed it until further notice. The strike had begun, and with it a contest for public support across Chicago and the nation.

Workers immediately set up a strike committee. A representative of the ARU advised Pullman workers against violence and drinking. Thomas Heathcoate, the chairman of the strike committee, told workers to stay away from plant gates. Daily meetings would be held at the Turner Hall in Kensington. The union placed three hundred men along the gates of the Pullman plant in order to guard it against any kind of damage. Pullman management called this picketing. The men stayed on watch until July 6 when the military replaced them to safeguard Pullman's property.

Labor leader Eugene V. Debs came to Pullman to evaluate the situation. On May 16, Debs, in a speech to the workers, compared Pullman's paternalism to slavery and characterized George Pullman as "a greater felon than a poor thief," and he promised to "strip the mask of hypocrisy" from Pullman's face. In a response to calls for help, supplies poured in to the Kensington Strike Headquarters. Public opinion supported the workers' struggle. The Chicago press, on the other hand, with the exception of the *Chicago Times,* referred to the strike as a hopeless mistake. George Pullman himself left town, making his way to Pullman Island in the St. Lawrence River. Later he joined his wife and daughter Florence in New York.[45]

The union organized a Strike Relief Committee and announced that Mayor John P. Hopkins's store, Secord-Hopkins, had donated goods worth $1,500 and $1,000 in cash. Hopkins had been a longtime foe of Pullman and had supported the annexation of Hyde Park Township, including Pullman, in 1889. Another Kensington merchant donated a storeroom, and Hopkins allowed a seven-room apartment to be used by strikers. South Side policemen asked for donations for the strikers. Hopkins replied to people who objected to such display of official favoritism by saying there was no rule against police soliciting for charity. The *Chicago Daily News* donated the use of a store as the city headquarters of the Relief Committee. On May 22, workers drew their last paychecks. Seven days later, brickyard workers, mostly Italians and Czechs, walked out. Newspapers wrote of the hovels that these unskilled workers lived in near the brickyards exposing Pullman to more embarrassment.

In early June the ARU held its annual national convention in Chicago and considered a national boycott of Pullman cars. Over four hundred delegates met at Uhlich's Hall on June 12, as strikers addressed the meeting. Debs wanted to avoid any action by the national union, especially a boycott. The union sent a delegation to speak with Pullman management, who turned them away. On June 20, the ARU gave the Pullman Palace Car Company notice that they would begin a national boycott on June 26 unless the company addressed the workers' grievances. This move set the stage for a national confrontation between labor and management.

The General Managers' Association came to the aid of the Pullman Company. Formed in 1886 by twenty-four railroads, the organization tried to establish common policies on common issues of concern. The Association held a meeting on June 25, and the railroads decided to act together against the boycott and established a temporary headquarters in the Rookery in the Loop. It directed the antilabor struggle and proved to be a formidable foe. On June 26, the national boycott began and quickly spread threatening to shut down the nation's railroads. Many ARU locals called strikes against their railroads, and by July 2, the General Managers' Association acknowledged a stalemate. Chicago was besieged. Prices of food first rose and then soared. Chicago's papers vilified "Dictator Debs" and his hold on the city. Across America, the workers' action now became the "Chicago Strike." Mayor Hopkins put his three-thousand-man police force on alert as disorder threatened the city and the threat of chaos intensified.

The boycott disrupted the movement of mail, making the strike a federal affair. U.S. attorneys, acting under orders of Attorney General Richard Olney, obtained an injunction against the ARU from the Circuit Court of Chicago on July 2. The injunction ordered ARU officers not to communicate with each other or anyone else concerning the boycott. Debs knew this meant the union's defeat, and he chose to ignore the injunction. Meanwhile violence began to breakout on the railroad lines. On the same day that the Circuit Court handed down the injunction against the union, about two thousand strikers and supporters gathered at the Rock Island Railroad yards in suburban Blue Island just to the south of the city. The federal marshal ordered them to disperse, and when they refused he cabled asking for troops, which arrived on July 4 from Fort Sheridan, just north of Chicago. President Grover Cleveland ignored the objections of Illinois Governor John Peter Altgeld and Mayor Hopkins, both fellow Democrats. Because Altgeld had granted clemency to the surviving Haymarket martyrs, some saw the president's action as a slap at him and the pro-striker Hopkins. The next day, a mob of ten thousand took over the rail yards that served the Union Stock Yards. The soldiers and police retreated before this mass of humanity. That night, a huge fire broke out in the deserted Columbian Exposition buildings on the lakefront. The next morning saw the destruction of $340,000 worth of railroad equipment (more than $8 million in 2007). More federal troops rushed into the city from as far away as New York and Nebraska, as local officials deputized more marshals and added more police. Altgeld called in the state militia. On July 7, the army cleared the tracks and escorted trains bringing mail and food into the city. Federal power smashed the strike, as troops occupied Chicago for the third time since the Civil War. The strike in Pullman continued, but the writing was on the wall, and on July 19, as the strike failed, most federal troops left Chicago.

George Pullman's reputation as an urban philanthropist and utopian builder also lay in ruins. He never settled the union question. In August 1894, the Illinois attorney general filed suit to force the company to divest its residential holdings. Pullman's lawyers fought back. Governor Altgeld tried to raise Pullman's taxes and then sought to regulate sleeping car rates. Other states also attempted to control the company, but nothing came of their efforts. On October 19, 1897, George M. Pullman died at the age of sixty-six of a heart attack. His family buried him in Chicago's Graceland Cemetery under tons of steel and concrete to prevent labor radicals from desecrating his grave. Solon Beman designed a lone Corinthian column to mark the grave. The following October, the Illinois Supreme Court reversed a lower court's decision and ordered the Pullman Palace Car Company to sell all of its land not needed for car production. The town began to be dismantled immediately. By 1908, the company had no relationship with the town except as a major employer.[46]

As Pullman's perfect town lay destroyed by 1897, a new movement came out of the cauldron of the 1890s. Progressivism was born of the tragic struggles of the 1890s. The 1892 Homestead Strike in Pennsylvania and the 1894 Pullman Strike in Illinois had brought national attention to the continued struggle to deal with the Industrial Revolution. Pullman's town may have become just another Chicago neighborhood, but the idea of planning for a more perfect city also emerged out of that struggle and out of the World's Fair. While Pullman may have been discredited, his ideas concerning the influence of the urban environment sparked other experiments such as nearby Harvey, Illinois, which was organized around Christian principles at the time of the fair and the strike. To the northwest of the city, the Swedish settlement of North Park grew around the Swedish Covenant Church's North Park College. Eighty-eight percent of the neighborhood's early residents were born in Sweden, and another 10 percent were American born of Swedish parentage.[47] Although they would distance themselves from Pullman, both Daniel Burnham and Jane Addams had learned from the experiment. No one would attempt such a totally undemocratic experiment again, but the concept that planning might restore order to the chaotic city and that experts could use science to perfect the city emerged as major themes of the coming century.

The Progressive and Not So Progressive City

In 1901, self-professed anarchist Leon Czolgosz assassinated President William McKinley. The chaos and violence that had marked the relationship between labor and capital now touched the White House as the assassin's political beliefs shocked the nation. For the third time in thirty-six years, an assassin had struck down an American president. As the nation buried the man who had led the country to victory in its first global war in 1898, Americans waited to see how the already legendary young "Roughrider," Teddy Roosevelt, would fill McKinley's shoes. Roosevelt quickly proved to be his own man. Unwittingly, Czolgosz, the young Polish American anarchist from Detroit, had inaugurated a new era in the history of the United States. Progressivism, long gestating both in the halls of academia and on city streets of Europe, America, Australia, and New Zealand, suddenly found itself born into the White House in the person of Roosevelt. The voice of Jane Addams and countless others who were determined to solve the problems of urban industrial capitalist society might now be heard in the highest corridors. Chicago remained at the center of this process.

The Continued Clash of Social Classes

With the death of McKinley, Chicago and the nation entered the Progressive era. The era of urban chaos did not disappear; indeed the creation of U.S. Steel from the merger of the Carnegie and Morgan steel interests in 1901 produced yet another huge monopoly determined to smash unionism. Predictably, labor reacted, and the Amalgamated Steel and Iron Workers struck the new company. The 1901 steel strike ended in defeat for the union, and the once powerful Amalgamated slipped into irrelevancy. Chicago's steel mills remained unorganized, yet U.S. Steel tried to sidestep Chicago radicalism by developing a whole new town just across the border in Indiana. Gary, Indiana, became the center of the region's steel industry. Not overtly planned in the tradition of Pullman, but nonetheless a company town, U.S. Steel named the town after the president of the new industrial behemoth, Elbert H. Gary, whose hostile attitude toward labor was well known.[1]

Trends toward monopoly continued as the nation entered the new century—one marked by ever more labor conflict. The new corporate model attempted to expand its control over the labor force, and so clashed with workers. Craft unions fought hand-to-hand with corporations over the control of the new production system. The Chicago building trades lockout of 1899–1900 showed corporate power in conflict with craft interests. In 1899, the creation of the Building Contractors' Council (BCC) marked management's defiance of union and craft rules for the building trades, such as brick layers, carpenters, and others necessary for construction projects. Company owners hoped to reshape the construction industry in a new corporate image. The power of the BCC came from the support of suppliers of raw material, architects, and most of Chicago's bankers. The organization led to a conflict with the Building Trades Council, which represented traditional craft unions, and the struggle soon turned violent, bringing the financial community into the fight on the side of the BCC and forcing Mayor Carter Harrison II to move against the craft organizations. For the time being the BCC had won, but the unions recovered quickly and prelockout conditions concerning wage rates and craft prerogatives again prevailed.[2]

Progressivism in Chicago had deep roots, as it did across the northern Atlantic economy. Reform had been in the air for over twenty years. Industrialized European nations as well as New Zealand and Australia led the way toward corralling unbridled industrialism, where corporate profits always trumped the safety, income, and rights of workers. Even autocratic Germany had put a social safety net in place for its citizens in order to prevent any attraction to socialism. American Progressives looked toward the European states for ideas concerning problems presented by the industrial capitalist economy.[3]

Yet, American workers seemed more disorganized than ever. The glory days of the Knights of Labor were long gone. Terrence Powderley, still titular head of that organization, now worked as a minor federal bureaucrat. Craft unions, united under Samuel Gompers's American Federation of Labor (AFL), seemed powerless in light of the new industrial monopolies emerging across the country. The labor movement remained fragmented by ethnic, gender, racial, and craft issues. Still, workers continued to hope that organized labor would provide a weapon to corral in the behemoth of monopoly stomping across the nation.

Meanwhile, union organizers appeared once again in the Stock Yard District. Ten years earlier during the Pullman Strike, the Back of the Yards had broken out in violence, and federal troops patrolled Packingtown's streets. Various small strikes erupted throughout the 1890s. The Back of the Yards, with its seemingly endless dirty gray mud-filled streets lined with saloons, balloon-frame tenements, and small churches, provided a home for new groups of immigrants and new union activity. Michael Donnelley, a skilled butcher and leader of the Amalgamated Meat Cutters and Butcher Workmen, a union founded in 1894 to organize both meat cutters and packinghouse workers under the auspices of the AFL, walked into neighborhood saloons and halls with a new message of labor solidarity that included the increasing numbers of unskilled packinghouse workers not traditionally organized by unions.

By 1904, the Amalgamated developed into an important factor in the relationship between capital and labor in the stockyards. That summer, packinghouse owners moved against Donnelley's organization, and a strike broke out in the slaughterhouses. When the two sides reached a settlement, management refused to extend it to unskilled workers and also fired some union organizers. Donnelley and his men walked out again, in what was perhaps the first strike by skilled laborers for the rights of unskilled workers in the country. The union lost the strike but set a precedent for future union organizing drives to recruit the unskilled.[4] A barrier within the labor movement between the skilled and unskilled had been broken.

African Americans remained, however, the one group that presented an ongoing dilemma to union activists. The packers brought many black strikebreakers into their plants. They let most go after the strike, but African Americans came to be seen as another social group that could be used to foment fragmentation in the labor force and prevent unionization. This dangerous mixture of race, ethnic, and class issues haunted the city throughout the twentieth century.[5]

The word "ghetto" in 1900 did not yet conjure up images of black Americans trapped in urban slums but rather invoked immigrants in general and East European Jews in particular. The shift in the source of immigration from northern and western Europe to southern and eastern Europe had brought tremendous changes to Chicago's neighborhoods. But one fact had remained constant: immigrants and their children made up the overwhelming majority of the city's population. All along city streets, they attempted to build a sense of community in order to deal with the reality of the new industrial city.

In this diversity lay both the city's strength and its weakness. Polish and Lithuanian gangs stared each other down across Morgan Street in Bridgeport. Czechs and Germans avoided each other on the Lower West Side. The Irish feared the arrival of Jews and African Americans on the South Side. On the North Side, Gold Coast residents feared their Sicilian neighbors in Little Hell just to the west. No one group truly occupied any one neighborhood; rather, an ethnic cluster dominated its main streets while side streets showed a great mixture of ethnicity. Blacks, Asians, and others also walked along Chicago streets. Sometimes, the conflict between groups reached dangerous heights, but often neighborhood change happened silently, as one group moved out and another moved in—a story that continues today.

The streetcar city allowed various ethnic groups to at least attempt to segregate themselves from others. Germans fled before the Slavic invasion of many of their old neighborhoods on the West Side, especially along Milwaukee Avenue. The Irish remained the most dispersed group in the city, although as the twentieth century began they dominated various North Side, West Side, and South

Figure 51. Emil J. Brach and his two sons founded Brach's Palace of Sweets in 1904. This store, located at the intersection of North Avenue and Town Street, sold candy produced onsite for both the retail and wholesale trade. Many small neighborhood establishments soon prospered and grew into larger businesses. (Chicago Public Library, Special Collections and Preservation Division.)

Side neighborhoods. As the century progressed, Poles came to control the West Town community, along with much of Bridgeport, Back of the Yards, South Chicago, and Hegewisch. Their presence could also be felt in other neighborhoods. Czechs dominated Pilsen, as well as what would become known for the first half of the twentieth century as "Czech California" in South Lawndale. Here too, however, Czechs shared these streets with others, especially Poles and Germans.

While they lived on the same streets, these ethnic groups had their own institutions. Thus they were spatially integrated, but socially segregated. Irishmen, Poles, Czechs, Germans, Slovaks, and others might live together in Pilsen or West Town, but they lived separate social lives in their own churches, parochial schools, saloons, clubs, and stores. This social fragmentation hindered those who would organize these disparate ethnic and immigrant groups to bring about change.[6]

Middle-class reformers looked with some dismay at the immigrant neighbor-hoods with their poverty and local fragmentation. How was it possible to unite these groups for change? Could a Pole, an Irishman, an Italian, and a Jew be brought together to seek out common needs and possibilities with native white Americans? Was there any hope for real democracy in the out-of-control in-dustrial city? The problem of public space seemed central. Where was there neutral territory in the ethnic industrial city? The American city did a fine job at providing private space but not public space. Furthermore, ethnic groups felt uncomfortable and often threatened in those public spaces that did exist such as Chicago's large parks and boulevards. These spaces remained middle-class American preserves rather than meeting places for the working class. The city's churches, saloons, and club halls retained their ethnic identities and therefore were only semipublic places. Indeed, middle-class reformers felt uncomfort-able with most of these institutions, especially the saloon. They saw alcohol as a monster that stalked Chicago's immigrant wards, stealing immigrants' pay in exchange for moral oblivion. The whiskey rows and corner taverns of the city did not hold out the promise of republican virtue for those who hoped to rec-reate the democratic town hall meetings of a golden small-town New England past. For many, the saloon threatened the morality and stability of the com-munity by endangering the family, especially women and children. While some saw the bars as a stabilizing factor, reformers tended to look down upon this institution as a harbor for vice and dissolution.[7]

Chicago's Progressive Politics

Progressivism in Chicago and across the country took various paths. The most obvious one was political. New York, Cleveland, Detroit, and other municipali-ties saw at least short-lived reform administrations. Chicago, on the other hand, although referred to as "the most radical city in America" after the election of Edward F. Dunne to the mayoralty in 1905, saw little in the way of reform ad-ministrations. The five (two-year term) elections of Carter Harrison II, son of the assassinated mayor, are seen by some to constitute a Progressive administra-tion. But many would disagree, given Harrison's alliance with the "gray wolves," the city's corrupt aldermen, who had also supported his father's organization. Certainly, there were reform organizations in Chicago, but they often fought with each other over the details of various issues.[8]

In 1897, Carter Harrison II, the "harmonizer and unifier," won his first elec-tion as mayor of Chicago. The thirty-five-year period before the outbreak of World War I saw Harrison, or his father the original "Our Carter," win ten of seventeen mayoral elections. They did this without the benefit of a citywide po-litical machine. Both, however, were champions of the politics of compromise and understood the shifting ethnic and class alliances across the city's wards.[9]

Chicago had a long-standing reform tradition dating back to the Great Chicago Fire. The city's elites founded the Civic Association in 1874 as a response to the second Chicago fire and the insurance crises that came in its aftermath. The Union League Club, organized five years later to promote a third term for President Grant, also became involved in electoral regulation. And William T. Stead helped organize the Civic Federation of Chicago in 1893 as an all-encompassing reform organization, but it soon focused on the issue of civil service reform.

The city's most successful reform group, the Municipal Voters League (MVL), attempted to bring labor and elite reformers together over franchise issues, of which transit played a central role. As Chicago developed, especially with the advent of modern transportation, communication, and power technologies, it became necessary to grant local monopolies or franchises to various companies providing the public with mass transit, telephone, and telegraph lines or gas and electricity, and the city council generally granted such franchises in Chicago. Indeed, the MVL's leadership tended to be made up of, not Chicago's powerful capitalists, but second-level and second-generation businessmen and experts such as architect Allen Pond and social workers Jane Addams and Graham Taylor. Chicago's most powerful magnates, such as Marshall Field and Philip D. Armour, often opposed the MVL as they had ties with both the traction companies owned by Charles Yerkes and politicians that they had worked hand in hand with before. The good government people, or "goo goos," hoped to bring about reform in a city well known for corruption. They sought efficiency in government and were often not that enthralled with democracy as they felt that the masses were not capable of making intelligent decisions. They often also saw a connection between vice and local politicians, especially the notorious John Coughlin and Michael Kenna of the First Ward. The use of public franchises further enriched these politicians.[10]

Public transportation had long been a problem in Chicago. Various franchises and state laws governed the relationship between these privately owned corporations and the public spaces in which they must necessarily be built. As early as 1853, the state legislature divided Chicago into three sections based on the North and South Branches of the Chicago River. The North, West, and South Divisions, more popularly referred to as the various "Sides" of the city, then became territories for the horse car lines put in place in the late 1850s. In 1865, the state legislature agreed to replace the twenty-year franchises with ninety-nine-year agreements. An 1870 state constitution withheld this power from the state legislature, and in 1875 the city brought back the twenty-year leases. This became the regular practice of the city council. Three years later, the transit companies were required to pay for the use of city streets. In 1883, not wishing for a court fight over the old ninety-nine-year leases, the city extended the franchises for another twenty years.

Figure 52. This is Chicago's first electric streetcar or "trolley," which began operation in 1890. Notice the similarity in design to the cable cars. (Chicago Public Library, Special Collections and Preservation Division.)

Transit became a very profitable business in the city. By 1900, more than 1.25 million passengers rode the streetcars on ten privately owned surface lines. Charles Yerkes, who came to the city in 1881 and owned the West Chicago Company and the North Chicago Railway Company, two of the largest traction companies, had a tremendous amount of influence among the gray wolves of the city council. In 1897, Yerkes supported the unsuccessful Humphrey bill, which would have extended the transit leases for another fifty years. His political allies then passed the Allen Bill, giving the Chicago City Council a chance to extend transit leases for either twenty or fifty years. The council soon followed Yerkes's lead and passed fifty-year leases. Carter Harrison II vetoed the measure. In a session on December 19, 1898, calling for the override of the mayor's veto, angry crowds of Chicagoans gathered outside city hall and threatened to lynch any Chicago alderman who voted to override Harrison's veto. Yerkes's manipulation of the city council and of the state legislature was perhaps not as real as widely believed, but he certainly fell short of the reformer's idea of a proper relationship between capital and the democratic political processes.

Yerkes soon left Chicago for London, where he made another fortune by help-ing to build the city's celebrated subway or "tube." [11]

The MVL played a large role in the defeat of the franchise extension bills and supported aldermanic candidates based on their signing of an anti-Yerkes pledge. Reformers had targeted the transit king for some time, and the MVL achieved its greatest victory in the 1898 elections, as forty-two of the sixty-eight aldermen agreed to oppose Yerkes. Between 1901 and 1911, 85 percent of candi-dates elected to the city council had the support of the MVL. Many times, the MVL would be practical in their endorsements, supporting the lesser of two evils. The MVL saw itself as a machine of the righteous, supporting no party but only individual candidates. It did not prove very effective outside of the traction issue. [12]

The transit issue gave rise to the political career of Edward F. Dunne, Chi-cago's one truly Progressive mayor, elected in 1905. Dunne, the only person to serve as both mayor of Chicago and governor of Illinois, was the first child of Patrick W. Dunne and Mary Lawlor. His father took part in Irish national poli-tics before fleeing Ireland for the United States in 1849. The Dunnes eventually moved to Peoria, Illinois, where "Eddy" grew up and graduated from Peoria Public High School. Dunne then went to Trinity College in Dublin in 1871 but did not matriculate because of the family's financial troubles. Dunne's father joined the Illinois House of Representatives in 1876, and the following year the family moved to Chicago.

Figure 53. The corner of State and Madison Streets provided a major transportation hub for the city's trolley system. (From a Chicago Railways Company Bond, Author's Collection.)

After finishing law school in 1877, Dunne became involved in local Chicago politics. Judge Murray Tulley sponsored Dunne among the leadership of Democratic politics and brought him into reformist political circles. In 1892, voters elected Dunne to the judiciary. Dunne became a Bryan Democrat by 1896, and while he remained on the outskirts of municipal political power, his star rose quickly, and in 1905 Democrats elected him mayor.

Dunne's election was based primarily on the transit issue. He was interested in civic reform: he saw government as a positive force in society that could bring about change for the betterment of everyone not just the business elite or the masses. He promised the immediate municipal ownership of the traction companies and pledged that the city would eventually own the gas and electric utilities. The idealistic Dunne soon found himself in the real world of Chicago politics. He counted among his sponsors Democrats Bathhouse John Coughlin and Hinky Dink Kenna, as well as their rivals the Hopkins-Sullivan branch of the party who hoped to get control from the Harrison forces. The "goo goos" hardly trusted him because of this regular party support. Dunne's campaign was a mixture of traditional ethnocultural, partisan, and pragmatic ward-based politics with ideological appeals to independent voters.[13]

Labor turbulence greeted the new mayor's first one hundred days. Chicago's Teamsters had grown in power over the years. By the early 1900s, they began to reach across union lines and attempt to influence labor across the spectrum of Chicago's work world. There had been a teamster strike in 1902 against the meatpackers and again in 1904 in support of striking packinghouse workers. Now, in 1905, the Chicago Teamsters took on their most powerful opponents in a 105-day strike that saw over 415 serious injuries and the death of twenty-one people. The Employers Association (EA), funded in 1903 by some of Chicago's richest companies, was an outgrowth of the Chicago Association of Commerce. The EA, in turn, created the Employers' Teaming Company to destroy the Teamsters' Union in 1905.[14]

The strike took up much of Dunne's attention. He formed a committee to study the issues involved, but by the time the report came out, public opinion had been swayed against the unions. On May 10, 1905, under the threat of yet another federal occupation of the city, Dunne mobilized 1,700 emergency policemen to protect the nonunion delivery wagons. By July, the Teamsters had lost the strike. This crisis took the momentum away from Dunne on the issue of traction ownership because in some circles it led to the impression that Dunne was weak.[15]

Other problems quickly emerged for Mayor Dunne, including an argument over education in the city and his appointments to the school board. The Chicago Federation of Teachers (CFT), founded in 1897, stood at the center of the storm. The CFT, led by Mary Haley and Catherine Goggins, successfully attacked several big businesses over their refusal to pay school taxes, collecting some $600,000 in back taxes and then forcing the Board of Education to raise teachers' salaries. Mayor Dunne, while still a judge, had ordered the school board to hand the money over to the teachers in a celebrated court case in 1902. Shortly after his election, Dunne appointed seven new school board members; five of these appointments were made with special reference to the controversy between Superintendent Edwin Cooley and the union, including Jane Addams and Dr. Cornelia Bey, both close friends of Haley and Goggins. Arguments and division quickly broke out on the board, and the question of textbooks became a disaster. Dunne again seemed to be incapable of taking decisive action, and his foes accused him of running an inefficient administration.

In relation to transit, Dunne vacillated between his early promises for immediate municipal ownership and various compromise stands. He at first hired an outside expert to give advice about the possibilities of Chicago's ownership of the traction lines. This decision was a disaster as James Dalrymple, the manager of the municipally owned system in Glasgow, Scotland, issued a report advising against municipal ownership. The Dalrymple Report played directly into the hands of Dunne's opponents, including Carter Harrison II, who, while tentatively in favor of municipal ownership, had warned of moving too quickly on the issue. More confusion broke out over Dunne's instruction to Charles Werno, the chairman of the Committee on Local Transportation, to enter into an agreement to purchase the various transit lines and to build new lines. This letter led to an agreement with the transit lines, which the mayor then rejected, and again Dunne seemed to be running a confused administration.[16]

Dunne soon also became involved in the liquor issue, a thorny problem for Democrats. An Irish Catholic, Dunne understood the role that the saloon played in immigrant communities and preferred personal temperance to legislative prohibition. Mayor Dunne realized that a Democratic politician could not risk making concessions to the antisaloon movement, but he also recognized that politicians abused how they handed out liquor licenses. The moral reform camp put pressure on his administration, and so he attempted to take a middle course and proposed to enforce the Sunday closing laws and raise the license fee from $500 to $1,000. He revoked over one hundred saloon licenses, and his police even closed one of Alderman Kenna's saloons for a short time. Dunne promised to give the licenses back if the saloons would clean up their act and follow city ordinances, especially with regard to gambling and prostitution. The state legislature, however, would not let him restore the licenses.

Despite Dunne's actions, the Sunday Closing League and other antisaloon groups forced a grand jury investigation of the administration and the police. As a result, his fellow Democrat Anton Cermak, a fast rising Czech American politician, formed the United Societies for Local Self-Government in 1907, a multiethnic organization that claimed over two hundred thousand members pledged to personal liberty, which included the freedom to have a beer on a

Sunday. The saloonkeepers, ward bosses, and others sought revenge against the mayor. Cermak worked for the defeat of Dunne, and in 1907 the Republican Party ran Fred Busse, who promised a wide-open city.

The Dunne administration posed a serious challenge to the status quo in Chicago. His appointments to the school board represented teachers and the working class. He believed that "labor and middle class people are better able to determine what is good for their children than the merchants club." He brought outsiders into city government. Dunne, however, came up against the fractured nature of the Chicago political system. Real power still lay with the ward bosses. In many ways despite what seemed to be an erratic administration Dunne reached the limits of reform in Chicago. Much of the opposition to him came from the fractured reform group itself. Moral reformers stood against him. Once he upset the ward bosses and saloonkeepers who had originally supported him, Dunne was finished. The system of using franchises and contracts for money, jobs, and votes remained firmly entrenched in the city. Dunne seemed to be moving away from that system, and yet some feared with the traction issue he would just be creating another source of patronage jobs.[17]

Dunne's 1907 platform opposed settlement with the traction companies. Busse, a German American coal and ice dealer, endorsed the traction settlement. The traction companies spent freely to defeat Dunne, as did the liquor interests. Estimates of their spending ran as high as $600,000. The Chicago City Railway Company spent $350,000 alone in promoting the settlement and the defeat of Mayor Dunne. Much of that money helped Democratic candidates who supported the traction agreement. Busse won the election with 164,702 votes to 151,779 for Dunne. The settlement ordinances were adopted by 167,367 votes to 134,281.

Busse was a practical choice for the Republican Party who held on to the mayoralty for one term; and then Carter Harrison II returned, recapturing the office for the Democratic Party in 1911. For the time being, Anton Cermak continued to build his organization. The curious dance in Chicago between reformers and professional politicians continued. Certainly, the city council passed progressive measures. Even Busse supported some reform measures. During his administration, the first four-year term in office for a Chicago mayor—itself a progressive reform—Burnham designed the Chicago Plan of 1909. The city was in the throes of the Progressive movement, even as it rejected Dunne. The movement for a new municipal charter and the continued agitation over the municipal ownership of the utilities, as well as drinking and the future of education, remained important issues.[18]

The Progressive Accomplishment

Chicagoans were better at instituting Progressive era reform than taking control of the political system. The city became a showplace of reform early in the epoch owing to Jane Addams's and others' influence on public policy. The political machine, seeing value in some of these changes, often supported them and helped bring about structural change on the neighborhood level. Chicagoans played a lead role in the development of city planning, housing, working conditions, construction of playgrounds and parks, reform of the court system, advanced education, and the role of the university in the modern city. The Progressive community acted as the conscience of the city and helped to formulate policies that made Chicago a better place to live. Progressives such as Mary McDowell, the founder of the University of Chicago Settlement House in the Back of the Yards neighborhood, worked to clean the city in sometimes very elemental ways. She became known as the "Garbage Lady" as she struggled for better environmental conditions in her community.[19] Progressivism also showed its inherent limitations in this city that seemed to accept no limits as it tried to deal with moral issues such as liquor, gambling, and prostitution or with social questions such as poverty, immigration, and the constant issue in American society, race. Like the city itself, the Progressive movement had contradictions in its attitudes toward these varied concerns.

Often in Chicago's Progressive community, concerns about democracy came together with concerns about children.[20] In 1893, Illinois joined the ranks of the most progressive states with the passage of a child labor law. The new law forbade the employment of children under the age of fourteen and totally prohibited the employment of children in manufacturing. Children over the age of fourteen but younger than sixteen could not be employed at a job considered hazardous—any job that an insurance company refused to insure. Four years later, a new law extended the provisions of the 1893 act to commercial enterprises. The law limited the working hours of those under sixteen to no more than sixty hours per week and no more than ten hours per day. The new law also required a certificate from a doctor stating that the child was physically fit to work. By 1900, new laws regarding compulsory school attendance and stronger child labor laws, which no longer allowed children under sixteen to work more than eight hours per day, had been passed. Reformers soon discovered that enforcement would be difficult. On the one hand, the office of the factory inspector had a small staff; on the other, both age and health restrictions could easily be gotten around by families who contacted notary publics, doctors, and even priests and ministers who, aware of the dire financial standing of the family, often changed birth dates on official certificates.[21]

Governor John Peter Altgeld appointed Florence Kelley as the state's first factory inspector in 1893—an appointment that generated considerable protest. The *Illinois Staats-Zeitung* called Kelley "an extremist socialist agitator who hardly differs from an anarchist." At thirty-four years of age, Kelley had a chance to prove herself and her ideas and also to expand the role of government in the lives of individuals she knew needed the protection of the government. With the state's authority behind her, Kelley could eliminate child labor in Illinois, or so she hoped. She moved her office near Hull-House and chose Alzina Parsons Stevens as her chief assistant. Stevens, a longtime labor union

Figure 54. Many women and girls were employed in mass production industries such as candy making. Here women work coating bonbons at the Brach Candy Company Plant about 1919. (Chicago Public Library, Special Collections and Preservation Division.)

advocate, moved into Hull-House. With a great deal of energy, Florence Kelley actually enforced the law she saw as part of the larger class struggle. Kelley's office became a "revolutionary stronghold." Kelley wrote to Frederick Engels, Karl Marx's coauthor and a leader of the international socialist movement, that Governor Altgeld placed no restrictions on her freedom of speech and that three of her deputies and her assistant were outspoken socialists.

The child labor laws were quickly challenged in the courts. In 1895, the Illinois Supreme Court struck down the eight-hour provision for women in the 1893 law. The law had been gender specific but had helped workers in general get better conditions. The courts said that the law prohibited women from using their right to contract their labor on an employer's terms. The following year, Altgeld lost reelection, at least in part because he had issued pardons to the three anarchists still in prison for their roles in the Haymarket Affair. The new governor removed Kelley as factory inspector. Nevertheless the work of Florence Kelley and Progressive women connected to Hull-House did not go unnoticed and began a national movement to curtail child labor, which culminated in 1916 with the first federal child labor law, the Keating-Owen Act. The Supreme Court struck that law down two years later, but in 1921 Congress passed a second federal law creating the U.S. Children's Bureau.[22]

In the 1890s, Progressives continued to try and help women and children by expanding the role of government. This was part of a general reordering of the role of federal, state, and local governments and their relationship with ordinary citizens in the years after the Civil War. At the end of the nineteenth century, Progressive reformers, particularly women, often referred to as "child savers," helped to create special judicial and correctional institutions dealing with youthful offenders. The origins of the definition of delinquency are to be found in their ideas. These were "disinterested" reformers who saw the problem of juvenile delinquency as matter of morality and of conscience. They furthermore saw themselves as altruists and humanitarians with the highest ideals concerning children as they invented a new category of youthful misbehavior.

The growth of the theory of environmentalism—the idea that one's environment influenced one's morals—came directly out of the settlement house experience. As a result, the harsher aspects of Social Darwinism, or the so-called law of the jungle, were blunted and modified. The city became portrayed as a breeding ground for criminals. Reformer Lincoln Steffens proclaimed Chicago, "first in violence, deepest in dirt, loud, lawless, unlovely, ill-smelling, irreverent, new; an overgrown gawk of a village, the 'tough' among cities, a spectacle for the nation." The answer for many of the reformers was to look back to their rural upbringing and attempt to make the city more like the towns and villages they came from. It would not be America's final attempt to find the "blessed"

Figure 55. Pictured here about 1911 are boys learning wood crafting at the Jewish Training School on the West Side. Progressives often encouraged young boys to learn a trade before entering the work place. (Chicago Jewish Archives, Spertus Institute of Jewish Studies.)

community. For children, this seemed most important because the city offered amusements and temptations unknown to rural America. As William Douglas Morrison wrote in his 1897 book *Juvenile Offenders,* "The restraining eye of the village community is no longer upon them." Chicago's reformers and early sociologists pointed to the disintegration of traditional norms and the creation of a violent class.[23]

The legal status of children gradually changed over the course of the nineteenth century. Florence Kelley, in her innovative research done in the 1880s, saw the child as more and more a ward of the state. The definition of the proper relationship between the state and children became vital to Progressives. Illinois' Juvenile Court Act of 1899, generally recognized as the first in the nation, established a separate court and facilities for incarcerating young offenders. By 1917, all but three states passed similar bills, and by 1932 over six hundred independent juvenile courts operated in the United States. More than twenty nations had also established similar courts. When the state established the court, reformers saw it as a child welfare center and granted it a good deal of flexibility to deal with children's problems.

On July 3, 1899, the Honorable Richard S. Tuthill initiated the modern era in juvenile justice as he presided over the Juvenile Court of Illinois. Before him stood an eleven-year-old boy, Henry Campbell, accused by his parents, Frank and Lena Campbell, who felt they needed the state's help in disciplining their boy. The Campbells pleaded that the child not be sent off to an institution but instead to his grandmother in Rome, New York. Tuthill agreed and sent Henry east. From the very start, this case showed the flexibility that had been written into the Juvenile Court law. The court could provide individual treatment for the children brought before it. On that first day Tuthill spoke out on the problem of delinquency and asserted that he presided over a court of last resort.

The Juvenile Court Committee (JCC) established the Juvenile Detention Home on the Near West Side at 625 West Adams. Lucy Flower, the major proponent behind the Juvenile Court Law, established the JCC as an outgrowth of the Chicago Women's Club. The JCC raised money for the court that was at first largely privately funded. In 1904, 1905, and 1907, reforms expanded the original law and the court's jurisdiction. Many traditionalists feared the Juvenile Court and saw it as an opening for the state to control the private lives of its citizens. Catholics worried that the largely Protestant reformers controlled the court and that the staff of the Juvenile Detention Home would proselytize their children.[24]

The Progressives who worked for the establishment of the Juvenile Court believed strongly in science and the power of the state to do good. They believed in academic experts. Ethel Sturgis Dummer, a member of one of Chicago's founding families, continued the fight on behalf of Chicago's children when she called a meeting at her home in 1908. The meeting resulted in the creation of the Juvenile Psychopathic Institute to fight the sources of juvenile delinquency. Headed by Julia Lathrop, it brought together activists, scientists, and philanthropists, like Dummer, to deal with social problems. Progressives believed fervently that the state could right the wrongs of society. With roots in the social gospel movement, which rejected the fatalism of Social Darwinism and replaced it with the brotherhood of Christ, and in municipal housekeeping, which preached that women as mothers knew best how to clean up the mess of the city, these Progressives felt an obligation to improve society. The creation of the Juvenile Court can be seen as a crucial event in the creation of the liberal welfare state.

For these reformers, individual rights were secondary to societal rights. Experts should control society for the benefit of all. Lucy Flower believed that the state, in extreme cases, had the right to sever the parent-child bond. The Juvenile Court became the hub of a whole series of reform laws, including acts establishing a home for delinquent boys (1905), county detention homes, state investigation of jails and almshouses (1909), the investigation of children's homes and orphanages, the court of domestic relations (1911), the Boy's Court (1914), and the separate hearing of girls' cases. To shore up the Juvenile Court the state legislature passed reform measure after reform measure.[25]

The fight over the Juvenile Court and its eventual establishment in Chicago mirrored yet another legal struggle: the fight to establish municipal courts in the city. The Industrial Revolution and urbanization had changed basic societal relationships, and social institutions often lagged behind new realities. At the turn of the century, much of the justice system in Chicago played itself out in the old justice of the peace courts. Referred to by the working class as "justice shops" where outcomes could be bought for the right price, this antiquated system, more appropriate for an agrarian society, dated back to English medieval law. In the last half of the nineteenth century, these fifty-two local courts presented apt symbols of confusion and corruption. The governor appointed the judges, who charged a fee, whether for a marriage or a criminal case. Originally the justices were seen as representatives of their local community. No legal training was necessary. They simply had to have reached the age of twenty-five. The justices held court in their offices or places of business, mostly located in the low rent districts of the city. Supposedly, these "prominent" citizens knew their neighbors well enough to settle minor cases. In a city of over 1 million residents, this proved unrealistic and ultimately unworkable. On top of the justice of the peace courts, the mayor chose eighteen of the fifty-two justices to serve as police magistrates. These magistrates received a salary, but here too the custom of fees prevailed. These police magistrates met in police stations and settled minor criminal cases. Both courts were rather informal affairs. In the modern city this ancient system of legal democracy quickly broke down. Justices could not know their constituents intimately and often did not represent, respect, or speak the same language of immigrant communities. Corruption ruled the day. The police magistrates often operated as arms of the political party in power

Figure 56. Chicago's City Hall was the target of many Progressive reformers in the 1900s. (Author's Collection.)

and often insured party discipline. For Progressive reformers, the courts were an abomination open to all forms of corruption and political interference.

State and federal lawmakers quietly transferred many of the issues originally handled by the justices of the peace to administrative agencies. A complicated urban society called for various types of supervision. By 1900, a general consensus prevailed that the old system had to be replaced. Reformers called for "business management for the courts." These Progressives connected the establishment of a new municipal court system to other Progressive reforms, especially the city charter movement.[26]

Political consolidation provided the main goal of the Chicago charter reform movement. Constitutional restraints dating back to the 1870 state constitution and an often hostile state legislature, dominated by downstate rural Protestants, hampered Chicago's ability to rule itself. State laws concerning the Sunday closing of saloons in particular irked many Chicagoans, if not Progressives. In 1902, the Civic Federation led reformers in a movement to secure a new municipal charter. Two tears later, seventy-four male civic leaders presented an enabling amendment that Chicagoans ratified. During 1906–7, a charter convention assembled and drafted a new municipal charter that significantly reduced the number of governing bodies in the city, increased the city's financial and taxing powers, and provided a considerable amount of home rule for Chicago. The Illinois legislature drastically changed the charter and returned it to Chicago. Many upper-class organizations backed passage of the charter—especially the Republican Party—but others dismissed the document as undemocratic, including Cermak's United Societies for Local Government who worked against it because the charter would not free Chicago from the state laws concerning the Sunday closing of saloons. Democrats opposed it because they claimed it rearranged the city's ward system to benefit upper-class voters, thus hurting their chances in ward and mayoral elections; suffragists opposed it because it did not provide municipal suffrage. In September 1907, the city charter went down to defeat.[27]

The municipal court reform, however, continued. In part, the justice of the peace system was the problem of governmental consolidation writ small. The reformers succeeded in doing away with the justices of the peace, and the new Municipal Court opened on December 3, 1906. Like the Juvenile Court, it quickly became a national model.

Green Spaces for the Poor and Great Plans

In 1898, Charles Zueblin of the University of Chicago published an article in the *American Journal of Sociology* outlining Chicago's social problems and presenting the playgrounds movement as one possible solution. Zueblin pointed out that the boulevards and parks system in Chicago was inadequate for the industrial city that had developed since Frederick Law Olmsted had begun to work on the South Park System in 1869. The parks and boulevards were largely inaccessible to the working poor, so Zueblin called for an intricate system of small parks and playgrounds in Chicago's industrial neighborhoods. The professor made the point that between six and seven hundred thousand Chicagoans lived in areas untouched by the city's system of parks. They also lived in some of the most crowded districts in urban America.[28] Settlement house playgrounds and a few public school playgrounds provided some services to the river wards, but generally speaking these areas remained underserved by public facilities.

The question of beauty and utility soon presented itself. Jane Addams was most determined about her vision of the small parks and proposed a solution to the problem that combined both the concepts of the playground and that of a breathing space. The Hull-House resident felt that nature uplifted the individual and that a park would provide a green setting that would give slum dwellers a chance to enjoy the beauty of the natural world while having a place to sit quietly and think. Addams also understood the need for play space in these overcrowded working-class wards and therefore wanted to create playing fields for the children of the poor. In addition, she hoped to make the parks active neighborhood centers in which ideas and issues could be discussed, creating a central place to focus neighborhood life. Addams explained, "The most

Figure 57. This view of the monumental flower sculptures in Washington Park in the 1880s helped set the atmospheres in the large Chicago parks as middle- and upper-class public spaces. (Stereopticon, Author's Collection.)

Figure 58. Landscape architects Frederick Law Olmsted and Calvert Vaux designed Washington Park as a retreat from the growing city in 1869. Working-class patrons, in contrast, wanted sports fields and picnic groves. Notice the middle-class couple in the rowboat and the herd of sheep used to cut grass in the park in the 1880s. (Postcard, Author's Collection.)

desirable thing is to reserve say a quarter of the space in a strip around the edge of the playground for trees and grass and for benches where the elders can sit. The London playgrounds reserve several rods around the edges in this way."[29]

Whatever their individual views concerning the nature of the new parks, observers generally agreed on where the parks should be located: Chicago's crowded working-class wards. Reformers aimed the legislation for small parks, passed in 1901, at these neighborhoods. These "reform" parks were part of a general movement to deal with the problems of the industrial immigrant city. A fieldhouse, intended for use by neighborhood residents, proved central to the proposal.[30]

The South Park commission built a fieldhouse and small ten-acre park, Davis Square, near the Union Stock Yards in 1904. In February the *Chicago Tribune* printed an artist's rendition of the park and playground, which designers had laid out much in the fashion that Jane Addams had proposed. Architects created large play areas, surrounded by green spaces for adults to sit and watch the activities in the center. It included a large fieldhouse with a swimming pool. The park provided a good model for the movement. It did not include lavish landscaping, nor did it have a lagoon, as did other larger neighborhood parks. Nevertheless, it provided most of the amenities asked for by reformers. The centerpiece fieldhouse made Davis Square a year-round neighborhood center that contained gymnasiums, showers, meeting rooms, a library, and even a cafeteria. The Chicago fieldhouse ideal presented a model for parks all over the nation.[31]

Figure 59. Pictured here is the Sherman Park fieldhouse, ca. 1907. Park fieldhouses developed into important community centers serving generations of Chicagoans from the youngest to the oldest members of the neighborhood. Progressives located this park just south of the Union Stock Yards. (Postcard, Author's Collection.)

The organization of the parks manifested the symbolic intent of the reforms. Park personnel tightly regulated activities. They established athletic leagues in various types of sports around strict rules of fair competition. The intent of both the recreational and hygiene facilities was to create a new kind of industrial resident, a new Chicagoan who played by the rules. As one newspaper proclaimed, out of the slums would come "clean, healthy men and women." Progressives thought these parks could ameliorate the realities of industrial districts.[32] The parks quickly became neighborhood centers as they provided space for all manner of activities. The West Park Commissioners opened Pulaski Park in 1914, in the heavily populated Polish district on the Near Northwest Side. It occupied a space that had formerly held ninety buildings and opened up the area directly in front of the Polish Catholic church of St. Stanislaus Kostka with its companion school.[33] In many ways Pulaski Park and neighboring Eckhart Park, across the street from St. Boniface Catholic Church, provided village squares for this densely populated immigrant neighborhood. The parks proved to be very lively village squares. Chicago's ethnic groups had long looked toward the larger and older parks as places in which to display their ethnic pride. The new small parks, however, provided a public place to gather and celebrate or protest in one's own neighborhood. As reformers hoped, the parks were a site for public recreation and entertainment, as well as spaces for attempts to assimilate the city's various ethnic groups. American plays, dances, and movies, for instance, were aimed at the younger members of the ethnic communities. The assimilation of these ethnic groups was of course a goal of the park designers and reformers, who were largely of Protestant American stock.

In addition to this system of small parks, the Chicago Board of Education established schoolyard playgrounds. The schoolyard program evolved out of an earlier playground project championed by Jane Addams. In the summer of 1901, the first public playground opened on the grounds of the Moseley School at Twenty-fourth and Wabash. Three others soon followed in various congested parts of the city. Within a few years, forty-six playgrounds opened citywide. In 1917, the Board of Education requested and received permission from the state legislature to operate the playgrounds on Board of Education property. By 1936, the Board of Education maintained sixty small playgrounds adjacent to school buildings.

Parks and playgrounds are now seen as a rather common feature of city life in Chicago neighborhoods, but they were rare in the nineteenth- and early twentieth-century city and stand today as a testament of the influence of Progressive reformers. Their planning and creation combined the talents of many of those who tried to deal with the era of urban chaos, including settlement house workers, architects, academics, and politicians.

Daniel Burnham's work on the Columbian Exposition and on the small parks led him to think about the planning of cities. He and Edward Bennett were inspired by Georges Eugène Haussman's renovation of Paris. They agreed

Figure 60. Pictured here is the first graduation class, St. Mary's School of Nursing, in 1903. Despite extreme poverty many ethnic communities created an institutional web to help the community through every stage of life. The Polish community pooled its resources to build St. Mary of Nazareth Hospital on the city's North Side. Ironically none of these first graduates of the nursing school were of Polish ancestry. (St. Mary of Nazareth Hospital Archives.)

with Haussman's approach and hoped to do for Chicago what the baron had done for the French capital. Like the Parisian innovator and most Progressives, the two Chicagoans believed in experts as the true leaders of society. The Burnham and Bennett 1909 plan expected Chicago to continue to grow at the rate that it had in their lifetimes. They predicted that within fifty years Chicago would be larger than any existing city. Therefore, they insisted that Chicago must plan for this future development. Burnham's famous quote, "Make no little plans they have no magic to stir men's blood," is apt, since this plan has shaped Chicago for nearly a century. The City Beautiful movement drew on the themes of order and beauty that were evident in Burnham and Bennett's plan. The plan's connection to the 1893 World's Columbian Exposition is central. As the authors point out, the fair provided the "beginning of . . . the orderly arrangement of extensive public grounds and buildings." Given the disaster of the 1894 Chicago strike, Burnham may have been hesitant to point out that George Pullman's plan for his model town, as well as other such utopian plans, predated the fair. But Pullman's experiment influenced Burnham, as sure as Haussman's Paris.[34]

The city's business elite, in the guise of the Commercial Club, had sponsored the plan. They saw it as a way of stimulating business growth by taming the city. Nevertheless, the City Beautiful movement's scattered leadership often

Figure 61. Irish immigrants John and Johanna Aylward married in Chicago and settled in the Back of the Yards where John found employment working on one of the railroads that entered the stockyards. They eventually built a home on West Fiftieth Street near Peoria Street. (Courtesy of Richard A. Rosenthal.)

seemed uneasy about the relation between commerce and the plans for public spaces in the city. What place did commercialism have in their plans for clean artistic open spaces, parks, and plazas? Should commercial establishments be allowed to operate in public spaces? Was there a way to integrate commercial ventures without debasing public beauty? All of these questions entered into the Chicago Plan.

The lakefront provided the most valuable part of the Chicago Plan. Burnham and Bennett planned to improve the city's waterfront and turn it over to the people. This proved to be the most important long-lasting effect of the plan. New bathing beaches and parks were built. The plan itself was a direct beneficiary of the campaign by A. Montgomery Ward to keep Chicago's lakefront park "forever free and clear." By 1890, Ward and his friend and attorney George P. Merrick waged a crusade to save the downtown lakefront from industrial or commercial developers. Ward's business stood across from Lake Park (Grant Park) on the northwest corner of Michigan and Madison Streets. The merchant initiated a lawsuit against the city to protect the park, especially from the Illinois Central Railroad. After various lawsuits the city council turned the park over to the South Park Commissioners (SPC). In turn the Illinois legislature gave all of the submerged land between Randolph Street and Twelfth Street (Roosevelt Road) out to the Chicago Harbor line to the SPC. Lawsuits continued, contesting the SPC's rights to lakefront land. For ten years, the commissioners fought off claims against their control of the land. The Federal Commission on Public Lands finally settled the cases in favor of the park commissions. After the settlement, the SPC went about their project of expanding and enhancing the lakefront along the South Side. In 1901, they renamed Lake Park as Grant Park; and it contained 201.88 acres. After 1905, the SPC built beaches at Twenty-second and Fifty-first Streets. The newly created Committee on Bathing Beaches and Recreation Piers called for the creation of seven beaches from Montrose Avenue to Seventy-ninth Street. The South Park Commission saw a chance to link Jackson Park on the South Side with the North Side's Lincoln Park via lakefront improvements, with Grant Park as the city's front yard and a centerpiece for the project.

Burnham and Bennett had a chance to build on previous plans. The two planners, however, tied beautification and civic promotion to commercial growth.

This put them at loggerheads with many reformers and with Ward, who hoped to keep all construction, especially the newly proposed Field Museum and the Crerar Library, out of Grant Park. The Olmsted Brothers proposed that these two link with the Art Institute to create a cultural center for the city. Marshall Field died in 1906, leaving $8 million for the construction of a new museum. Ward immediately acted against the Field plan despite almost unanimous support from the newspapers and civic leadership of the city. The Illinois Supreme Court upheld Ward's position once again in 1909. The Illinois Central Railroad provided a solution, which gave the city a tract of land south of Twelfth Street for the new Field Museum. Thus technically not in Grant Park, the new museum could overlook the city's front yard.

While Ward battled the city to preserve the lakefront as a public park, Burnham and Bennett got the backing of the Commercial Club to move forward on the Chicago Plan. The plan called for the centralizing of all cultural institutions in Grant Park. The two connected the cultural center to the small neighborhood parks on which Burnham had already worked with the Olmsted Brothers. The city could move into the forefront of American cities with the creation of a more extensive band of green throughout and around Chicago. Burnham and Bennett sought to create an Outer Drive along the lakefront as a pleasure drive and disagreed with Ward that the introduction of buildings in Grant Park would disturb its natural beauty. It would be part of an ideal city that would be built through the cooperation of commercial elites and city leaders for the benefit of all classes.[35]

The plan of course dealt with much more than the lakefront. It proposed to unite all of the various train stations into a Union Station just to the west of the Loop, with another to the south and no tracks north of Twelfth Street (Roosevelt Road). All freight traffic would avoid the downtown, and vacated train yards would provide land for future Loop expansion. Burnham and Bennett also saw a chance to revive the West Side. They proposed a massive civic center that resembled the Administration Building of the Columbian Exposition to be erected at the intersection of Blue Island Avenue and Congress Boulevard. This "Chicago Circle" would include a new city hall, so the crowds who worked or went to government buildings would not have to travel into the city center, thus relieving much of the Loop's business-oriented congestion. Burnham and Bennett also planned Chicago's forest preserves on the city's outskirts to provide a green belt for city dwellers to enjoy.[36]

Burnham and Bennett envisioned Chicago as the "Metropolis of the Midwest" and argued that there was no excuse for Chicago to continue to grow in a haphazard way. They saw Chicago as the intellectual, economic, and cultural capital of a vast area larger than the Austro-Hungarian Empire, Germany, or France. The Chicago Plan called for a beautiful, orderly, and logical city. The problem with uncontrolled growth seemed obvious. "Cheaply constructed dwellings" and "ugly apartment houses" line streets as a testament to the

Figure 62. This look at the Burnham and Bennett 1909 proposal for a Chicago Civic Center clearly shows the influence of the World's Columbian Exposition on the Beaux-Arts movement in city planning. The domed structure closely resembles the Fair's Administration Building. (Chicago Public Library, *Plan of Chicago*, by Daniel H. Burnham and Edward H. Bennett, 1909.)

developer's greed, resulting in slums. Uncontrolled growth like uncontrolled industrialism might result in massive profits but hurt society as a whole. Burnham and Bennett pointed to England as an example of how to manage the situation by means of town planning rules. They recommended that Chicago follow the English example of regional planning, taking into consideration the land that the city was likely to annex in at least the next decade. Public and semipublic buildings, as well as libraries, parks, and playgrounds, should be provided for. They pointed out that "the question of creating pleasing conditions in a suburb is not primarily a matter of money, but of thoughtful cooperation." The entire region should be connected by a system of highways constructed for both heavy loads and pleasure driving.[37]

The Problem of Housing the Poor

Burnham and Bennett's plan was a magnificent attempt to chart a course for Chicago and the outlying region that would guarantee a beautiful and orderly future. The plan had its detractors, including labor leader John Fitzpatrick, and social workers Jane Addams and Mary E. McDowell, who sought more justice for the immigrant working class. They questioned why the city needed a beautification plan while the poor lived in squalid conditions. Certainly, the plan did not address the question of housing. McDowell warned that housing was central to the problems faced by her neighbors in Back of the Yards. Fitzpatrick objected to the new partnership between the Commercial Club and the city's government and claimed that the Chicago Plan recalled a form of government controlled by elites. Jane Addams, while supporting the idea for a general plan, objected to the location of all civic and cultural institutions in the downtown area.[38]

But the supporters of the 1909 plan outnumbered the critics. Mayor Fred Busse established the Chicago Plan Commission to enact Burnham and Bennett's vision. The new commission had 328 members to help promote the plan and advise on its execution. Charles H. Wacker, a prominent brewer, acted as chairman. Walter D. Moody, the plan's publicist, wrote an eighth grade textbook summarizing the plan, and the Chicago Public Schools distributed this so-called Wacker Manual. School children learned the benefits of city planning and spoke to their parents, or so the planners hoped as the parents would be asked to vote for bond issues to pay for it all. Lecturers spread the word to numerous organizations across the city, and films about the plan even bombarded nickelodeon customers. The plan proved to be a source of jobs and growth in the years ahead, as politicians both used and misused it in the name of progress.

For all his desires to plan cities, Burnham believed that housing remained within the realm of private developers. But four years after the unveiling of the Chicago Plan, the City Club of Chicago sponsored a competition on urban housing. The plans were to deal with a quarter section of undeveloped land eight miles from the center of the city. The city, despite its continued growth, had large tracts of land to the southwest, southeast, west, and northwest of the Loop, which had never been filled in with housing. Developers who had promoted various suburban developments owned much of this land, but when the economy collapsed in the 1890s, interest in this land had also declined and never recovered. Attention was now beginning to grow in these areas once again. Wilhelm Bernhard, who, like most of the entries, abandoned the traditional grid system and favored the curving road and spaces of the English Garden City movement or the diagonal streets that marked the Burnham Plan, won first place in the City Club of Chicago's competition. Another entry, Hugh J. Fixmer's plan, did neither of these, but instead carried through Chicago's grid system. Criticized for being unimaginative, Fizmer's plan represented much of what actually occurred as developers began to bring housing to Chicago's open spaces. The bungalow belt began to spread across the city's edges and into the suburbs during the Progressive movement.[39]

But housing remained a major problem for the city. The poor lived in terrible conditions. A 1901 study by Robert Hunter for the City Homes Association saw widespread problems of poorly constructed and overcrowded dwellings across the city. Ten years later, Sophonisba P. Breckenridge and Edith Abbott of Hull-House again surveyed housing in the poorer wards of the city. They included the area of the West Side that Hunter has examined and found increased overcrowding especially in the Italian and Jewish neighborhoods. The six most densely populated wards in the city all stood on the West Side. Rates of over four hundred residents per acre were not unknown, and most areas had between three and four hundred per acre. Furthermore, industry and commercial businesses had moved across Canal Street into the Italian and Jewish quarters of the West Side and occupied a good deal of space in formerly residential areas. The whole district between Halsted and the Chicago River seemed opened to this invasion. Indeed, landowners before World War I did not make improvements on residential buildings because they hoped soon to sell their property for industrial purposes. Some improvements had been made, such as Jefferson Park (Skinner Park) on the West Side on Adams Street and the construction of the new Juvenile Court, but old houses remained in disrepair and horrible conditions, which included overcrowding, faulty plumbing, and vermin infestation, prevailed over much of the area. In many cases when improvements were made or factories built, owners simply sold the wooden frame houses that had occupied the lot, and the buyers moved them to new sites. This relocation of slum buildings led to even more overcrowding, as some West Side lots contained as many as three buildings. The Jewish neighborhood had no alleys, so that rear tenements often stood next to neighboring tenements, providing an almost continuous row of houses across the block.

Breckinridge and Abbott canvassed one block on the Jewish West Side between Canal and Jefferson, Liberty and Maxwell. It contained 2.8 acres with 1,033 residents, or 369 residents per acre, an increase of 116 residents since 1901. Another block in Czech Pilsen provided homes to 1,239 people. On the Polish Northwest Side a block near St. Stanislaus Kostka church, on Noble Street, had similar densities, although here the numbers had gone down since 1901. Researchers pointed out that all these numbers might not be totally reliable because rumors that the canvassers wanted to rid the neighborhood of boarders percolated through the immigrant districts and many residents may not have reported lodgers. Therefore, the returns in all districts, but in particular on the Polish Northwest Side, probably underestimated the terrible congestion problem.

Despite this statistical problem, investigators found extensive overcrowding. Men slept in closets that could just fit a bed. Whole families slept in one bed while they rented other rooms to boarders. The types of buildings provided evidence of the true state of overcrowding. The Jewish West Side was among the oldest settled areas in the city, and the dilapidated two-story wooden-frame buildings had long outlived their purpose. The Polish neighborhood to the north and the Czech neighborhood to the south contained more brick buildings. These structures tended to be newer and were built higher. Even here, however, old housing that rarely conformed to the 1902 tenement laws predominated. A high percentage of the land was occupied by structures, with few lots covered less than 50 percent. Single-family homes were rare in all three neighborhoods, never reaching above 5 percent, and the four-room apartment predominated. Researchers also found a large number of illegal cellar and basement flats. Over the ten-year period between Hunter's study and the Breckenridge and Abbott study, conditions had once again worsened.

The elimination of the indoor privy, a simple hole cut into the ground under the house, provided the one improvement in facilities over the decade. The West Side privies had just about disappeared after 1901, although yard closets or outhouses, not indoor plumbing, often replaced them. The privy remained an issue in Back of the Yards and other outlying industrial districts. Toilet amenities, however, remained unsuitable and multiple households often used a single backyard or indoor facility. In one case, thirty individuals used a single yard closet in the Polish district.

Dark and gloomy bedrooms prevailed throughout working-class neighborhoods. Landlords and residents frequently ignored the amount of space legally required for each individual in an apartment. Breckenridge and Abbott admitted that this law was hard to enforce, given the traditional narrow and long Chicago lot and the poverty of the residents. The local population paid high rents, especially in the Jewish neighborhood. Here despite dilapidated conditions, Jews tended to pay more for apartments comparable to those in the

Figure 63. The Maxwell Street Market on the Jewish West Side pictured here in 1917 developed after the fire as the area became known as the Jewish Quarter or Ghetto, which became home to many Russian, Polish, and Lithuanian Jews at the turn of the century. (DN-0068696, Chicago Daily News negatives collection, Chicago History Museum.)

Czech and Polish districts. The authors claimed that this was largely a result of Jewish clannishness forcing rents upward, as Jews wanted to live among other Jews, although they did admit it might have been a result of ethnic prejudice. They also pointed to the lodger or boarder issue that often resulted in higher rents. The boarder rate seemed to be considerably higher among Jews.

In the end, housing remained a big problem for Chicago throughout the Progressive era. While paved streets, cement sidewalks, the elimination of the privy, and later the outhouse, with the construction of an effective sewer system provided some hope, immigrant districts remained overcrowded and often stalked by disease. The 1918 influenza epidemic hit these neighborhoods especially hard. The solution to the problems seemed to be found at the edge of the city. Here empty lots beckoned to Chicagoans. The desire for affordable housing remained only an unfulfilled dream for many working-class and immigrant Chicagoans at least until after World War I.[40]

Big Bill Thompson and the End of Progressivism

While one might call Carter Harrison II a Progressive, no one would call William Hale Thompson one. The colorful South Side Republican was elected as mayor for the first time in 1915. Born in Boston in 1867 to a well-established New England father and the daughter of one of the original incorporators of Chicago, he moved with his family to the city in 1868. His father, William Hale Thompson, Sr., dealt in real estate and became a Republican member of the Illinois state legislature and was known for passing the first state law to prevent cruelty to animals and for helping to establish a state militia.

The younger Thompson thus came from a distinguished background, a scion of Chicago's elite Republican class. Living on the West Side, Thompson met the Irish and other ethnic groups that clustered around Twelfth Street. The boy got into trouble with the police, and his family tried to send him off to boarding school. Instead, Bill Thompson got a job and saved his money to go west. At the age of fifteen, Thompson signed on as a "hood," the driver of a wagon that carried cowhands' bedding, hauled wood and water, and assisted the camp cook. He had decided to live the life of a western rancher. In 1888, his father bought a ranch in Ewing, Nebraska, and asked his son to take it over. On the way to the ranch, Thompson was almost killed in a brothel brawl due to a case of mistaken identity. He eventually made it to Ewing and managed the ranch. Three years later his father died, and Big Bill Thompson returned to Chicago for good at the age of twenty-four.

Well situated financially due to his father's estate and business, Bill Thompson began a career as an athlete, and Chicagoans first knew him as a baseball star, a leading water polo player, a handball champion, and the winner of several swimming and diving trophies. Thompson made a reputation as captain of the Chicago Athletic Association (CAA) football team, and in 1894, the CAA, with Thompson at its head, defeated Princeton and Dartmouth, although they lost to Harvard and Yale in very hard fought games. By Thanksgiving, the team was hailed as the champion of the western athletic clubs. On Thanksgiving they faced the Boston Athletic Club for the national championship, but just before the game a scandal broke out. A member of the CAA had been providing free meals for six of the club's members, something forbidden by the Amateur Athletic Union's strict rules. Thompson moved to expel the players. The *Tribune* proclaimed that Thompson and the CAA had taken a stand for "clean" football. Thompson then led the truncated team to the championship none-theless. William Hale Thompson instantly became a Chicago hero. Chicago children flocked to the CAA to see him work out with the water polo team. By 1897, Thompson was a nationally known athlete. In 1900, when he decided to enter politics, Thompson ran for Alderman of the South Side's Second Ward, just beyond the vice empire of Hinky Dink Kenna and Bathhouse John Cough-lin in the First Ward Levee District.[41]

The Second Ward was going through a great deal of change in 1900. Prosti-tutes and other denizens of the vice district moved south to the district once home to fashionable homes. On Prairie Avenue many of Chicago's elite still lived, and they looked for someone to save them from the rapid manifestation of urban decline and moral chaos. Here too in the Second Ward lived Chicago's growing African American population. The new aldermanic candidate sup-ported municipal ownership and civil service reform. Thompson defeated the Democratic incumbent by four hundred votes.

In that strange Chicago way of politics—where party affiliation usually means very little—the two Democratic leaders of the First Ward, Coughlin and Kenna, enabled Thompson's victory, by controlling the "flop-house" vote. They punished the Democratic incumbent, Charles F. Gunther, for not allow-ing them to run vice in the Second Ward. Shortly thereafter, the two convinced the political novice to agree to a ward redistricting plan, which placed vice as well as Thompson's home, in the First Ward, thus ending his days as alderman. But before he left office Thompson supported the creation of a playground in the Second Ward that benefited the growing African American population. This relationship with Chicago's growing black population would come to help him in his later career.

William Lorimer, the "Blond Boss," who ran the city's largest Republican organization, became Thompson's political mentor and had him giving "tent" speeches in 1902. Lorimer represented the heavily industrial West Side in Con-gress. The West Sider—an immigrant, a convert to Catholicism, and a coalition builder—reached out to the growing West Side Jewish population. On several occasions, Lorimer and others encouraged Thompson to run for mayor. Thomp-son, however, preferred his new sport, sailing, to politics. In 1912, Lorimer finally convinced him to run for the Cook County Board of Review. Thompson lost the election but further endeared himself to the GOP by his stump speeches. In 1912, the U.S. Senate expelled Lorimer on corruption charges, and Fred Lundin, the Swedish American politician, took over the remnants of the Republican or-ganization. The new boss chose Thompson to run for mayor in 1915, and this time he agreed.

Thompson won the Republican primary largely on the votes of African Americans from his old Second Ward, defeating the Englewood leader Charles Denneen's choice for mayor, Judge Harry Olson, by 2,500 votes. Thompson promised a "Square Deal" for all party factions, echoing Theodore Roosevelt's presidential campaign. In the Democratic mayoral primary, County Clerk Robert M. Sweitzer defeated Carter Harrison II as Democrats split along factional and ethnic lines, with reformers supporting Harrison and seeing Sweitzer as a pawn of the regular party organization. The Democrats expected to win the general election on the mere strength of numbers. Harrison in defeat gathered more votes than Thompson had in victory. Republicans, however, united behind the former cowboy and football star. Thompson understood Chicagoans, and he could read national election returns as he continued to make various allusions to Roosevelt. The wards that had supported the former president in 1912 all went for Thompson. Sweitzer lost by 147,000 votes. "Natural" Democrats did not yet see themselves that way, and a candidate for mayor could still ignore ethnic voting blocs. That would soon change.[42]

Thompson proved himself an able politician. His first two years in office, he emphasized middle-class reforms. The new mayor seemed like a caring politician as he raced home to take over relief operations in the wake of the Eastland disaster that claimed 811 lives on July 24, 1915. Labor also concerned him. In June 1915, he mediated a traction strike largely because the middle class rode the lines to the Loop. Thompson, however, was no friend of labor. He moved often and harshly against unions, particularly those who hoped to organize municipal workers. He refused to see clothing workers leader, Sidney Hillman, and attacked the Chicago Teachers Federation. In yet another move against working-class and ethnic neighborhoods, he forcibly closed over seven thousand saloons on the first Sunday in October, enforcing a law long ignored by both Democratic and Republican politicians. The Protestant middle class saw Thompson as a hero.

The race issue soon emerged in Thompson's first administration. In September 1915, blacks and Italians clashed over the increased employment of African Americans on city work gangs. The mayor had paid back black support with an increase in municipal jobs. Thompson addressed fifteen thousand blacks in the Coliseum and defended his hiring practices to the welcoming crowd. Anti-Thompson forces began to refer to city hall as "Uncle Tom's Cabin."[43]

Various corruption charges soon surfaced against Thompson and his allies. Police Chief Charles Healey was indicted on gambling charges. Oscar De Priest, the black South Side politician, was also indicted. Democrats saw this as an opening to attack Thompson as a protector of vice, gambling, and prostitution. The suicide of Dr. Theodore Sachs, the former head of the Municipal Tuberculosis Sanitarium, further muddied the waters as he left a note behind was addressed to "The People of Chicago" criticizing Thompson. Sachs had resigned from the sanitarium stating that he refused to make it a "political football." He firmly stated that he was leaving because he did not believe in the "political management" of hospitals. When Sachs committed suicide by taking poison, his note expressed his love for the Municipal Sanitarium and its patients. Sachs wrote, "The institution should remain as it was built, unsoiled by graft or politics, the heritage of the people." Thompson dismissed the note and repeated that his original appointment of Sachs was the worst he had made as mayor. Thompson claimed to be the target of both the old bosses and the new Progressive reformers.[44]

Like other twentieth-century mayors, Thompson saw himself as a builder. He embraced Burnham and Bennett's Chicago Plan of 1909 as his own because he saw that it gave him and his supporters a political opportunity. In his 1915 campaign, Thompson had praised the plan and the work of Charles Wacker, and he proposed his own additional plan for Chicago, calling for subways and underground utility conduits. For Thompson, city planning meant the power to build. Workers got jobs and businessmen received the public works they wanted; it also meant patronage jobs for the Republican Party to reward supporters. A "builder" mayor could be forgiven much by his constituents. The city would look better, business would flourish, and Thompson could control contracts and patronage, which brought him votes to stay in power. He opened Municipal Pier (Navy Pier) with fifty thousand people in attendance to see the first real results of the 1909 plan. Not even World War I could stop the Burnham Plan, as the Twelfth Street project was successfully executed, and planning got under way for a massive bridge across the river at Michigan Avenue that would open up the North Side to development and might allow the Loop to grow northward. In 1919, Thompson moved to make the lakefront a recreational center in accordance with the Chicago Plan.[45]

William Hale Thompson was the consummate politician. He was well aware of his image and worked hard at perfecting it. He knew the city and its people well. While coming from a privileged background, he also knew the rough and tumble streets of the West Side and of the Levee on the South Side. Thompson knew his constituents and often played to their prejudices—especially against Catholics and immigrants—when it benefited him. Often called a demagogue, Thompson set the stage for twentieth-century mayors in Chicago. He was the first to go after and capture the African American vote. While his use of patronage was clumsy (especially in the case of the Municipal Tuberculosis Sanitarium but also in the schools and on the police and fire departments), he did attempt to build a citywide machine against the old ward bosses. Even Progressives who rallied behind the Hyde Parker Charles E. Merriam could agree with Thompson on his use of big government. After all, he had originally run as an alderman who championed the cause of municipal ownership. Yet Thompson was in many ways as contradictory as his city. His first two terms would include war, race riots, the start of city planning, and strikes, as well as the Black Sox scandal. Both the White Sox and the Cubs would be at the height of their powers during his term in office, winning three pennants and one world championship between them. As World War I and then the 1920s appeared on the horizon, Chicago and Thompson continued their brash ways. Both would leave their mark on the 1920s.

7—1071

The Immigrant Capital and World War I

Chicago had long been the destination for wave after wave of immigrants primarily from Europe, as well as the Middle East and Asia. Though not always welcome—Chicago was the home of much anti-immigrant, anti-Catholic, and anti-Semitic behavior—immigrants nevertheless created a home for themselves on the southwestern shore of Lake Michigan. By the beginning of the nineteenth century, immigrants had made their way across the cityscape and created viable neighborhoods. In 1910, the foreign born and their children made up almost 80 percent of Chicago's population. Before World War I, it was not even hinted at that this great era of immigration would come to an end within the next ten years, nor that immigrants would face competition from a native-born population at the bottom of the workforce, but these trends began in the Progressive Era. The new century brought dramatic changes to both Europe and America, and then in Chicago, at the capitalist world's economic heart.

Immigrant City

Many Americans feared immigrants, and the murder of President McKinley by the Polish American anarchist Leon Czolgosz only increased their concerns. On July 4, 1905, the South Park Commission dedicated a statue of the slain president in a Stock Yard District park at Archer and Western Boulevard that had recently been named after him. Charles J. Mulligan had recast the statue from the melted-down bronze of an unpopular statue of Christopher Columbus, and it depicts McKinley championing a protective tariff while a member of Congress. Some five thousand persons attended the ceremony; in a largely Polish working-class neighborhood McKinley was portrayed as a protector of the American worker, not as president, but as a congressman. The stockyard workers who enjoyed the park did not miss the irony of this dedication less than a year after their defeat in a hard fought strike.[1]

Another local incident shows how deep these ethnic and political pressures ran. On March 1, 1908, a young Russian Jewish immigrant, Lazarus Averbuch,

Figure 64. Third grade boys at St. Stanislaus Kostka Parochial School in 1917. Lessons are written in both Polish and English on the blackboards. (Courtesy of Theodore Swigon, Jr.)

attempted to deliver a package to the Chicago Police Chief George Shippy. Witnesses provided conflicting accounts of what happened that evening, but the police chief apparently thought that Averbuch intended to deliver a bomb and shot him dead in the hallway of his home. Seven gunshots riddled Averbuch's body. The city had been in considerable agitation over East European anarchists at the time, and so the police brought in over three hundred suspects, including Emma Goldman, attempting to prove there was an anarchist conspiracy in the city. Rabbi Abram Hirschberg of the North Chicago Hebrew Congregation immediately condemned Averbuch as a misguided youth who had fallen away from the tenets of his religion, reminding Chicagoans that Judaism opposed anarchism and held "no sympathy for the teachings of Emma Goldberg and her brood." In reality, Averbuch had no political connections and was an unlucky young man cut down at the beginning of his life while merely trying to deliver a package. The case, widely discussed in the American press, raised the specter of an anti-Semitic crusade disguised as anti-anarchist politics. Jane Addams became involved, as did the lawyer and future New Dealer Harold L. Ickes. The Jewish community raised money to support the investigation and to properly rebury Averbuch in a Jewish cemetery.[2]

Chicago remained a center of strife and even revolutionary agitation, as the new century proceeded. Immigration hit a high point during the 1910s, as immigrants, their children, and grandchildren made Chicago home. On the Northwest Side, Polish immigrants built churches, parochial schools, and institutions throughout the Milwaukee Avenue corridor, while Swedes settled heavily in the Andersonville neighborhood to the north. In 1917, East European Jews organized the Covenant Club as an answer to German Jews who barred their coreligionists from membership in the prestigious Standard Club. In the Back of the Yards, ten Catholic churches of various ethnic traditions divvied up the neighborhood. Pilsen remained the largest concentration of Czechs in the city, and both the Poles and Czechs made their way across the Lower West Side to South Lawndale and then to suburban Cicero with its huge Western Electric plant. South Chicago was an amalgam of ethnic groups that worked in the steel mills. Everywhere ethnic groups shared neighborhoods with others, but within these neighborhoods, they created their own institutions—synagogues, parishes, parochial schools, bars, meeting halls, and fraternal organizations. They nonetheless often shared the physical space of a neighborhood, the streets, parks, sidewalks, and even houses with other groups. Residents who later would simply say everybody was Polish or Czech or Irish in the old neighborhood later forgot this combination of spatial integration and social segregation. Social segregation provided a feeling of exclusiveness and muted the realities of the way ethnic groups divided limited urban space in the crowded immigrant districts.[3]

While the city remained a heavily German and Irish city, the so-called new immigration from southern and eastern Europe transformed Chicago. As the city entered Carter Harrison II's final term in 1911, it contained huge populations of newly arrived eastern and southern Europeans. These communities constantly faced the daunting task of welcoming and integrating newcomers into their communities. Union organizers, priests, ministers, and rabbis, as well as politicians, faced neighborhoods whose populations seemed to turn over ceaselessly. The problems associated with bringing so many different individuals into established ethnic institutions at times proved daunting. Old-country regionalism and religious differences could often disrupt relations within an ethnic group that seemed monolithic to outsiders. Italian immigrants often regarded themselves as Calabrians, Sicilians, or Tuscans first and Italians second; but the hardships they faced in the United States made them Italian. Germans and Czechs found themselves divided by religion and ideological beliefs. The country and region of origin as well as religious practices separated Jews. Poles were divided by regionalism and even by differing definitions of nationalism. Social fragmentation along ethnic lines in the workplace slowed and complicated efforts to organize labor.

To the outsider, immigrant Chicago must have seemed very confusing. Streets divided ethnic enclaves, and crossing one could be a dangerous thing

Figure 65. East European Jews formed the Covenant Club in the Loop as a response to being barred from the more prestigious Standard Club dominated by German and West European Jews. (Chicago Jewish Archives, Spertus Institute of Jewish Studies.)

to do except at certain times of the day. Ethnic street gangs glared at each other across these invisible boundaries. And while some street gangs combined and perhaps Americanized ethnic groups, others maintained a strict ethnic identity based on parochial school attendance, which reinforced ethnic identification well into the twentieth century. To non-Catholics, the more than thirty parishes circling the Union Stock Yards were simply subdivisions of Catholicism, but to residents they mapped out strict ethnic borders that were crossed only with trepidation. Parish priests sometimes reinforced these lines and consolidated their own positions by demanding that parishioners confess and receive other sacraments in their ethnic languages. Parochial schools—with the exception of the Irish Catholic schools, which referred to themselves as English speaking—spent half of the day teaching students in the languages spoken at home by their parents. This arrangement played itself out all across the city and the working-class suburbs.[4]

Figure 66. Pilsen Park on Twenty-sixth and Albany was located next to the Pilsen Brewing Company. It served as an ethnic space for the Czech community in Chicago and a rallying place for the Czech independence movement during World War I. (Advertisement, Author's Collection.)

In addition to ethnic parochial schools, immigrants created a vast array of institutions designed to help the ethnic communities to reinforce ethnic boundaries and so survive in the new industrial city. Small businesses such as grocery stores, delicatessens, and taverns served these purposes as well as economic ones. This creation of semipublic space proved crucial in Chicago, especially the ethnic saloon played a vital role in these communities.[5] Sometimes these institutions could develop into large businesses, which employed their co-ethnics while also creating a middle class of managers and entrepreneurs. On September 3, 1903, a group of Czech saloon owners formed the cooperative Pilsen Brewing Company as a protest against what they considered to be the monopolistic practices of the Milwaukee-based Schlitz Brewing Company. They elected John A. Cervenka, a Pilsen saloonkeeper, president of the company, capitalized at $100,000. By 1910, the Pilsen Brewing Company had 164 stockholders, each a bar owner. The company's modern plant stood on the corner of Twenty-sixth and Albany in the South Lawndale neighborhood, commonly referred to as "Czech Albany." Adolph Lonek designed the structure, and the company employed primarily Slavic workers. Cervenka was close to the fast-rising Czech Democratic politician Anton Cermak, who had taken on Edward Dunne with his antiprohibition organization, the United Societies for Local Self-Government. In August 1907, the Pilsen Brewery's stockholders decided to open a recreational park and beer garden next to their sprawling plant at a cost of up to $25,000. It opened the following spring and quickly developed as an important gathering place for people from across the Chicago Czech community including Catholics, Protestants, and Free Thinkers. Pilsen Park offered a legitimate semipublic space— comparable to the German North Side Bismarck Park—that gave the Czechs a place to rally and organize within the confines of their own community. Conveniently located along the Twenty-sixth Street streetcar line, it stood close to various Czech halls, churches, and schools, and the community used the site as well for lectures. In July 1913, over 1,200 people heard Vaclav J. Klofac lecture on the topic of the Balkan War and its potential meaning for the Slavic nations. The following year, Pilsen Park provided the site of a massive rally to mark the beginning of World War I. By that time Cervenka had begun his career as an important local politician, tied to Cermak as a candidate for Clerk of the Probate Court. But in July, the attention of the Czech community turned from local politics to the international stage as war clouds gathered over Central Europe.

World War I

When war broke out in Europe in the summer of 1914, most native-born Americans seemed disengaged and isolationist in their response, but Chicago's ethnic population stood on edge and openly supported either the Allies or the Central Powers. Anti-Austrian Czechs chose Cervenka's Pilsen Park as a rallying space for a demonstration the evening that war broke out between the Hapsburgs' Austro-Hungarian Empire and the Kingdom of Serbia in the Balkans. This time, war between the two states would spread like a wildfire across Europe and cause millions to die in the fighting of the First World War, changing the broad course of world history in its wake. On July 26, 1914, a group of Czech leaders met at a small Czech restaurant on the corner of Twenty-sixth and Trumbull Streets to plan for a response to the expected Austro-Hungarian declaration of war on Serbia. As a result of their radical ideology these Czech nationalists had been expelled from universities or lost positions in Europe. In America they felt free to speak out against the Hapsburgs and in defense of both a free Bohemia and of Serbia, a neighboring Slavic state. They hoped to resurrect a Czech state free from Austrian or German dominance. The next day the leaders called for the Pilsen Park rally. The rally, held on the evening of July 28 as Austro-Hungarian troops marched into Serbia, proved to be a great success, enabling the various Slavic communities of Chicago to protest the Haps-burg war effort. Some four thousand Czechs, Serbs, Croatians, and others came to Pilsen Park that evening.

As the crowd gathered they noticed two large metal shields hanging from the rafters of the pavilion. On them were insignias that the crowd immediately identified as the Hapsburg coat of arms including the two-headed black eagle. Cervenka later denied that they were Austro-Hungarian symbols, but the Czechs had long been subjects of the dual empire, and Cervenka himself had been proud of his father's service in the Austro-Hungarian cavalry. The crowd tried to pull down the shields but could not until a group of Czech Sokols, a nationalist gymnastic group, formed a human pyramid and then ripped down the offensive emblems. The crowd trampled the escutcheons in an orderly fash-ion by forming two lines so that everyone could wipe their feet on the shields. Leaders eventually restored order, and the meeting progressed with the passage of a resolution in support of Serbia and called for the dissolution of Bohemia's ties with the Hapsburgs.

Chicago Czechs demanded independence and encouraged those back in Bohemia to resist service in the Austro-Hungarian army. On the following day, the Austrian consulate in Chicago announced that subjects of the Empire should be prepared to be drafted into the army and leave Chicago for their homeland in order to serve in the armed forces. Chicago's Czech leaders openly scoffed at these demands in the English-language newspapers. V. A. Gerringer, the publisher of the oldest Czech daily in Chicago, *Svornost,* called for an upris-ing against Vienna. Far from the battlefields of Europe, the cry for Czechoslo-vak independence rose up first from Chicago's South Lawndale neighborhood.

Many of Chicago's ethnic communities were in an uproar over the war. Rus-sian steelworkers began to hold impromptu military drills. Croatians, who also lived in Pilsen and were subjects of the Hapsburgs, held a mass meeting on August 1, 1914, at Congressional Hall at Eighteenth Street and Racine Avenue. In turn, Chicago's Germans and Austrians held patriotic rallies at Turner Hall at North Avenue and Clark Street on the North Side. Chicago's West Side Irish met at Emmett Hall on the corner of Taylor Street and Ogden Avenue and promised to send troops to fight the British in Ireland. Socialists also re-sponded by calling a mass meeting attended by ten thousand workingmen at Pilsen Park on Monday August 3, 1914, to protest the Austrian action. After the November 15, 1915, Czechoslovak demand for independence made in Paris, Pilsen Park quickly became a rallying point for the raising of funds to support independence. The community organized with other Slavs to hold bazaars to raise money.[6]

Chicago's German community also responded quickly to the war. On August 14, 1914, the Chicago *Abendpost,* reacting not only to the Russian declaration of war against the German Empire but also to events in Chicago, declared, "A victory of the Slav means death to education, constitutionalism, liberalism and

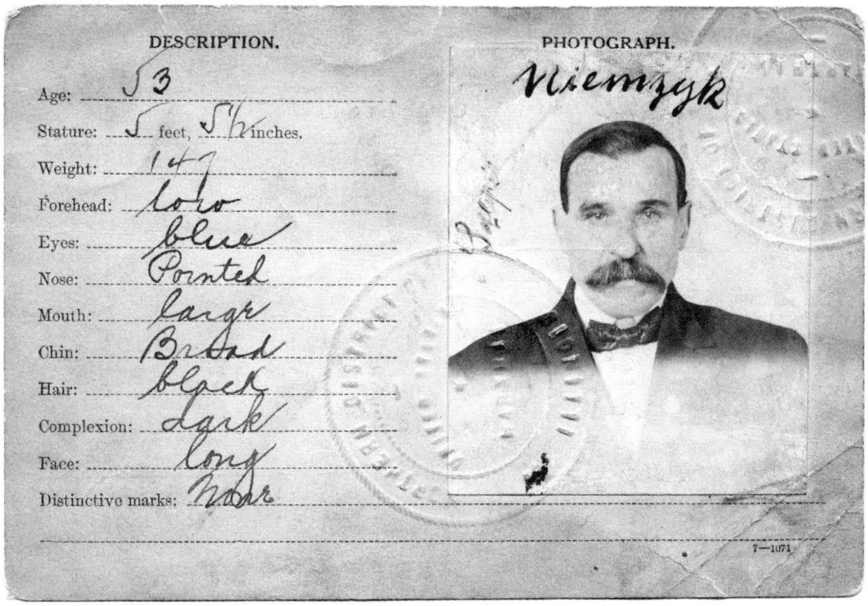

DESCRIPTION.

Age: 53

Stature: 5 feet, 5½ inches.

Weight: 147

Forehead: low

Eyes: blue

Nose: Pointed

Mouth: large

Chin: Broad

Hair: black

Complexion: dark

Face: long

Distinctive marks: None

PHOTOGRAPH.

Niemczyk

7—1071

Figure 67. Frank Niemczyk came from the German Partition of Poland before World War I and settled in the Back of the Yards neighborhood. He worked for Swift and Company, first in the North House Tankroom and then as a teamster. In order to get a job in the German-dominated teamster department he changed his name to Leyman and passed as a German immigrant. (Courtesy of Lawrence Trickle.)

free thought. A Slav victory means the obliteration of four centuries of European culture." Of course the *Abendpost* meant four centuries of German culture and ignored the cultures of France and Britain, which fought alongside Slavs in the war. The city faced the possibility of Old World violence on its streets.

In 1914, the population of Chicago stood at about 2.5 million people. Of these only 752,111 were classified as native born, children of parents born in the United States. Germans provided the largest ethnic group with 399,977 first- and second-generation residents. The group would have loomed even larger if the third generation was counted. Austrians comprised 58,843 Chicagoans, with 140,560 Irish making up a substantial part of the local population. These groups were among the most powerful and influential of the city's population. In addition, Jews made up the overwhelming majority of Chicago's 166,134 Russians, and most of these remained openly hostile to the oppressive czarist regime, which had allowed or even encouraged pogroms, leading many to come to America. German Jews quickly rallied to the German cause. Scandinavians openly supported the Central Powers of Germany, Austria-Hungary, and Turkey at the beginning of the war. The more than two hundred thousand Poles in Chicago were at first divided in their sympathies, as all of the East European combatants occupied some part of Poland, but they quickly moved into the anti–Central Power camp along with the 102,000 Czechs and the Serbs and others from Slavic Europe.

Mayor Thompson saw a political advantage to be gained in the war. Chicago's many ethnic groups stood divided, but the Germans and the Irish were the largest and therefore politically the most influential, so Thompson quickly took an antiwar stand. In August 1915, a crowd of Republican picnickers in Aurora greeted the mayor. Big Bill disagreed with the other speakers, who had assailed Wilson for not fighting after the sinking of the Lusitania. He praised Wilson but stated, "We have not gone far enough into the middle of the road. I believe that we should not send any armaments or munitions." He stated that he did not care who rose to power in Europe. He reminded the crowd of the commandment "Thou shalt not kill" and went on to say that America should sell anything to the combatants, except the means to wage war.

Republican Boss Fred Lundin encouraged Big Bill to speak out, considering him a possible candidate in 1916 for the White House against any war-minded Democrat, and began to bolster Thompson's views with the publication of the *Republican,* a weekly newspaper. In reality, Thompson simply urged traditional American isolationism, the kind favored by his core of supporters in the Protestant middle class. Thompson, always aware of his audience, also saw this as a way to reach out to the German and Irish voters who opposed Britain and the Allies. As war continued Thompson's views grew even more controversial.[7]

Chicago's Germans held huge rallies as the fighting began. The corner of Clybourn and North Avenue in the heart of the North Side German community, the city's largest and most compact, saw crowds gather to discuss the fighting. German Americans decked out their homes with German flags. The *Illinois Staats-Zeitung* called for a rally at the North Side Turner Hall to raise money for Germany's fallen heroes, and German reservists soon marched down neighborhood streets. By August 3 some seven hundred reservists clogged the ninth floor offices of the German Consulate in the People's Gas Building volunteering to fight for their fatherland. On August 5, Germans held a huge rally at the Auditorium Theater and raised sizeable funds for war relief, while also criticizing the English-language press and vowing support for Germany and Austria. Five thousand protestors took to the street to assert themselves at the offices of Chicago's major dailies and sing "The Watch on the Rhine." That night, a pro-German crowd gathered in Grant Park. No Chicago ethnic group had ever displayed such an outpouring of nationalist enthusiasm for their homeland. Business leaders, such as brewer Charles Wacker and meatpacker Oscar F. Meyer, helped raise money for the German Red Cross. Meanwhile, German American organizations berated the Slavic countries, many of which were subject to German and Austrian rule. The war had broken out between Austria and Serbia, but the Germania Club insisted that the fighting was between Teuton and Slav, calling Germany's neighbors the natural "serf" races of Europe. Irish nationalists saw the war as an opportunity to gain Ireland's independence form Great Britain. The August 2 rally at Emmett Hall on the corner of Ogden and Taylor on the West Side recruited one thousand Irishmen to prepare to fight England in two regiments and a medical corps, which would wait for Dublin's "call of help." In mid-August, Chicago's Germans and Irish held a combined picnic and listened to nationalistic speakers harangue the British.

Meanwhile, Chicago's Slavs fought back well beyond the July 28 rally at Pilsen Park. The Czechs, Chicago's oldest and in many ways economically best-positioned Slavic group, picked up the Slavic mantle, reminding Germans that Prague had a university long before Germany did. They warned their German neighbors that Chicago's Slavs were fed up with insults. Meanwhile, Serbians rallied at Best Hall, and fights between Serbs and Germans broke out in South Chicago and Gary. At an outdoor rally at Milwaukee and Division in West Town on the Polish Northwest Side, thousands of Poles heard the Serbian side of the story. In mid-August the Polish National Council advised young Polish males not to respond to the Russian call to arms and said that Poles should wish a pox on all the warring powers. Casimir Zychlinski, president of the Polish National Alliance (PNA), called Russia, Austria, and Germany all "rapacious vultures" for partitioning Poland in the eighteenth century. The PNA, founded to help restore Polish independence, saw the war as a chance for a new Poland to emerge.

The conflict even spilled over to Chicago's playgrounds and to its premier cultural institution, the Chicago Symphony Orchestra. On September 2, 1914, Mrs. Ella Flagg, superintendent of Chicago schools, issued an order to stop the fighting among children of warring nationalities on Chicago's school playgrounds. Strife rocked the Chicago Symphony Orchestra when musicians began to argue over the war. In an effort to appear neutral, the conductor scheduled several nationalist songs for a mid-August concert at Ravinia. Germans made up the majority of orchestra members, but their French, Belgian, and Russian associates erupted over the thought of playing "The Watch on the Rhine." German musicians played sour notes during the playing of the French anthem "Le Marseillaise," and a free-for-all among these representatives of high culture almost broke out at Ravinia. The members eventually agreed to not play any patriotic songs for the duration of the war.

The German American press defended Germany's war actions, including the invasion of Belgium, even when these became extremely unpopular in the United States. Furthermore, it attacked Americanizers and agreed with German intellectuals that German *Kultur* was superior to so-called American culture. German Jews also supported the German war effort. On December 10, 1914, Rabbi Emil G. Hirsch said, "Our hopes are with those German and Austro-Hungarian soldiers in the trenches over there. . . . If you win, the best there is in the human race will also have won, and with you the German element of America." His words, spoken before the American entry into the war, would later come back to haunt him. An anti-Zionist, Hirsch was later pushed out of his position in Mount Sinai Temple because of his disloyalty to the American cause.

The German American public seemed impervious to broader public opinion. When newsreels portraying German aggressions played in theaters in German neighborhoods the audience would applaud. U.S. congressmen of German ancestry spoke out against the Allies and warned that America should not enter the war against Germany. Even the terrible news surrounding the sinking of H.M.S. Lusitania, in which 128 Americans died, saw Chicago's *Abendpost* stating that Americans would now understand that when Germany spoke it meant business. The Teutonic Sons of America held a meeting in Chicago in February 1916 and passed a resolution condemning President Woodrow Wilson for hypocrisy.[8]

Right up until the American declaration of war on April 4, 1917, German leaders warned of a race war breaking out in the United States if it entered the war on the Allied side. On the eve of the declaration, German Chicago sent a delegation of twenty-five to Washington, D.C., to argue against it. Numerous German congressmen voted against the declaration, including six from Chicago. One Chicago Congressman, Fred Britten—who portrayed himself as German but was actually of Irish descent—recommended that Germans be exempt from the draft. Shocked by the declaration of war, the Missouri Synod Lutheran Church refused to distribute Liberty Loan literature in their churches.

Perhaps more frightening than the ranting of the German American press or of various leaders was the real possibility of sabotage both before and, especially, after the American entry into the war on April 2, 1917. In 1915, a German-born former Harvard professor tried to kill millionaire J. P. Morgan in New York in order to prevent him from loaning money to the Allies. Various plots uncovered before and after the war seemed to implicate members of the German community. The Zimmermann Telegram, which offered a German alliance and a return of territories to Mexico lost to the United States nearly eighty years earlier, did not help the position of German Americans.[9]

Poison, Hysteria, Politics, and Ethnic Conflict

Events during February 1916 shocked Chicagoans and resurrected old fears of an international anarchist conspiracy. That year the Vatican named George William Mundelein the third Catholic archbishop of Chicago. Mundelein, a German American, carefully arranged his arrival in the city to impress upon believer and nonbeliever alike his image as a bold and decisive leader of the Catholic Church. The festivities began on February 3, when a group of sixty-three Chicagoans arrived in New York to escort the new archbishop to their city. Six days later, Archbishop John Bonzano installed Mundelein as the Chicago archbishop. Three receptions followed over the next few days.[10] On February 10, nearly three hundred Chicagoans gathered at the University Club on Michigan Avenue to honor their new archbishop. The group of male civic, church, and social leaders would have a night they would not soon forget.

About twenty minutes after waiters served the soup, a guest got up and left. Soon everyone's faces began to turn white. The city librarian, Henry E. Legler, then stood up and headed for the door. He took only a few steps before he fell unconscious. Bank presidents, nationally known politicians, and church-men began to flee the room in pain. Some made their way to the back alley to vomit. Dr. John B. Murphy set up what he called an "emergency field hospital" as groans and sounds of distress could be heard up and down the corridor. The press speculated about ptomaine poisoning. Eventually most of the ill guests returned to their tables to continue the dinner, though they passed on eating the other courses. Archbishop Mundelein jokingly addressed the crowd by say-ing, "While we have seen one hundred or more of the great men here tonight falter and fall by the wayside, it is to be noted that the church and state re-mained serene. It augurs well for Illinois." Even though the speakers' table had not been served the soup, he went on to say, "You know it takes something stronger than soup to get me." In actuality something stronger than chicken soup had been served. Someone had laced it with arsenic. The next day police sought Jean Crones, whom the club manager had identified as the soup cook.[11]

Although about one hundred became ill, providentially none of the guests died. The Church had planned the dinner for two hundred guests but at the last minute enlarged the guest list to just fewer than three hundred men. Like all canny cooks, the University Club staff simply diluted the soup, which had been prepared the day before. Crones had not included enough arsenic to poison the diluted batch. Police soon arrested a close friend of Crones, John Allegrini, and the subsequent investigation and interrogation of Allegrini exposed the world of radicalism in which Crones lived.

Police searched the boarding house at 2201 South Prairie, where Crones rented a room from a woman identified as Mrs. Howard, although she also went by the name Ziegenfeus. Crones himself was born in Cologne, Germany, of Belgian parents; a search of his room found a makeshift laboratory and a large collection of anarchist literature. Evidence suggested that Crones had enrolled as a correspondence student in chemistry at the Scranton Correspon-dence School, and police found test tubes and a gas plate in his room. Dr. John Dill Roberston's mistaken claim that the room contained enough gun cotton, an explosive, to blow up the entire building brought back memories of the Hay-market Affair.

Crones had not been seen since Wednesday, when he prepared the soup. He had worked as a cook in various places across the United States since arriv-ing from Germany. The accused would-be mass murderer, a drifter, had been employed at the University Club since September. Rumors had it that Crones belonged to the Industrial Workers of the World (IWW), but the union flatly denied his membership. For his part, Mundelein denied the importance of the event and said, "Such a man is equally the enemy of the Church and the state and of the home." The archbishop said that anti-Catholicism in Chicago did not worry him.[12]

Four hundred men scoured the city looking for Jean Crones. Meanwhile, 150 Chicago detectives, mounted officers, and police protected the Sunday gathering for the laity at the Auditorium Theater, while interest revolved around John Allegrini, as the Italian anarchist remained in police custody. The press sketched the details of Crones's movements the days prior to the banquet. Allegrini told police that he and Crones had gone to hear Emma Goldman speak at the Fine Arts Building, but that he never believed that Crones would take a life. On February 15, the *Tribune* headline shouted, "Huge Bomb Plot Exposed." The Chicago police claimed to have uncovered a conspiracy to destroy public buildings in the city, including the People's Gas Light and Coke Company building on Michigan Avenue. The plot targeted landmarks in other cities, with St. Patrick's Cathedral in New York prominent among them. The police further asserted that the international conspiracy centered on anarchist circles in Rome. Crones had threatened to kill President Wilson as well as various Catholic dignitaries. Furthermore the police tried to connect some thirty mysterious fires in Chicago churches to Crones, although this link seemed highly unlikely because of his recent arrival to the city.

People reported various sightings of Crones in Chicago, in New York, and in Boston. The New York City police started getting a series of taunting letters supposedly from Crones, explaining his method for the poisoning and his habit of walking near police stations. Meanwhile Chicago police tried to connect Crones to the Haymarket Affair by association with the widows of two of the martyrs, Lucy Parsons and Nan Spies, as well as with other anarchists in the city. Emma Goldman remarked, "It is to laugh, the man is not an anarchist. He is a lunatic." On March 17, Judge La Buy released John Allegrini for a lack of evidence, as the Italian immigrant obviously knew nothing of the poisoning. In May, reports of sightings of Crones in Pittsburgh hiding as a Catholic nun emerged. While such stories provided good copy for the Chicago press, Crones simply had disappeared. As a result of the event, the Irish Fellowship Club appointed an official food taster for the annual St. Patrick's Day Dinner. On March 17, 1916, between the hours of 5 and 6 p.m., one William J. Healy tasted all ten of the courses to be served in the kitchen of the La Salle Hotel, for the sake of former President Taft, Archbishop Mundelein, and other dignitaries who attended the event.[13]

While Mundelein might have laughed off the Crones affair, other events soon grabbed his attention. Anti-immigrant and anti-Catholic sentiment often raised their ugly heads in Chicago and across the country. The American Protective Association (APA) and other groups such as the so-called Guardians of Liberty actively campaigned against Catholics and immigrants. In early March, three days of rioting broke out among his flock as a result of anti-Catholic lectures

Figure 68. Orders of Catholic Sisters such as the Polish Sisters of the Holy Family of Nazareth served the various Catholic ethnic neighborhoods throughout the city. (Archives of St. Mary of Nazareth Hospital Center.)

being presented on the South Side by Joseph and Mary Slattery. The Guardians of Liberty brought the former Catholic priest and his wife to Chicago to give a series of lectures. The first talk was scheduled for Boulevard Hall near Garfield Boulevard and Halsted Street, in the Englewood neighborhood just down the block from one of the most important Irish Catholic parishes in the city, the Church of the Visitation.[14]

More than six hundred people jammed Boulevard Hall on the evening of Wednesday, March 1, 1916. The Guardians of Liberty counted many important people among their group, one that purportedly supported free speech, including Chicago school board member Charles H. Young. The meeting opened a little after 8:00 p.m., and trouble broke out as Slattery rose to speak. About twenty young men attempted to enter the hall without paying and were turned away. At that point some two hundred of the attendees became boisterous. The hall quickly filled with so much noise that no one could speak, and Young claimed that the trouble was premeditated. A policeman stood up and said that no one would be allowed to speak. Several witnesses claimed that the police also taunted Slattery as cries of "down with the APA" rose from the crowd.

Violence erupted as the meeting then broke up and crowds attacked several men escorting women, including Charles H. Young, who had tried with his wife to board a streetcar when a mob attacked the car, pulling the trolley off the wire and beating the riders. Young took refuge on a quiet side street, but someone hit him with brass knuckles. Up and down the streets local residents stood on their front porches and cheered the crowd on. The Slatterys got in a cab and drove back to the Sherman Hotel in the Loop under police escort, while rioters cut telephone wires in the neighborhood so that more police could not be called. Someone pulled a fire alarm box, and two fire companies arrived on the scene. Police from the Englewood Station arrived as did police from the Stockyard and Thirty-fifth Street stations. Older audience members tried to hide in a drugstore until the police could escort them out. W. A. Gibson, an attorney, complained that a number of policemen were "perniciously active in the noise in the hall." Police made only one arrest that night, and various residents told reporters that Visitation's pastor and parishioners objected to the speech and decided to act on it.[15]

The next evening saw another outbreak of violence on the South Side as the Slatterys attempted to give a talk at the Oakland Music Hall at 3977 South Cottage Grove, near Holy Angels Catholic Church. When the Irish formed the parish in 1880, the district was heavily Protestant, and the property had to be purchased secretly through third parties. In 1916, Auxiliary Bishop Alexander J. McGavick served as pastor.[16] As tensions rose that night the police decided to prevent the meeting. Several people tried to force their way into the hall, but police pushed them back. William F. Bigelow of the Guardians of Liberty crossed the street to Drexel Hall and tried to rent it but to no avail. Once again, the throng beat people on streetcars. Several rioters hit Soren Nelson, a dairyman from Englewood, on the Cottage Grove car. He heard yells of APA, and then the men attacked him.

On Friday afternoon, Mary Slattery hoped to address a group of women on "Convent Life" in Thornton Hall, once again in Englewood, on Sixty-ninth and Normal, but found the hall closed. Groups of Catholic women surged around the building, and rumors of a riot had convinced D. H. Harper, the hall's owner, to cancel the event. Police stopped Paul Schult, a member of the Guardians of Liberty, and searched him for a weapon, while various groups of Catholic and Protestant women hurled arguments at each other. Englewood had just recently gone through a tremendous transformation in ethnicity and religion, and tempers flared, many over past wrongs. Mrs. C. H. Hummy, past president of the Protestant Women's National Association, called for free speech. In turn, Mrs. G. W. De Grasse argued, "We have the right to come to meetings and stop them, too, when our priests and nuns are attacked as a whole in glittering generalities." The Women's Party of Cook County adopted resolutions condemning the police for preventing the previous night's meeting, and they offered a $100 reward for Charles Young's assailant. For his part Archbishop Mundelein refused to discipline the pastor of Visitation Parish for saying the first lecture in Englewood was unacceptable to the local parish.[17]

Obviously the era of chaos remained a part of life on Chicago's streets as World War I did much to activate ethnic and religious strife in the city. The war and the transformations that it brought created yet more conflict. Furthermore, the actions of the Chicago police—many of them devout Irish Catholics—in the three days of riots, would not augur well for future civil strife. Ethnic and religious conflicts were nothing new to Chicago. Neither was the taking of sides by the police who often had friends, neighbors, and relatives involved in labor union activities or even in mob action. What proved new about the World War I era was how one ethnic group in particular was singled out and its patriotism questioned.

The German community had played an arrogant and dangerous game. With American entry into the war they would pay a price for their support of the Central Powers, one quick and devastating to German American culture. The community was attacked from all sides. Slavs, especially Czechs and Poles, stood in the first ranks of those attacking Chicago's *Deutschtum.* Even before the 1917 declaration of war, both communities had launched a massive anti-German propaganda campaign. Polish composer and patriotic leader Ignace Jan Paderewski worked both in public and behind the scenes to secure American support for the Polish cause. On January 22, 1917, as the United States edged closer to war, President Woodrow Wilson gave his famous "Peace without Victory" speech in which he called for Polish independence, which assured Polish American loyalty to both the American and the Allied cause.

As Chicago went to war in 1917, near hysteria broke out about German espionage as the American Protective League snooped through German neighborhoods and vandals defaced the Goethe statue in Lincoln Park with red chalk. Mayor Thompson, however, did not change his attitude about the war. Lundin, despite the collapse of Thompson's nascent presidential ambitions, continued to believe that the antiwar stance might get Thompson national support. Thompson marched in a preparedness parade down Michigan Avenue and talked about a "power boat" defense against German attacks. On April 15, 1917, Thompson spoke out directly against the war. He decried the war hysteria and proclaimed that he did not believe that the American people favored sending an army to Europe. In a question posed about inviting French Marshal Joffre, hero of the Marne, to Chicago during his national tour, Thompson hedged and instead attacked the draft. Banging his fist on the desk, the mayor heralded Chicago's diversity and angrily explained that a mayor would be presuming a lot by speaking for all the people of Chicago in extending such an invitation to a hero of France.

The outcry against Thompson was loud and strong. The city's newspapers immediately attacked him and asked the U.S. district attorney's office to investigate the mayor. Even Teddy Roosevelt attacked his former imitator at a rally at the Stock Yards Dexter Park Pavilion, as the crowd sang, "We'll hang old Thompson to a sour apple tree." The city council finally sent an invitation to the

French delegation. Not to miss a public relations occasion, on May 7, Thompson greeted them and welcomed them to Chicago. Hours after the Frenchmen left, however, the *Republican* offered an editorial once again loudly criticizing the war. Thompson referred to the fighting as "the federal government's war."

In September, a pacifist group, the People's Council of America for Democracy and Terms of Peace, asked Thompson if they could meet in Chicago. Various other cities in the Midwest had already blocked their meeting. Thompson agreed that they could gather in Chicago, but Illinois Governor Lowden promised to send troops to stop the assembly. In turn the mayor promised to use Chicago police to fight the state militia. Before such a conflict could happen the group held its rally and left town. The city council almost went to war over the issue, and they passed a resolution barring any other such meetings. Thompson then vetoed the resolution. A mob of thousands hung Thompson in effigy along the lakefront and sang "Hang Big Bill! Hang Kaiser Bill!" Nonetheless, Lundin and Thompson saw his growing national reputation as a chance to once again promote Thompson for national office, and he ran for the Senate in the September 1918 Republican primary only to be soundly defeated by Medill McCormick of the Tribune family. After the war, Big Bill ran successfully again for the mayoralty in 1919.[18]

Chicago's Poles and Czechs led a multifaceted crusade against German Americans. In one instance, they campaigned against a "Kaiserized" speller used in the Chicago public schools. The Slavic press had been agitating since 1915 for its removal from the Chicago public schools, and as the press carried on its battle in 1917 thousands of Slavic students reacted and tore out the offending pages, which praised Kaiser Wilhelm. In turn, Polish and Czech leaders began to agitate against the Bismarck School, a public school named for the German chancellor, now situated in a Polish neighborhood. In March 1918, students petitioned to have the name changed, and the school board agreed. Polish and other Chicagoans demanded and the city council complied in the changing of street names such as Berlin, Hamburg, Coblenz, Lubeck, and Rhine Streets.

That year proved to be a high point of anti-German agitation. German *Kultur* found itself under attack from both organized and unorganized groups in what was once one of the most Germanic cities in the nation. In May 1918, the Germania Club changed its name to the Lincoln Club, the Bismarck Hotel became the Randolph Hotel, and the Hotel Kaiserhof changed its name to the Hotel Atlantic. The Goethe statue in Lincoln Park, dedicated a scant six weeks before the war broke out in 1914, had to be taken down under threats of destruction. The Schiller statue got a yellow coat of paint. Vendors no longer sold frankfurters but hot dogs. Sauerkraut became "liberty cabbage." Even private individuals changed their names and denied their ethnic heritage. In April 1918, one of the most powerful ethnic fraternal organizations in the country, the National German-American Alliance, disbanded, as did its local Chicago chapter.

Figure 69. Soldiers, nurses, and civilians encourage the purchase of savings stamps for the war effort in 1917. (Chicago Public Library, Special Collections and Preservation Division.)

Chicago's Slavs largely reached their war aims. An independent Poland and Czechoslovakia now appeared in Central Europe. Serbia became Yugoslavia and united the South Slavs. Chicago's Poles gained in prestige if not in total acceptance. The first Chicagoan to die under fire in the war was Peter Wojtalewicz of St. Adalbert's parish at Seventeenth and Paulina. Two Polish boys from Milwaukee and Chicago captured the first German prisoner of war taken by the U.S. Expeditionary Force. The Poles raised an army of some twenty-five thousand men from the Polish diaspora to fight under French command on the Western Front. Three thousand of these soldiers came from Chicago alone.[19]

World War I and the Labor Movement

The war presented a unique opportunity for the American labor movement. Both the Knights of Labor and the American Federation of Labor (AFL) had argued for immigration restriction. They saw newly arrived immigrants as competitors for jobs and as a force owners used to depress American wages. In 1885, largely through their lobbying, Congress passed a law against contract labor. After a long campaign, whose leadership included the AFL, Congress passed in 1917 the literacy test for immigrants, the first real curtailment of European immigration in American history.[20] The war in Europe also strangled immigration. Chicago's ethnic groups found themselves cut off from their homelands for the first time. The fighting separated families, and labor shortages occurred, especially as American industry began to fill orders for the Allies' war needs. Some immigrants made their way back to their homelands to fight, but most stayed in the United States, particularly those Slavic groups whose homes were occupied by the two great Germanic powers, Austria-Hungary and Germany.

War news remained big news in the various neighborhoods of the city. It also meant big news in union halls. Might this break in immigration give labor leaders a chance to organize industries where they had failed before? If the army of new arrivals no longer gathered at factory gates to take jobs from strikers, would that force management to deal with a resurrected labor movement? Organizers posed these questions especially after the American declaration of war. The draft and the emergence of a great army needing clothing, food, and arms constrained the labor market even more.

Two men played a crucial role in creating a new labor movement in Chicago: William Z. Foster and John Fitzpatrick—the latter the president of the Chicago Federation of Labor (CFL). Founded in 1896, the CFL emerged as a powerful central labor council that gave Chicago workers a strong local organization. By the end of 1903, the CFL had a membership of 245,000 workers, including thirty-five thousand women. According to Foster, the idea of organizing the stockyards came to him as he worked as a car inspector on the Soo Line on July 1, 1917. The AFL, still licking its wounds from the 1904 packinghouse strike defeat, basically ignored the stockyards. Foster, a former member of the IWW, felt that because of the labor shortage, the time to organize the Chicago meatpacking industry had arrived. He approached Fitzpatrick, and on July 23 the CFL formed the Stock Yard Labor Council (SYLC), a new organization of various craft unions, including the Amalgamated Meat Cutters and Butcher Workmen, who had led the 1904 strike.[21]

The plan called for a federation of all the locals in the stockyards, rather than the "one big" union called for by the IWW and labor radicals. Foster knew that the big union approach would only result in opposition from the traditional trade unions and would result in fragmentation of the workforce. Nevertheless the SYLC faced the ethnic and racial realities of the meatpacking workforce, where workers had long been divided by ethnicity, race, and gender. More and more African Americans came to work in the yards as European immigration ceased. Black leaders, hesitant to join a white-controlled union, demanded their own locals. The Poles and Lithuanians also organized their own combined local. Nevertheless these separate ethnic locals remained members of the SYLC and the Amalgamated, and so broader action seemed possible, and indeed it seemed as if unionism had finally succeeded in the stockyards as workers flocked to the SYLC. Eventually, because of the wartime emergency, the

Figure 70. Chicagoans erected a War Memorial Arch in Grant Park to mark the deaths of American troops in World War I. (Postcard, Author's Collection.)

government forced arbitration on management, and the union gained most of its demands, at least temporarily.[22]

The success of the SYLC soon led Foster and Fitzpatrick to look to Chicago's other important industry, steel, as a target of organizers. On August 1, 1918, while the war continued to rage in Europe, thirty union leaders met in Chicago with Samuel Gompers of the AFL to form the National Committee for Organizing Iron and Steel Workers. Foster and Fitzpatrick planned to use the same methods that had succeeded in the stockyards. The advantages of industrial unionism could be had without raising the fears of the traditional AFL unions. Leaders recognized that the drive would have to be national in scope and not just take place in Chicago, as it had in meatpacking. The unions, however, did not adequately support Foster with necessary funds, and this forced a fatal decision to concentrate on the Chicago mills alone.

The national committee launched its campaign in Chicago in September 1918. Unionists held mass meetings, and workers flocked to union halls. Steelworkers in Chicago had never acted this way before so something was obviously in the air. The change in attitude resulted from the war and from the policy of the federal government during the conflict. The Wilson administration hoped to avoid labor problems, and in meatpacking conflicts, federal judge Samuel Alschuler made decisions favorable to the workers. In July 1918, the War Labor Board handed down a ruling favorable to steelworkers at Bethlehem Steel in Pennsylvania. The federal government now seemed to recognize, for the first time, workers' rights. This shift gave momentum to the unions as they faced U.S. Steel and the other smaller steel companies. The tight labor market also reinforced the position of the men as they threatened to strike, and no employer opposition seemed evident during the initial organizational drive. Steelworkers still worked the twelve-hour day and brought their grievances to the unions. In reality, however, organized labor was running against the clock of war. When negotiators signed the armistice and it went into effect on November 11, 1918, many of the conditions that had helped Foster and Fitzpatrick organize the stockyards disappeared instantly. Within a week, Bethlehem Steel announced it no longer felt obligated to recognize the agreement with the War Labor Board since the war was over. With the arrival of peace, the unions faced the steel companies without the support of the government that had seemed so important.[23] Chicago's economy was obviously connected to worldwide events. Peace in Europe might now mean industrial warfare in Chicago.

The Great Migration

While World War I cut off European immigration, it increased the need for labor, especially unskilled labor in Chicago's vast packinghouses, steel mills, and factories. Another migration took the place of the waves of European immigrants newly cut off from the American market, as African Americans made their way north to Chicago and other northern cities in search of freedom, individual mobility, and jobs. The first wave of the Great Migration transformed Chicago and set patterns in racial relations that would last for most of the twentieth century.

African Americans tended to follow rail lines north. The Illinois Central Railroad tied Chicago to New Orleans and the entire Mississippi Valley, extending to Birmingham and through other spur rail lines such as the Yazoo and Mississippi Valley Railroad and the Central Georgia Railroad, as far east as Savannah. Chicago's black population prior to 1916 tended to come from the Upper South—Kentucky, Tennessee, and Missouri—but as the war demanded more and more blacks for the city's labor market, the majority of African Americans came from the Deep South: Mississippi, Louisiana, Arkansas, and other more distant southern states touched by the Illinois Central Railroad. These southerners found homes in the Chicago ghetto.

The Illinois Central Railroad provided not only a transportation system but also a communications system for distributing news, especially the *Chicago Defender,* which had a national circulation of fifty thousand in 1916 and proved to be an important factor in promoting the Great Migration. Founded by Robert

Sengstacke Abbott in 1905 as a four-page handbill, this institution soon became the largest-selling African American newspaper in the United States. Calling itself "the World's Greatest Weekly," the *Defender* brought news of Chicago to the southern countryside and helped to spur migration fever. In 1919, the *Defender*'s circulation jumped to 130,000 nationally, with three-quarters of its readers in the South. Some circulation estimates had the number considerably higher, perhaps as much as 230,000 in 1919. Banned by some southern towns and cities, Pullman porters and others working on the Illinois Central lines secretly distributed the *Chicago Defender* despite attempts at censorship.[24]

From 1890 to 1915, Chicago's African American population grew from fewer than fifteen thousand to over fifty thousand people. The growing African American population made up about 2 percent of the city's population in the years before the war. More confined as a group residentially after 1890, blacks tended to settle south of the Loop. The creation of the South Side Black Belt was already seen in outline by 1914, but as late as 1910 African Americans remained less segregated from native-born whites than Italian immigrants were. That year, blacks did not entirely occupy more than twelve city blocks. In several neighborhoods, blacks and whites lived together without much hostility. This peace would be short-lived.

Violence did break out on various occasions. The public school system, legally integrated since 1874, saw frequent outbursts of racial violence, especially after 1890. Much of the opposition to African Americans in schools came from white students and their parents, rather than from school officials. In 1905, white children, transferred to a predominantly black school, rioted. Three years later, 150 white students stayed home when the school board transferred them to a school attended by African Americans. In 1909, white students harassed and beat two black children enrolling in a previously all-white school. A school strike in 1912 resulted in more racial tensions. Wendell Phillips High School, the first predominantly black high school in the city, was often the scene of racial violence. The color line remained a source of tension particularly on the South Side, and white groups periodically called for racial segregation of the schools. Catholic schools in the city were openly segregated. Only black students attended St. Monica's parochial school, established for African American Catholics in 1912. Private universities had various policies. Both the University of Chicago and Northwestern University admitted black students, but witnessed minor disturbances when blacks entered dormitories.[25]

As black settlement spread east of State Street on the South Side, violence increased. By 1910, the emerging South Side ghetto stretched south on State Street from Twelfth Street to Thirty-ninth Street (Pershing Road), and that year 78 percent of Chicago's black population lived in this district known to whites as the "Black Belt." The 1910 census counted 34,335 African American residents in this district, which had expanded on both its southern and eastern boundaries. The remaining number of black Chicagoans lived on the West Side

(3,379) and in smaller enclaves including Englewood, the Near North Side, and several other scattered settlements.

Between 1910 and 1914, the limited housing stock of the Black Belt absorbed another ten thousand migrants. Most of these new arrivals settled in the area between State Street and the Rock Island and New York Central Railroad tracks to the west. This area, known as the Federal Street ghetto, was the poorest and most rundown section of the Black Belt. Most African Americans coming north knew where to go as they got off the train at the Illinois Central Railroad Station at Twelfth and Michigan Avenue: they faced south and started walking. As it had European immigration, chain migration marked the black move to the city, and many came to join family and friends on the South Side. The racial line in Chicago grew stricter as the Great Migration continued. For the most part, by 1915, black Chicagoans lived with other black Chicagoans and sent their children to predominantly black schools. Whites also excluded African Americans from most white business establishments.[26]

As the wartime influx from the South occurred, housing demands and costs skyrocketed. Even before the war, rents were high in the Black Belt. In 1912, the *Journal of American Sociology* published a survey of housing conditions in both the South Side and the smaller West Side black communities. It revealed that African Americans paid higher rents than any other ethnic group for comparable housing. Half of the residents of the Back of the Yards, Polish North Side, and the Czech Lower West Side paid less than $8.50 per month for a four-room apartment; half of the tenants in the part of the Black Belt studies paid $12.00! Also these homes were in poorer condition than those in either Back of the Yards or South Chicago.[27]

African Americans nonetheless attempted to build their own city in the middle of Chicago, and, like other ethnic groups, they created their own local institutions. As blacks became more excluded from Chicago's institutions, the community made decisions based on northern segregation. Increased separation of the races opened up new economic opportunities for aspiring blacks in their own neighborhoods, and a new middle class appeared in the first decade of the twentieth century. This new middle class replaced an older elite that refused to give up the hope of integration and was therefore less likely to create separate black institutions. Businessmen such as Robert S. Abbott, political leaders like Louis B. Anderson and Oscar De Priest, and religious leader Archibald J. Carey, among others, dominated Chicago's black institutions and created the basis for what would be called the Black Metropolis or Bronzeville by the 1920s. The roots of this black Chicago were already visible before and during World War I.[28]

In a long-lasting Chicago tradition, the new black leadership saw migrants as sources of votes and as customers for their businesses. In a city where public space was at a premium, especially for African Americans, African American entrepreneurs created "the Stroll," a section of State Street between Twenty-sixth and Thirty-ninth Streets; busy both night and day, the Stroll provided a sense of pride and even flamboyance off limits in other parts of Chicago. Black-owned businesses, both licit and illicit, filled the street. Vice, from prostitution to drugs and gambling, had become centered in the Black Belt after Carter Harrison closed down the old Levee in the South Loop in 1912. Many of these "leisure" institutions catered to both blacks and whites. Called "Black and Tans," nightclubs catered to people from all over the city and gave birth to Chicago as a center of jazz, a nascent form of urban music.[29]

As the black population grew, it began to put more pressure on neighbor-hood boundaries, particularly to the east. The Great Migration did more than transport blacks from one place to another: it also brought them into a new culture. In Bronzeville the various social classes lived next to each other due to the realities of housing segregation. With the rise of southern migration, Chi-cago's black middle class, while encouraging and welcoming these newcomers, often felt that the migrants had to learn new habits when they arrived on the South Side. Black newspapers such as the *Defender* and the *Whip* told rural and small-town southerners how to act in the big city. They reminded them that they no longer lived in the South and that the North had different standards of behavior, both in private and on the street. Old settlers, both northern blacks and those who migrated earlier from the Upper South, worried about the im-pact of the migrants on Chicago's always tenuous racial relations. This division caused tensions within the black community.

Unlike white Chicagoans, the black middle class could not move away from poor migrants. Even those who lived in the "best" black neighborhoods lived in close proximity to Federal Street and the southerners. The northern bourgeoi-sie often felt distaste for the newcomers, and longtime black Chicagoans re-jected socializing even with newly rich black migrants. When old settlers tried to move out of the ghetto, they encountered white hostility. Between July 1917 and July 1919, twenty-six bombs exploded at isolated black residences in once all-white neighborhoods, most of these in the middle-class white neighbor-hood to the east of Bronzeville along the lakefront.[30] As in the case of the im-migrant ghettoes, outsiders had a very narrow and prejudiced view of these Afri-can American settlements. They saw chaos and feared its spread, while blacks saw a new Black Metropolis growing in the middle of Chicago's South Side.

1919: *Annus Mirabilis*

The Latin term *Annus Mirabilis* means a "year of wonder" but can also imply one of fear and disaster. The year 1919 certainly did not begin any such way. World War I had ended, and Chicagoans joyfully celebrated the peacetime New Year. Americans saw a world now made safe for democracy as the vanquished Central Powers sued for peace. Troops set sail to return home, and immigrants looked forward to renewed immigration and the reunions of families separated by war. Those ethnic groups associated with the new Slavic republics of central and eastern Europe had high hopes for their homelands, and many would decide to emigrate back in the 1920s. Organized labor seemed strong in the stockyards and grew quickly in the steel mills and elsewhere. African Americans celebrated their home on Chicago's South Side, as their veterans returned as well. The year looked promising for the Chicago White Sox, winners of the first wartime World Series in 1917. Some billed the Sox as the greatest team in baseball history, with an offense led by Shoeless Joe Jackson and a pitching staff formed around ace Eddie Cicotte. The Cubs had won the 1918 National League pennant adding to its three previous league championships and World Series victories in 1907 and 1908. Chicagoans had much to look forward to and be optimistic about as 1919 began.

The year, however, proved to be a challenging one not only for Chicago, but for the nation. President Wilson traveled to Paris for the peace conference with many idealistic demands in his portfolio. Parisians greeted him with enthusiasm as the great American savior who had brought the war to a victorious end for the Allies. Wilson hoped his Fourteen Points would be the basis for the treaty and the peace. While events in the newly formed Soviet Union caused concern, the international scene could be looked upon with optimism. Soon that optimism turned to frustration, as Wilson faced allies eager for revenge and retribution against Germany and the Central Powers.

In Chicago, peace also brought economic difficulty. Industry had grown during the war years in order to supply the American and allied armies, but those war orders ended. Unemployment soared even as the celebration of the end of the fighting took place. Plants began to lay off workers, and returning soldiers found their jobs gone. Many whites coming home from the Western Front felt that African Americans had stolen their jobs and racial animosity began to grow. Blacks felt that they were the first to be let go in any downturn and resented whites that remained on the job.

The packinghouses had become a major employer for African Americans, and much of the ill will between the races played out on the city's kill floors. Black employment in Chicago had been largely built upon war orders, and so African Americans were among the first to feel the pain of the postwar economy. In late January 1919, a black official of the U.S. Employment Service complained "there has not been a single vacant job in Chicago for a colored man." He noted that "nothing would tend to cause race friction" as much as unemployment. By May 1919, total employment fell in the stockyards from over sixty-five thousand in January to fifty thousand and would continue downward. Moreover, returning soldiers added to the numbers of unemployed. Black workers hesitated to unionize during this period, as they knew it would hurt their chances of employment given the anti–organized labor attitude of management.[31]

In the stockyards, despite the gains of the Stock Yard Labor Council, the packers had refused to sign an agreement directly with the unions. Judge

Alschuler had to prepare separate agreements to be signed by the unions and management. Union leaders realized that the principle of collective bargaining would have to be established before the Alschuler agreement faded into history. In mid-February Alschuler granted his second award increasing wages and granting better working hours. On April 12, the packers asked the federal government to extend the Alschuler agreement for one year after the declaration of peace. Stockyard management obviously did not want a conflict with their workers right after the war. The union did not want the extension. In June, the SYLC kicked off a drive to organize more workers in the packinghouses. On July 6, black and white workers paraded through the streets and congregated in Davis Square Park near the yards. The goal of organizing all workers in the stockyards, particularly newly arrived southern migrants, still seemed out of reach. Many blacks did not trust the unions. Ninety percent of white workers in the stockyards were unionized while three-quarters of African Americans had not joined the movement.

Meanwhile, a violent strike broke out on July 8 in the Argo Corn Products plant just to the southwest of the city. Many Polish, Russian, and Lithuanian workers in the stockyards had friends or relatives working at Argo, and they marched out to the plant to support them. Rumors circulated that management planned to hire blacks to displace these strikers. The rumors proved true, as some six hundred black workers arrived to work in the plant. This labor conflict set the stage for a wider racial confrontation in the city.

Industrial unrest broke out across the city and the United States in the summer of 1919. Close to 250,000 workers in Chicago struck, threatened to strike, or found themselves locked out in July 1919. The division between labor and capital seemed insurmountable as the middle classes feared the growth of the Communist Party. The Russian Revolution promised a utopian working-class society, and Chicago's old fear of anarchy and radicalism again raised its head. In June 1919, Chicago police arrested Dinilo Mari, an eighty-year-old anarchist who operated a clearinghouse for the mail of anarchist leaders at 1837 West Grand Avenue. The *Tribune* reported that the police had finally cleared the city of all the "master minds" of the anarchist movement. The paper also reported the arrest of George Markstall of North Troy Street, for making seditious comments about President Wilson on the streetcar. The forty-seven-year-old Markstall was married to Lucy Parsons, raising yet again the old ghost of the Haymarket Affair.[32]

Instead of a working-class revolution, a race riot broke out. The summer had been hot and sticky, and Chicagoans flocked to the lake to get some relief from the heat. Traditionally, the Twenty-sixth Street beach had been reserved for African Americans. Just to the south at Twenty-ninth Street lay the first of a string of white beaches. There had been several clashes between whites and blacks on the two beaches during the day. On Sunday, July 27, Eugene Williams, a sixteen-year-old black boy, went to swim with his friends in Lake Michigan.

Williams and his friends floated on a raft off the black beach when the lake's current took them across the invisible boundary line in the water off of the Twenty-ninth Street Beach. A white man began to throw rocks at the boys and yelled the usual racial epithets. Eugene Williams and his friends yelled back and ducked the rocks. One hit Williams in the head, and the lake's powerful currents pulled him under and he drowned. Thus began the fiercest race riot in the city's history.

Gangs, particularly Englewood's Ragen's Colts, played a central role in the riot. Called social athletic clubs, or sacs, these white groups ran the districts surrounding the Black Belt to the west and south. The police seemed to re-store calm on Monday as Chicago went back to work. This lull proved illusory as white crowds gathered to meet black packinghouse workers trying to make their way home from the stockyards. The long-anticipated race riot now be-came a terrifying reality, as white mobs stopped streetcars and pulled blacks off, beating and killing several. African Americans also committed atrocities in the street fighting as black gangs attacked white peddlers and businessmen.

White gangs sped through the Black Belt, firing guns from their cars as they quickly passed through the Bronzeville neighborhood, which was only a few blocks wide at various intersections. The corner of Thirty-fifth and Wabash—site of the Angelus House, a white boarding house in the Black Belt, and of De La Salle Institute, a white Catholic boys high school—became the center of rioting. A mob of some 1,500 blacks gathered outside the Angelus House as rumors spread that white snipers had fired from its windows. Police found no arms in the building. A confrontation took place between police and the crowd. Shots rang out and several black men lay dying.

Chaos spread throughout the South Side, the Loop, and parts of the West Side. The police could not control the crowds. Evidence pointed to the fact that police sympathies often lay with the white gangs. Some probably had been members of the Colts, Aylwards, Our Flag, Hamburg, or Standard Clubs—white gangs involved in the fighting. Certainly they knew members and many had family members in the gangs. In particular, observers accused the police of the Stockyard Station on Halsted near Forty-eighth Street in the Canaryville neighborhood of looking the other way as the gangs went looking for African Americans. Police often arrested victims rather than rioters in the neighbor-hoods surrounding the stockyards, and police bullets killed no whites despite the widespread fighting.

Monday's death toll reached seventeen as the city braced for a transit strike the next day. Both surface and elevated trains stopped running at 4 a.m. on Tuesday. Blacks stayed away from work in droves, as they feared walking through the white ethnic neighborhoods to their jobs in the yards. That day, violence spread to the Loop with white soldiers and sailors joining the fighting. Mobs beat and shot blacks in the streets. Despite the violence authorities did

Figure 71. African American men gather at the corner of Thirty-fifth and State Street during the 1919 race riot. (DN-0071297, Chicago Daily News negatives collection, Chicago History Museum.)

not bring the state militia into Chicago as rumors of even greater atrocities made their way about the city.

Mayor William Hale Thompson claimed that the police had controlled the situation and refused to request help from the state militia. Meanwhile, the newspapers and prominent Chicagoans called for the troops. Governor Lowden refused to act unilaterally stating that it was up to the mayor: so politics played a part in the riot's death toll. Meanwhile, Alderman Joe McDonough of Bridgeport warned the police that he would recommend that his constituents arm themselves unless something was done right away. Finally, after long resisting, on July 30 Thompson asked for troops. He had given in to employers who wanted protection for their African American workers. That evening shortly after 10 p.m. militiamen moved out of the armories into the region bounded by Eighteenth Street and Garfield Boulevard, Wentworth and Indiana. Later that night rain began to fall. After the soldiers arrived violence continued only sporadically. Troops promised to bring black workers into the yards on the following Monday. That weekend, someone set a fire in the Back of the Yards neighborhood that resulted in over nine hundred, primarily Polish and Lithuanian, immigrants losing their homes. White gangs had burned the buildings in an attempt to rally immigrants against the African Americans. The Polish newspapers blamed not blacks, but white gangs, particularly the Irish, from the eastern section of the Stock Yard District. The Poles and other eastern Europeans had stayed out of the fighting up to this point. Finally, on Thursday, August 7, African Americans returned to work under the protection of the police; the militia withdrew the next day. Some ten thousand white union members walked out in a strike.[33] The fighting lasted on and off until August 3 and resulted in thirty-eight dead—twenty-three black and fifteen white—and about five hundred injured. Objects hurled by the crowds hurt a handful of women. The conflict was a young man's riot, and resulted from competition between whites and blacks over jobs, housing, and politics. The new black presence in the city made African Americans a threat to various white groups, especially on the South Side, which had the largest concentration of African Americans and of industry that welcomed them. Many of the South Side's older white ethnic groups, such as the Irish, Germans, and Scandinavians, had made their way up the ladder of mobility in Chicago and felt threatened by black competition. Other cities also witnessed racial combat, but Chicago's proved to be the fiercest. The clash mapped out racial lines, which would endure in place for the next twenty years and which influenced race relations in the city for the rest of the century.

The year 1919 dragged on, with more unemployment and sporadic racial violence. The nation endured a Red Scare, and immigrants feared deportation. On the South Side, trouble began to brew again as steelworkers prepared for a confrontation with U.S. Steel. The steel companies seemed determined not to have the industry organized—by Foster and Fitzpatrick or by anyone else. Elbert H. Gary headed U.S. Steel and warned his stockholders that they must be fair to workers in order to counter the union movement. Management encouraged the creation of Employee Representation Programs that gained popularity during the war. The companies also encouraged local authorities to act against the union organizers. Nevertheless, owners could not stop the national committee's efforts, especially in the Chicago District. The steel managers branded the committee's leaders as dangerous radicals and claimed that only the foreign born had joined the union thus bringing up the specter of international revolution and the communist threat. The companies especially targeted Foster as dangerous. Fitzpatrick and the SYLC came to his aid, and Judge Alschuler spoke up for the labor leader.

Samuel Gompers approached Gary and asked for a parley. The AFL leader wrote Gary telling him that one hundred thousand steelworkers were union members on June 30, 1919. Gary ignored the letter. On July 8, Gompers reported this to the national committee, and local unions threatened to walk out of the mills. On July 20, rank and file leaders forced the national committee to call for a strike vote. The strike began on September 22. Immigrant communities rallied to the unions involved in the action, including the Amalgamated Association of Iron and Steel Workers. The American-born workers proved to be more reluctant to strike. In South Chicago, on the city's Southeast Side, the committee employed organizers from the various language groups in the mills, including Poles, Croatians, and Italians.

Violence broke out in the Chicago Steel District. In Hammond, Indiana, police opened fire and killed five Polish workers at the Standard Steel Car Company during a strike that preceded the big steel walk out. On September 25, some eighteen thousand workers struck the South Chicago plants; in response over five hundred police and forty mounted police patrolled the streets. Fighting occurred as crowds attacked strikebreakers at the U.S. Steel South Works plant. On September 29, a gun battle broke out early in the morning near the South Works. Angry mobs continued to greet strikebreakers. On October 5, strikers congregated near the Eighty-third Street Illinois Central commuter station looking for scabs. They also stopped cars, especially to look for African Americans, as rumors had it management had prepared to import black strikebreakers. On October 4, the CFL newspaper, the *New Majority,* claimed that 95 percent of the men remained on strike.

But the odds were against the union as they faced the huge U.S. Steel trust and a united front of smaller plants. By November, all the mills in the Chicago district except those in Waukegan and Joliet operated at between 50 and 85 percent capacity. On December 10, only eighteen thousand men out of the original ninety thousand remained on strike. As Christmas approached, workers already felt the sting of defeat. On January 8, 1920, the unions called off the strike that had been broken weeks earlier.

The year 1919 marked the end of the great labor-organizing drives of the World War I years. Two years later the meatpackers would destroy the Amalgamated Meat Cutters in another strike that erased the gains made by Foster and Fitzpatrick with the Stock Yard Labor Council. Organized labor almost disappeared from the American political scene in the 1920s. It would take the trials of the Great Depression to bring organized labor back into the packinghouses and steel mills of the South Side.[34]

As the steelworkers went on strike, the Chicago White Sox won the 1919 American League pennant and looked to be favorites in the World Series against the Cincinnati Reds. The South Siders had won the 1917 World Championship, and Chicago seemed assured of another baseball crown, but it was not meant to be. When the Sox lost the best-of-nine-game series to the Reds, rumors spread that they had lost deliberately, that gamblers had influenced the outcome. Baseball always had a dark side connected to gambling, but nothing as serious as a World Series had ever been at stake. The courts eventually found eight White Sox ballplayers not guilty, but the newly named baseball commissioner, Chicago-based Judge Kenesaw Mountain Landis, barred the men from baseball for life. The White Sox did not win another pennant for forty years and did not win a World Series during the rest of the twentieth century. Nineteen hundred and nineteen proved to be a very bad year indeed.

Twentieth-Century Metropolis

The transition from war to peace proved to be a difficult one for Chicago and the nation: race riots and strikes broke out across the country in the wake of the war; a Red Scare resulted in the arrest, imprisonment, and deportation of thousands of immigrants; and many Americans yearned for a mythic calm that they called "normalcy." If normalcy meant the class and ethnic conflict of the prewar period, then that is exactly what they got in the four years after the signing of the armistice. On the streets of American cities, chaos threatened to reign again, and Chicago—with its large foreign-born population—braced for the worst of times. Soldiers raided union halls in Gary during the steel strike, and across the area "patriots" searched for evidence of another conspiracy. The Ku Klux Klan reemerged as a largely urban midwestern and western organization, tracing its roots back to the American Protective Association and the so-called Guardians of Liberty. In Chicago, the Klan's headquarters stood in Hyde Park near the University of Chicago. Racism, anti-Semitism, and anti-Catholicism still poisoned the waters of American society.

The Attack on Immigrants

Progressive reformers had a checkered relationship with America's immigrants. While sympathetic to their plight, they loathed the power political bosses wielded thanks to immigrant voters and feared the Catholic Church, which many saw as antidemocratic and superstitious in its basic beliefs. The Immigrant Restriction League, led largely by Senator Henry Cabot Lodge, had campaigned for a literacy test for immigrants since 1896, when President Cleveland vetoed the original bill. Both Republican and Democratic presidents had opposed its passage since then, but proponents of the literacy law finally prevailed over President Wilson's objections in 1917. Many Progressives supported more stringent immigration restriction as a way of battling slums and political bossism. Liberal Progressives saw immigrants as pawns in the struggle to clean up American cities, and they often blamed immigrants for Chicago's problems, such as slums, crime, vice, and alcoholism. Samuel Gompers, president of the American Federation of Labor, himself an immigrant, continued to back restriction as a way to strengthen the labor movement by minimizing competition from immigrants willing to work more cheaply than people already in the United States.

The opponents of anti-immigrant literacy legislation hoped to block the movement before World War I, with the demand for yet another congressional investigation into immigration. In 1911, Congress established just such a committee, popularly known as the Dillingham Commission. Three senators, three members of the House, and three presidential appointees made up the commission over three years at a cost of over $1 million; ultimately a staff of over three hundred people compiled the massive forty-two-volume report. The findings of the commission supported restriction, as did the 1916 publication of the popular book by Madison Grant, *The Passing of the Great Race*. At the time the different nationalities of Europe were classified as belonging to separate races: Poles, Czechs, and Russians were classified as part of the Slavic race. The undesirability of the "races" of eastern and southern Europe seemed obvious to most native white Americans, who saw themselves as Anglo-Saxons.

When the Republican Party took control of Congress in 1919, Albert Johnson, a friend of both the Immigration Restriction League and of Madison Grant, became the new chairman of the House Committee on Immigration and immediately called for immigration restriction. The House again held hearings from 1919 to 1921 and proposed limitation, but President Wilson pocket vetoed the bill. The law finally passed on May 19, 1921, with President Harding's approval, as the first bill to curb European immigration of all kinds and to put in force a quota system. The bill hoped to reverse certain trends in European immigration and created quotas based on the 1910 census. In 1924, the National Origins Act surpassed this temporary law and used the 1890 census as the baseline for immigration and quotas. This law literally cut immigration from southern and eastern Europe to a trickle of both the prewar and postwar numbers. Years of Social Darwinist theory, nativist diatribes, academic and popular attacks on immigration and general American fears had shaped the immigration restriction movement. The so-called Golden Gate to America slammed shut.[1]

For immigrant Chicago, this terrible blow cut off the city's ethnic and immigrant populations from family and friends. The recent race riots and the continued growth of the African American population seemed also to threaten the city's white ethnics. Many feared that upward mobility was not possible in the bleak years immediately following World War I. While some Poles, Czechs, and others had returned to their newly independent homelands, the vast majority stayed in America. Indeed, many found their native lands not as welcoming as they had expected. Poles looked on the former immigrants as "Americans" and did not want their advice on how to rule the new nation. Indeed, in reaction to both nativism in the United States and European attitudes, Chicago's ethnic

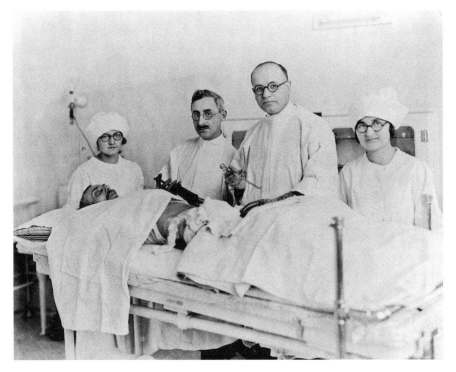

Figure 72. Operating Room, St. Mary of Nazareth Hospital, ca. 1910. By the early twentieth century ethnic doctors and nurses began to provide a wide range of medical services to the Polish community. (Archives of St. Mary of Nazareth Hospital Center.)

populations pulled back from their national ethnic identities and Americanized but also ironically became more insular at the same time, embracing the idea of becoming "hyphenated Americans," still proud of their ancestry, but now permanently tied to life in the United States.

For many ethnic Chicagoans, immigration restriction created opportunities as well as problems. The problems were obvious: the cutting off of the steady flow from the homeland meant that freshly arrived immigrants would not constantly renew ethnic cultures. Some feared the disappearance of their distinct communities. Others saw the new reality as a way of settling into American culture and of building communities not constantly burdened by having to assimilate newcomers. Few outsiders recognized that new immigrants presented a challenge to the ethnic communities themselves. How do recent arrivals react to labor unions? Will they join fraternal groups? How will they take part in the political system? Will they have habits that are easily assimilable to the larger ethnic culture? Will they support the parochial schools? How will immigrants from another region of the homeland interact with those already established in Chicago? Ethnic communities had to bring in and assimilate new immigrants if they were to maintain and improve their status. Now, with immigration cut off, as harmful and hurtful as that might have been, these communities could set down roots in American society, much as older groups had. In the four-hundred-thousand-member Chicago Polish community and in many others as well, leaders began to look at the American communities as permanent not temporary sojourns, or ever-changing outposts of Poland. Many echoed the Polish words, *Wychodźtwo dla Wychodżtwa,* immigrants for immigrants.[2] As was so often the case, large-scale political change had unintended consequences on the streets of Chicago.

The Bungalow and the New Ethnic Metropolis

While the military economy of World War I had slowed down the construction of new housing on Chicago's periphery as early as the 1910s, the bungalow fad began to transform these outlying neighborhoods and suburbs. New transit lines connected far-flung areas to the Loop and opened up residential expansion. The traction settlement ordinance of 1907 had placed regulation of mass transit under the Board of Supervising Engineers, and for the first time at least some regulation of the transit system was in the hands of professionals. In 1913, the Unification Ordinances were passed, unifying the system and creating the Chicago Surface Lines. The elevated railway system, originally developed in the 1890s but by this time owned by electric company magnate Samuel Insull, circled the downtown with a new Union Loop. While financial problems continuously plagued the system, the construction of new electric interurban lines, streetcar lines, and elevated lines increased the possibilities for residential con-

struction. The new "Bungalow Belt" depended heavily on mass transit. Much of this development occurred before the full impact of the automobile in the later 1920s; the northward construction of the electric elevated lines reached Evanston in 1908, with additional stations added over the next ten years. In the city, the Ravenswood extension reached Kimball Avenue in 1909. Streetcars continuously expanded along the city's streets.[3]

The city's narrow lots and inclement weather largely shaped Chicago's peculiar brick version of the bungalow, although examples of stucco, wood frame, and the more expansive California-style bungalows also could be found. They joined the traditional balloon-frame apartments and cottages: the Queen Anne, Victorian, and American Four-Square residences of the late nineteenth and early twentieth century. Rectangular and standing about one and one-half stories in height, with many windows, bungalows stood squarely on the twenty-five- to thirty-seven-foot-wide traditional

Figure 73. The Union Loop, which circled Chicago's downtown, is pictured here on Wabash Street about 1910. (Postcard, Author's Collection.)

Chicago lot, providing a small front lawn and a backyard. To a large extent the creation of the bungalow resulted from technological changes in the process of home building. Advances in millwork lumber production, plumbing, and consumer products powered by electricity made the new housing possible.[4]

Bungalows were the first truly modern houses to be mass produced in twentieth-century Chicago. These detached single-family homes included central heat, electricity, and modern bathroom facilities. Eventually many included a detached garage facing a rear alley or occasionally a side driveway. The new designs of Frank Lloyd Wright's Prairie School influenced Chicago's mass-produced bungalows, as their interiors included woodwork, built-in cabinets, and hardwood floors that provided an easy to clean environment. A gracious and inviting front door and entry hall greeted visitors. Between 1910 and 1930, developers built roughly eighty thousand of these brick homes across the city in a crescent-shaped area that extended from the north lakefront to the Indiana border soon called the Bungalow Belt. Approximately twenty thousand appeared in the inner-ring suburbs, with fine examples in Cicero and Berwyn. By the end of the 1920s, these homes had filled in much of the open spaces of Chicago's outlying neighborhoods and suburbs.[5]

Bungalow Belt developers included small family-run ethnic businesses, as well as large developers, such as Charles Ringer in South Shore, William H. Brittigan on the Southwest Side, or A. J. Schorsch and William Zelosky on the Northwest Side. The bungalow became a symbol of upward mobility for Chicago's white ethnic population in the 1920s. White Protestants made up many of the original inhabitants of Bungalow Belt neighborhoods; they had moved out of older communities such as Englewood or Jefferson Park, looking for better housing and to get away from what they considered undesirable ethnic groups. The new neighborhoods supported new public schools, as well as Catholic, Jewish, and Protestant congregations. Many of these institutions no longer carried an identifiable ethnic character, but more often than not ethnic Chicagoans still laid claim to these new neighborhoods and institutions. While George Cardinal Mundelein discouraged ethnic parishes, many, such as St. Turibius—a Polish American parish on the Southwest Side—remained openly ethnic if not officially organized as an ethnic parish. But in the 1920s the new neighborhoods were seen as American, distinct from the original settlements of Chicago's immigrant communities.

In the years after 1920, neighborhoods just beyond the old industrial core began to see phenomenal growth. Gage Park, just south and west of the stockyards, more than doubled in population to 31,355 residents. Chicago Lawn, just to the south, increased by more than 300 percent to 47,462 residents. Portage Park on the Northwest Side jumped from 24,439 in 1920 to 54,203 ten years later. Norwood Park saw its numbers increase from fewer than 3,000 residents in 1920 to over 14,000 in 1930. Austin's population increased to that of a good-sized city as it reached more than 131,000 people by 1930—thanks largely to

Figure 74. Builders constructed some eighty thousand bungalows in Chicago and twenty thousand more in the suburbs during the period 1915–30. These homes provided all the modern conveniences to residents including central hearting, indoor plumbing, and electricity. Pictured here is a row of bungalows on the 1700 block of West 100th Street in the East Beverly neighborhood. (Photograph by D. Pacyga.)

the opening of the Division Street carline in 1915. Cicero and Berwyn saw their populations jump dramatically between 1910 and 1930; Cicero's population more than quadrupled from 14,557 to 66,062. The opening in 1903 of the massive Hawthorne Works of the Western Electric Company attracted many to the industrial suburb, as did the new housing stock of bungalows and brick two-flats. Berwyn, just to the west of Cicero, grew from 5,841 residents in 1901 to 47,027 in 1930 as the Bungalow Belt expanded across the prairie. By the beginning of the Great Depression, Berwyn was by and large filled up with housing. The town's close proximity to Cicero and Chicago helped it to develop as a dormitory suburb, much like, but not nearly as prestigious, as nearby Riverside.[6]

Three communities—LaVergne, Upsala or Swedetown, and Berwyn—originally made up the suburb later known as Berwyn. In 1902, residents incorporated the area as a village. Six years later Berwyn became a city, receiving its charter from the state of Illinois. Berwyn had a population of 5,841 in 1910. Within ten years, Czechs moved into the area in large numbers, as did developers who built bungalows for them. The central portion of the town developed quickly as newcomers built thousands of new homes each year. The 1920s construction boom saw farms and fields replaced by rows of bungalows, many of them more

Figure 75. This greenhouse on the edge of the city in 1910 shows the vast amount of land still open for development during the 1920s. Various developers moved quickly to develop these properties with bungalows. (Chicago Public Library, Special Collections and Preservation Division.)

substantial "super" bungalows. Berwyn claimed to be the fastest growing city in the United States in the 1920s with a population increase of 222 percent.[7]

These western suburbs demonstrated the connection between bungalows and upward mobility. The early twentieth century saw the continued expansion of industry along the South Branch of the Chicago River and the Illinois and Michigan Canal. In 1900, the opening of the new Sanitary Drainage and Ship Canal expanded this concentration of industry. The crowded streets of Pilsen provided homes to two generations of Czechs, Poles, and other East Europeans, but many now looked further west. Czechs, Poles, and other east Europeans had settled in large numbers in the Pilsen and Heart of Chicago neighborhoods, both located in the Lower West Side community area. In the 1920s, these neighborhoods remained vibrant centers of ethnic culture, but prosperous residents soon began to move away from the original centers. The community area had reached residential maturity in 1895, and lost nineteen thousand residents by 1930. By 1920, South Lawndale to the southwest of Pilsen had taken on the name of Czech California and was home to 84,030 residents. This area of second settlement also lost population during the 1920s, although not as intensely as the older Pilsen settlement. In 1930, 76,749 Chicagoans lived in South Lawndale. Twenty-sixth Street was referred to as the Bohemian

Broadway, but like all American streets, Twenty-sixth Street led out of town and in this case into Cicero and Berwyn. The Czechs and Poles followed the tug toward the suburbs.

Czech institutions followed the new residents to the suburbs. As in Chicago, the Bohemian community quickly became important in the political life of the western suburbs, and Czech gymnastic fraternal groups built the Sokol Slavsky Building at Cermak Road and Lombard Avenue in Cicero. Sokol Tabor constructed its own building in Berwyn, as did the Sokol Berwyn. Sokol Stickney, founded in 1927, operated out of its new building in that suburb. Czech Freethinker or Rationalist schools also operated in the suburbs, including the Masaryk, Burnham, and Ales Schools in Cicero. In Berwyn the Havlicek and Jirasek schools served the Rationalist Bohemian populations. East European churches quickly appeared in Cicero and Berwyn as well.[8]

While developers built a few bungalows for African Americans, mostly in the Morgan Park area on the city's Far South Side, the Bungalow Belt remained exclusively white. These neighborhoods certainly did not welcome blacks, and in some cases even Catholics and Jews faced Protestant prejudice. Still Catholics and Jews found their way to the Bungalow Belt and settled in large numbers near Marquette Park. Catholics founded St. Rita, St. Nicholas of Tolentine, St. Clare of Montefalco, and the Lithuanian church of the Nativity. Lithuanian Catholics even opened a grammar school, high school, and hospital in Marquette Park. In 1928, Dr. E. Charles Sydney came to serve as rabbi of the Lawn

Figure 76. Nick Adlar, Jr. (right), owner of Fort Dearborn Lithograph, 2846–54 North California Avenue, stands next to the company's first press as it began operation in 1923. Many young men tested the waters of Chicago's economy during the 1920s. (Courtesy of Fort Dearborn Lithograph.)

Manor Community Center at 6641 South Troy, also in the Marquette Park neighborhood. The congregation grew rapidly, and two hundred new members enrolled in two months as Jews moved into the neighborhood. Race, however, remained a source of conflict long after the 1919 race riot.

In March 1927, the local Chicago Lawn newspaper, the *Liberty Bell,* ran a story titled, "Color Line Scare Stirs 60th Street." A Loop attorney, Cameron Latter, had purchased some property along the Grand Trunk Railway tracks; he hoped to open an icehouse. Residents quickly opposed the scheme. They filed petitions to keep the business out of the neighborhood, claiming that the new zoning laws prohibited industrial uses. The Chicago City Council had introduced zoning laws in 1923 that proved popular in the Bungalow Belt as a way of keeping certain businesses out.[9] Mr. Latter's attorney protested that the zoning laws had been established improperly in this case and that even the Zoning Board of Appeals had admitted the problem. In fact a concrete block manufacturing plant currently stood on the land. Latter then made a threat that he knew would get the attention of local residents. The attorney threatened to build three bungalows on the property and rent them to African Americans. Residents let Cameron build the icehouse. They preferred horses and men hauling ice on residential streets to African American neighbors. The following December, the Southwest Federation of Improvement Clubs met at the Clearing Town Hall at 5634 West Sixty-third Street and announced that they hoped to prohibit "colored folks" from moving into any Southwest Side neighborhood and called for the imposition of racial covenants. Ironically enough, in February 1929 the Chicago Lawn Presbyterian Church at Sixty-second and St. Louis observed Lincoln's birthday by hosting "Inter-Racial Sunday," inviting black ministers and an African American quartet to pray together with neighborhood whites. Sing, preach, and pray they could, but African Americans could not live in Chicago Lawn in the 1920s.[10]

Black Metropolis

Restrictive covenants, contracts signed by white homeowners who agreed to neither sell nor rent to blacks, became popular in the 1920s in order to control racial change in the city, as they made aesthetic, architectural, and especially racial restrictions possible. In the 1920s, covenants, along with zoning and subdivision regulations, developed as key ways to control development of all sorts both in the city and suburbs. For African Americans this meant that much of the city's residential market would be closed to them, as racial covenants covered middle-class white areas across the city. In 1926, the Supreme Court dismissed *Corrigan v. Buckley* and upheld these private segregation agreements. In the fall of 1927, the Chicago Real Estate Board sent speakers across the city to promote such agreements. Within a year, these covenants stretched across the South Side. Even suburbanites signed the agreements, as developers made such language routine in contracts. Working-class districts generally did not have racial restrictive covenants, as they did not attract middle-class blacks and the threat of violence discouraged African Americans from looking for housing in these areas.[11]

While violence and restrictive covenants limited housing options for African Americans, they continued to build their community within the boundaries of a segregated Chicago. One thing proved obvious: the growing black population needed more housing. Generally speaking, after the 1919 race riot the Chicago Real Estate Board, while limiting black housing options, did recognize the need for a larger area of black housing generally in the area between Cottage Grove and Wentworth Avenues as far south as Sixty-third Street, along with the Lake Street area on the West Side. Whites fled these districts in the early 1920s. In 1920, blacks made up 15 percent of the inhabitants of the South Side's Washington Park community; a decade later the neighborhood's population had increased by nearly six thousand residents, and African Americans constituted 92 percent of the population. State Street remained the social class border in Washington Park, as the African American middle class moved into the better housing in the eastern portion of Washington Park.

Just to the north in Grand Boulevard, racial change had begun earlier, but still in 1920 blacks comprised only 32 percent of the community area's populace of 87,005. Irish and Jews still lived here in large numbers. Ten years later, the ghetto solidly claimed Grand Boulevard as its population rose to 103,256 with African Americans making up 94.6 percent of the population. Grand Boulevard's borders stretched from the New York Central and Rock Island Railroad tracks on the west to Cottage Grove on the east, and from Pershing Road (Thirty-ninth Street) on the north to Fifty-first Street on the south, and it provided the core of the expanding Bronzeville community. These two districts in many ways set the pattern for racial turnover in the city after 1919. The black middle class desired better housing and moved into areas abandoned by the white middle class. Despite Caucasian resistance, racial change occurred rapidly. White Chicagoans hoped that the restrictive covenants would limit black residential expansion.[12]

Excluded from the wider city, African Americans attempted to build their own city on Chicago's South Side. Black leaders built institutions that helped to create the "Black Metropolis" or "Bronzeville." Much like the European immigrant groups, Chicago's African Americans set down the foundations for many complex institutions on the South Side. At the turn of the century Chicago had a dozen black churches; fifteen years later the number had doubled, and black churches stood as the oldest institutions in Bronzeville. Black Chicagoans organized Quinn Chapel (AME), Chicago's oldest black church in 1847. Three years later, black Baptists founded Xenia Baptist Church (renamed Zoar Baptist in 1860). In 1850, other African American Baptists founded Mount Zion Baptist Church, and it soon combined with Zoar Baptist to create Olivet

Baptist Church. This church played a central role in the Great Migration, acting as a central clearinghouse for southern migrants searching for jobs and housing. In the 1920s, Olivet had some ten thousand parishioners, called itself the largest Protestant church in the world, and along with Quinn Chapel maintained preeminence among Chicago's black residents. As other churches quickly established themselves in Bronzeville, class relations often played themselves out in these houses of worship, which ranged from the well-established Protestant congregations to small storefront churches.

Secular institutions also grew in Bronzeville. Provident Hospital, founded by Dr. Daniel Hale Williams in 1891, was the most ambitious black secular institution in the city. Originally conceived as an integrated hospital, the realities of race in the early twentieth century meant that Provident would develop as an almost entirely black institution. By 1916, African Americans made up all of the nurses with the exception of the supervisor and almost all of the doctors. Women's clubs, the YMCA, the Illinois National Guard Armory, and the Douglass Center all served the community providing institutional resources in Bronzeville.[13]

Other types of businesses also flourished on Bronzeville's streets: groceries, barbershops, haberdasheries, and other small businesses lined the busy avenues. Taverns and nightclubs gave the Black Belt much of its character. By the 1920s, the Stroll along State Street south from Thirty-fifth Street went into decline, and African American entertainment venues moved southward to Grand Boulevard, and soon Forty-seventh Street east from State to South Parkway became the entertainment mecca for the community. The first large commercial dance hall for Bronzeville, the Savoy Ballroom on South Park Way (King Drive), opened on November 23, 1927. In 1928, the Regal Theater opened; the 3,500-seat movie house, part of the Balaban and Katz chain, provided a home for generations of black entertainers as it featured both live stage shows and motion pictures.

Chicago quickly became the focal point for a new type of urban music, jazz. Popular belief has it that New Orleans jazz musicians began to come to Chicago only after the closing of the infamous Storyville red light district, by the U.S. Navy in mid-November 1917. In reality, New Orleans bordellos and dance halls simply dispersed into other parts of the city; musicians had no impetus to flee the city. Chicago attracted African American jazz musicians on its own merits as a city. Chicago simply offered more opportunities for black musicians, especially during and after World War I, as the Great Migration changed the complexion of much of the South Side.

The *Chicago Tribune,* never afraid to echo or amplify the prejudices of an era, proclaimed as early as 1906 that "the Negro has a future in music." While the newspaper was probably referring to the minstrel shows and vaudeville acts familiar to whites, it also indicates that the entertainment industry presented

Figure 77. Chicago's Black Metropolis even fielded its own major league baseball team, the Chicago American Giants pictured here in 1905. (SDN-009529, Chicago Daily News negatives collection, Chicago History Museum.)

a socially acceptable career for African Americans. White prejudices acted to create a nightlife African American world on the South Side as black and white promoters played up the Black and Tan fantasies of the exotic other. For black musicians, this world provided an outlet for their talents, and for entrepreneurs it provided an excellent investment.

Black business investors were banned from many investment opportunities, so they focused an unusual amount of energy on the gambling and entertainment business. Twentieth-century jazz was intimately connected with these associations, including the so-called sporting life. Cabaret life, first on the Stroll and then later in Grand Boulevard, proved to be attractive, and an integrated "Sporting" fraternity provided much of the audience for these businesses. Many Black and Tans, clubs that catered to a racially mixed clientele, opened in the city. The popularity of the clubs made the Stroll and later Forty-seventh Street twenty-four-hour destinations. Poet Langston Hughes commented that "midnight was like day," when he visited Thirty-fifth and State Street in 1918.

While outsiders often pointed to vice in these establishments, the Black and Tans did not sell vice as much as the hint of interracial sensuality. After the 1919 race riot some of the Black and Tans stopped welcoming white customers and became African American neighborhood institutions. Others were Black and Tans only in early morning hours when whites would go "slumming" on the South Side.

The nightclubs also often tied themselves to local Republican Party politics. Since the Civil War, the vast majority of African Americans supported the GOP, and the party of Lincoln, the "Great Emancipator," held their loyalty well into the 1930s. William Hale Thompson, who owed much to black voters, often looked the other way when it came to the Black and Tans just as he ignored white organized crime. In 1919, Virgil Williams held the "Big Second Ward Harmony Dinner" at his Royal Gardens dance hall on the South Side, where he feted both black and white politicians. When the Republican Party held its national convention in Chicago he turned the Royal Gardens over to the politicians as an entertainment center. In return Thompson protected South Side speakeasies, and while overworked federal agents sometimes closed the joints, Thompson kept them going with the quick issuance of licenses to operate, mostly as "soft drink" parlors.

By 1926, despite the opposition of white unions, African American musicians began to be hired by downtown hotels and clubs. Louis Armstrong played at the famous Blackhawk Restaurant on Wabash Avenue. Clubs like the College Inn and Bal Tabarin featured jazz. While blacks could perform at white clubs, they remained closed to African American customers. Segregation persisted and fostered the growth of a separate black musical movement on the South Side, creating a very intricate form of urban jazz often influenced by the diverse culture of Chicago.

Jazz musicians symbolized the urban elite for African Americans coming to Chicago. They dressed in elegant tuxedos, as opposed to the shabby way that blacks had been portrayed in vaudeville. Men like Earl Hines represented the finest in style and sophistication to both black and white audiences. The cosmopolitan nature of cabaret performances required musicians to be on time, to be well dressed, and to remain awake on stage. One African American orchestra leader, Dave Peyton, never tired of pointing out bad habits to be avoided by his musicians, including lateness, smoking and drinking, and loud behavior. Earl Hines fined his players the extremely high fee of $5 per minute if they were late. Cabaret musicians learned quickly to pay attention to details and enforce strict codes in Chicago cabarets. These rules for musicians reflected in many ways the new industrial codes imposed by mass industrialism on workers in Chicago's factories as well as other business establishments.[14]

Popular Culture

While the Black and Tans attracted the "sporting crowd" to Bronzeville, the 1920s brought about many changes in the way that all Americans entertained themselves. A new urban-oriented mass culture developed based on older forms of entertainment revolutionized by new forms of communication technology. Movies became instantly popular, attracting crowds. Major Loop theaters drew thousands weekly to see the films and lavish stage shows that often included the best vaudeville performers. In 1927, a weekly average of 46,000 patrons attended the Chicago Theater, while 22,700 visited the McVickers and 43,400 watched the "shows" at the Oriental. Ethnic and working-class culture had been locally situated in Chicago's neighborhoods. In Pilsen and other working-class districts, local troupes of actors put on plays dealing with local class and ethnic concerns in venues like Thalia Hall on Eighteenth Street. From early on, German, Czech, and other groups created theaters in local halls, saloons, and schools. With the development of the nickelodeon in the early 1900s and large neighborhood movie palaces by the 1920s much of this localized culture gave way to a broad mass popular culture. Movie houses brought "American" entertainment to ethnic groups newly cut off from their homelands by immigration restriction. Theaters such as the Alvin Theater on Chicago Avenue, the Peoples Theater on West Forty-seventh Street, and the Arrow Theater on Fullerton Avenue entertained generations of ethnic working-class Chicagoans. Some occasionally screened ethnic films, but standard American films helped to create a popular culture that transformed American cities.

In addition to the major theaters, many smaller movie houses opened in the Loop such as the Bijou Dream Theater, the Band Box Theater (for women only), and the Adams Theater, which figured prominently in two early civil rights cases. The Adams refused to seat African Americans on the main floor. In 1923, the NAACP sued, and the theater and owners agreed to seat blacks, but once again a civil rights violation occurred as an usher attempted to force African Americans to sit in the first row. While the court cases had mixed results, they presaged court actions that would later bring down segregation.[15]

Records and radio were part of the communications revolution as well as film. The city's first radio station, KYW, owned by Westinghouse, opened in 1921. The following year on April 13, the *Chicago Daily News* and the Fair Store went on the air with WGU, later renamed WMAQ. In turn, in 1924, the Tribune Company operated WGN Radio, with its call letters reminding Chicagoans of the newspaper's masthead motto, "World's Greatest Newspaper."[16] Others quickly followed, as the city became a major broadcasting center. Like local theater, radio included ethnic broadcasting, and the airwaves brought religious, ethnic, and cultural programming into Chicago's homes. Eventually WCFL, the voice of the Chicago Federation of Labor, brought class issues to listeners' radio. The new form of communication proved very flexible and democratic in its early days. Programming such as that by Bruno "Junior" Zielinski entertained ethnic communities. Zielinski played a hilarious Chicago Polish American character, the son, in a program called *Kłopoty Rodziny Siekierków* (Troubles of the Siekierki Family) on radio station WEDC.[17] The 1930s would be the heyday of this type of programming as Yiddish, Lithuanian, German,

Czech, African American, and other ethnic broadcasts filled the airwaves of Chicago and other big cities. While the radio maintained this local ethnic culture, it also introduced national programming that brought new ideas into Chicago's parlors and eventually undercut much of the ethnic and class-based programming. Still, in the 1920s and 1930s, ethnics resisted the national mass culture, and for a while at least the new technologies provided fruitful outlets for the continuation of local entertainment traditions.

For male youth, baseball united the masses from neighborhood sandlots to the big league stadiums. In 1901, the new American League joined the National League, founded in 1876. Two years later, the two league champions played the first baseball World Series, and a mere three years after that the two Chicago teams, the White Sox and Cubs, found themselves competing against each other for the championship. But it was Babe Ruth's Yankees in the 1920s that truly electrified the American public and brought about the renewal of the game after the disastrous 1919 Black Sox scandal. The Yankees won six American League pennants in the 1920s and three world championships. Charles Comiskey found it profitable and therefore necessary to put up an upper deck in the outfield at Comiskey Park in order to hold the crowds that wanted to see the White Sox play Ruth and the Yankees.

But Chicago would soon have a champion of its own: in 1929 the Chicago Cubs won their first National League pennant in eleven years. This proved to be the beginning of a second golden age for the Cubs, who had dominated baseball in the 1880s and 1890s, as they would make a habit of winning a pennant every three years after that through the 1930s. That 1929 team seemed cursed as Hack Wilson lost a ball in the sun and the Cubs blew an eight-run lead in the eighth inning of the fourth game losing 10 to 8. Connie Mack's Philadelphia Athletics won that World Series in five games over manager Joe McCarthy's Cubs. Wilson's miscue brought back memories of the 1918 World Series when Cub right fielder Lefty Tyler dropped a line drive in the second inning of the sixth and final game allowing two Red Sox runs to score. Unfortunately the team would be plagued with misplays throughout the century.[18]

The Automobile

In 1913, Henry Ford transformed both the automobile industry and the nation when he introduced the assembly line at his Highland, Michigan, plant. The Model-T quickly became a household word as America began its long love affair with the motorcar. The automobile was now affordable to the great middle class and not totally beyond the reach of some workers. While few understood the impact of the modern assembly line in 1913, the American city would never be the same.

Chicagoans had been early proponents of the new horseless carriage. In 1895, automotive pioneer J. Frank Duryea won America's first auto race. The event, organized by H. H. Kohlsaat, the publisher of the *Chicago Times-Herald,* was originally to run from Chicago to Milwaukee, but bad roads north of Racine, Wisconsin, necessitated a less ambitious contest. The race ran from Jackson Park to Evanston and back, on Thanksgiving Day. Only two cars completed the entire course, and Duryea won the $5,000 prize, with an average speed of seven miles per hour over the 54.36-mile distance. Despite a snowstorm that dumped a foot of snow on Chicago, he accomplished this on a mere 3.5 gallons of gas. In conjunction with the race in what may have been the first automobile show, a modest exposition of twelve automobiles took place in the Studebaker Company wagon showroom at 623 South Wabash.[19]

Some farsighted souls saw the automobile as a great benefactor for the city. Alderman Charles F. Gunther made various proposals in 1897 that would give the automobile and the horseless omnibus preeminence on city streets. As part of the street railway franchise renewal, he proposed asphalt-paved streets. The alderman prophesized streets cleared of horses and their voluminous, reeking droppings, streets on which people and goods moved quickly and quietly by rubber wheeled vehicles. Gunther stated, "The horseless carriage solves the problem in my mind." Gunther called Chicago the Paris of America, implying that like the French capital it should take the lead in the new mode of transportation. E. P. Ingersoll, editor of the *Horseless Carriage,* visualized city streets eventually rid of streetcar tracks, what he called "an incalculable improvement."[20]

Chicago became an early center for the manufacture of automobiles. In the first decade of the new century, entrepreneurs formed twenty-eight companies that produced sixty-eight models of horseless carriages, and the city became known for developing the popular "highwheeler." Sears, Roebuck and Company even sold the automobiles through their catalog. Chicago's automobile industry declined by World War I, but in turn the city became more important for the production of automobile parts.[21]

As the new century went on, the automobile, largely used as a toy by the wealthy for Sunday drives through the park, began to present both an opportunity and a problem for Chicagoans. Like many new inventions, local government initially did not know how to deal with the new contraption. Many still classified the automobile with the bicycle, which seemed to be a much more viable transportation alternative. Bicycle drivers insisted on better paved roads and brought these issues before local and state governments. In 1899, bicyclists won a special bicycle path along Archer Avenue out to Worth. Wealthy automobile owners now joined the bicyclists in their demands for asphalt-paved roads rather than Chicago's usual cobblestone streets. Early automobiles backfired frequently, startling both horses and pedestrians. Drivers showed little courtesy to pedestrians, often parking on sidewalks.

In June 1899, wealthy drivers planned an automobile club to promote their interests. They took as its prototype a similar Parisian club. Organizers hoped to defend automobile interests against what they considered to be "unprogres-

Figure 78. This 1908 photograph portrays presumably the first automobile in the Englewood neighborhood. (Chicago Public Library, Special Collections and Preservation Division.)

sive" actions of the South Park Board, which had banned the automobile from its streets and boulevards. Robert Shaw and C. E. Woods (the general manager of the Fischer Equipment Company, an early car manufacturer) organized the club, and about fifty members joined at first. The overturning of the South Park Board's decision presented the first goal of the club. On June 16, 1899, South Park Police stopped Montgomery Ward and Robert Shaw from driving on Michigan Boulevard. Others, however, flaunted the law, and police made no attempt to stop them.

The city and state attempted to regulate the new devices and their owners. In 1899, Mayor Carter Harrison II called for the corporation counsel to draw up an ordinance to provide for the examination and licensing of all persons who intended to drive a car through the streets or parks. The *Chicago Tribune* lauded the mayor, pointed to a similar law in Paris, and claimed that some day drivers would have to be regulated as to speed and skill. It further editorialized that "it is certainly desirable for the general public that none but competent men be allowed to manipulate the new vehicles, especially for the next few years, while the Chicago horse is becoming reconciled to the new order of things." The ordinance requiring a license in Chicago went into effect on May 8, 1900. Four women held licenses, including Julia Bracken, the first female to hold a license in Chicago.

Figure 79. This advertisement for the Chicago School of Motoring appealed to female drivers. (Postcard, Author's Collection.)

Chicago drivers protested strongly when, in December 1902, the city council called for each motorcar to be marked with numbers so that they could easily be identified, claiming the licenses would disfigure their automobiles. Other cities were far ahead of Chicago in requiring license plates in some form. Cab driver A. C. Banker led the fight against the city ordinance. In 1905, the Chicago Automobile Club drafted a law to be presented to the legislature in Springfield. It called for the regulation of speed and for all cars to be licensed by the secretary of state. The law set the speed limit at ten miles per hour in crowded districts and fifteen miles per hour in less populated areas and set fines and provided for the revocation of the new state licenses. The proposed law also called for slow vehicles to stay to the right and let faster vehicles pass them on the left. This nuance was aimed at farmers who "drive leisurely along the country road and refuse to get out of the way for fast automobiles." Apparently city residents out for drives in the country did not want to be slowed down by locals. By 1907, the secretary of state issued licenses to motorists as local government continued to look for ways to deal with the new machines. Problems continued, as some reported that over five thousand unlicensed vehicles operated in Chicago in 1910. Part of the problem was the lack of legislation that required licenses be displayed. With both the city and the state licensing automobiles, and the difficulties with enforcement, the dilemma continued. In 1913, the Illinois Supreme Court found the state licensing law invalid. While the state law remained in limbo, the court in turn upheld Chicago's licensing fees. By 1916, the state law had been rewritten and a $6.00 fee attached to state licenses. That year the state reported nearly 250,000 licensed vehicles in Illinois.[22]

In 1901, the city hosted its first Chicago Automobile Show at the Coliseum on South Wabash. That year only one out of every ten thousand residents owned a car. It was the first large-scale indoor exhibition of automobiles held in the city. The first night, Friday, March 22, was by invitation only, with twenty thousand persons expected to attend. The exposition opened to the public the following evening at 7 p.m. Organizers expected the trade fair to be the largest in the country, with eighty manufacturers displaying their automobiles, and it included an indoor track on which the public could ride in any of the automobiles exhibited. The *Chicago Tribune* predicted that the show would "rival the horse show as a society event." One visitor proclaimed that attendance at the opening was three times greater than the New York show.[23]

Despite the legal and other complications, the city and the nation embraced the automobile. By the 1920s, the automobile seemed to be everywhere. Burnham and Bennett's 1909 plan, with its wide boulevards and plans for the widening of Michigan Avenue, encouraged the new form of transportation. Newspapers included special columns devoted to motoring, such as J. L. Jenkin's "Motordom Today" in the *Chicago Tribune.* In January 1925, as the nation entered the boom years of the 1920s, Eugene S. Taylor, manager of the Chicago Plan Commission, addressed a session of the American Roadbuilders Association at the Congress Hotel. Taylor, a proponent of bigger and better roads, called for a highway circling the city. The city planner optimistically pointed to the advancements already made in Chicago on behalf of the motorist. In spite of his claim of a fifty thousand annual increase in the number of autos on Chicago streets, Taylor felt the city did a good job handling the growing congestion. He pointed out that the new Michigan Avenue Bridge that opened in 1921 had increased traffic flow 700 percent. Frank T. Sheets, chief highway engineer, also addressed the meeting and spoke on state roads emphasizing the importance of maintenance. A "Good Roads Show" opened in the Coliseum in conjunction with the convention. Organizers expected some twenty thousand spectators to visit the exhibit. Two hundred and eighty exhibitors brought tons of heavy machinery and steam shovels to display to the public. At a growth rate of 137 new cars on city streets every day Chicago had entered the auto age with gusto.[24]

H. J. Rosenberg, president of the Chicago-Flint Company, proclaimed later that month, "The automobile has changed the complexion of the civilized world." Industrialist C. H. Wills, president of Wills-Sainte Claire, Inc., went even further, proclaiming the auto as a "priceless boon to mankind." He pointed to the growth of the city's suburban fringe. "Without the motor car, what is now endless outlying city property would still be farmland." Wills claimed that, even more importantly, the car had "dynamited" the farmer out of his isolation and increased his wealth. Wills maintained that the automobile transformed human nature and made America "just one big town." He went on to assert that the motorcar meant to the nation what the circulation of blood meant to the human body and even made reference to the founding fathers, claiming that the new transportation form helped put into practice the "theory of Adams

Looking South from Bridge, Michigan City, Ind.
Crowd Gathering to witness the Arrival
of Passenger Boat from Chicago.

Figure 80. Michigan City, Indiana, and the surrounding dune lands provided Chicagoans with a nearby vacation destination. Pictured here are automobiles waiting for the passenger boat to arrive from Chicago in the days before well-paved interstate roads. (Postcard, Author's Collection.)

and Hancock and Jefferson." The car had united the country and fulfilled the prophecy of its founders, or so proponents argued.

While such proclamations from industry leaders were to be expected, the down side of the automobile also soon appeared. Lincoln Park Commissioners found themselves overwhelmed by the traffic problem in the park, which provided the only direct route between the Loop and the residential areas of the North Side. From 7 a.m. until 7 p.m., an hourly average of 3,506 cars made their way along Lincoln Park's Lake Shore Drive. The traffic on Stockton Drive inside Lincoln Park amounted to a minimum of 1,544 cars per hour for a total of over 5,000 cars passing through the park every hour. Motorbuses added to the congestion. In 1924, 1,420 cars were damaged in accidents in the park and boulevards of the Lincoln Park System. Lincoln Park had originally been laid out for horse carriage pleasure driving only, so park commissioners had to redesign it. In the eight years before 1925, they widened entrances to the park, eliminated many of the curves, and created a beach drive from Ohio to Webster Street, with plans for a continuous drive to extend all the way to Irving Park Boulevard. Plans included connecting the Lincoln Park System with the South Parks to allow motorists coming from the South Side to the North Side to avoid the Loop.

The West Side also suffered from congestion. In 1929, the West Park Board sought to widen and pave Augusta Boulevard. Local taxpayers revolted against the assessments that would come with the project, claiming that more traffic actually hurt land values. Observers pointed out that autos even clogged side streets. The West Side apparently had the slowest boulevard traffic in the city, according to tests conducted by the Chicago Motor Club. Some saw a proposed elevated expressway, the Austin-Kinzie elevated boulevard, as an answer to at least part of the problem.[25]

The car presented trouble beyond congestion by the mid-1920s, when it was called the "most potent agent of violent death" in Cook County. In 1924, 684 men, women, and children died in Cook County as a result of motor accidents, a reduction of 5 percent from the 1923 record of 721 deaths. County Coroner Oscar Wolff blamed speed as a major reason for the deaths. Wolff proposed a bill calling for the "mental and physical examination" of all motorists in Illinois. He pointed out that East Coast states had licensed all motorists and death rates had declined. Coroner Wolff said that the pedestrians killed tended to be either older or very young and that a small bit of caution on the part of motorists would save lives. He warned that cars should slow down when children were near.[26] The issue of auto-related deaths continued throughout the 1920s. The numbers continued to rise until 1929, when there was a 6 percent downturn. That year, 1,022 people died in Cook County from auto accidents. In 1927, the figure stood at 969, and in 1928 a record 1,089 died because of automobiles. As a result of the 1928 fatality numbers, Chief Justice Harry Olson of the municipal court reopened traffic court early in 1929. Olson pointed out that "motorists are killing three times as many persons as murderers." The decrease in 1929 was due to a sharp decline in city accidents that had numbered 916 in 1928 and fell to 799 the following year. Coroner Bundesen, echoing his predecessor, claimed that safety education had helped. Accidents also frequently occurred at railroad crossings where drivers were expected to stop and get out of their cars to see if trains were approaching.[27]

By 1928, the growth of the automobile had reshaped the American industrial scene. In that year the industry (manufacturers and parts) took the lead from railroads as the largest user of steel. The following year purported to be an even greater year for the industry. Predictions at the New York Auto Show early in January of the production of 6 million cars in 1929 did not seem out of line as Jazz Age prosperity boomed. Chicagoans in turn looked forward to their own automobile show later that month. Indeed, despite predictions of a downturn in demand, that following October automobile sales set a new record. This would come to an end as the optimism of the 1920s screeched to a halt with the stock market crash that October.

In response to demands for better roads, the state imposed the first tax on gasoline in 1929. Illinois was the last state in the union to charge a tax on gaso-

Figure 81. Trucks quickly replaced horse-drawn wagons. Here trucks of the Emil J. Paidar Company at 1214–18 North Wells Street, makers of barber chairs and beauty parlor equipment, are loaded with merchandise in 1925. (Photograph by Hoffman; ICHi-16826, Chicago History Museum.)

line. Many gas stations were found near the borders of Wisconsin and Indiana because Illinois attracted drivers from taxed states. Chicago fought the gas tax, but lost; at midnight, August 1, 1929, Illinois legislators imposed a three-cent tax on a gallon of gasoline. This resulted in a run on gasoline stations the night before. Motorists filled their tanks, as well as tins and drums, with fuel as gas stations reported record sales.[28]

Despite the growth of automobile ownership, the Chicago area still relied heavily on mass transit in the 1920s. The Loop remained the center of this vast system that had developed since the introduction of the omnibus in the nineteenth century. For all of its problems, the city maintained a serviceable mass transit system. Electric streetcars cruised up and down Chicago's major business streets. Motorbuses that for the most part made their way on the city's boulevard system joined them. The "L" roared overhead, while proposals for a new subway system seemed to come and go every year. A vast system of electric interurbans, largely in place before 1915, connected Chicago with outlying suburbs and cities from Milwaukee in the north and DeKalb in the northwest to Joliet and Aurora in the southwest, even reaching out to South Bend, Indiana. Chicagoans could make the journey all the way to St. Joseph, Michigan, and as far north as Janesville or Watertown, Wisconsin, by switching between interurbans. On the South Side, one interurban connected the far south suburbs to

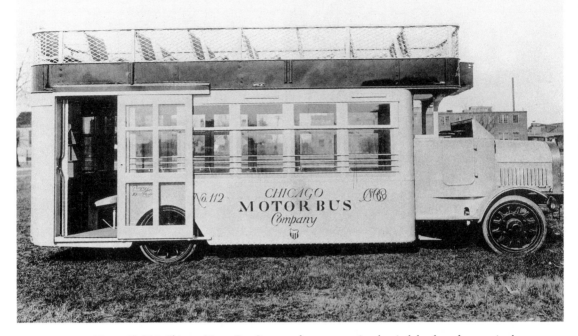

Figure 82. This Chicago Motor Bus Company began to service the city's boulevard system in the 1920s. Other forms of mass transit had always been kept off these thoroughfares. (Chicago Public Library, Special Collections and Preservation Division.)

the intersection of Archer and Cicero Avenues, while yet another tied Kankakee to the huge neighborhood shopping district at Sixty-third and Halsted. Passengers could then take other forms of mass transit into the Loop.[29]

Many commuter railroads also knit the region together. By the 1880s, fifteen railroads fanned out from the city to the ever-growing suburbs. In 1925, as eighteen commuter railroads asked for a 20 percent increase in fares, Chicago area residents reacted sharply. One commuter lauded the Illinois Central Railroad (ICRR) for electrifying its line and asked that others follow suit. He said, "Take your 20 percent, but give us electrification." Suburbanites felt that the old smoke belching steam railroads needed to be replaced by modern clean modes of transportation. Records from the ICRR showed that electrification actually made the trip downtown substantially faster for commuters and also eliminated the dirty and obnoxious smoke that covered passengers in soot. City dwellers joined with suburbanites to protest the fare increase. When railroads tried to increase revenues by posting advertisements in the cars, commuters complained again. The Northwestern Railroad took out bundle racks on the coaches so that commuters would have an unobstructed view of ads the advertisers required. What suburbanites had viewed as a right—that is, to sit without their bundles and suitcases crowding them in seats—now seemed to be taken away and at a time that the railroads asked for higher fares. The president of the company quickly rescinded the order, giving in to north suburban

Figure 83. By 1915, a large system of electric interurban trains connected Chicago with other midwestern towns and cities. Pictured here is the Aurora, Elgin, and Chicago interurban train about 1907. (Postcard, Author's Collection.)

protest. Meanwhile, the railroads continued to complain that they lost money on commuter trains. That the automobile cut into passenger numbers on the railroads is probable, although numbers did not show this in the 1920s. In reality, suburban growth initially offset those who left the commuter lines to drive to work. The automobile, however, began to expand suburbs not connected to the old rail lines. As early as 1916, versions of suburban automobile shopping malls appeared with the construction of architect Howard Van Doren Shaw's Lake Forest Market Square, a blend of retail and office space along with residential apartments and extensive parking facilities, and the Spanish Court in Wilmette (1926). By 1930, one out of every eight Chicagoans owned a car. It would take time, but the internal combustion engine redefined the Chicago region.[30]

The impact on leisure and entertainment began almost immediately. The car gave individuals unprecedented mobility. Chicagoans drove out to roadhouses on the edge of the city for both licit and illicit activities. Several suburbs catered to clienteles who might act differently under the watchful eyes of city neighbors and Chicago police than they would in the "country" settings of suburban Calumet City, Cicero, or Burnside. Roadhouses along Archer, Ogden, and Milwaukee Avenues began to attract the "sporting" crowd with illegal alcohol, gambling, and prostitution. Parents worried about "car" dates and the sexual morals of their children who were now courting away from the family porch or parlor.

Gangsters were a more immediate concern. It is hard to imagine the Capone gang without automobiles. Automobiles made drive-by shootings possible. The legendary 1929 St. Valentine's Day massacre occurred in a Clark Street garage. John "Dingbat" Oberta, the so-called inventor of the "one-way" ride, obviously

Figure 84. Pictured here are both the old steam-powered engine and the new electric trains of the Illinois Central Railroad in the mid-1920s. (Chicago Public Library, Special Collections and Preservation Division.)

depended on the automobile. (In the end rival gangsters gunned down Oberta and his driver Stanley Malaga at 103rd and Roberts Road in 1930.) Hooligans who could not afford their own automobiles often committed taxi murders. Stockyard labor leaders John Kikulski and Stanley Rokosz both died after being attacked by thugs who arrived and departed in taxis.

Gangland

Chicago's reputation as the gangster capital of America developed in the 1920s. In 1927, William E. Dodd, a historian at the University of Chicago, told his audience at the LaSalle Hotel that Chicago now reaped the results of its history of looking the other way when it came to lawbreakers. Dodd claimed that the tradition of stealing from the Indians, the state's later claim it could ignore federal laws, and the manipulation and corruption of the municipal government by nineteenth-century robber barons had all resulted in a pervasive atmosphere of corruption. "Immigrants read the screaming headlines telling of lawless actions. They tried to break the laws and got away with it. Of all the places in the Middle West, all these influences for lawlessness are strongest in Chicago. Where Crime is common, crime grows."[31] That same year Edward R. Litsinger, a candidate for mayor, called the city the nation's "Crime Capital." The city had seen a 93 percent increase in murders. He pointed to politics as the source of corruption, especially the candidacies of Mayor Thompson and State's Attorney Robert E. Crowe. Certainly crime and politics had long been connected in Chicago. During Thompson's first two administrations, city hall protected vice. When William Dever won the mayor's office in 1923, he declared war on beer runners and other gangsters, which resulted in a wild outbreak of violence both between gangsters and between police and the various gangs that ruled Chicago's underworld. In his 1927 reelection campaign Thompson pledged a wet city, continuing what Dodd had characterized as a local disrespect for federal laws. Thompson stated in regard to his opponents, "Dever is dry, Litsinger is dry, and Doc Robertson is so dry he never even takes a bath. The Doc used to boast he didn't take a bath in years. But read Thompson's platform—you can't find anything wetter that that in the middle of the Atlantic. It's the only wet platform in the campaign."[32] Thompson now obviously courted many ethnic Chicagoans who had always opposed prohibition.

The arrival of Alphonse Capone from Brooklyn in 1921 proved to be a central event in the growth of organized crime in the city. Even before Capone's arrival, Chicago gangsters began changing the usual nineteenth-century way of doing things. Technology and a new kind of corporate organization revolutionized the everyday lives of mobsters, as the telephone, automobile, and eventually the Thompson submachine gun made life easier for what Chicagoans called the "Outfit." From the time of the Columbian Exposition, Michael Hinky Dink Kenna and Bathhouse John Coughlin controlled vice in the First Ward. When they needed help they often received it from local thugs. In the late 1890s, the duo brought Jim Colosimo into the organization to deal with both the madams and the growing Italian presence in the district. Colosimo, born in Consenza, Italy, quickly made himself at home in Chicago as Kenna and Coughlin's "bagman" or "collector." He also had a parallel career as a street sweeper and union organizer, and quickly moved into the First Ward's power structure and opened Colosimo's Café at 2128 South Wabash Avenue. By 1912, Colosimo controlled the South Side's vice industry. He made friends with opera singer Enrico Caruso and the lawyer and reformer Clarence Darrow, both regular patrons at the café. The gangster-entrepreneur operated mini-brothels all over town, and newspapers estimated that Colosimo garnered $50,000 a month from operating his various "resorts." "Big Jim" lived large, buying mansions staffed by liveried servants for himself and his father. A product of the Gilded Age, he loved the publicity associated with his success in the city's vice industry. Colosimo brought Johnny Torrio from Brooklyn to operate his business while he attended to his flamboyant lifestyle.

Unlike Colosimo, Torrio was an organized quiet man who valued his private family life and preferred to work behind the scenes. He had been a successful gangster in Brooklyn, operating a vast organization behind the facade of the John Torrio Association. His New York neighbors knew Torrio as a small, shy, and "almost dainty" man who ran a successful numbers racket. Few knew that the quiet little man also controlled several brothels and developed a modern businesslike form of racketeering that soon transformed crime across the country. Occasionally Torrio employed a young neighborhood boy named Al Capone to run errands for him. After testing Capone on several occasions, he brought him into his organization. Eventually Capone went to work for another Brooklyn mobster Frankie Yale (Francesco Ioele). Yale introduced Capone to the more violent side of the mob. After a while Capone, now married with a child, went to work in Baltimore as a bookkeeper for the Aiello Construction firm and seemingly left the mob behind him. After his father died in 1920, however, Capone returned to Brooklyn and resumed his relationship with Johnny Torrio, who by this time had decided to work with Colosimo. As in so many other American success stories, Capone moved west to find his fortune.

Torrio quietly and efficiently built his empire in Chicago, even as Colosimo continued his gaudy lifestyle. Colosimo had become involved with a singer named Dale Winter and was so infatuated that he left the running of his business to Torrio. In March 1920, Colosimo divorced his wife and longtime vice partner Victoria Moresco and married Winter. Back in Brooklyn the everdangerous Frankie Yale watched Colosimo's folly and decided to move in on the Chicago organization. On the morning of May 11, 1920, Colosimo said goodbye to his new wife and went to his office trying to catch up with the business he had neglected over the last few months. That afternoon an assailant, probably Yale himself, gunned him down in the lobby of his office building. Four days later, five thousand mourners followed Colosimo's hearse to his final resting place in Oak Woods Cemetery. It was the first of Chicago's many grandiose gangster funerals. While Yale hoped to take over the Chicago organization, Colosimo's death instead solidified Torrio's position.

Colosimo's money went to his father, but Torrio inherited his crime machine and eventually controlled literally thousands of speakeasies, brothels, and gambling houses. Prohibition created a perfect opportunity for Torrio and others to supply the city and the nation with now illegal beer, wine, and spirits. Like other big businessmen Torrio searched to expand his marketplace. His suburban businesses thrived outside of the occasional Chicago crackdowns on vice. Torrio cleared several million dollars a year despite the need to payoff various police forces and political organizations, including Chicago's growing Republican machine under the leadership of Big Bill Thompson. The Brooklyn mobster employed eight hundred people in the Chicago area alone, and in 1921 he brought twenty-two-year-old Al Capone to Chicago to help him control his growing empire.

Capone's brother Ralph arrived in the city the next year. The two Capone brothers operated several of Torrio's brothels, and less than a year later Torrio raised Al Capone to the premier position in his vice empire: as manager of the Four Deuces club in the old Levee District, at 2222 South Wabash Avenue. While Capone now worked as Torrio's partner, with an annual salary of $25,000, he still primarily acted as a pimp. Capone invented a legitimate business as a front and printed business cards that claimed he was a secondhand furniture dealer at 2220 South Wabash. He opened a second office up the street, hidden behind the phony front of one Dr. Brown's office. This doctor's office became the nerve center of the Torrio-Capone machine. Records taken from a raid of Dr. Brown's office in 1924 showed that the Torrio-Capone gang made annual profits of around $3 million (more than $36 million in 2007 dollars).

In 1922, Al Capone moved his wife, mother, and child to Chicago, and the rest of the family soon followed. He bought a modest two-flat on the South Side at 7244 South Prairie, in a neighborhood that had few Italians. Ralph continued to live on the North Side in the apartment he once shared with his brother. Neighbors knew Al Capone as a successful secondhand furniture dealer and the family as big and friendly, with Al often inviting them in for a pasta dinner. Like Torrio, Capone valued his private life and donned the trappings of middle-class respectability.

To avoid unnecessary and unprofitable violence, Torrio had advanced the idea that there was room enough for all the gangs in Chicago. He helped divide the city up into various territories and encouraged peace among the various criminal organizations. Yet neighborhood violence escalated as small-time mobsters took control of local businesses, resulting in the political backlash that helped elect reformer William E. Dever to the mayoralty in 1923. Dever intended to enforce the federal prohibition laws. Warfare quickly broke out between the police and the various gangster organizations, as well between the various gangs. Torrio and Capone decided to move their organization to nearby Cicero. In October 1923, Torrio opened a brothel on Roosevelt Road. Police soon shut it down along with another Torrio operation in Cicero. Torrio, always the practical businessman and peacemaker, sat down with Cicero's gangs and other rivals and worked out an agreement to divide the control of vice in the suburb. Johnny Torrio soon left with millions of dollars for Italy, where he settled his mother in an estate staffed by thirty servants. Capone took over Cicero with the help of his brother Frank. Ralph opened a brothel in nearby Forest Park and control of the western suburban vice trade went to the Capones.

Al Capone made Anton's Hotel his headquarters in Cicero. The Torrio-Capone gang took control of the Hawthorne Race Track and operated speakeasies, brothels, and gambling dens throughout the suburb. His control became complete, even organizing a municipal parade for Peter Aiello, whom Capone

Figure 85. Rogues Gallery photograph of Al Capone, who organized a citywide crime machine in the 1920s, building on the work of his predecessors Johnny Torrio and Big Jim Colosimo. (DN-0094945, Chicago Daily News negatives collection, Chicago History Museum.)

had once worked for in Baltimore as a bookkeeper. The Capones supported the local Republican organization, as Colosimo and Torrio had supported the party in Chicago. The 1924 Cicero elections proved violent as mobsters worked to control the results. County Judge Edmund Jarecki attempted to intervene by deputizing Chicago police to enter Cicero ostensibly to protect the workers at the massive Western Electric plant from gunfire, but the election went by a slight margin to the Capone-backed Republicans. The newly deputized police, in plainclothes and unmarked cars, shot and killed Frank Capone. Dion O'Bannion provided $20,000 worth of flowers for Frank Capone's funeral, one of the most opulent in Chicago's history.

Shortly afterward, Al Capone moved his headquarters in Cicero to the Hawthorne Inn at 4833 West Twenty-second Street just west of the Western Electric plant. The fortress-like Hawthorne Inn symbolized Capone's machine in the suburb. At the age of twenty-five, Capone ruled Cicero and much of Chicago's underworld. Instead of their own guns the Capone organization used Cicero's police to take care of problems. Life seemed to return to normal on the streets of the working-class suburbs. The *Cicero Tribune* carried out a crusade against the gangsters including an expose of Capone's houses of prostitution. Capone eventually purchased control of the newspaper and the crusading editor, Robert St. John, left town after rejecting a bribery attempt and enduring a beating. The *Cicero Tribune* became Capone's house organ under the leadership of Louis Cowen, who later became known as the "King of the Slot Machines." In 1932, assassins killed Cowen as he delivered the proceeds from the Hawthorne Race Track to the organization.[33]

Capone continued to solidify his position in the crime world, especially in Cicero. But on April 27, 1926, unknown assailants gunned down the "Hanging Prosecutor," William H. McSwiggin, in front of a Cicero dive, the Pony Inn, along with two of his friends, John "Red" Duffy and Jim Doherty. All three men were the children of policemen. Edward Hanley, along with William "Klondike" O'Connell and Myles O'Connell, survived the attack. To the public it seemed as if McSwiggin and Capone had known and worked with each other. The brilliant twenty-six year-old assistant state's attorney obviously fraternized with the gangsters from whom he supposedly protected the public. Capone's name immediately surfaced in the investigation, and various Capone brothers were arrested, but Al Capone disappeared. He stayed in self-imposed exile for four months before finally calling the Chicago authorities and giving himself up on July 28, 1926. The gangster was soon cleared of McSwiggin's murder, which remained unsolved.[34]

Gang warfare continued as Capone abandoned Torrio's policy of coexistence and attempted to solidify his control on Chicago's underworld. He endeavored to make peace with Hymie Weiss (Earl Wajciechowski) by offering him control of all beer concessions north of Madison Street. Weiss turned it down, wanting vengeance for the murder of Dion O'Bannion, whom gunmen had killed in his florist shop across from Holy Name Cathedral in 1924. Capone then decided that Weiss also had to die. On October 11, 1926, Weiss crossed State Street south of Chicago Avenue with four companions, lawyer W. W. O'Brien, bootlegger Patrick Murray, politician Benjamin Jacobs, and Sam Peller, their chauffer. Capone's men opened fire from a second-story window. The twenty-eight-year-old racketeer died in a hale of bullets, which scarred the facade of Holy Name Cathedral. Another lavish gangster funeral made Chicago's reputation as the gangland capital of America. Nine days later, Capone called a peace conference at the Sherman Hotel close to City Hall. He first offered Judge John Lyle a chance to act as peacemaker, but the judge turned him down, so Capone turned to Thompson, the former mayor. The conference was a success, and peace was restored.[35]

By 1927, it appeared as though gangsters had taken total control of Chicago. Gang members openly disregarded the law. After being arrested in a police crackdown, Tim Murphy told reporters: "Listen the cops in this town couldn't track an elephant through the snow. I begin to think that the one that pinched me was the original Scotty, the guy that was eating a sandwich and bit his arm down to the elbow before he found out his mistake." Big Tim went on to complain that it seemed to be a big deal to arrest him. He said the policeman who brought him in was a Boy Scout named Sherlock. "He ought to start an agency. If he does I'd hide my watch and see if he can find it."[36]

In April 1927, Big Bill Thompson won the mayoralty for the third time with a plurality of eighty-three thousand votes. The Capone crowd celebrated as their candidate bragged that he would punch the king of England in the nose if he ever came to Chicago.[37] The tumultuous election included stolen ballot boxes as well as the shooting of an election worker during the February primary, and in April two Democratic headquarters in the North Side's Forty-second Ward were bombed. Although no one was hurt, the message was clear: certain parties in the underworld did not want a second Democratic Dever administration.

Even when enforcing the law, Chicago appeared crooked. On the afternoon of April 4, policeman Dan Healy shot Vincent "The Schemer" Drucci, a gangster formerly affiliated with O'Bannion, who had led the gangs that had terrorized other elections. National Guardsmen stood ready to enforce the law on the city's streets as the threat of more violence hung over Chicago. Meanwhile, five thousand Chicago policemen guarded polling places and patrolled the streets. Police arrested Drucci on an order to pick up troublemakers and investigate the break-in into the office of Forty-second Ward Alderman Dorsey Crowe, a supporter of Mayor Dever. The break-in resulted in the killing of a watchman, and rumors abounded that gangsters planned to kidnap Crowe and other Forty-second Ward Dever Democrats. Officer Healy shot Drucci while the gangster was in custody, in a police car taking him to the Criminal Court Building. Drucci and Healy argued, and Healy shot Drucci four times. A coroner's jury found Healy's actions justified and cleared the detective sergeant of any wrongdoing, but Healy testified that he had received eight or nine death threats after the shooting. Having one gangster shot to death while under arrest, even as others ran wild, did not alleviate the reputation for corruption that police had earned.[38]

Violence continued despite the so-called peace conference. In November a huge bomb exploded at 823 West Adams Street—a "resort" operated by the Bertsche-Skidmore-Zuta vice syndicate—supposedly as a warning to the faction not to operate south of Madison Street. Fifteen prostitutes ran out of the wrecked building, along with several male patrons, and the police later arrested several Capone henchmen. Ira Sherman, the operator of the bombed club, said he knew of no reason why anyone would try to put him out of business. Several days later a bomb exploded at John Remus's "soft drink parlor" and restaurant at 5315 West Fullerton Avenue. Remus, the former Republican state representative from the Twenty-fifth District, said the bombing resulted from his refusal to buy alcohol from three men who demanded he buy their product. Bombs later hit the Adams Street resort again, as well as a soft drink parlor at 323 North Ashland. Seven bombs had gone off in the weeklong violence. Meanwhile Al Capone went on a hunting trip. He seemed interested in maintaining his distance from the violence and establishing an alibi as his forces moved on rival gangs.[39]

About two weeks later, Capone announced he was sick of the business and was leaving Chicago, perhaps never to return. The gangster complained, "I've been spending the best years of my life as a public benefactor. I've given people the light pleasures, shown them a good time. And all I get is abuse. . . . Well now that I am going away I guess murder will stop. There won't be anymore booze. You won't be able to find a crap game, even let alone a roulette wheel or a faro game. . . . Public service is my motto. . . . But I'm not appreciated." He then went on to laud Cicero as a fine town. Chicago Police Chief Hughes wished Capone a Merry Christmas and said he would not be angry if Capone never returned. Capone, however, did not leave town for long. By December 18, Capone returned to the city and lived under virtual house arrest in his family's home on South Prairie Avenue. The police had orders to arrest anyone coming in or out of the building. Joe Saltis, the Polish beer runner, sat in a police cell after being arrested in a saloon at Fiftieth and Hermitage in the Back of the Yards neighborhood. Both Capone and Saltis claimed that their constitutional rights had been denied. Meanwhile, a bomb hit the Churndale Creamery, another business operated by the Bertsche-Skidmore-Zuta vice syndicate.[40]

The ongoing gang warfare and the competition between Capone's forces and those allied with the old O'Bannion gang, now led by Bugs Moran, continued. As 1928 came to an end, Capone's bodyguard, "Machine Gun" Jack McGurn (Vincenzo Gebaldi), plotted to start another turf war on behalf of his boss. McGurn had risen quickly in the Capone organization, and Moran's henchmen tried to kill him. By the beginning of 1929, McGurn recovered from the shooting and asked Capone for his blessing to destroy Moran's gang. This vendetta set the stage for the city's most infamous mass killing, the St. Valentine's Day massacre.

McGurn imported killers from out of town to make the hit on the Moran gang. They rented a room across the street from the S. M. C. Cartage Company, at 2122 North Clark Street, where Moran's gang had used the garage as a distribution point for the delivery of liquor and beer. To establish his alibi, Capone rejoined his family at the Palm Island Villa in Florida, but kept in touch by telephone with McGurn until just a few days before the planned attack. McGurn lured the gang to the garage with a promise of a delivery of Canadian whiskey. Capone's men scheduled the hit for 10:30 on the morning of February 14.

At that time, the lookout spotted a man they mistakenly thought was Moran enter the garage. Capone's men arrived in a stolen police car, with two of them dressed in police uniforms. As they entered the building, they announced a police raid and lined the seven men up against the garage wall. The phony police disarmed Moran's men and then opened fire, killing all except Frank Gusenberg who survived despite being shot twenty-two times. Police took him to a hospital where Sgt. Clarence Sweeney attempted to interrogate him before he died. Gusenberg stayed true to the gangster code and refused to talk, stating

"No one—nobody shot me." Capone's men did not get Moran: he had overslept and so survived.

The mass killing chilled Chicago. Newspapers reported that the city's gangsters left town in record numbers. On February 18, the Chicago train deposited at least fifty gangsters in Miami. The *Chicago Tribune* estimated that five hundred hoodlums fled to Florida. The Chicagoans' arrival resulted in the quick inflation of Miami's hotel rates as rooms, paid for in cash, rented at a premium rate. Police never found anyone guilty of the murders that cold February 14 morning. When asked who had killed his associates Moran said, "Only Capone kills like that." Chicago's gang warfare would go on as the 1920s came to a close.[41]

8

Years of Crises

Depression and War

The stock market collapse of Black Thursday, October 24, 1929, signaled the beginning of an unprecedented economic panic and depression that did not end until the outbreak of World War II. The "high" living days of the Roaring Twenties soon turned into the gray somber days of the Great Depression. American institutions, especially the capitalist free market economic system but also democracy, came under question as the country looked for a way out of the economic shambles. Chicago quickly felt the pressure of the financial collapse. By 1930–31, the unemployment situation in the city reached epic proportions, and Chicago struggled for a way out of the crisis. The Great Depression saw the end of Republican control of both local and national governments. Herbert Hoover, who entered the White House in March of 1929, had promised a growing American economy, a promise that proved hollow in the months after the economic crash. Big Bill Thompson, mayor of Chicago, who had attempted to build a Republican political machine, could not adjust to the new economic reality. Meanwhile Anton Cermak, his Democratic rival, lurked in the wings, hoping to build a new permanent Democratic Party majority in Chicago.

Unemployment

Throughout the Great Depression, reliable unemployment statistics proved hard to obtain. The Department of the Census played down the catastrophe, and various reports further muddied the waters; the public, however, clearly understood the problem.[1] Joblessness grew as the city and the nation sank deeper into the economic morass. Almost immediately, the forces of conservative reaction moved against those in the city who attempted to organize the unemployed. The *Chicago Tribune* reported attacks on "communist agitators." Judge Herbert G. Immenhausen fined Albert Goldman, an attorney and leader of a demonstration by the unemployed at City Hall, $100 for whispering in a defendant's ear in his courtroom. The judge made it clear that he did not care for "Russian sympathizers."[2] Several days later, the Chicago Police Department carried out three raids against suspected radicals involved in organizing the city's unemployed, arresting ten men and two women. At 2021 West Division Street, police wrecked the office of so-called Reds, destroying chairs and desks as well as books, printed material, and records. Another police raid at People's Hall, 2457 West Chicago Avenue, closed a screening of a movie about Czar Ivan the Terrible. Police made arrests and questioned people attracted by the free film and made a third raid at the Lithuanian Auditorium, 3133 South Halsted. The *Tribune* claimed that the raids proved that six radicals from the Communist Party of the United States led the unemployed demonstrations at City Hall, tying them to the World War I era labor leader, William Z. Foster, now head of the national Communist Party.[3] In March, the *Tribune* urged caution on police and warned that First Amendment rights should be held sacrosanct but still condemned radical agitators. In June, union printers beat two Communist organizers handing out pamphlets pertaining to the Trade Union Unity League, a group claiming to represent the unemployed. One of the men died, while police reported the other could not identify his assailants. Demonstrations of the unemployed touched a nerve in a city that recalled the Haymarket Affair and the massive labor strikes of the immediate post–World War I years.[4]

Communist organizations had been active in Chicago throughout the 1920s but had little success. The deepening financial crises gave the movement new life. Chicago's working-class neighborhoods were hardest hit. North Side communists gathered at various locations, including the famous Dill Pickle Club, Finnish Workers Hall, Viking Temple, and in numerous ethnic halls run by Scandinavians and Ukrainians. Many attended open-air meetings in Washington Square Park, popularly known as "Bughouse Square." The party organized around various North Side factories, including the Stewert-Warner and Deering plants. On the South Side, massive marches were common. Washington Park provided a meeting ground for communist speakers. In February 1931, three thousand peaceful marchers "of all races and nationalities" marched from Thirty-first and State Street to Fiftieth and Federal Street, where organizers held a giant open-air meeting. Some twenty children led the march carrying banners condemning child labor. The communist Trade Union Unity League called it a "Hunger March." More than one hundred Chicago police kept order along the route. The next year an interracial group marched from Forty-seventh and Federal Street through the stockyard neighborhoods to Forty-third and Ashland Avenue in another massive hunger march. Again a veritable army of police stood by to keep order.[5]

Despite its wide industrial base, Chicago suffered from the worst jobless rate in Illinois. Close to 60 percent of the unemployed men and women in the state lived in Chicago. Between October 1 and October 25, 1930, 22,609 people made applications at free employment bureaus set up by the state government; of these, 12,426 came from Chicago. Less than 25 percent of Chicago's applicants found jobs, compared with two-thirds of downstate applicants who

received work. The city set up ten homeless shelters for unemployed men. Payrolls in the city shrank by 25 percent from 1927 to 1933. Only half of the people employed in manufacturing in 1927 still had a job in 1933. In 1931, Chicago's overall unemployment rate stood at 30 percent, much higher than the national rate, which would hit 25 percent in 1932–33, the worst years of the Depression. African Americans suffered disproportionately, and by 1932, 40–50 percent of Chicago's black workers had no job.[6]

During the early years of the Depression, Chicagoans largely relied on private charity to attempt to deal with poverty. In typical fashion the Edgewater Committee on Unemployment called for all neighborhood organizations to meet at the Trumbull School at Foster and Ashland Avenues to discuss relief on the North Side in October of 1931. The Edgewater meeting was believed to be the first in the city to try and unite all the neighborhood's organizations in their local relief efforts. Dr. M. H. Bickman of the governor's commission on relief efforts, Roy Jacobson of the Workers Committee on Unemployment, and local leaders addressed the meeting. Organizers set the date of the Rogers Park Charity Ball for October 28, and various groups established relief stations. Officials urged churches and schools to take care of their own communities and to refer all others to the Governor's Joint Relief Fund in Chase Park. Meeting organizers hoped to get Governor Emmerson to release public works funds to get people back to work. The Uptown Lions planned to open their own relief station on Leland Avenue to take care of the needy in their community. According to the Lions' plan, anyone with a note from a local pastor, a Lions Club member, or someone of "recognized" standing could get relief at the relief station. Officials of the club said that their method would cut red tape and make it easier for the needy to get relief. The North Shore Hotel Association promised to support the relief station. At this early point, businessmen were still able to help fund local relief efforts. The management of the Adelphi Theater at 7074 North Clark donated 10 percent of its weekday receipts for one week to relief efforts.[7]

On the South Side, Chicago's African American community tried to deal with the dire situation. The economic downturn had hit Bronzeville especially hard. Black leaders planned an outdoor concert to raise relief funds for their needy neighbors, which organizers hoped to hold at Comiskey Park. Congressman Oscar De Priest stressed that Chicago's African Americans had suffered the most from the Depression. He claimed that black Chicagoans had lost

Figure 86. (*Facing*) This view of La Salle Street from the top of the Chicago Board of Trade Building shows the busy urban canyon below. The large art deco building on the left is the Field Building, completed in 1933; it was the last big construction project in the Loop for more than twenty years after the stock market collapse in 1929. (Photograph by Charles W. Cushman; Indiana University Archives, P02220.)

between $6 and $8 million in bank failures. Planners hoped to raise $50,000 in funds to be turned over to the Governor's Unemployment Commission for use in the black community. Black institutions responded to the crisis. Billiken Clubs, youth groups organized in Bronzeville, passed out Christmas baskets and collected toys for poor families, while the Good Shepherd Congregation Church at 5700 South Prairie fed over three hundred men daily at the outset of the Depression. Rev. Harold M. Kingsley's parish offered coffee and bread for breakfast and a full lunch to anyone who came to the church door. Local leaders ran a Relief Station at 5039 South Indiana, supported by Governor Emmerson's Relief Commission. Individuals in Bronzeville worked hard to help the poor. A social worker, Joseph D. Bryan, and his wife distributed 1,600 articles of clothing to the children of poor families during Christmas 1931. The Chicago Church Federation and the Episcopal City Mission sponsored a Christmas party to help the Bryans pass out trousers and other articles of clothing. Bryan told the *Chicago Defender* that over two thousand children had sought help for food, shelter, and clothing over the year.[8]

For workers, the answer to the relief problem was simple: provide work and not charity. On Labor Day, September 7, 1931, more than forty thousand union members marched down Michigan Avenue to Soldier Field calling for more jobs. The parade, which lasted for one and one-half hours, demanded an end to Prohibition as one answer to unemployment. Bystanders cheered placards stating "Give Us Beer and Employ a Million Workers" and "What the Country Needs is a Stein of Real Beer," and a sign carried by the egg inspectors union that read "Prohibition had Reduced the Consumption of Eggs," presumably due to the lack of bars serving pickled and hard boiled eggs to patrons. Horseshoers, elevator operators in uniform, and white-smocked meat cutters marched among the diverse group of workers. The building trades unions' sign proclaimed "Start a Building Program by Remodeling the Slums." The following month on October 31 some fifty thousand marchers, including many communists, again descended on the Loop. Marching from the North, South, and West Sides they gathered at City Hall where a group of seventy met with Mayor Anton Cermak to present their demands while the rest of the demonstrators went on to hear speeches in Grant Park. Cermak promised to try and meet their demands but confessed that there was little he could do.[9]

Despite state, city, and neighborhood efforts to raise funds for relief, the crises proved overwhelming as the flow of money began to dry up. On January 11, 1932, police battled more than three hundred men and women who threatened to storm the Governor's Relief Station at the Abraham Lincoln Center at the intersection of Oakwood Boulevard and Langley Street in Bronzeville. The confrontation resulted in the injury of three policemen and a number of protestors. Rent relief had dried up, and the crowd demanded aid. Afterward members of the International Labor Defense, the League of Struggle for Negro Rights, and the Unemployed Council gathered at 4000 South Federal Street

Figure 87. The financial panic and Great Depression had a direct impact on many local stores and businesses. This is the interior men's furnishings department of the Baer Brothers and Prodie Store in the 1930s. (Chicago Public Library, Special Collections and Preservation Department.)

and met at a communist organization's headquarters. Police swooped down and arrested nineteen of the members. By the summer of 1932, Chicago's relief funds had all but vanished, and relief stations were threatened with closure. Chicago and Illinois officials met with representatives of the Reconstruction Finance Corporation (RFC) to try to negotiate a loan and avoid the closing of all relief stations in Cook County. These stations spent $100,000 per day, and the last $200,000 in state money had already been granted. The state desperately sought a federal government bailout. Much hope involved possible federal legislation that would give an additional $45 million to Illinois for relief.[10]

The state faced constant crises as the economic situation worsened. In October 1932, the Illinois Emergency Relief Commission again reported a lack of funds and the possible closing of relief stations for the winter. The commission lived hand to mouth, barely getting by each month. The RFC asked for additional state legislation to raise funds before it would help Illinois. Talk of a statewide sales tax sparked much of the debate. RFC had already loaned Illinois over $20 million and had set $45 million as the most it would loan any state.

A gasoline tax held little promise for a city already hard hit by the Depression. The numbers simply did not add up, while the situation worsened. During the month of September, unemployment cases grew by five to six hundred per day. The month saw a total increase of over eight thousand cases, and the city council considered a proposal for a jobless parade. The parade was to protest the 60 percent reduction in orders for perishable groceries by relief agencies in response to demands by the state of Illinois to trim costs. They also protested the giving out of ration boxes, a procedure seen as more economical by state agencies rather than letting the unemployed buy their own food.[11]

Chicagoans and Americans in general blamed their woes on the party in power. First in Chicago, and then across the country, the Republican Party found itself on the losing end of the national debate. Chicago's Big Bill Thompson, who had built a machine based on Chicago's refusal to reform, seemed to hope that the Depression might simply go away. In October 1930, Thompson proclaimed the economic downturn as "all psychological." He proposed a Chicago Prosperity Drive to turn things around. A flier distributed by city hall promised to "double business, wipe out bread lines and create jobs for the unemployed." Thompson wanted Chicagoans to spend money in participating stores and take part in a $1 million drawing. Protest by the Association of Commerce and the refusal of School Superintendent William Bogan to publicize the lottery along with a general outcry killed the scheme by year's end. Thompson seemed to hope that parades and rhetoric would encourage voters to reelect him in 1931, but the newspapers kept playing up his relationship with Al Capone and the city's underworld.[12]

Anton Cermak and the Birth of the Democratic Machine

By the stroke of midnight January 15, 1931, sixteen candidates for the mayoralty of Chicago placed themselves on the primary ballot. One surprise appeared on the list, Oscar De Priest, the African American Republican representative from the First Congressional District. Most observers saw this as a political maneuver, perhaps to get more favors for the black community from Republicans. The only opposition to Democratic Boss Anton Cermak was James C. Mullen a boxing promoter. Charles V. Barrett called for unity among the many Republicans to unseat Thompson, now seen as a corrupt holdover from the Roaring Twenties.[13]

Thompson treated the election as a giant show in which he offered the masses bread and circuses. In regard to Capone, Thompson laughed, "I can't see Capone in my lap." He treated the city council to a visit by a cowboy and a cowgirl on horseback. At the Cort Theater, Thompson rode on stage on a horse, and he paraded a menagerie down Chicago's streets with animals symbolizing his various primary opponents. His vaudeville antics had pleased Chicagoans in the past; Big Bill trusted they would work again.[14]

The contest for the Republican nomination finally narrowed to a fight between Thompson and Judge John H. Lyle, whom many Chicago Republicans saw as their only hope to rid city hall of corruption. The *Chicago Tribune* endorsed Lyle in the primary. Newspaper articles proclaimed that all eyes focused on the Republican primary and the struggle against corruption represented by Lyle, who had fought against gangster influence in the Thompson administration. Thompson had an army of payrollers working the streets and getting out the vote and an almost unlimited war chest. Lyle charged that Thompson received funds from Al Capone.[15] Despite corruption and charges that Thompson embarrassed the city, Big Bill won the February 24 GOP primary by over sixty-seven thousand votes. But this time Republicans elected Thompson with only a plurality. Alderman Arthur F. Albert finished a poor third, but captured enough anti–city hall votes to secure the Thompson victory. Cermak won the Democratic primary, as expected, and hoped to capture the mayoralty.[16]

On the evening of March 23 nearly twenty-six thousand Cermak supporters jammed the Chicago Stadium in a mass rally. Speakers accused Thompson of "prejudice, bigotry, and intolerance." Thompson's attempts to "stir up" the German, Irish, and Jewish communities were condemned as a disgrace. Speakers assailed Thompson's "buffoonery" as a scandal and again pointed out that the whole world watched the Chicago election.[17]

Population shifts had remade the Chicago political scene. Republicans had long relied on their white American-born base and on African American votes. The Great Depression eroded GOP support, but perhaps more importantly, the growth of eastern and southern European ethnic communities began to have an impact on elections. In 1930, the foreign born and their children made up 64.3 percent of Chicago's population. This was actually lower than in 1910, but the growing ethnic groups showed a predilection to become citizens and vote Democratic. Czechs, Poles, Jews, and Germans increasingly saw their fates tied to the Democrats; the Depression simply reinforced this decision on the part of thousands of Chicagoans. With the death of Democratic bosses Roger Sullivan and then George Brennan, in 1928 Czech-born Anton Cermak took control of the Democratic Party. He built a masterful coalition that included groups previously outside of the party structure. Many Chicagoans identified with his immigrant biography, and Cermak acted as the ultimate "broker" politician as he worked ethnic wards to create a powerful multiethnic machine. The Irish continued to try and retake control of the Democratic Party, but Cermak always beat them back, even on the eve of the 1931 election.

Cermak had a wide range of weapons, but most importantly he had a strong base in the Czech wards of the Lower West Side. Cermak, after ten years of work for the Twelfth Ward Regular Democratic Organization, won election as a representative in the Illinois General Assembly at the age of twenty-nine. As a state representative from 1902 to 1909 Cermak widened his political base. At this time, many immigrant communities had begun to feel the threat of prohibition. The German community responded by calling a meeting of various immigrant groups including the Czechs and Poles, which resulted in the creation of the United Societies for Local Self Government, an organization devoted to stopping prohibition, both in the neighborhoods of Chicago and nationally. Chicago's precincts could vote themselves dry, and many had already done so as an anti-immigrant measure. Cermak quickly sided with the "wets," those who opposed any attempt to control the consumption of alcohol. The United Societies grew quickly, and members elected Cermak president in 1907. From this point on Cermak was recognized as the most important of the "dripping wets" in the state. He quickly recognized the importance of his position and the power it presented him in Chicago politics, and in 1908 he became committeeman of the Twelfth Ward Regular Democratic Organization. His stature grew, and in 1909 the people of the Twelfth Ward, in a special election to fill a vacancy, elected the former miner and pushcart operator, with a fifth grade education, as their alderman. He attempted to hold both his position in the state legislature and on the city council but finally gave up the legislature in 1910 after being elected to a full term as alderman. Residents of Czech California recognized him as a familiar and respected man. He dabbled in real estate and in the savings and loan business, each of which required face-to-face contacts with his neighbors. All of his enterprises operated on Twenty-sixth Street near Pilsen Park, an important public space for Czechs, Cermak, and the Democrats.

Cermak's prestige and power grew. He ran for increasingly more influential offices, with his eye on city hall. Voters elected him president of the Cook County Board in 1922. Six years later, Cermak lost the race for U.S. Senate, but then he solidified his control of the Cook County Democrats, leading them to their greatest victories since the Civil War. Cermak, a great coalition builder, worked to build a far-reaching alliance of immigrant ethnic Democrats. The Irish, led by Michael L. Igoe, continued to hold out against the Cermak forces, but Cermak outmaneuvered him and his allies and eventually ran virtually unopposed for the Democratic nomination for mayor.[18]

As the campaign proceeded, Cermak showed his wide ethnic coalition. On March 26, 1931, Polish women rallied for Cermak at the Sherman Hotel. Republican women also attended and spoke to the gathering about the need to clean corruption out of city hall. On April 2, labor unions rallied for Cermak. In supporting Cermak in the general election, the *Chicago Tribune* wrote that he promised a "New Deal" for Chicago, more than a year before Roosevelt promised such a New Deal for the country. Just before the mayoral election agents of the state's attorney raided the offices of the city sealer, Daniel Serritella, a known Capone associate. This last scandal sealed Thompson's fate.

On April 7, 1931, Cermak beat Thompson by 191,916 votes, and the West Side Czech who Thompson had referred to as a "Bozo" and a "Bohunk" won all but five wards as Chicago placed the Democrats in power and set the stage for the 1932 presidential election. Thompson carried three African American and two gangster-dominated wards. Even before officials announced the election results, telegrams from across the country and even the world reached the city, congratulating it for throwing Thompson out of office. Cermak's organization had won a handsome victory, and the Chicago Democratic machine was born. Few, however, would have predicted that Democrats would hold city hall from 1931 well into the next century. Importantly, the only Irish ward that delivered among the largest majorities was Joe McDonough's in Bridgeport where the alderman's aide was Richard J. Daley, a young and ambitious Democrat who worked hard for the organization as he made his way through law school at night.[19]

The city's thirty-eighth mayor—and the first immigrant mayor, as well as the first of neither Irish nor Anglo-Saxon ancestry—faced a difficult job. Despite the Democrats' jubilation, Chicago remained deep in economic depression. Cermak realized the vastness of the task. A taciturn man, his only expression of triumph came when he saw his name over the door of the mayor's office. "That's the name my opponent didn't like. But it's there and the majority of people seem to like it." Cermak took office within forty-eight hours and got to work.

Saving the city from fiscal disaster certainly provided the basic theme for the new administration, as Cermak understood the full scope of the economic situation and the crucial need for state and federal aid. By October 1932, about 750,000 Chicagoans had joined the ranks of the unemployed. Of the eight hundred thousand still employed in the city, many only worked part-time. The collapse spanned across the economic spectrum. Rents fell spectacularly as evictions skyrocketed. Riots broke out in neighborhoods as those evicted refused to leave and, often with the help of neighbors, stayed in their apartments. By September 1931, of the city's 228 banks, only fifty-one remained open.[20]

The inability of local government to pay its workers stood out as one symbol of the Great Depression in Chicago. This was especially true for the city's public school teachers. Up until April 1931, teachers still received payment in cash. The April 1 paychecks came in cash in May. By the summer of 1931, the school board offered to pay teachers in scrip. Between April 1 and July 16, 1931, the Chicago School Board had defaulted on twenty-four payrolls. It owed over $15 million in salaries and unpaid bills. While Governor Emmerson's revenue committee attacked the board as wasteful, the board members denied the allegations and blamed the economic downturn. The board issued over $5 million in scrip. Lawyers for the teachers union warned that the scrip might not be legal, although Commonwealth Edison announced that it would accept the Board of Education's scrip as payment for its services. Five hundred members of the teachers' union petitioned the board to stop the proposed scrip plan. Margaret Haley, business representative of the teachers' union, warned merchants not to accept the board-issued paper money.[21]

Dissatisfaction grew as the new school year began in September. On September 29, some seven hundred teachers rallied at Hyde Park High School to protest the scrip system. Henry W. Sumner, principal of the Scott School, acted as temporary chairman of the new organization. Chicago's fourteen thousand teachers had been paid in scrip since April, their plight grew, and area businesses forced teachers to take larger and larger discounts on the nearly worthless paper, giving them pennies on the dollar. Meanwhile, more lawyers joined the chorus complaining about the illegality of the board-issued money. Many teachers took out loans at high interest rates. Others found ingenious ways to get cash for scrip. Finally, the circuit court stopped the payment system after a lawsuit by the Chicago Teachers' Federation. Payless paydays followed. By August 1933, the Chicago School Board owed its employees, including teachers, $26 million in back salaries. Teachers did not sit by idly. On January 4, 1932, the teachers' organization rented the Chicago Stadium and held a huge mass meeting of more than twenty-seven thousand people, including Mayor Cermak and other dignitaries. By January 7, they presented a truckload of petitions to the Illinois State Legislature, asking it to pass laws that would restore public credit so that public obligations could be met and schoolteachers could be paid. The petition laid the hopes of teachers and students alike on the representatives. Over nine hundred thousand voters signed the petitions. In November the *Chicago Daily News* pointed out that the city owed fourteen thousand teachers and four thousand other public school employees over $20 million in back pay. The newspaper reported that on various occasions teachers passed out because of a lack of adequate food. The *Daily News* had organized its Aid to Neediest Families fund in 1928 before the full financial collapse. It reported a great growth in numbers of families needing help.[22]

Besides teachers, firemen, police, and other municipal employees often went unpaid. The city's business community began to put pressure on the city government to bring about an end to the crises in the summer of 1933. The Board of Education approved a retrenchment policy and fired 1,400 teachers, increased the workload of principals and high school instructors, shortened the school year, and closed the city's one junior college. Trustees also abolished the junior high school system, cut the number of kindergartens in half, and cut or eliminated many other programs. Citywide protests followed. Over thirty thousand citizens attended a mass meeting at the Chicago Stadium on July 21 to remonstrate against the changes. In September, the schools opened in confusion. Police patrolled high schools with more than one hundred officers at Phillips High School alone. Ten new high schools opened in former junior high schools, with no programs and no equipment. Chicago's schools had hit rock bottom.

Cermak tried to deal with the deepening crisis, although he never completely won the struggle to get more funding from the state legislature to deal not only with the school crises but also with unemployment relief. The new mayor looked to Washington, D.C., for help, setting a trend that would gain momentum with the election of Franklin Delano Roosevelt in 1932. Mayor Anton Cermak warned of thousands of hungry and desperate men in the streets of Chicago. In January 1932, the Democratic leader urged support of emergency relief legislation in Springfield that would add $20 million to relief aid. Cermak pointed out that private charity had been pushed beyond its limit. "In the past our charitable organizations have had a reserve for emergencies. That has been depleted in the last two years." He added that where one family might have sought aid now five had joined their ranks. In particular Cermak talked about the plight of the former white-collar worker and small homeowner who now joined the legion of the impoverished. Cermak warned that many who would have ignored communist appeals now listened to revolutionary talk and called the proposed relief legislation "civic fire insurance." Later that year, Cermak told the U.S. House of Representatives Banking and Currency Committee that they had a basic choice between sending money or troops to Chicago.

A year after becoming mayor, Cermak appealed for a federal "prosperity loan" to deal with the Depression. Without knowing it, Cermak encouraged a Keynesian solution to the Depression. He approached the Hoover administration with hope of "priming" the economic pump. In addition, Cermak cut the city's payroll letting go of many Thompson men but not replacing them. He pushed for public works and began to negotiate a loan from the Reconstruction Finance Corporation to finally build Chicago's subway. Cermak took a European tour to push the idea of a Chicago World's Fair in 1933. The West Side Czech knew the value of good public relations and how it might be used to attract investment to Chicago.[23]

Cermak moved to take control of the city council. Aldermen had a long tradition of independence and of creating their own ward organizations. The new mayor would not tolerate such autonomy; Cermak made clear who was boss. When he stepped down as county board president to run for the mayoralty, he made sure that Emmett Whealan, his longtime ally, took his place. While he gave up the chairmanship of the Cook County Democratic Party he placed it in the hands of Pat Nash, a loyal member of Cermak's group. He continued to sit as a member of the committee and controlled every section of local party authority. Cermak was no buffoon; he tightly held the strings of the party organization together and moved to take advantage of every gain made by the Democrats either in Illinois or across the nation. He intended to take and control power for a long time. The mayor masterfully dominated the state Democratic Party in 1932, defeating his old nemesis Michael L. Igoe and nominating Henry Horner for governor.

Cermak's main interest in the Democratic nominee for president in 1932 was that he would support the "Wets" in their desire to do away with prohibition. Although he initially supported Senator James H. Lewis, he also favored Al Smith who came from much the same background as the immigrant mayor. Smith was Catholic, working class, and in touch with the new immigrants who had swept Cermak into office. He was a self-made man and as "wet" as Cermak. Even though Franklin D. Roosevelt won the nomination, Cermak succeeded in including in the Democratic platform the "Wettest of Wet Planks," often called the "Illinois plank." Cermak continued to play the ethnic card, and his actions at the Chicago Democratic Convention guaranteed the unity of his local machine. During the general election Cermak and the Cook County Democrats delivered for Roosevelt, giving the New York governor the largest presidential vote in Chicago and Illinois history. On top of all that, Cermak had done what many had seen as impossible: he elected a Chicago Jew as governor of the Prairie State. Cermak and Chicago seemed in a good position to gain from the Democratic victory of November 1932.

The presidential campaign had been a difficult one for FDR, and he took a rest in Florida before being sworn in as president. On February 15, 1933, Roosevelt landed from a yachting trip off the Florida coast, and that night supporters held a reception in Miami at Bayfront Park. While a huge crowd gathered to meet the president-elect, Anton Cermak sat in the first row of the reviewing stand. Roosevelt rode in the usual open car waving to his constituents. As he approached he beckoned to Cermak to come to the car, but Cermak held back until after FDR gave a short speech. At the end of the talk, Cermak and other dignitaries approached the car. The two Democrats exchanged a few words, and as Roosevelt's car prepared to leave, shots rang out hitting Cermak along with four others. Pandemonium broke out, and Cermak yelled for the car to take off. Police rescued the would-be assassin from the vengeful crowd as FDR's car stopped a short distance away and Cermak, with the help of two companions, walked to the vehicle. The automobile sped to the hospital with Roosevelt cradling Cermak in his arms. Cermak allegedly told the president, "I'm glad it was me instead of you." Over the next nineteen days Cermak struggled for his life, dying on March 6. The martyred mayor's funeral included thirty thousand marchers, while twenty-three thousand attended ceremonies at the Chicago Stadium and fifty thousand witnessed his burial at the Bohemian National Cemetery in near zero temperatures.

Rumors immediately circulated that Chicago gangsters had sent Giuseppe Zangara to shoot Cermak and not Roosevelt. Talk of Cermak's involvement in Chicago's underworld circulated, and everyone knew that corruption had long reigned in city hall. Though Cermak had promised to wipe out gangster influence before the Chicago Fair, gossip persisted that he favored some mobsters over others, which could have endangered him. Still, a full investigation ultimately revealed that the assassin had in fact targeted the president and not Chicago's mayor.[24]

Figure 88. A horse-drawn wagon carrying Mayor Anton J. Cermak's coffin passes a crowd of mourners on March 10, 1933. (DN-0010531, Chicago Daily News negatives collection, Chicago Historical Society.)

Kelly-Nash: A New Democratic Day

Chicago's Democrats quickly gathered together to find a new leader. Ethnic factions made their appeals. Some mentioned Jacob Arvey, the city's most powerful non-Irish politician, but to name a Jewish mayor after Horner, a Jew, had defeated an Irish Democrat in the last primary seemed, as Arvey put it, "rubbing it in to the Irish."[25] Pat Nash proposed Francis J. Corr, alderman of the Seventeenth Ward, as a temporary mayor; he served for one month, and on April 14 the city council voted Ed Kelly, the South Parks Board President, into the mayor's office. Thus began a remarkable run in the history of Chicago politics that spanned both the Great Depression and World War II. If Cermak was the George Washington of Chicago's Democratic machine, Kelly was its Andrew Jackson, building it into a powerful and permanent force in city politics. Just as the old urban machines seemed to be dying off, Chicago's came on the scene and quickly grew into one of the most successful urban political organizations in the nation's history. Ed Kelly and Pat Nash could take much of the credit for its development.

Kelly had worked on the fringes of electoral politics. Raised in Bridgeport, the son of an Irish immigrant, he started working for the city as an ax man chopping down trees for the Sanitary District. Over the years Kelly received various promotions, always developing his political ties, including a friendship with Robert R. McCormick, publisher of the *Chicago Tribune* and onetime president of the Chicago Sanitary District. Despite his lack of formal training, the Sanitary District promoted him to chief engineer. In 1922, he joined the South Park Board, and two years later he began a ten-year reign as the board's chief executive. Despite his reputation as a respected political figure, he had held only appointed positions, and most did not see him as a major political player. That all changed with the assassination of Anton Cermak.[26]

Kelly proved to be the Chicago Democratic Party's true organizational genius. He nurtured his Washington connection with the Roosevelt White House and used it to strengthen his organization in Chicago. Circumventing critics in the Roosevelt administration, Kelly and Nash used New Deal programs as patronage farms that, while they helped Depression-plagued Chicagoans, also solidified support for the Democratic Party. Kelly and Nash did not have complete say as to who would be hired or fired under New Deal programs, but they also were not shy about taking credit for the jobs created by the Public Works Administration, Works Project Administration, or other Washington economic initiatives.[27]

The trials of the Great Depression released forces that few understood in Chicago, or for that matter in the nation or the world. Chicagoans faced these hardships with a sense of determination. Before he died, Anton Cermak began preparations for the 1933 World's Fair—usually called the "Century of Progress" Fair—to celebrate the one hundredth anniversary of the city's incorporation as a town and to once again bring the world to the shores of Lake Michigan. The Cermak assassination meant that Ed Kelly took on the role of World's Fair mayor. Unlike the Columbian Exposition of 1893, the 1933 fair looked to the future for its architectural inspiration and displayed a wide range of vibrant colors and building materials. The "Rainbow City" illuminated at night by white and colored lights captured the public's imagination.

The Century of Progress Exposition opened on May 27, 1933, on 477 lakefront acres just south of the Loop. It closed on November 12, but reopened for a second year on May 26, 1934, and ran again until October 31. The fair's popularity in part necessitated the extension, but so did the realities of the depression, as organizers hoped the second year would help retire its debts, as private investors had largely funded the fair. Organizers offered founder and sustaining memberships at $1,000 and $50, each raising $171,400. Legion memberships, opened to the general public, raised an additional $637,754. For $5.00, a certificate of membership good for ten admissions could be purchased. The Century

THE SKY RIDE
CHICAGO WORLD'S FAIR
1933

Figure 89. The Sky Ride at the Century of Progress World's Fair in 1933 gave riders a bird's eye view of the colorful and futuristic buildings. (Author's Collection.)

of Progress Board of Trustees authorized a $10 million bond issue on the day before "Black Tuesday" in 1929. Within a month of the fair's final closing, the trustees retired all remaining notes. The Century of Progress proved to be a success, especially given the economic hardships of the times. Because of its two-year run, fair attendance far surpassed the 1893 Columbian Exposition with 48,769,221 visitors.[28]

Even as Chicagoans and guests from all over the world visited futuristic structures such as the Chrysler Building, the Sears, Roebuck and Company structure, and the House of Tomorrow and rode the Cyclone roller coaster or walked the streets of the Belgian Village, the Great Depression continued to wreak havoc on the city and the nation. Other political strains also became evident, as Hitler took power in Germany and both Mussolini and Stalin solidified their positions in Italy and the Soviet Union. Chicago's Jews raised fears as the Nazi regime began attacking Germany's Hebrew community. Soon, however, the city's Slavs also felt threatened by political developments in Central Europe. The Italian community split between fascists and antifascists. Among the city's Germans, who had largely become a rather invisible ethnic group after World War I, German American Bund activities appeared, as Hitler raised German pride and expectations.

In Chicago, pro-Nazi sympathizers met mostly on the North Side in various halls and taverns. In February 1938, as war threatened Europe, one thousand

Figure 90. The Sears, Roebuck and Company Building at the 1933 fair contained futuristic lines. Unlike the 1893 Columbian Exposition, fair planners during the Great Depression looked forward to a technologically advanced world. (Author's Collection.)

Figure 91. Fair goers in 1933 celebrated "Chicago Day" on October 9, the anniversary of the Great Chicago Fire of 1871, as their predecessors had in 1893. (Author's Collection.)

Nazi supporters gathered at the Germania Club as speakers attacked the Jews and advocated fascism. Chicago police arrested five people for disorderly conduct, including two Nazis, and the Germania Club quickly banned Nazi meetings at its hall.[29] In July, the Bund planned to hold a folk festival and rally at the Riverview Amusement Park at Belmont and Western Avenues. Anti-Nazi organizations, including the German-American League for Culture, the American Jewish Congress, and the B'Nai Brith protested the plans. Still Riverview Park officials indicated that they planned to go ahead with the folk festival, perhaps because the Chicago Bund's Headquarters stood at 3855 North Western Avenue, just north of the amusement park. Eventually, the Nazis moved their picnic to the Ukrainian National Park on Higgins Road near the edge of Park Ridge. Protests followed, but this time the picnic took place.[30]

Violence hounded the German American Bund and other pro-Nazi organizations wherever they rallied in and around Chicago. In October 1938, more than 150 policemen broke up a near riot at the Lincoln Turner Hall at 1019 West Diversey Avenue. Inside the Bund had held a celebration marking the "freedom of the Sudentenland" after Germany seized the territory from the crippled Czechoslovak Republic. Some two thousand protestors clashed with Nazi sympathizers, as police pushed through the crowd. Rose Sebek threw a tomato and hit a policeman in the face, and police took Mrs. Sebek and twelve others into custody. Eventually, some five thousand protestors walked neighborhood streets. Despite violence and protest, the German American Bund continued to hold rallies even as war seemed imminent in Europe. In June 1939, some four thousand persons gave the Nazi salute at Kolze Electric Park on Irving Park Road. Several hundred boys and men walked the grounds of the park in Nazi uniforms, as one hundred police stood in reserve at the Jefferson Park police station.[31]

While a relatively small minority of Chicago's Germans supported the German American Bund, Chicago's Czechoslovaks came out in force to defend their homeland from Nazi claims. Rose Sebek and her friends were only among the most active demonstrators. Pilsen Park, in Czech California on Twenty-sixth and Albany Street, again became a focal point of Czech patriotism. Chicago's Czech community met en masse in Pilsen Park after the September 29, 1938, Munich Agreement dismembered Czechoslovakia. They sent a resolution to President Franklin D. Roosevelt supporting Czechoslovak freedom and condemning Nazism. On March 15, 1939, as Nazi Germany swallowed what remained of Czechoslovakia, organizers held another mass meeting at Pilsen Park. The Chicago chapters of the Czech-American National Alliance, the Alliance of Bohemian Catholics, and the Slovak American Alliance arranged the rally; as a crowd filled Pilsen Park's auditorium "almost to suffocation," police finally closed the doors and turned hundreds away. The tense crowd of about five thousand Bohemian and Slovak Chicagoans sat in an "almost death like silence, as during a funeral." The faces of men twisted grimly in emotion, and women wept openly as the speakers once again addressed a Pilsen Park gathering about Czechoslovak freedom.[32] Obviously Chicago's ethnic groups were still concerned with events in their homelands.

The Urge to Organize: Neighborhoods

Chicagoans began to organize themselves throughout the 1930s, and a reinvigorated labor movement, in the guise of the Congress of Industrial Organizations (CIO), soon provided a voice for many of Chicago's workers. As early as 1930, sociologists from the University of Chicago attempted to figure out ways of dealing with youth delinquency in the city's neighborhoods. In the 1920s, Clifford R. Shaw and his colleagues formulated a new theory of the causes of juvenile crime that rejected the imposition of middle-class values on immigrant and working-class communities. They hoped to attack the problem from the inside out, using the institutions and values of the ethnic working-class neighborhoods themselves. Earlier studies had clearly demarcated the areas of gang activity in Chicago and argued against ethnic guilt, positing instead the idea that the physical environment and social situation of the inner city itself acted as a natural breeding ground for gang activity. Only a change at the community level could lower crime rates.[33]

When Clifford Shaw began to search for an inner-city community on which to test this thesis, he settled on the Bush neighborhood in the northeast corner of South Chicago. It lay cradled between Carnegie–Illinois Steel's massive South Works, now part of the U.S. Steel Corporation, and the tracks of the Illinois Central Railroad. The mill separated the Bush from the upper-middle-class community of South Shore and the University of Chicago's home in Hyde Park. More railroads cut it off from the rest of South Chicago to the south. Shaw wanted a part of the city with well-defined boundaries and a distinct local culture; the Bush satisfied his needs. Looking for social disintegration and the slum, Shaw came upon an intricate working-class neighborhood already possessing many of the tools it needed to create a better future.

St. Michael's Polish Catholic Church stood at the center of its social life. The church's steeples challenged the South Works' smokestacks for dominance of the sky. Wooden two-flats and an occasional brick building huddled close together, seeming to embrace the mill. The Church dominated the community as it had the Polish villages from which the immigrants had left to make their living in Chicago's steel industry. At first, the sociologists thought they would ally themselves with the local settlement house run by the Baptist Church, but they soon figured out where the real institutional power in the community lay: not with the interloping Protestants, but with Rev. John Lange, the Catholic pastor of St. Michael's.

James McDonald arrived in South Chicago to head the program and soon recognized the importance of Lange and St. Michael's. Through a local chiropodist, Dr. Adam S. Mioduski, McDonald began to make contacts in the Polish community. Clifford Shaw came down to meet Father Lange, and the Bush Area Project, later called the Russell Square Community Committee, was born. In 1933, the St. Michael's Boys Club opened, and in about fifteen months the Bush Area Project was fully operational. Shaw hoped that local institutions such as the parish and the boys' club would provide an alternative to the gangs of the neighborhood. The Chicago Area Project proved to be immensely successful in minimizing juvenile delinquency. McDonald and Shaw saw the people of the Bush as saving themselves with only minor outside help.[34]

Saul Alinsky, who worked with the Chicago Area Project, as well as in the Back of the Yards, to establish youth committees, soon abandoned Shaw and the project as too conservative in their approach. He looked to the Back of the Yards neighborhood, just west of Chicago's Union Stock Yards, to test his own organizational theories. In the Back of the Yards a handful of young energetic leaders emerged in the 1930s, looking for ways to empower the community. Alinsky arrived in the neighborhood in late 1938 and early the following year met Joseph Meegan after a Packingtown Youth Committee meeting. The youth committee was a spinoff of the Packinghouse Workers Organizing Committee (PWOC) of the CIO. The new union felt that it was as important to organize neighborhoods as shop floors. The radical CIO approach in many ways threatened the political order of the city, as well as the economic relationship between worker and management in the stockyards. Young union members made up the youth committee, supposedly to improve recreational facilities in the neighborhood. Meegan was the supervisor of Davis Square Park just west of the packinghouses on Forty-fourth and Marshfield Avenue. Alinsky felt that a meeting of community and labor representatives without church and ethnic leadership present would accomplish little. The two men became quick friends and in many ways represented two sides of the same coin. Alinsky, a Jew and an outsider as well as a University of Chicago graduate, was enamored with the new labor movement and understood PWOC's leadership. Meegan, an Irish Catholic who grew up in Fuller Park just the other side of the yards, understood the ethnic and religious world of the Back of the Yards. In the late 1930s, these two young men forged an alliance that eventually included Chicago's powerful Catholic Archdiocese.

The official motto of the new group, "We the People Will Work Out Our Own Destiny," implied a type of agency that had a much more radical potential for change than the youth committees and boys' clubs envisioned by Clifford Shaw. The Back of the Yards Neighborhood Council (BYNC) would prove to be a formidable political player in Chicago over the next few decades. In the Back of the Yards, the alliance of such potentially powerful forces as organized labor, the Catholic Church, and ethnic organizations meant that the new group would have to be taken seriously.

The first meeting took place on July 14, 1939, at Davis Square Park, and Father Ambrose Ondrak, a young Slovak American priest, opened it with a prayer. The older pastors remained cool to the new organization, but younger priests like Ondrak, Roman J. Berendt, Joseph Kelly, and Edward Plawinski rallied to the cause. Bishop Bernard J. Sheil's unqualified endorsement further encouraged the pastors, who often saw themselves as ethnic rivals, to cooperate. Meegan and Alinsky agreed that the BYNC should be run by democratically elected local leaders and not by outside investigators and reformers. They limited memberships to local organizations, including women's and youth groups, each of whom would have three representatives on the council and one vote. The stated goal was to unite the community and promote the welfare of all residents regardless of their race, color, or creed. The council meetings provided a forum in which neighborhood problems could be openly discussed. Here was the root of Alinsky's dream: the idea that a neighborhood could affect its own future through united action.[35]

The Urge to Organize: Labor

After the defeat of organized labor in the wake of World War I, union representation in the city's major industries disappeared. The coming of Roosevelt's New Deal in the 1930s and the passage first of the National Recovery Act and then the Wagner Act (1937) revived the labor movement, especially in the mass production industries where it even predated the creation of the CIO. In 1933, only about 2 percent of the city's steel workers had a union contract. Many more found themselves represented by so-called Employee Representation Plans, which were little more than company controlled front organizations. The creation of the early CIO in 1935 called for industrial unionism—that is, anyone who worked in an industry, regardless of the trade they practiced, should join one union. The old Amalgamated Iron and Steel Workers union soon affiliated with the Steelworkers Organizing Committee (SWOC) of the CIO. By 1936, conservative unionists in the American Federation of Labor moved to oust the industrial unionists from their organization. The following year the CIO targeted U.S. Steel's South Works. On July 16, 1936, three thousand members of the old company representation plan joined the Amalgamated Iron and Steel Workers en masse. Some nine thousand steel workers at the mill waited to see what would happen. Over the next year the CIO drive spread through the Chicago District plants of U.S. Steel. SWOC organizers used the many ethnic clubs in the steel plants to reach out to laborers. CIO organizers also attempted to win over the wives and sisters of workers, to influence community organizations, and to attract African Americans to their organization.[36]

Figure 92. The Carnegie-Illinois Steel South Works located in the South Chicago neighborhood was part of the U.S. Steel and Steelworkers Organizing Committee contract in 1937. (Photograph by Charles W. Cushman; Indiana University Archives, P02192.)

On March 2, 1937, roughly nine months after the beginning of the union drive, Benjamin Fairless of the Carnegie-Illinois Division of U.S. Steel signed an agreement with Phillip Murray of SWOC. The contract resulted from secret negotiations between John L. Lewis, president of the CIO, and Myron Taylor, chairman of the board of the U.S. Steel Corporation. The contract had an immediate impact on the labor movement, as SWOC became a major union with a contract to represent the workers of one of the nation's largest and traditionally most antiunion companies. With the U.S. Steel contract, the CIO became a major player in the American economy. Within two months time, SWOC bargained contracts with eighty-eight other companies and had a membership of 288,000 nationwide. Organizers had their hands full with thousands of steelworkers joining the union daily. By May, membership in Chicago alone topped thirty thousand.[37]

While Big Steel agreed to a contract with SWOC, largely because the threat of war in Asia and Europe promised larger sales, Little Steel remained determined to fight labor organizers. On May 27, 1937, SWOC struck the Republic Steel Corporation and the Youngstown Sheet and Tube Company, two of the steel industry's "Little Sisters." In Chicago twenty-five thousand steelworkers walked off their jobs. On Memorial Day SWOC held a mass meeting of workers and supporters at Sam's Café, which served as a union command post for the Republic Steel strikers. Activists led a march of 1,000–2,500 unionists to the gates of the company to throw up a picket line. Roughly fifty Chicago police met the protestors and demanded they disband. The police then began to fire indiscriminately into the crowd. Ten people died, and sixty-eight lay wounded. The Chicago police moved quickly to stop any bad publicity from the massacre as the Police Movie Censor Board refused to allow a film of the conflict to be shown in the city.[38]

SWOC reacted immediately, and Chicago's city hall began to feel the heat. On June 8, SWOC organized a rally in the Civic Opera House, and on June 17 a mass meeting was held at the Chicago Stadium. Van A. Bittner referred to the "damnable beastly police" and "crazy hoodlum policemen." The Memorial Day Massacre quickly developed into a threat to the Democratic machine. Mayor Kelly needed to react quickly to conditions on the Southeast Side, and he eventually developed a policy more favorable toward SWOC and the CIO. Democratic leaders, facing a mayoral election in 1939, worried about the new political power of the industrial mass production workforce. Kelly seemed ready to grant the CIO more clout, and he also knew that they had influence in Roosevelt's White House. After the massacre, union leaders felt a shift in their relationship with the Chicago Democrats away from either indifference or outright hostility to cordiality and even friendship. Kelly endorsed the CIO and even aldermen began to speak well of the union organization.[39] Chicago's politicians could feel that the political winds had shifted and that the industrial working class was beginning to exert its political power.

A very different outcome for the city's meatpacking industry and the PWOC resulted from this "new" relationship. The National Labor Relations Board (NLRB) decision dissolving the Armour and Company employee representation plan in 1938 set the stage for a CIO contract. The company asked to open up negotiations after the CIO held a mass meeting of representatives from all of Armour's plants, yet management hesitated to sign a contract. The NLRB election proved successful for PWOC, and in November 1938 the workers celebrated a huge victory. The Chicago police did not interfere in the stockyards as they had in the Republic Steel strike. Like the U.S. Steel contract, the victory at Armour and Company signaled other stockyard workers to flock to the CIO. Soon workers at Wilson and Company, Roberts and Oake Packing, and the Union Stock Yard and Transit Company formed PWOC locals. To workers, the corner of Forty-third Street and Packers Avenue became unofficially known as "CIO Corner," while the union's detractors referred to the intersection as "Red Square." In March 1939, Mayor Kelly openly supported PWOC Local 44 in its struggle to sign a contract with the Union Stock Yard and Transit Company. Local 44 sent a unanimous resolution to Kelly thanking him for his support. Obviously the Democrats had quickly moved a long way from the events of Memorial Day 1937. In April 1939, a march through the Back of the Yards held banners that proclaimed "A Million Votes for Kelly and a Contract with Armour."

The CIO also supported the fledgling Back of the Yards Neighborhood Council. The urge to organize, felt both in the packing plants and in the neighborhood, merged nicely. In June 1939, the Packinghouse Workers Council of Chicago met to plan a far-reaching program to organize the entire neighborhood behind the Armour and Company workers attempt to get a contract. The company continued to refuse to negotiate despite the NLRB election the year before. CIO organizers planned to have block parties and dances as well as to work with both white and black clergy. With the new council, they also promoted union work among the neighborhood's Mexicans, through a PWOC Mexican Committee. The CIO planned a huge picnic at Birutis' Grove on July 23. A priest from a local Polish Catholic Church, Sacred Heart, spoke to PWOC members on behalf of the BYNC, while Catholic Bishop Bernard Sheil urged workers to organize in the plants.[40] Labor and neighborhood organizations soon saw themselves as full-fledged members of a powerful political organization. The dark days of monopoly capitalism began to fade somewhat.

World War II: Emporium of the United Nations

On September 1, 1939, the *Chicago Tribune*'s headline screamed "WAR! BOMB WARSAW!" and Chicagoans awoke to the news of a new and terrible chapter in the history of Europe and the world. Chicago's Polish community had been bracing for an outbreak of hostilities for some time. Now the horrific news from Central Europe poured in daily, as the Polish Army heroically fought the Nazi invasion. The world went to war and America, protected by two vast oceans and still disenchanted by the experience of World War I, seemed to pull away from the unfolding tragedy.

American isolationism had no place in Chicago's many ethnic communities. Poles, Czechs, and others mobilized their communities immediately. On October 4, 1939, Chicagoans announced the formation of a Chicago Branch of the Commission for Polish Relief. The organization's goals were to be strictly humanitarian. The Legion of Polish Women, a newly organized group, sponsored a concert on October 8 at the Civic Opera House to raise money for the new relief fund. Meanwhile another organization, Polish Civilian War Relief, representing seventy-two churches and Polish organizations in the city, brought more than ten thousand women of Polish extraction together to make clothing for the suffering citizens of Poland. The group opened its headquarters in the center of the Northwest Side's Polish community at the intersection of Ashland and Division Avenues. All of the clothing was to be turned over to the Red Cross for distribution in occupied Poland.[41]

Figure 93. Polish American women carry a large Polish flag during the traditional Polish Constitution Day Parade on May 3, 1942. The marchers used the flag to catch coins as a contribution to Polish war relief. (Photograph by Charles W. Cushman, Indiana University Archives, P02610.)

Meanwhile, a group calling itself the Polish All-American Council held a two-day meeting at the Polish Roman Catholic Youth Hall at 984 North Milwaukee Avenue. Leaders stressed their convictions that Poland would survive and regain its independence. In February 1940, the group organized a mass rally at the Chicago Stadium that attracted eighteen thousand people to raise funds for Polish Relief. The Polish tenor, Jan Kiepura, appeared on the program along with Gen. Joseph Haller, minister without portfolio of the new Polish government-in-exile and a leader of the Polish forces that had resisted the Soviet invasion in 1920.[42]

Fund-raising activities grew as the war continued. The Amalgamated Clothing Workers donated $2,000 to the Red Cross for Polish relief. Meanwhile the community organized everything from card parties to fashion shows at Loop hotels to raise money. The first relief shipment, sent to Poland in April, consisted of 1,600 tons of food and supplies including 15,000 gallons of cod liver oil for Polish children. In June 1940, the Commission for Polish Relief sent 6,000 tons of food to Poland via Italy. Reports said that 7 million women and children faced famine in Poland. By September 1940, the Polish Civilian War Relief of Chicago contained 105 units with 8,000 active members. A High Mass, held at Our Lady of Perpetual Heart Church in Bridgeport on Sunday

September 22, marked the opening of an all-day meeting to review the war relief work of Chicago's Polish community. That afternoon the meeting moved to the headquarters at the Polish Women's Alliance building at 1309 North Ashland Avenue.[43]

Whether or not the general American public agreed, ethnic Chicagoans of all types quickly realized the threat of war. Several of Chicago's largest ethnic groups faced the horrors of the Nazi regime and attempted to sway American pubic opinion toward intervention. Mayor Ed Kelly also seemed certain that the United States would get caught up in the fighting sooner rather than later. As the fascist onslaught continued both in Europe and Asia, Kelly prepared the city for the coming conflict. Critics felt that Kelly moved too fast and that war might still be avoided, but the mayor's office positioned itself to take the lead on the home front should the United States join the fighting. On March 5, 1941, Kelly created and chaired the Chicago Commission on National Defense. Seventy-one business leaders sat on the commission, which worked to prepare the city's industry for war and to make every neighborhood a part of the defense program. The commission undertook an industrial survey of the city as one of its first tasks and organized an aluminum drive that summer, establishing a central collection point at Congress Plaza on the lakefront. Guarded by three naval reservists the "dump" grew slowly into a mountain of the precious metal. In addition police, fire, and gas stations throughout the city collected aluminum. Several hundred members of the Cloak and Dressmakers Union paraded through the western end of the Loop on July 23 and deposited aluminum on a pile at Franklin and Monroe Streets. During the first two days of the recycling campaign, the city collected eighty thousand pounds of aluminum.[44]

Kelly's commission looked hard at industrial production. Small businesses' response to the war effort proved a major concern. The Depression still haunted the American economy that had not yet been jump-started by the war. Commission members called a meeting of four thousand small manufacturers at their headquarters at 174 West Washington Street on October 2. The mayor hoped to instruct these producers on how to pool their resources in order to bid on government work. Kelly feared that those who did not take part in war production would be forced to close because of a lack of material for nondefense products, ultimately throwing thousands of Chicagoans out of work.[45]

The responsibility for preparing the public for war lay with the new civil defense system being put in place by Washington, D.C. Kelly's close relationship with Roosevelt assured him an important position in the organizational framework being created for Chicago and northern Illinois. On May 20, 1941, the federal government established the Office of Civilian Defense, which designated Chicago as one of the civilian defense districts with Kelly at its helm. The mayor's new domain extended beyond the city's boundaries across the entire metropolitan area and gave him a tremendous amount of authority. Chicago's complex transportation and communication system proved crucial to the war effort.[46]

After the Japanese attack on Pearl Harbor on December 7, Chicago police guarded bridges in the hope of stopping any saboteurs who might throw the city into a panic. The next day, federal and local agents descended on the shops of Chicago's Japanese community. The owners and employees of the city's twenty-five Japanese lunchrooms and caterers seemed confused when Mayor Kelly closed their establishments. Across the country 726 Japanese nationals had been taken into custody. Japanese Chicagoans anticipated the same treatment. Employees huddled in the backroom of one of the largest Japanese establishments in Chicago, the Tokyo Lunch at 551 South State Street. On the entrance were a heavy lock and a sign that read, "Closed for short duration by the mayor's order." Goro Tsuchida, a thirty-year resident of the United States, and his Kentucky-born Japanese American wife sat gloomily in their lunchroom at 1130 North Clark Street as their two sons waited to be drafted. Madame Shintani's Restaurant at 743 North Rush sat darkened as anti-Japanese sentiment ran throughout the city. Meanwhile, war news sharply boosted livestock prices in the Union Stock Yards.[47]

The war that many feared, and that some hoped for to liberate their homelands, was now a reality. The emergency presented unprecedented problems, even greater than the Civil War. Chicago played a key role in both providing manpower to fight the war and industrial production to ensure the success of allied forces. The Emporium of the West now became the Emporium of the United Nations as the United States entered the fighting. This proved to be no easy task as Chicago's factories, plants, and mills remained largely orientated toward a peaceful market at the end of 1941. The threat of Japanese bombs transformed the economy nearly overnight from one still not fully recovered from the Great Depression to one of full employment and manpower shortages.

The change to wartime production proved daunting and had a tremendous influence on the city's demographic, social, and economic future. By early 1942, Chicago firms filled $2 billion in war orders. Just three years earlier the amount of money spent on military equipment in Chicago stood at roughly zero. The city's manufacturing base grew faster than ever before. Chicago's role as a transportation center made the location of defense industries there inevitable. From June 1940 through the end of the fighting in the Pacific, both private companies and the federal War Plant Corporation spent $1.3 billion on factory construction, a third of it spent on new buildings. Construction crews transformed parts of the city and suburbs, which still had a rural character, into massive industrial areas.

During the first two months of the war, Chicago stopped producing some six hundred consumer products, a result of almost immediate cutbacks in material. These manufacturers were more than glad to take up war production as they could no longer meet their traditional markets. War transformed the plants

Figure 94. Chicago's young men volunteered in large numbers for the U.S. Armed Forces. Pictured here is a young cavalry soldier from Back of the Yards, ca. 1942. (Author's Collection.)

from making roller skates, juke boxes, can openers, and Radio Flyer wagons to the nose sections of bombers, five-gallon gasoline "blitz" cans, and M-I rifles. This took a good deal of retraining for laborers at the same time that the workforce fluctuated massively, as recruitment campaigns and the draft took workers into the military. While the initial war orders came into the city at an excruciatingly slow pace, Mayor Kelly and leaders of the Chicago Association of Commerce made many trips to Washington, D.C., in an attempt to divert investment to the city from the two coasts. Within two years the idle factories of early 1942 were a thing of the past, as Chicago became a major producer of war goods.[48]

Chicagoans quickly had to face the realities of war. Sons and husbands left for the military. Women too would find roles as Army WACs (members of the Women's Army Corps), Navy WAVEs (members of Women Accepted for Volunteer Emergency), and volunteers helping the military by doing traditional service such as wrapping bandages, but their role in the wartime home front economy proved crucial. While "Rosie the Riveter" became an iconic wartime figure, working-class women had long worked in the packinghouses, factories, and warehouses of the city. In 1920, female employees made up as much as

20 percent of the stockyard workforce. The war, however, pulled middle- and upper-class women into industrial employment as more and more felt it their patriotic duty to help the nation fight the war on the home front.

One year after Pearl Harbor, over three hundred thousand Chicago-area women worked in war plants of one sort or another, an amazing 19 percent of the female population. Women collected approximately $870,000 for war relief organizations, knitted 276,112 garments, made or remodeled 4,906,200 articles of clothing, and packed 71,600 comfort kits for the armed forces. Red Cross workers made 4 million surgical dressings. In addition women donated over 8,000 pounds of cookies and 150,642 cakes to servicemen's centers and USO clubs. Women collected over 300,000 tons of scrap metal and saved 3 million pounds of grease and fat for recycling for the munitions industry. They also helped to purchase several ambulances and stuffed 75,000 Christmas stockings for grateful GIs. The Red Cross coordinated many of these activities from its main office at 616 South Michigan Avenue. School authorities in Joliet announced that woman teachers could ignore the pre–Pearl Harbor rule that they must leave teaching after marrying. The school board informed both public grade and high school teachers that they could stay on the job if they married a serviceman. The *Chicago Tribune* asked women to be patient with the various aid organizations as it took some time to place everyone who wanted to help. As they did during the Depression, neighborhood residents banded together. Women in Edgewater volunteered through the Edgemere Club to aid the war effort. Some three hundred women gathered on Mondays and Wednesdays at the Edgewater Beach Hotel to sew, knit garments, and make bandages and surgical dressings.[49]

Early in 1942 the Chicago Public Schools offered a ten-day national defense training class for women at the Chicago Vocational School on Eighty-seventh and Anthony Street. Twenty women from the Pullman Standard Car Company's Aircraft Division comprised the first six-hour class designed to train students to perform the 2,500 operations necessary for the construction of bomber wings. The demand for more industrial workers worried the Roosevelt administration, and training of war industry personnel remained a paramount problem as the war went on.[50] The economic transformation continued throughout the war. In May 1943, a major push was made by the War Manpower Commission to bring women into defense industries as male workers left for the armed services and a labor shortage loomed. Mayor Kelly made a personal appeal to Chicago's women in 1944, the first "women only" labor recruiting call in the city's history. Some companies sent teams of employees door-to-door to recruit women. Pay rose as Chicago's unemployment rate fell to 1 percent in 1944.[51]

On October 28, 1942, the city held its first successful air raid alarm test. In May of the following year the Illinois Civil Air Patrol staged a mock air raid on the city. By this time, however, the fear of a real air raid had basically disappeared from the city as Chicago seemed to be too far from the fighting to be in direct danger. Nevertheless, Kelly's block captains appeared everywhere, as did demonstrations of America's military might. Downtown Chicago became an outdoor military museum as the war effort dominated the Loop. Store windows urged the purchase of Liberty Bonds, and Marshal Field's opened a "Victory Center" that included an educational program on gardening, food conservation, and cooking. Chicagoans knew the corner of Van Buren and State Streets, site of noontime bond rallies, as "Victory Corner," and the west face of City Hall as "Victory Plaza." The Navy placed a captured Japanese mini-submarine on display at the corner of State and Madison. Servicemen's centers defined much of the Loop's nightlife as uniformed soldiers, sailors, and marines looked for a "night on the town" before shipping out.

Chicagoans officially kicked off the Third War Loan Drive in September 1943. Organizers held a rally at the Civic Opera House on the evening of September 7, while officially beginning the drive two days later. At noon on September 13 every church bell in the city rang to usher in a four-day house-to-house push by local civilian defense captains to sell war bonds. The wardens asked every family to buy two more $25 bonds. Meanwhile as the city made plans to make the loan drive successful the Allied armies accepted the surrender of Fascist Italy. On the corner of Taylor and Halsted Streets Italian merchants took to the streets waving flags, creating a spontaneous parade through Little Italy's streets. The victory in Italy distracted Chicagoans for only a short time from the loan drive. Soon a Hollywood Cavalcade of Stars arrived in Chicago to breathe more life into the campaign. Eight thousand people welcomed a host of movie stars including Mickey Rooney, Harpo Marx, Judy Garland, and Betty Hutton at Union Station on September 15. Mayor Kelly greeted the celebrities at Randolph and State Street. Over $15 million dollars in bonds sold at two rallies including a huge rally at Soldier Field on the evening of September 16. Meanwhile Chicagoans could inspect tanks, antiaircraft guns, bulldozers, and jeeps that lined State Street. A paratrooper landed on State Street to the amazement of the crowds. Chicago businesses and ethnic groups enthusiastically responded to the drive. Wieboldt's employees purchased $7.5 million in bonds. The Polish Roman Catholic Union bought $1 million in bonds adding to the $5 million in bonds the organization already held. Major C. Udell Turpin, a well-known African American businessman, headed up the Negro Division of the Illinois bond drive. He was credited with raising over $10 million for the various bond drives in the black community. The African American youth organization the Billikens supported bond drives throughout the war. The fifteenth annual Bud Billiken parade in 1944 included a huge war bond rally in Washington Park. Other rallies were held at Bronzeville ballrooms and nightclubs.[52]

Rationing hit families and neighborhoods. As consumer products disappeared, scrap metal drives, newspaper drives, and animal fat collections took place across the city. In 1942, Chicago led the nation with 113.7 pounds of scrap

Figure 95. Corner War Memorial in Back of the Yards, ca. 1942. (Author's Collection.)

metal collected per capita. Chicago's city hall dominated the salvage drives for the entire region. In August 1944, while the collection of scrap metal and fat declined in the city, Chicagoans still collected five thousand tons of paper, or 38 percent of the national total. Victory Gardens, corner War Memorials, and Honor Rolls listing local servicemen marked all of Chicago's neighborhoods and suburbs. Everywhere the war cast its shadow on the nation.

While situated far from the actual fighting and with little threat of long-range air raids or naval bombardments, Chicagoans did fear Nazi efforts to sabotage local industries and hurt the war effort. Early in the war, the Chicago police padlocked the Haus Vaterland, home to the German American Bund on North Western Avenue. That same summer of 1942, the arrest of Herbert Haupt in Chicago made headlines. Haupt, a twenty-two-year-old naturalized German immigrant, had grown up in the city. He attended a school for spies in Germany and returned to the city to blow up defense plants. Arrested on June 27, Haupt was tried and found guilty; he was executed on August 8. Authorities also took his parents and an aunt and uncle into custody and sentenced them to life for harboring a spy. The Haupt case shocked the city and the nation and showed the German population in Chicago, a community that had already witnessed a good deal of scrutiny during World War I, in a dangerous light. In response to such suspicions, Chicago's German Americans went out of their way to prove their loyalty to the United States.

Thousands of relocated Japanese Americans from the West Coast arrived in Chicago during the war. Before Pearl Harbor, only about 350 Japanese lived throughout the city. The first evacuees arrived in June 1942, and soon Chicago became the most concentrated destination for West Coast refugees. Two large Japanese neighborhoods centered on the North Side intersection of Clark and Division Streets and in the South Side's Kenwood-Oakland neighborhood east of Cottage Grove Avenue, between Forty-third and Forty-seventh Streets. The two communities acted as "buffers" between sometimes hostile African American and Caucasian neighborhoods.

Figure 96. The Hawthorne plant of the Western Electric Company in Cicero was the largest producer of telephone and communication equipment in the United States, an industry vital to the war effort. Here Western Electric's Victory Girl and her court raise the Treasury Department's Minute Man Flag awarded to the company for its production efforts. (ICHi-39371, Chicago History Museum.)

The war years greatly influenced the city. Chicago played a central role in the war of attrition against the Axis Powers; only Detroit manufactured more war products. By mid-1944, the city's industries had contracted to produce $7.8 billion of the total $23 billion of ordnance produced in the Chicago Ordnance District. Chicago's industries proudly displayed the Army-Navy E-Awards for excellence in wartime production. Only about 5 percent of the nation's eighty-five thousand defense plants won awards. Over two hundred of them operated in Chicago, and seventy-five in the suburbs.[53]

Fifty local companies manufactured parts for the B-29 super-fortress bomber, the superweapon that the military claimed would bring final victory to the Allies. Over half of the plane originated as aluminum sheeting from ALCOA in suburban McCook. Dodge-Chicago on South Cicero Avenue built its four engines. Chicago firms assembled much of the rest of the plane, and even if workers finally put together the airplane elsewhere, Chicagoans felt ownership of the craft. They took a great deal of pride in its construction. One young woman, Pauline, a Dodge-Chicago inspector, wrote a letter to a parts packer who had put her name on some of the cartons of material arriving from New Jersey to be assembled in the Chicago plant: "So you see my friend, on those little parts, that sometimes seem unimportant to us and on the work we do, Victory depends; so let's keep up the good work together from far and near because our boys depend on the work we do here and let's keep them supplied so they can end this war the sooner the better and come back to us with the ultimate Victory that we are all hoping and praying for."[54] In Chicago and elsewhere, the war industry knit people together overcoming regional, racial, class, and ethnic divisions.

Despite Chicago's jump in industrial production during the war, the federal government's investment on the West Coast signified a dilemma for the postwar city. The first of three Pacific wars, World War II set in motion vast economic changes that shifted the nation's industrial base away from Chicago, and the Midwest and Northeast. Enormous reallocations of investment by the federal government resulted in the permanent transfer of industries and populations. The incredible movement of people across the country to defense plants on the West Coast remade postwar America. Millions of Americans went West between 1940 and 1945. In 1948, the Census Bureau stated, "Probably never before in the history of the United States has there been internal population movement of such magnitude as in the last seven eventful years." During the period 1940–47, some 25 million people (21 percent of the population) migrated from their homes to another county or state. African Americans and Hispanics made up much of this population, and their movement to Oakland or Los Angeles rearranged the racial landscapes of those cities. Racial conflicts such as the Zoot Suit Riots in Los Angeles, as well as various other clashes, left a troublesome legacy. The importance of the Bay Area for wartime shipping can-

Figure 97. Chicago's Jewish community collects clothing and canned food for survivors of the Holocaust, 1945. (Chicago Jewish Archives, Spertus Institute of Jewish Studies.)

not be overstated, leading to the creation of modern Oakland. The production of "Liberty Ships" at the Kaiser Shipyards did much to win the war.[55]

Once-sleepy towns and small cities now boomed with war production plants and migrants from across the United States. West Coast cities played national, rather than regional, economic roles for the first time. Boeing's massive airplane factory transformed Portland. The aircraft industry expanded in Los Angeles, and San Diego—once a shabby bus stop on the way to Tijuana— became a major embarkation point for the Marine Corps. Cities became the engines of the new West Coast, and by 1990, 80 percent of all westerners lived in urbanized areas. Hardly the Wild West of the romanticized American imagination, the New West presented a highly industrialized urban setting.[56]

Furthermore, in the postwar years the West Coast emerged as a destination for many returning GIs and their new families as its economy expanded at the expense of Chicago and other older industrial areas. As industries followed the federal largesse to the West and the South, many of these new industrial centers proved to be hostile to organized labor and pro–big business in their tax policies. Numerous Chicagoans who had left home during the war decided that the warmer parts of the country might be better places to raise their children and find upward mobility. Chicago witnessed more population growth in the 1940s, reaching its peak population to date in 1950 with some 3.7 million residents, but the writing already appeared on the wall, and the city fell into a population decline that only further immigration would reverse at the end of the century.[57]

The war proved to be a turning point in the history of the city as well as the nation. In many ways Chicagoans and their city would never be the same after playing such a crucial role in war production and supplying so many men and women to the armed services. Pauline, and other women like her, left the manufacturing plants and became wives and mothers. Many had been war brides and now saw their husbands return. Still the wartime experience could never be forgotten and would have a tremendous impact on the lives of women and their families as the twentieth century progressed.

Social change was also an issue for returning servicemen. They had left often insular ethnic communities to be mixed in barracks and aboard ships with others from across the country. For the first time, these young Chicagoans visited foreign lands and other parts of the country. New experiences presented themselves and many did not wish to return to the familiar two-flat on Forty-seventh Street, the apartment in Rogers Park, or the bungalow in Berwyn. Many hoped for something better than "sticking pigs" in the stockyards and sought out jobs in other industries. Others took advantage of the GI Bill and finished high school or went to college. Yet others settled in different areas of the country. Some returned but never recovered from the horrors of war. Most however, did come home to Chicago, searched out the new opportunities, and lived routine lives. Often they began to leave their old ethnic communities and looked for new housing on the outskirts of the city or in the once distant suburbs.

Chicago's black populace soared and continued to grow during the thirty-year period following the war. During the war itself roughly sixty-five thousand African Americans from the rural South came to Chicago. Crowded into the South and West Side ghettoes, they arrived to take advantage of wartime prosperity. In 1940, blacks made up only 2.8 percent of workers in Cook and DuPage Counties. Five years later they comprised nearly 14 percent of the workforce. Of those women at Armour and Company, whose numbers had doubled during the war, many, if not most, were black. Hundreds of black women benefited from a CIO–Chicago Urban League program that placed them in all kinds of industries. Chicagoan A. Philip Randolph, president of the Brotherhood of Sleeping Car Porters and an early civil rights leader, threatened a march on Washington if war manufacturers continued to discriminate against blacks. This showdown resulted in President Roosevelt's Executive Order 8802, which forbade racial discrimination in defense plants and government agencies across the nation, an incredible step for a federal government that still supported segregation in the South and across the land in public housing projects. Despite executive orders and the great need for wartime workers, discrimination persisted, as the *Chicago Daily Defender* frequently reported. Black women seemed

Figure 98. This house built as a single-family cottage in the nineteenth century was typical of the kind of housing that African Americans found available as they migrated to Chicago during World War II and after. Located at 3621 South Federal Street in the heart of the black ghetto it housed several families in the 1940s. (Photograph by Charles W. Cushman; Indiana University Archives, P04229.)

to be especially victims of both racism and sexism by employers. When the city and the federal government proposed to build housing for black war workers in the Calumet area, white real estate organizations protested.

In 1965, more blacks lived in Chicago than in Mississippi, and public housing alone housed a larger African American population than Selma, Alabama. The movement of blacks from the South to Chicago would not end until the mid-1970s. Still, blacks faced discrimination, particularly in those new wartime industries located on the city's outskirts and suburbs. The vast majority of white Chicagoans resisted integration, especially in housing. Race would present a major conflict for Chicagoans in the postwar era.[58]

Chicago after the War

Changing Times

To both visitor and resident alike, Chicago in 1945 seemed a dreary, worn-out city. Years of neglect, first as a result of the Great Depression and then World War II, had its impact on the Loop and neighborhoods. Prosperity had come in the guise of new wartime industries, but Chicago's infrastructure sat in disrepair. Outside of the construction of some public housing for war workers, little wartime residential construction had taken place. Migrants flocked to the city, straining the housing stock to a breaking point. Many returning veterans moved their new families in with parents or in-laws. Racial tensions again flared as the African American community saw its greatest growth and yet remained restricted to a ghetto only slightly expanded since 1930.

Little construction had taken place in the Loop since the completion of the Field Building in the early 1930s. The Works Progress Administration built the new subway in the early 1940s, but public transportation remained in poor shape and was financially exhausted. Highways had been planned, but not yet built. Chicago, like many other American cities, faced immense problems. Many Chicagoans saw the suburbs as better places to live and work than their old urban neighborhoods. Others hoped to remake those neighborhoods with a new vision born of both the New Deal and the organizational experiences of the prewar era.

The Postwar Democrats

For Richard J. Daley, a politician few Chicagoans outside of the South Side's Bridgeport neighborhood would have recognized in 1945, the postwar world bristled with opportunity. Daley grew up the only child of Irish immigrants. A boyhood friend once remarked of the young Daley, "His family was a little better off than the rest of us, Dick was the only kid in the neighborhood who had a handkerchief."[1] Daley went on to De La Salle Institute, the Christian Brothers' school on Thirty-fifth and Wabash just east of Bridgeport. He graduated from the business program and went to work in the Union Stock Yards, using his education and connections to get a job with the Dolan, Ludeman and Company Livestock Commission Firm. In later years Daley often portrayed himself as a stockyard cowboy, but he largely worked in Dolan's office in the Exchange Building.

An Irish Catholic boy from the South Side learned some basic truths very quickly on the street, in school, and in the ward offices. One was the virtue of loyalty. Daley had learned from his Christian Brother teachers at De La Salle Institute the power of loyalty: loyalty to one's friends; loyalty to the neighborhood; in Chicago Catholic terms, loyalty to the parish; and loyalty to the universal Church and the Democratic Party. Another basic value was to never tell on one's colleagues whatever their transgressions. Boys would be punished at De La Salle for telling the Brothers about their classmates' wrong doings. Daley and his fellow Catholic South Siders seemed to be born with an almost natural talent for politics. In the pietistic Irish world of popular religion, you most likely couldn't even go to your eternal just reward without help from a heavenly friend. You had to know someone to get past the pearly gates. A patron saint, or perhaps the Virgin Mary, could help a sinner get into heaven. It was sort of like being someone from the Eleventh Ward who needed a job; he or she needed the help of a patron, someone with political clout. Daley understood that structure, and he planned to be that patron, to be the greatest worldly patron of all in Chicago.[2]

Patronage provided much of the power behind Chicago's politics and had since the fire first brought the city to its knees. Simply put, patronage was the placing of political allies, friends, and even family members into government jobs. A longtime American tradition that dated to the first days of the federal government and even to the colonial governments, the system had fallen out of favor nationally after the assassination of President James A. Garfield in 1881 by a disappointed office seeker. Chicago's Mayor Carter Harrison suffered the same fate twelve years later. Still, despite attempts at civil service reform on both a national and local level, patronage remained an important source of political power in Chicago and across the United States. Daley understood both the crude and the more sophisticated customs of the system. He also knew that controlling patronage provided the most political power possible. The young Daley began his political career working for Big Joe McDonough, Bridgeport's legendary football hero alderman. In 1924, Daley won his first political contest, elected as president of the Hamburg Athletic Club, the local community's own borderline street gang and McDonough's political army. The Hamburg AC played sports and had been involved in the 1919 race riot, but their main job was to knock on doors and get the vote out for Democratic politicians. Daley's election assured McDonough's continued support of the club and their continued support of the alderman.

Over the years, Daley worked hard, kept his mouth shut, and remained loyal to Nativity of Our Lord Parish and the local Democratic Party. Years of graft and corruption had made many a Chicagoan cynical and less trusting of local politicians. Then in 1931, with the overwhelming election of Anton Cermak, Daley had his chance. McDonough had supported Cermak and had considerable clout in the new administration. He began his slow rise in the local party structure, eventually getting elected to his first state office in 1936—as a Republican! Only in the strange ways of Chicago and Illinois politics could such a thing happen. Under the law at the time, every state congressional district had three representatives, and one had to be from a minority party. So in overwhelmingly Democratic Bridgeport, the local party put Daley up to fill a Republican seat vacated by death. He won handily, and the Democrats actually had three votes from Bridgeport. This was the beginning of his career in electoral politics.

Daley thus got his start as a Cermak Democrat in the middle of the Great Depression and Franklin Roosevelt's New Deal. He learned lessons from both Cermak and Roosevelt. From Cermak, Daley learned the importance of control of Chicago's immigrant and working-class neighborhoods and the party organization. He also learned that the aldermen were generally an uncontrollable and corrupt bunch. From Roosevelt, the young Daley realized that government could be an active force in the lives of ordinary citizens. FDR's New Deal provided an example of how the federal government could guarantee better lives for the nation's citizens—at least in theory. In turn Daley learned from Kelly how to manipulate the new federal largesse. Daley was indeed a man of his times. His experiences as a young politician, watching the elders of Chicago's Democratic Party formed much of his public life. After World War II, he was ready to make a greater contribution.[3]

Certainly, the experience of the previous fifteen years had taught Daley, as well as most Chicagoans and Americans, the necessity of a strong federal government that could rally the nation. The creation of the Veterans Administration and the GI Bill of Rights generated this viewpoint. The long-term impact of these laws, like those of the Home Owners Loan Corporation and the Federal Housing Authority, were not yet apparent. GIs, who wanted desperately to live the good life that they felt they had earned on the beaches of the Pacific and across the battlefields of Europe, believed the programs insured a better life. Americans black and white, female and male expected a better America. What each of those groups meant by this was another question. Those separate ideals could, as they had in 1919, mean conflict—especially between the races.

The Problem of Race

Racial problems existed across the city, but particularly on the South Side. Woodlawn, the neighborhood just to the south of Hyde Park and the University of Chicago, provided a point of conflict between the races in the years directly after the war. In 1920, the U.S. census counted only 2 percent of Woodlawn's population as African American. This small group of largely middle-class blacks lived among a population dominated by Chicagoans of Irish, German, and English descent. Blacks tended to be concentrated in an area that ran from Sixty-third Street south to Sixty-seventh Street and from Cottage Grove Avenue west to South Park Way, one of those areas that white real estate dealers had agreed to cede to blacks in the post-1919 era. This census tract recorded 16.6 percent of its population as African American that year. Ten years later, blacks made up 13 percent of Woodlawn's total population, and as the black population increased so did segregation; the district west of Cottage Grove, known as West Woodlawn, reported over 80 percent of its population as African American.[4]

In the 1920s the blocks bordering Sixty-third Street took on a rather transient character. Many people who worked in the Loop moved to Woodlawn. Many buildings were subdivided into kitchenette apartments, which along with boarding houses and apartment hotels dominated the district nearest Sixty-third Street. The street itself became a major shopping and entertainment strip for South Siders. Mass transit and the emerging urban entertainment culture nurtured many of the businesses on the street. Chicagoans from throughout the city converged on this "Bright Lights" district.

Woodlawn's close proximity to the University of Chicago resulted in roughly half of the university's faculty living in the neighborhood by 1930. Other prominent Chicagoans also called Woodlawn home. This mixture of white ethnics, a growing middle-class black population, white university professors and administrators, plus a largely white-collar transient population led to a very diverse and vibrant community area. Residents mingled with Chicagoans from all over the city along Sixty-third Street. This mixture, however, proved to be temporary especially under the dual pressures of postwar American prosperity and racism.

Between 1930 and 1960, Woodlawn's population grew from 66,052 residents to 81,699. African American inhabitants jumped from 13 percent to nearly 90 percent of the community in the same time period. In 1940, the area to the west of Cottage Grove Avenue had almost no white residents. After World War II, blacks moved east of the old racial dividing line at Cottage Grove Avenue. The 1948 Supreme Court decision outlawing racial covenants, in which landowners agreed not to sell or rent to African Americans or other supposed undesirables, opened up Woodlawn and other South Side neighborhoods on the edge of the ghetto to black residents. The postwar years also witnessed immense growth at the edge of the city. Upwardly mobile whites left neighborhoods like Woodlawn for the city's outskirts and the suburbs. Chicago's growing African American population in turn looked for more housing beyond the crowded and worn down ghetto. Massive racial turnover occurred in Woodlawn during the 1950s as forty thousand whites left the area and African Americans, along with some two thousand Puerto Ricans, replaced them. As the 1950s began, the authors of

Figure 99. As the number of African Americans grew they found themselves living in buildings originally intended for fewer residents. Developers originally built the Hawthorn Apartments at 500–520 East Thirty-third Place for middle-class residents, but by 1946 the apartments had been subdivided into crowded slum dwellings. (Photograph by Charles W. Cushman; Indiana University Archives, P03497.)

the sensational book *Chicago Confidential* referred to Sixty-third Street as the "main street of Bronzeville's toniest section."[5]

The events in Woodlawn and across the South Side heralded the remaking of the ghetto after the dislocating effects of World War II. The war had had a tremendous impact on Chicago's black population. First of all it revived the great migration. The numbers of African Americans moving north between 1940 and 1975 would dwarf earlier migrations from the South. The races renegotiated boundaries during a long, agonizing, and sometimes violent period. While Chicago's population rose from 3,396,808 in 1940 to 3,620,962 ten years later and then went into decline to 3,550,404 in 1960, the African American population rose from 278,000 in 1940 to 813,000 in 1960 and continued to grow. White Chicagoans rarely considered voluntary integration in the postwar era. Instead, they constantly reestablished, even if only temporarily, a shifting racial boundary line clearly delineating the "Second Ghetto," a reality of life in Chicago by 1960.[6]

Englewood: Angeline Jackson's Neighborhood

When he returned from serving in the U.S. Army at the end of World War II, the senior George Jackson felt unhappy and dissatisfied with Greenfield, Mississippi. The Army experience had changed him, and he wanted a better life than he felt he could have in the South. In 1952, Jackson decided to follow his sister north to Chicago. At first the Jacksons lived on the West Side with George Jackson's sister. Soon Jackson started work at the huge U.S. Post Office downtown. Finally the family found an apartment on the 5500 block of South Wentworth through some friends who lived nearby on La Salle Street. Jackson eventually purchased the two-flat with a storefront and remodeled the store as a small apartment.

Wentworth Avenue was a lively street with a streetcar line that allowed the Jacksons to explore the city. Nearby stood St. Anne's Roman Catholic Church and parochial school, both of which came to play an important role in the Jacksons' lives. Born a Catholic, Angeline Jackson attended parochial school and Catholic high school in Mississippi. For the Jacksons, the old Irish church on the corner provided an anchor in the new urban environment. Angeline Jackson had heard about shootings and violence in Chicago and worried about her children. Chicago's crowded anonymous streets seemed very different from small town life in the South, where Jackson felt she knew were she stood with white neighbors. "They either liked you or they didn't and you knew it." Race relations in Chicago seemed more complicated. Whites might smile at blacks but still hate them. Certainly Chicago was an intricate and sometimes frightening place. St. Ann's provided a haven in that strange world.[7]

By the late 1950s, the urban world of the Jacksons shifted, or to be more precise, became displaced. Change moved in directly across the street from the family home. The record shop that played Sam Cooke albums, the pastry shop, the Certified Grocery Store, and the Uptown Drugstore, where their oldest son, George, worked, disappeared, replaced by the gapping hole created by the Chicago Land Clearance Commission for the South Side Expressway. Clouds of dust blew across what looked like an old war zone. The remaining white families left as the bulldozers arrived. The new racial dividing line became the Pennsylvania Railroad tracks to the west. Construction crews built the future Dan Ryan Expressway just outside the Jacksons' door, and huge earth-moving equipment thundered by daily, much as the millions of trucks, cars, buses, and eventually a new rapid transit line would after the expressway opened in 1962.

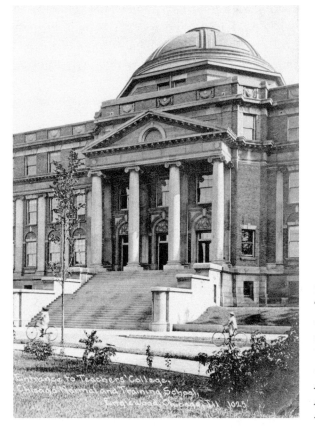

Figure 100. Chicago Teachers' College or Normal School had provided an important institutional base for Englewood and even gave a street, Normal Avenue, its name. (Postcard, Author's Collection.)

A fourteen-lane expressway appeared as Mrs. Jackson's front window now overlooked the Garfield Boulevard off-ramp of the Dan Ryan Expressway. The Jacksons found themselves trapped in the midst of urban renewal.[8]

Just to the north and east of them, construction crews worked building massive high-rise towers. First demolition of the old Federal Street slum and then construction of the Robert Taylor Homes radically shifted the Jacksons' world. For the Jackson children the whole orientation of the neighborhood changed from west to east. George Jr. and his brother Prentiss had often played football on the grassy boulevard in front of St. Anne's and the Uptown Drugstore. Now a bridge spanning the Dan Ryan Expressway stood at the site. The Uptown Drugstore moved farther south to Sixty-first and State Street. St. Ann's white working-class population disappeared. The expressway built a wall across the South Side. South of Thirty-fifth Street the wall, however, could not contain the exploding black population. The southern half of Armour Square, Fuller Park, and Englewood became African American neighborhoods despite this new barrier in the cityscape. North of Thirty-fifth Street Comiskey Park with its parking lots provided an additional boundary between blacks and whites. The power of the Eleventh Ward Regular Democratic Organization also helped hold the racial dividing line. South Side neighborhoods saw much change in the 1950s as urban renewal shifted boundaries of racial and ethnic neighborhoods.

According to the census, the Jacksons lived in Englewood, which stood squarely in the center of demographic and economic change. For years the neighborhood remained a racial hot spot where conflict broke out periodically. By 1952, when the Jacksons moved to Fifty-fifth and Wentworth, change was in the air, but Englewood would go through a long transition as blacks and whites met each other on the streets of the South Side. By the mid-1950s Englewood was a "changing" neighborhood. Southern whites and blacks poured into the district as many white ethnic working-class residents moved south and west or abandoned the city altogether. They left behind a neighborhood of older homes at a time when Victorian simply meant old-fashioned and not worth much. World War II, with its kitchenette conversions and overcrowding, had broken down many parts of the neighborhood. Workers flocked to it because of the good transit lines and its proximity to both the stockyards and the expanding wartime industrial belts to both the southeast and southwest. In general, newcomers arrived in the most rundown parts of Englewood first, so the changes became most obvious in the oldest sections of the neighborhood. Local institutions mirrored transformations on the streets and in the two-flats, cottages, and old Victorian homes. By 1960, whites made up only 36.6 percent of Englewood's population. The whites that tended to remain in Englewood lived in Visitation Parish on Garfield Boulevard. "Viz" remained a white, particularly Irish American, holdout into the 1960s. The Roman Catholic parish maintained both a coeducational parochial school and a girl's high school.[9]

Ted Swigon's Back of the Yards: A Shifting Landscape

Just northwest of Visitation Parish and Englewood, Ted Swigon lived in a Polish American world, a world that his parents and grandparents had lived in. His father, Theodore Sr., grew up in St. Stanislaus Kostka parish up on the North Side in another neighborhood now being transformed by the expressway fever raging in Chicago and across America in the late 1950s. The elder Swigon had the good fortune to marry a South Side Polish girl, Ann Zon, who lived in St. John of God parish near the stockyards. As Polish American young women preferred to live close to their mothers, the Swigons made their lives in Back of the Yards.

As an altar boy Ted Swigon came to know St. John of God's Church well. He knew every nook and cranny of the huge structure as he climbed the bell towers, knew the small hiding places only an altar boy could find. Swigon and other altar boys assisted the priest as he put on the vestments, saying a precise prayer with each one, kissing his mantle, and preparing for the liturgy. Swigon came to know the seasons and rituals as he grew up. St. John of God's choir

Figure 101. St. John of God Catholic School altar boys, ca. 1956. Ted Swigon is in the center. (Courtesy of Theodore J. Swigon.)

was renowned in the neighborhood, and on holy days the choir entered in a procession from the rear of the massive limestone church with its huge towers and rose window.[10]

While the parish church provided sacred space for the neighborhood, other types of public, private, and semipublic space abounded in Back of the Yards and other Chicago neighborhoods. Like most urban neighborhoods, the Back of the Yards was filled with places where people gathered for social, political, and cultural reasons. Taverns, parks, halls, and the ever-present stores on both the busy major thoroughfares and the side streets furnished haunts for residents. On Fifty-first Street, a hardware store near St. John of God's was the site of an ongoing card game. The narrow, dimly lit store smelled of cigar smoke as neighborhood men gathered in the back to try a hand or two. They joked in Polish, and the proprietor often ignored customers, especially neighborhood children sent by their fathers to buy nails, screws, or some other piece of hardware. The owner's son took care of patrons once the older men dealt the cards.[11]

Influenced by the Felician Sisters, especially Sister Daniella, who guided the altar boys at St. John of God Parochial School, Ted Swigon and several of his classmates went to Quigley Preparatory Seminary to study for the priesthood. After two years he decided against the life of a Catholic priest, and he transferred to De La Salle Institute. So eventually did the other boys from his class who went to Quigley; countless young men of Swigon's generation decided to forgo the priesthood just as the Catholic Church seemed triumphant in urban America. Many young women who thought they might become nuns also changed their minds. Changes in religious attitudes crept silently and almost unnoticed through the parishes and neighborhoods of Catholic America.[12]

That transformation did not yet seem worrisome as the 1950s came to an end. The vast majority of Catholic Chicagoans attended Mass on Sundays; their children went to parochial schools and Catholic high schools; Latin, the ancient language of the Church, endured as the language of the Mass and sacraments. Various orders of sisters, many with strong ethnic roots, maintained the Chicago Catholic school system, the largest private school system in the world. The Sisters of Mercy maintained loyalty to the community that had carried them to Chicago from Dublin. In addition to grade schools and high schools, they operated St. Xavier College, Illinois' first institution of higher learning, founded in 1846. The college moved in 1956 to a new location on the Far Southwest Side in the Mount Greenwood neighborhood, following the Irish to the outskirts of the city.[13] The Felician Sisters tended to Polish American children. The Sisters of St. Casimir served the Lithuanian community. Many of these orders of nuns had a long established presence in the schools, hospital, nursing homes, orphanages, and other such institutions of Catholic Chicago.

Religious vocations still seemed abundant. In April 1958, the Archdiocese ordained thirty-four new priests. Eight more priests received Holy Orders later that year. On August 16, 1958, three groups of young Sisters of Mercy participated in ceremonies of profession at St. Xavier College and Queen of Martyrs Parish on the Southwest Side. At 7:30 a.m. in the college chapel, twenty-seven sisters made their temporary profession taking vows for a three-year period, exchanging the white veil of a novice for the black veil of the professed sister. Three hours later in Queen of Martyrs Church, twenty-six more sisters pronounced their final vows putting on a silver ring to be worn for life. Finally in the afternoon, nineteen postulants received the white veil of a novice, acquiring the habit of a Sister of Mercy and beginning their study toward the permanent sisterhood. Also that August, thirteen women took final vows as Felician Sisters at the Felician Mother House on Peterson Avenue. About two thousand young men and women attended the Archdiocese of Chicago's various seminaries and scholasticates. The more than three hundred thousand students in Catholic grammar and high schools seemed to assure a continual source of vocations in Chicago.[14]

The neighborhood Ted Swigon grew up in was a familiar one of ethnic churches, taverns, grocery stores, soda shops, candy stores, delicatessens, and

Figure 102. New Sister of Mercy novices exit St. Mary Queen of Martyrs Church in Evergreen Park, ca. 1955. These young women took their first vows upon entering the Roman Catholic sisterhood. (Sisters of Mercy Chicago Regional Community Archives.)

parks. Each ethnic group maintained an almost complete set of institutions that served members from cradle to grave and beyond. In Back of the Yards, Lithuanians were baptized, educated, confirmed, married, and buried from Holy Cross Church with a short stop at Eudeikis Funeral Parlor on Hermitage Street on their way to St. Casimir Lithuanian Cemetery. Polish mountaineers or *Polski Górale* sought the same services at Sacred Heart and the Wolniak or Bafia funeral parlors as they buried their dead at Resurrection Cemetery to the southwest of the city. Three Polish Catholic churches joined Lithuanian, German, Czech, Slovak, Mexican, Ukrainian, French Canadian, and two Irish parishes in the neighborhood. Non-Catholic churches also existed, including the German Lutheran St. Martini church, the Russian Orthodox St. Michael's, and a Polish National Catholic parish, a group that broke with the Roman Catholic Church in the early 1900s. At one time a small synagogue also operated in the neighborhood, but it was closed by the 1950s. While assimilation had taken place, especially in the wake of World War II, ethnic identification remained strong in these working-class neighborhoods. This connection with being Polish or a member of any other ethnic group provided a sense of community and even of political power in a city where such categorizations mattered in the neighborhood, the union hall, and at the voting booth.[15]

There seemed to be a sense of permanence to this way of life, yet already shifts had occurred in the structures of the city. Older residents of the Back of the Yards saw their children move to the "new" neighborhoods of the Far Southwest Side or even to the suburbs. Veterans returning from World War II and the Korean War shunned work in the packinghouses and searched out better, cleaner jobs and housing on the rapidly expanding fringes of the city. Still in the 1950s many stayed and had been joined by new immigrants after the Second World War including displaced persons from Poland, Lithuania, and other places torn by war and Communist takeovers. These "D.P.s," allowed into the United States by special post-1945 legislation, rejuvenated many of the older Polish and Lithuanian institutions as they came to the older industrial neighborhoods of Chicago's core. In many ways the arrival of the refugees masked the long-term changes taking place under the impact of prosperity and technological change. Polish could still be heard on Back of the Yards' streets, even if many former residents now lived a good car ride away in the Bungalow Belt or suburbs. Some came back on Sunday or holidays to visit their old parishes or attend fraternal club meetings. Others returned to play bingo at St. Augustine's community center. More returned to witness the ongoing rites of passage at places like St. Joseph's Church or Patka's Funeral Parlor or to dance at a wedding at Columbia or Pulaski Halls. But the children and grandchildren of immigrants from the great waves of immigration that changed Chicago after 1880 had become more American in culture and outlook. The World War II experience transformed them. They simply became white Americans even if most still had a rudimentary knowledge of an ethnic language, had a preference for a certain kind of food, and enjoyed a polka at a wedding or a Sunday afternoon picnic in the Dan Ryan Woods, Tarnow's Grove, or Polonia Grove on Archer Avenue. Change and continuity simultaneously marked the lives of most Chicagoans.

In the late 1950s the Back of the Yards remained a working-class white ethnic enclave, centering on the intersection of West Forty-seventh Street and Ashland Avenue. After World War II, the familiar world of neighborhoods remained intact even if under stress. It was obvious that both population changes and decisions being made in city hall, Springfield, and especially Washington, D.C., might alter the realities of this familiar world. A second ghetto, although that is hardly what Chicagoans would have called it, emerged on the South and West Sides. Many Chicagoans hunkered down to try and prevent, or at least slow, those changes.

Reaction to Change

Average Chicagoans faced the everyday realities of the new city emerging around them. For some it presented positive choices; for others it threatened disaster. Constant vigilance was necessary on the part of some communities to protect themselves from real or perceived threats. Social class played a tremendous role in this situation. Some neighborhoods, like Hyde Park, the Gold Coast, or Lincoln Park, were better able to manipulate the socioeconomic system and control their destinies. Other neighborhoods, such as Bridgeport, relied on political clout; Back of the Yards relied on community organizing while some areas used violence to try and preserve their communities. In any case, the large forces changing Chicago in the immediate postwar years created situations in which many Chicagoans, black and white, felt helpless. Huge economic, demographic, and political forces seemed to be moving people and changing urban realities. Change brought about by the war and by government agencies, often in the guise of urban renewal projects such as the expressway system or public housing, carved up whole parts of the city.

One of the traditions that did not change was the rule of color on the streets. Chicago, like most of the nation, remained strongly segregated in the 1950s, and the civil rights movement had not yet touched northern cities. The movement of African Americans into the neighborhoods west of Wentworth Avenue had brought sporadic violence, resentment, and fear to fuel the fires of racism across the South Side. While urban renewal changed the face of the Federal Street slum in the guise of massive public housing projects and ploughed through the neighborhoods across the South Side and into Englewood with the advent of the Dan Ryan Expressway, other neighborhoods tried to tame the beast of change and "conserve" their districts. In Hyde Park the powerful University of Chicago and its offspring the South East Chicago Commission launched a campaign to preserve the lakefront neighborhood. While Hyde Parkers wrapped themselves in liberal notions about integration, they displaced working-class and poor whites and blacks alike with their plan to save Hyde Park. Politically powerful elites made designs to control, if not eliminate, them in the neighborhood that included the University of Chicago and the Museum of Science and Industry. The Hyde Park urban renewal plan announced in 1958 was obviously designed to control black and lower-class white populations. An activist University of Chicago administration pursued a plan that would "protect" the university from the encroaching ghetto. The scheme hit on nine hundred acres in the South Side community and called for the demolition of six hundred buildings as planners expected the project to take five years. Groundbreaking took place in 1958, and the Hyde Park A and B Project called for the erection of 550 apartments, 250 row houses, and a shopping center at an estimated cost of $15 million.

Figure 103. Robinson's Delicatessen, located at 244 East Thirty-fifth Street, served Chicago's Bronzeville neighborhood in the late 1940s. Located just east of State Street, these buildings became prime targets of Chicago's postwar urban renewal program. (Photograph by Charles W. Cushman; Indiana University Archives, P04242.)

Various groups, including the CIO, openly criticized the urban renewal plan even as both university officials and city planners publicly denied racial and social class biases. At times the racial antagonism in Hyde Park erupted into the open. On October 1, 1958, the *Hyde Park Herald,* a neighborhood weekly that supported the urban renewal plan, printed an anonymous letter attacking African Americans as "savages" and as "screaming brawling, whining low incomes who make a slum wherever they light." The black press reprinted the missive, which played on white prejudices referencing to the "primitive beat of the tom-tom and the agonized wail of the saxophone in pain." The writer called for Hyde Park to "scrape off the effluvia of the spilling slums to provide a clean beautiful sanctuary for those to whom life is a search for meaning." In Back of the Yards and in West Woodlawn white and black working-class residents organized to try and conserve their neighborhoods, to stop the "beast" of urban renewal.[16]

Middle-class African American leaders, who saw Woodlawn as an escape from the traditional ghetto, joined white businessmen and the few remaining white residents in the 1950s in an attempt to stabilize the community and help it maintain its middle-class character. In 1958, the Community Conservation Board began developing a program for the rehabilitation of West Woodlawn, where high unemployment matched a drop in city services in the neighborhood. African American leaders in West Woodlawn had waged a long struggle against blight and pointed out that the area contrasted sharply with other South Side communities that had turned into slums. Still, blight appeared along commercial streets, especially Sixty-third Street. The 240-acre site might prove to be a test case as an example of black Chicagoans taking control of their future and saving their neighborhood. Leaders quickly clarified that they wanted the area "conserved" and not bulldozed. The African American leadership of West Woodlawn showed the way to their neighbors east of Cottage Grove.[17]

The people of East Woodlawn felt that they had much to fear from a University of Chicago–led conservation program in the Hyde Park and Kenwood. Middle-class African Americans felt that the university intended to dump poor black residents into Woodlawn. In April 1958, African American community activist Ruth Porter wrote Julian Levi, "The interracial character of the community [Woodlawn] is fast receding." She complained that unscrupulous landlords accelerated racial transition as they engaged in the wholesale turn over of tenancy from white to black and raised the rents excessively: "The residency of the stable white people is becoming more tentative every day." Many felt that the powers that be did not care.[18]

About a fifteen-minute drive northwest from Woodlawn in the Back of the Yards, Joseph Meegan emerged as an important player in the neighborhood conservation movement. Meegan, the primary organizer behind the Back of the Yards Neighborhood Council (BYNC), could see his neighbors looking for housing beyond the Stock Yard District. Former neighborhood residents often said they would stay if better and newer affordable housing existed in the district. Meegan hoped to build new housing that would keep his working-class neighbors in the neighborhood and preserve its character.[19] He convinced the city to allow the construction of single-family homes on lots smaller than the traditional twenty-five-foot Chicago lot. This opened up odd parcels of land across the South and Southwest Sides for new housing. The BYNC leader had a simple plan, and the council based its actions on Saul Alinsky's beliefs that working-class people had a right to determine their own future. In the 1940s and 1950s, journalists, sociologists, and the Catholic hierarchy hailed the organization as an example of real democracy being developed on a grassroots level. Still the question of race haunted Meegan and the BYNC. Council officials publicly proclaimed, "Negroes don't have anything in common with the people who live here."[20]

Between 1953 and early 1958, the BYNC program erected over 150 new homes and remodeled more than four thousand older ones. Home financing and repair did not pose a problem in Back of the Yards. Twenty-two local banks and lending institutions pledged to continue to finance the BYNC Conservation Program. A heavily Catholic area, the Catholic Church had much to lose if the neighborhood changed to a Protestant African American one. Cardinal Stritch supported the BYNC program. He asked all forty-three local priests also to support it. An editorial in the *New World* lauded the conservation programs in the Back of the Yards and in West Woodlawn as examples for the rest of the city: "These two programs are helping to conserve their own neighborhoods, but even more important, they are not creating new problems for other neighborhoods. Because there were no vast demolition projects the people are remaining in their own neighborhoods, not spilling out into surrounding neighborhoods to cause new housing problems. By conserving their own neighborhoods, these programs are giving stability to surrounding neighborhoods." The Catholic newspaper attacked the Hyde Park urban renewal program, claiming, "Programs which may help one neighborhood but spread problems to other neighborhoods are open to question."[21] Put simply, all neighborhoods were connected, and the problems should be addressed both locally and city-wide without upsetting traditional residential patterns and institutions.

Arguing over Urban Renewal

Chicago's Catholics faced a quickly changing city. Church leaders attempted to shore up inner-city parishes threatened by racial change and urban renewal. Cardinal Stritch named Rev. Msgr. John Egan director of conservation for the Archdiocese of Chicago, in 1958. Egan attacked the Hyde Park renewal plan and the highway builders. In an obvious reference to the impact of the South Side Expressway the monsignor said, "When the superhighway is rammed through such a neighborhood, it takes with it more than the buildings it demolishes for its right of way. It abolishes a human community and a way of life, which has much to be said for it. No churchman, be he of whatever faith, be he a pastor or a Bishop, can look at this destruction of healthy social cells with equanimity." Monsignor Egan and the Conservation Commission lauded the self-directed example of the BYNC and tried to make it as a model to the rest of the city and perhaps even the nation. The racial question remained, but while Egan pointed to black housing problems as the major moral issue of the times, he focused on Hyde Park, a not very Catholic neighborhood, where the removal of poor blacks would mean forcing them into other neighborhoods, most likely those of the Catholic working class who might then flee to the suburbs. The Catholic

Figure 104. Beulah's Eat Shoppe restaurant located at 400 East Thirty-first Street occupied an old bus and served food twenty-four hours per day in Bronzeville in the late 1940s. (Photograph by Charles W. Cushman; Indiana University Archives, P04269.)

leader called for more housing and less segregation. He claimed that African Americans were the "victim of a gigantic silent conspiracy." Egan asserted that "when handled correctly urban renewal will be an inestimable blessing for all of us." It was not urban renewal per se, but the methods of the experts and bureaucrats that Egan objected to. Plans called for some 4,500 housing units to be removed in Hyde Park alone. The priest called urban renewal as urban planners practiced it a "Second Trojan Horse" and pointed to the fact that cities had been changing at an accelerated pace in the years after World War II. The priest quoted D. E. Macklemann, consultant to Chicago's Planning Department, who estimated that twenty-five thousand dwelling units had been cleared from 1950 to 1958, and that probably more than one hundred thousand residents had lived in those units. Mackleman estimated another twenty-five thousand units would be pulled down by 1961. Egan worried about the demographic spillover into previously stable areas, areas that were overwhelmingly Catholic in population.[22]

Labor leaders joined the Catholic Church in condemning the Hyde Park/Kenwood plan. The Congress of Industrial Organizations found "much to regret" in the plan and claimed that Hyde Park was reimposing the outlawed racial covenants. Labor leaders accused planners of forcing economic segregation on the lakefront neighborhoods. The plan was blatantly unfair to certain groups and, according to union leaders, was another step in removing middle-income workers from the lakefront. They tied the race riots in Trumbull Park, a white steelworkers community, to the Hyde Park plan, pointing to the hypocrisy of the upper classes. The CIO called for breaking up the ghetto, although they did not give a formula for doing so. A Catholic mayor and a largely Roman Catholic legislative body politely listened and went on with business as usual, supporting the plans.[23]

Violence: The Murder of Alvin Palmer

The Back of the Yards had long been a center of industrial and racial conflict. Street gangs maintained a strong presence in the neighborhood. Area teenagers often attended both public and Catholic high schools with mixed ethnic populations where racial and ethnic tension filled the corridors. Teenagers found themselves in social situations their parents did not know or understand. These working-class families sent their children, especially boys, to public high schools such as Tilden Technical, Lindbloom, and Gage Park High Schools. Particularly in these public high schools, ethnicity meant less, and race more, as white and black violence frequently erupted.

Seventeen-year-old Joseph Schwartz worked as a freight caller in the rail yards near the Chicago Stockyards and lived nearby at Fifty-second and Laflin. A high school dropout, Schwartz had argued with his father over paying his family rent and had moved in with his brother Bill. He started hanging out at a candy store owned by Michael Perun at Fifty-first and Wolcott near Cornell Square Park. Joe Schwartz joined the Rebels, a local Back of the Yards street gang.[24]

Alvin Palmer, another seventeen-year old, attended Farragut High School on the West Side. As World War II ended, Alvin's father, Elijah, decided to move to Chicago from Cleveland, Alvin's birthplace. They lived on the West Side until 1956 when Elijah Palmer went into the secondhand furniture business in Englewood. The young boy, a good student, and a member of the Boy Scouts, the Junior Red Cross, the Farragut Student Council, and the high school U.S. Marine Corps Reserve, continued to attend the integrated West Side high school as a senior who expected to graduate that June 1957.[25]

On the night of March 11, 1957, Palmer rode the Kedzie Avenue bus south from his old neighborhood. He got off at Fifty-ninth Street just before 10:00 p.m. and waited for the eastbound bus in front of a tobacco store. Across the street stood the Colony Theater, the local movie house, and Gertie's Ice Cream Parlor. Wilmore Johnson, a black grocery clerk who lived on Fifty-ninth and Wentworth also waited for the bus on the corner. Suddenly a car filled with teenagers, all members of the Rebels, drove past. When the car returned, Joe Schwartz, who had been drinking heavily, jumped out and leaned against the stoplight, glaring at the two blacks. The white teenager grabbed Palmer in an arm lock and began to beat him on the head with a three-pound ball-peen hammer. Johnson ran toward the two, and Schwartz hit him on the arm with the hammer before fleeing down the street. Alvin Palmer died ten hours later.

The Rebels quickly drove back to their candy store hangout in Back of the Yards, where Schwartz showed off the bloodstained hammer. The weapon itself belonged to another gang member, Larry Adas. Later Schwartz gave the hammer to Jerry Bandyk and Ronald White, two other Rebels. After trying to destroy the hammer, Bandyk hid the weapon in his father's garage.[26]

The murder stunned the city, and it broke the "conspiracy of silence" that had prevailed in the Chicago press's coverage of racial conflict. The randomness of the event and the obvious involvement of youth gangs shook Chicagoans. The police combed the Southwest Side looking for the offenders, making sweeps of white teenage hangouts.

Meanwhile a young police officer, just on the force twenty-two months, Joseph Mildice, who lived in the Gage Park neighborhood, began to do some investigating on his own. His work paid off when two telephone calls to his home tipped the twenty-six-year-old policeman off to the identity of the murderer and his accomplices. The Chicago police held six Rebels, all of whom lived in Back of the Yards. Most of the accused attended Gage Park High School. The randomness of the attack appeared more and more evident as the teenagers spoke to police. When Joe Schwartz saw Palmer on the southwest corner of Fifty-ninth and Kedzie he simply said, "There's one" and sealed Palmer's fate.

The next day, Schwartz heard that Palmer had died; the Rebel got a hair cut and lost his sideburns. It made him harder to identify, but other Rebels quickly told their story to the police. On March 15 the *Chicago Tribune* ran a huge headline announcing that the police had arrested fifteen teens. Two cars of Rebels had cruised together that night looking to catch a black in a white neighborhood. State's Attorney Benjamin Adamowski called for the death penalty for all fifteen boys. Adamowski stated, "This is a cold blooded murder. There is no penalty we can ask, other than execution, that fits the crime." The incensed state's attorney said they should all be tried as murderers as they acted as a gang. Schwartz said, "It was just one of those things." Adamowski scoffed at the gang's name and said, "If that's what they want to be, we will treat them like rebels."

All fifteen boys were indicted for Alvin Palmer's murder: Joseph Schwartz, Ronald Rybka, James Adams, Lawrence Pavlik, Thomas Trybula, Frank Nowobielski, Edward Fron, Lawrence Adas, Donald Duchak, Alvin Zurek, Edward Gorski, Raymond Kozlowski, Andrew Budz, Ronald White, and Jerome Bandyk. All except Duchak lived in the Back of the Yards, and he had only recently moved to West Englewood just to the south. While the gang was of mixed ethnicity, like the Back of the Yards, Polish Americans dominated it as they did the neighborhood. Police booked Schwartz and ten of the Rebels on murder charges and handed four others over to juvenile authorities. When the Rebels appeared at the inquest, only six had relatives who made their presence known. Most of the boys faced the judge alone. Michael DeLaney, head of the Chicago Police Department's Juvenile Section, blamed their parents. DeLaney stated, "Any way you slice it Chicago's teen-age gang spree springs from delinquent parents."[27]

The Palmer murder raised racial tensions in the city. The *Chicago Daily Defender* editorialized that "this crime has burned shorter the fuse that may ignite the powder keg of racial tensions." Some acts of reprisal against whites by blacks had already occurred. Gerald D. Bullock, president of the Illinois NAACP, proclaimed that the perpetrators of the crime had directed it at all black citizens. The Rebels had killed Alvin Palmer because of his black skin. Bullock said that the murder symbolized "many Chicago attitudes toward racial minorities." The Palmer murder seemed more than gratuitous; it became a symbol of youth out of control. Blacks and whites generally did not live together, but they had to work together in the city. They attended schools together and worked in each other's neighborhoods. Palmer's death had a chilling effect on the always volatile racial order in a city already under stress. A racial killing so senseless, so unwarranted threatened the peace of the South Side and of all of Chicago.[28]

The Palmer family held Alvin's wake at a chapel at 1006 West Fifty-ninth Street, and the funeral on March 19 at the Church of God in Christ at Sixty-first and May Streets in Englewood. Over one thousand Chicagoans, black and white, attended the funeral. The senior class president, Claude Harrison, a white Farragut High School student, presented student donations to Palmer's parents to help with the funeral expenses. White and black students served as honorary pallbearers. Alvin Palmer's parents buried him in Cleveland. In June, Joe Schwartz received a fifty-year sentence. He broke down and cried in the courtroom. Years later Joe Schwartz wrote the Christian Brothers at De La Salle Institute, where he attended school for a short time, telling them of his remorse and sorrow for Palmer's death and his ruined life.[29] Alvin Palmer and Joe Schwartz symbolized the tensions of a city going through vast changes in the postwar period. The struggle to reach a new racial balance in the city continued throughout the era.

The post-1945 city saw a new ghetto emerging. The white power structure reshaped and reconstituted racial boundaries in Chicago. On the South Side middle- and working-class Chicagoans of both races faced an uncertain future. They resisted the Second Ghetto in their own ways. Chicago's South and West Side white communities saw themselves under siege. The city's African American population continued to grow rapidly, and forces outside the control of neighborhood leaders redrew ghetto boundaries. New expressways and housing projects reshaped the South Side, displacing families and creating new borders. Working-class and lower-middle-class whites did not see racial integration as an option in a rapidly changing postwar world. The Rebels, as senseless and violent as they became, were part of that reaction to a changing world that seemed to offer few options to white working-class neighborhoods.[30]

One alternative to violence, the hard work of neighborhood renewal, or dealing with race as a problem was simply to move. The years after World War II saw an unprecedented growth in Chicago's suburbs and their role in the political, social, and cultural life of the region.

Postwar Suburbs

As Chicago entered the postwar world, much on a neighborhood level seemed to remain the same, but massive structural changes had taken place during the war. After 1940, transportation changes altered the relationship between the city, the suburbs, and the region as a whole. Rail lines, canals, and mass transit had tied the area together to the Loop. After World War II, automobiles, trucks, and expressways began to have more of an effect on the region. New wartime industries brought change. Development took place in a much more diffuse and uncontrolled pattern.

Before 1940, there existed a kind of logic to the city's growth. Rail systems connected all residential and manufacturing areas. Naturally lowest land costs appeared at the fringe and fell away from rail lines. Both dormitory and industrial suburbs existed, and had since the mid-nineteenth century. Before the war, suburbs remained relatively stable with a mix of local and metropolitan functions. They tended to be homogeneous communities. The war shattered this old model. Rapid development sometimes meant haphazard development, with standards of zoning and regulation compromised. Suburban acreage more than doubled between 1940 and 1960. Fifteen years after the war ended the six-county metropolitan region included 6.1 million residents, about the number living in the Mountain States. It covered roughly 3,700 square miles, or about as much territory as Delaware. Chicago's share of the population of the area declined after 1920 when it had reached 80 percent. By 1960, it stood only at a little above par with the surrounding suburban areas. In the years ahead it would slip further yet.

Suburbanization has always been connected to the decentralization of industry in Chicago and most American cities. Developers marketed Melrose Park, to the west of the city, as a blue-collar suburb from its earliest days. In 1925, the *Chicago Evening Post* reported that "Melrose Park offers an ideal place of residence to thrifty people. It has not all the advantages in the catalog, but like all the communities in the Chicago district it has a good honest climate." Modest homes close to suburban factories such as the National Malleable and Steel Castings Company, the American Brake Shoe and Foundry, Edward Hines Lumber, Melrose Park Plating, and American Can provided a suburban home for workers and a ready workforce for industries.[31]

To the south of the city and in northwestern Indiana industrial suburbs saw the large scale development of heavy industry, especially steel. Harvey, Chicago Heights, East Chicago, and above all Gary, founded by the U.S. Steel Com-

Figure 105. Chicago Municipal Airport (Midway Airport) developed into the "World's Busiest Airport" after World War II. American attitudes toward air travel changed as a result of the war, and Chicago became the center of the nation's airline industry. The city maintained its dominance with the development of O'Hare Airport to the northwest of the city. Pictured here is a DC-3 landing as a Boeing 307 Stratoliner takes on cargo at the Municipal Airport in 1941. (Photograph by Charles W. Cushman; Indiana University Archives, P02543.)

pany, were among the largest. The town of Blue Island, just across the city's boundaries, owed its growth to the Rock Island Railroad, which established its repair shops there. The town then quickly drew industries attracted by the Rock Island and other railroads that crossed the prairie at Blue Island. To the southwest Midlothian, Robbins, and Posen appeared, while to the west Stone Park and Stickney joined Melrose Park.

Chief among those industrial suburbs to the west was Cicero where the Western Electric Company located its huge Hawthorne plant in 1906. The plant served as the manufacturing arm of the national Bell Telephone System, producing more than forty-three thousand varieties of telephone apparatuses. The plant also produced, at one time or another, typewriters, sewing machines, electric fans, vacuum cleaners, vacuum tubes, and a motion picture sound system that revolutionized that industry. At its height, right after World War II, some forty thousand people worked at Hawthorne Works, and it included ten miles of railroad tracks within its boundaries.[32]

Chicago entrepreneurs were among the first to establish whole industrial districts, setting a precedent for future suburban development. This creation of manufacturing districts continued up until the Great Depression, and even that era saw continued expansion into Chicago's outlying communities. Between 1935 and 1940, 75 percent of local manufacturers built on suburban locations. By 1940, it was clear that for a growing proportion of industrial concerns a city location was no longer necessary or even imperative. Workers in turn followed and settled in these areas. Many lived in homes they had built themselves; others purchased homes constructed by both small and large developers in the bungalow boom of the 1920s.[33]

After the war, planned industrial parks with one-story buildings and lots of parking appeared throughout the suburbs. Open land and nicely landscaped parks surrounded the plants. They seemed very modern when compared with the city's dark and dirty nineteenth-century factories. The new suburban locations attracted new growing firms. By the late 1950s an almost unbroken ring of industrial suburbs surrounded the city.[34]

The Chicago area had experienced spectacular growth in the housing market, mostly on the outer edges of the city and in the suburbs in the 1950s. In the fifteen years after World War II builders erected nearly seven hundred thousand new homes in the Chicago metropolitan area.[35] At first many suburbs suffered from haphazard development, with little control over housing standards. Until 1940, suburbs were rather homogeneous and had a nice mix of local and metropolitan functions usually including an active downtown. The war basically destroyed this model. Out of what was once prairie land near 211th and Western Avenue to the south of the city, the brand new community of Park Forest emerged in the 1950s with approximately four thousand new homes and three thousand apartments. Working-class suburbs, such as Hometown near Eighty-seventh and Cicero Avenue to the southwest of the city also emerged to serve the new class of better-off industrial workers. Suburbs such as Evergreen Park, Oak Lawn, Calumet City, Dolton, and Homewood saw phenomenal expansion. Across the border in Indiana the Gary/Hammond area witnessed the building of about twenty-two thousand new homes. Skokie to the north of the city proved to be the fastest growing suburb in Cook County. Arlington Heights, Des Plaines, Glenview, Park Ridge, Lincolnwood, Morton Grove, Mount Prospect, and Northbrook all witnessed enormous development. The western suburbs also saw expansion. Westchester, Elmhurst, Downers Grove, Wheaton, Lombard, La Grange Park, and Villa Park all chalked up housing gains as white families left the city for the suburbs.[36]

Industrial expansion continued on the periphery of the city. The Skokie Valley saw the greatest growth, with 163 new firms locating in suburban Skokie in the fourteen years after the war. Evanston and Des Plaines also saw expansion as part of the Skokie Valley investment pattern, with forty-four and eighteen new manufacturing plants, respectively. Schiller Park saw fifty-two new plants, Addison thirty-three, Harwood Heights twenty-five, Wheeling ten, Northlake

Figure 106. Many white Chicagoans left the city for the suburbs in the postwar years. Residential housing construction postponed by the Great Depression and World War II exploded in the period 1945–60. Evergreen Park was one of the inner-ring suburbs that saw tremendous growth during this period. (Photograph by D. Pacyga.)

seven including the massive Automatic Electric plant that employed seven thousand in the late 1950s, and Elk Grove Village saw the 770-acre Hotpoint plant tract open. These "drive to work" suburbs also included Hometown, Worth, Westchester, and Berkeley among others, all of which were easily accessible to the new industrial suburbs as a result of highway construction. Until 1950, all commuter communities remained dependent on rail service, but after that year the appearance of highways spurred the growth of outlying communities. The new highways determined the physical and economic landscape. New larger suburbs appeared independent of the traditional commuter lines. Some of the new automobile-oriented communities appeared as far as forty miles outside of the city. New industrial plants emerged with no rail connection, as did entire industrial districts. In 1950, railroads served all 102 of the Chicago area towns of 2,500 or more inhabitants. Ten years later at least six of the thirty-six or so new municipalities to reach the 2,500 population mark had no rail connections.[37]

Good roads made good sense in the postwar period. The Edens Expressway opened in 1951 and transformed the area to the north of the city. It set off a major residential and industrial boom in the surrounding area. Skokie, Morton Grove, Glenview, Northbrook, Northfield, and Deerfield grew rapidly. Industry too followed the Edens away from the city's high land costs and congestion.

The opening of the Tri-State Tollway, which acted like the old beltline railroads tying the expressway system together with a ring around the city, also spurred development after its opening in the 1950s.

The number of workers in Chicago and the suburbs reflected these changes. In 1947, Chicago manufacturers employed 532,130. Ten years later 389,607 workers labored in Chicago factories, a loss of 26 percent. In turn the suburban numbers grew by 43 percent to 276,893 from the 1947 total of 193,843. Estimates put the population increase in suburbia as a result of this growth in manufacturing as 500,000 out of a total residential growth of 1,250,000. Much of the development north of Chicago consisted of small manufacturing plants oriented toward the highway. In turn these new industries and populations attracted nonindustrial support services such as insurance companies and research concerns, many of which located in Evanston, Skokie, and Park Ridge. Also huge shopping malls opened in Skokie (Old Orchard) and in Mount Prospect (Randhurst).

Skokie became the model for suburban growth in the 1950s. In 1900, the suburb, then called Niles Center, had a population of just 568. In 1926, the "L" line from Howard Street was extended to Dempster in Skokie, followed a year later by the Skokie Valley Route of the North Shore Line, the region's electric interurban. This caused a residential boom in the town, and by 1930 Skokie's population stood at 5,007. While the Depression retarded further growth, the war years and their immediate aftermath once again stimulated growth. In 1950, Skokie had 14,836 inhabitants. The Edens Expressway led to further expansion, and ten years later the town stood at 59,358, drawing much of its population from Chicago's Jewish community. In the 1950s Skokie's employment base also skyrocketed with a 216 percent increase. Eighty-eight percent of Skokie residents, however, did not work in the suburb. Most Skokie citizens still worked in Chicago, and 90 percent used their cars to get to work. It served them as a dormitory suburb, however, one with a sound and expanding industrial tax base.[38]

This suburban industrial growth did not mean that Chicago had lost its industrial base. Even by the 1950s the city still dominated the industrial scene. Local industry still centered on the city. A large part of Chicago's problem, however, was a lack of space. In the 1950s, as expressways tore through the urban fabric, even more land was lost. The Congress Street Expressway (Eisenhower) removed fifty-nine manufacturing plants. The planned Northwest Expressway (Kennedy) would displace around 225 more manufacturing concerns as it moved across the Northwest Side's industrial belt.

There was land in the city, but much of it was in hard-to-reach places or under water. The 1952 survey found over seven thousand acres of vacant industrial land within Chicago's borders, almost eleven square miles. Of this only perhaps four thousand acres were really available, but there was a problem with the land. Nearly one thousand acres were in the Lake Calumet region, and it needed extensive landfill before it could be developed. Railroads owned

Figure 107. Many inner-city Jewish synagogues such as this one, Share Zedek, in Logan Square saw their congregations dwindle in the aftermath of World War II as Chicago's Jews moved in large numbers to the suburbs. (Chicago Jewish Archives, Spertus Institute of Jewish Studies.)

another 1,600 acres, and heavy train traffic crisscrossed the sites making them unattractive for new businesses. Finally there was an uneven pattern of the land for sale. Most was on the South Side, south of Ninety-fifth Street, and new businesses did not want to locate in this heavy industrial zone with its heavy pollution from steel mills, refineries, and difficulty of accessibility for workers from other parts of the city.

In addition, competition for land was great. In the postwar boom existing firms wanted to expand. A considerable amount of new industry had located in the city. The major problem was the design of postwar manufacturing plants. Like residential buildings, postwar changes in architecture, transportation, and manufacturing had impacted on modern factories. Many were designed in the "ranch house" manner: a sleek one-story plant rather than traditional multi-story plants. These were seen as more efficient and easier to maintain. Many times developers considered a rail connection unnecessary. In addition, firms wanted these new buildings built in a campus setting. The high land costs in the city often made this prohibitive. At older locations, buildings generally occupied about 66 percent of the land, while newer buildings occupied generally 47 percent of their sites. Setbacks, parking facilities, and possible future expansion necessitated a lower ratio of building to land area. This was much more possible in the suburbs than in Chicago. Industries located outside the

Figure 108. These rail yards occupied a good deal of space to the northwest of the Loop. Much land that might have been used for industrial expansion in the 1950s was already occupied with rail lines. (Photograph by Charles W. Cushman; Indiana University Archives, P03200.)

city used approximately four and one-half times the amount of land than they occupied at their former city location. Obsolete buildings, too costly to maintain or remove, posed another problem, as did congested streets, inadequate space, and urban blight, which drove many firms from the urban core. About one out of every three manufacturing plants stood outside of industrial concentrations in commercial districts and residential neighborhoods, a holdover from the days before zoning was enacted in 1923. Planners felt that these plants would have to be eventually relocated.

Hardest hit in this transformation was Chicago's Central Area industrial belt. This zone extended from Diversey on the north to Fifty-first Street and Garfield Boulevard on the south and from the lake to Western Avenue. Here lay much of the old industrial core of Chicago, including the fading Union Stock Yards. Fifty-eight percent of Chicago's industrial jobs were located in this district in 1952. The Central District contained slightly over half of all industrial employees with maximum concentrations of twenty-eight thousand workers per square mile. The average concentration was 160 workers per square acre, most worked in multistory buildings. In 1952 it was estimated that at least 6 million square feet of vacant industrial space in Chicago existed in seriously dilapidated buildings. Again most of these structures were in the Diversey Avenue to Garfield Boulevard area. It was not surprising that industries desired to leave this area. The movement took place both within Chicago and into the larger metropolitan area. Two hundred and forty three plants left Chicago for the suburbs from 1946 to 1950, with 52 percent of these leaving from the Central District. More plants moved from Chicago in the five years following World War II than in the previous twenty-one years.[39]

Postwar suburban development picked up on the demographic trends of the 1920s Bungalow Belt, making affordable large suburban tracts for those not poor, but also not part of the elite that dominated early Riverside or Oak Park. Along with the truck and car, cheap federal housing loan guarantees made suburbanization possible. Planners in the 1930s had worried about Chicago and other traditional cities as being too congested. The greenbelt towns and cities planned during the New Deal had influenced urban planning in the postwar years. As military personnel came home from World War II and overcrowding again became a national issue, many saw the suburbs as an obvious tool in decentralization. Suburbs seemed places where the American dream of a single-

Figure 109. Swift and Company cut back and then closed its massive Chicago plant just west of the Union Stock Yards in the postwar period. (Postcard, Author's Collection.)

family detached home could become a reality for the new America emerging after the war, and so developed acreage in suburbia more than doubled between 1940 and 1960.

To the south of the city stood an open prairie that would soon be developed into Park Forest, perhaps the most famous of Chicago's post-1945 communities. On October 28, 1946, Philip M. Klutznick, Nathan Manilow, and Carroll F. Sweet announced the creation of the suburb by American Community Builders at a press conference held at the Palmer House in the Loop. Elbert Peets designed Park Forest in the tradition of other planned communities; the English Garden City movement influenced him as did the American greenbelt tradition. The town quickly became known as "GI Town" because of the number of veterans settling in it. American Community Builders screened residents as to income, education, veteran status, and need. The first newcomers settled in August 1948 amid construction mud and chaos. On February 1, 1949, the town incorporated. By 1950, the village had a population of over three thousand families, all white. The first African American resident did not arrive until 1959. By 1960, nearly thirty thousand people lived in Park Forest. Returning veterans and their families came to the new community, attracted by a mix of affordable housing with a series of planned amenities, including a regional shopping center, Park Forest Centre, and a mixed ethnic population.[40]

Chicago's postwar housing shortage caused various problems for returning veterans and their families. One early Park Forest resident, Leona DeLue, lived with her family in the Sherman Hotel in the Loop until an apartment could be secured in Park Forest. Most new residents signed up on a waiting list, and homes filled up with families almost before construction crews completed the structures. American Community Builders held the first town meeting in a tent as both current and prospective tenants came to the meeting. With incorporation, residents moved to create a village government instead of a city government in order to avoid what they saw as Chicago's problems.[41]

Many older rural settlements jumped in population in the postwar period as they developed into suburbs rather than as independent farm towns. This resulted largely from the expansion of the commuting area for Chicago area residents. Old rural centers such as Arlington Heights, Lombard, or Downers Grove saw their populations jump from 2,500 to over twenty thousand between 1920 and 1960. Bedroom suburbs like Bartlett, Roselle, and Bloomingdale grew tremendously. Those that grew the most were both dormitory and industrial suburbs such as Naperville, Chicago Heights, and Bensenville.[42]

Deindustrialization: The Stockyards

Over the years one thing seemed to be constant: Chicago was the heart of the nation's agricultural-industrial life. Livestock marketing, meatpacking, and the various related industries played what seemed like a permanent role in Chicago's economy. The city had grown up with the meatpacking industry connected to the rest of the United States by a labyrinth of railroad tracks and a fleet of refrigerated railroad cars that tied the nation's meat markets to Chicago. From the very inception of the Union Stock Yards the city's livestock merchants controlled the national market. Farmers everywhere looked to Chicago to set the price for their hogs, cattle, calves, sheep, and, at one time, horses. The International Amphitheater, and its predecessor the Dexter Park Pavilion, were built to house the famous International Livestock Exposition, the nation's grandest show of prize livestock. Even the massive strikes that took place in the industry centered on the square mile five miles to the southwest of the Loop and bounded by Forty-seventh Street, Ashland Avenue, Pershing Road, and Halsted Street. Chicago seemed impossible to imagine without the smell of the stockyards wafting across the cityscape.

Of course in a dynamic economy like Chicago's, change occurred—and often. Chicago's meatpackers had long operated "off market" plants. Many of these tied to smaller stockyards such as those in St. Joseph, South St. Paul, East St. Louis, Kansas City, or the expanding Omaha market. These, however, played a secondary role to the flagship operations in Chicago. From 1893 until 1933, the Chicago packers ensured the success of the Union Stock Yard, and in turn it ensured the great number of livestock necessary to maintain their operations. Every year during that period at least 13 million head of livestock arrived at the Chicago stockyards. In the 1920s, however, the decentralization of the meatpacking industry had begun to make its mark. By the 1920s, Kansas City had developed as the second largest meatpacking center to Chicago.[43]

The Great Depression brought an end to the long run of high livestock receipts at the yards. After 1933, the annual numbers would never reach 13 million animals again; indeed livestock receipts would fall far below the record numbers of the 1920s when twice they peaked at over 18 million head. By the 1950s other markets often attracted more livestock, although the Chicago market remained the prime cattle market and the barometer for the industry.

In 1952, Wilson and Company replaced an old plant with a new modern facility in Kansas City. The one-story building proved to be more efficient than the old multistory plants, and while still tied to a central market, the Kansas City Stockyards, the direct buying of meat animals from farmers rather than livestock market purchases began to change the industry. Also farmers became less dependent on railroads to move their livestock to market. All of this, plus the increased western movement of the center of livestock breeding, meant changes for the meat industry. By the mid-1950s, Wilson, while maintaining its Loop headquarters, closed its Chicago plant, laying off thousands of workers, most of whom by this time were African American and Mexican. At the end of the 1950s, both Swift and Company and Armour and Company closed their slaughtering operations in Chicago.

The stories both of the Union Stock Yard and Transit Company (USY&T

Co.) and of Armour and Company in the postwar period are intimately connected to the life and fortunes of one William Wood Prince. Born William Wood, he was the son of a prosperous New York insurance executive, but at the age of ten became the protégé of his distant cousin Frederick Henry Prince, a brilliant speculator who invested heavily in railroads and controlled Chicago's USY&T Co. Frederick Prince's own son died in action as a member of the Lafayette Escadrille in World War I. When William Wood, after having attended Groton and Princeton, went off to war in 1944 as a captain of artillery the elder Prince wrote him and offered to adopt him so that someone of the same name would still control the Prince interests. William Wood thus became William Wood Prince. When Frederick Prince died, William Wood Prince ran the estate along with the elder Prince's longtime associate, James F. Donovan.

William Wood Prince eventually became the president of the USY&T Co. and began a program to modernize the stockyards to make them more competitive. New truck docks and facilities appeared along with a new hog market. The International Amphitheater also expanded as Chicago needed more exposition space for the large trade shows that made the city their home. On September 6, 1954, the one-billionth animal arrived at the Chicago stockyards, a steer called Billy the Billionth in honor of Prince. The head of the stockyards promised farmers a better, more modern facility and promised eastern "off market" packers faster transport of livestock to their kill floors. Prince hoped to stop the long downturn in business of the old Chicago institution.

In 1957, Prince left the USY&T Co. to run Armour and Company in which Prince Enterprises held considerable stock. Many in the yards hoped that this would reinforce Armour's commitment to Chicago and keep the packer on the market. Prince pushed Armour's pharmaceutical and chemical divisions and hoped to make the company diversify even more.[44] Within four years of taking the helm at Armour and Company Prince had the company turning large profits. His formula for success was to "decentralize, modernize, diversify." Armour became the fastest growing meat company in the nation as Prince put more than 40 percent of the company assets into more profitable lines such as chemicals, oils, and soaps. Armour also began to sell high profit frozen meals and freeze-dried foods. Prince soon decided to shutter five huge but unprofitable plants, including Chicago. At first Armour announced that refinery operations were to continue in Chicago and even hinted at the possibility of a new plant eventually being built in the city. But this was little solace to some two thousand Chicago Armour employees being laid off. Armour cited the regional shift in livestock operations, obsolete buildings, declining receipts at the stockyards, and excess production capacity and said it planned to continue to purchase livestock in Chicago for its eastern plants, but this too proved to be a short-lived promise. In what would become an increasingly familiar event, the equipment of the plant was auctioned off by Barliant and Company, the largest in Sam Barliant's auctioneer career.

Swift and Company also moved quickly to quit the Chicago Stockyards. Despite modernizing its dressed beef facilities in Chicago and other packing centers in 1956, the packer announced three years later the construction of a new plant in Rochelle, Illinois, and the closing of its Chicago kill floors. Swift and Company claimed the new plant would allow the company to serve the Chicago area more efficiently. Thousands of Swift workers might have disagreed. In 1962 Swift and Company's headquarters moved to the Loop from the Union Stock Yards where it had been located for seventy-six years. The *Butcher's Advocate,* the packing industry magazine, informed its readers in 1959 that central markets were losing their relative position as livestock suppliers for the nation's slaughterhouses.[45]

Eventually the game of hostile takeovers and big corporation ploys that marked the end of the twentieth century caught up with William Wood Prince. In 1969, General Host and the Greyhound Corporation took control of the company and forced Prince out as head of Armour and Company. The story of the decline and loss of Chicago's meatpacking industry foreshadowed much of the future for industrial Chicago and the nation.[46]

The Chicago stockyards never recovered from the loss of the Wilson, Armour, and Swift kill floors. The company celebrated its one hundredth anniversary in 1965–66 with all kinds of positive statements about its future as a fine cattle and hog market. By 1970, hog operations had been suspended, and in the summer of 1971 the cattle market closed, a victim of momentous changes in the industry. The long decline of the meat industry in Chicago could not be stopped.

Many in Chicago saw the passing of meatpacking as a positive sign for the city and not as a sign of deindustrialization. In 1947, Chicago produced over 5 percent of the total value added by manufacture in the nation. Chicago's proportion was equal to California's and twice that of Texas. It contributed more than 5 percent in nine of twenty major manufacturing groups. Its share was much greater in meatpacking, confections, iron and steel, communications equipment, and commercial printing.

But since 1939, Chicago's old-line industries had all declined. Food processing, furniture and fixtures, and apparel underwent a continuous decrease in production. These three industries accounted for more than 25 percent of the area's industrial workers on the eve of World War II. In 1947, they made up only 18 percent and by 1957 less than 16 percent, while the metals and machinery manufacturing industries continued to grow. In 1957, electrical and nonelectrical machinery manufacturing accounted for more than 25 percent of Chicago's industrial workers. By the late 1950s, two industries dominated Chicago's manufacturing base: the metals industry (primary and fabricated) and the machinery industry. Together they accounted for more than 50 percent of all manufacturing jobs and nearly 25 percent of all employment in the city. In 1950, 36 percent of Chicago's residents still worked in manufacturing.

By the mid-1950s the Chicago district was the largest steel producer in the

Figure 110. Despite the fact that many factories left Chicago in the immediate postwar years the city still maintained much of its industrial base. Here women wrap Curtiss Fruit Drops at the Curtiss Candy Company plant in 1952. (Photograph by Frank Silva; ICHi-39373, Chicago History Museum.)

world. Wrapping around the lake from Seventy-ninth Street on the city's South Side out to Gary, Indiana, 161 open hearths and twenty-six electric furnaces put out the nation's steel. The three largest mills in the country operated here: U.S. Steel's Gary Works and South Works (Chicago) and Inland Steel Company's Indiana Harbor Works. Mills of Republic Steel, Wisconsin Steel, and Youngstown Sheet and Tube rounded out a basic steel-producing area that not even Pittsburgh could match. In 1953, over $1.5 billion worth of steel rolled out of these plants and supplied employment for nearly one hundred thousand workers. U.S. Steel alone employed fifty-four thousand of these laborers.

In addition, in 1953 Chicago also dominated the candy industry. Every fourth candy bar made in the United States came from Chicago. This industry employed twenty-two thousand employees with an annual payroll of $86 million. Chicago led in the production of diesel locomotives, electronic equipment, plastics, and a host of other products. With this kind of diversity and industrial might, despite the loss of many manufacturing plants to the suburbs and some to the West Coast, Chicago seemed to be assured of a strong economic future with an expanding service sector economy and a secure industrial base. In the early 1950s deindustrialization seemed improbable, if not impossible.[47]

Still, parts of the city were being neglected, and some people called for planning of new industrial districts. One such proposed area was to the south of the Loop from Congress Parkway to Cermak Avenue and from the river to the lake. The South Side Planning Board (SSPB) in 1953 pointed to the dilapidated and abandoned residences and industrial buildings in the district and called for the city to create a huge industrial park. The SSPB's report called the location an outstanding one for a modern industrial district. It stated that "the Negro can be employed to advantage as has been fully shown by the great number of Chicago industries that have successfully adopted a non-discriminatory employment program. Many trade and technical schools on the Central South Side can help to provide necessary job training. Better housing and new community facilities will further serve to attract and retain this great potential labor force." Trying to overcome the racial prejudices that many believed took jobs out of the South and West Sides, the SSPB saw its proposal as part of a larger approach to the reconstruction of the South Side.[48]

Despite Chicago's powerful economy, the suburbs soon eclipsed the city. Better-off Chicagoans moved to the outlying areas largely as a result of growing racial antagonism, overcrowding, and the simple American desire to move on to something new. The city looked old and out of touch with postwar America. Chicago seemed to many a place of ethnic stores and churches and old industries that might fondly be remembered as the place "we grew up" but not as a place to raise the postwar generation. To both industrial developers and to upwardly mobile Chicagoans, the suburbs promised a modern and affordable alternative to the busy, grimy industrial city of the past.

Daley's City

Bridgeport's Richard J. Daley proved to be a cunning and tough politician. His most important career moves were first to become the Eleventh Ward Democratic committeeman in 1947, and then chairman of the Cook County Democratic Party in 1953. Raised on ward politics, he learned to trust few people, and his political adversaries soon learned the power of his sometimes violent temper. Allies also knew they could trust him as long as he could trust them. In 1955, Daley's patience paid off. The chairmanship of the Democratic Party of Cook County could have meant enough power and wealth for most men, but Daley showed little interest in wealth. He wanted power, the kind of power that could transform a city and bring respectability and influential friends. Daley wanted to be both party chairman and mayor of Chicago. Even Cermak had not achieved this goal as the bosses made him give up the chairmanship when he ran for mayor. They expected the same from Daley. They would be disappointed.

Martin Kennelly had replaced Ed Kelly as mayor in 1948, after Kelly had said that African Americans were free to live anywhere in the city. The negative reaction was quick—from racist whites as well as incredulous blacks—and Kelly was forced to retire. The committeemen floated Kennelly, another native of Bridgeport, as a reform candidate. He promised to bring the city into the modern era, but Kennelly also faced powerful aldermen who had business as usual in mind. The new mayor moved against the "numbers" racket in Bronzeville and earned the ire of William "Big Red" Dawson, the African American political boss who left the Republican Party in the 1930s and joined the Democrats, which proved to be the future, not only for blacks, but all Chicagoans. Dawson did not want police interfering in what was known elsewhere as the policy wheel. This gambling game made millions for various entrepreneurs in Bronzeville, but Kennelly saw it as corrupt and vowed to shut the popular diversion down. In turn, Dawson swore to shut Kennelly down. This conflict provided a chance for Richard J. Daley to make his move, and he knew

Figure 111. The Chicago skyline in 1941 is seen here from the top of the Board of Trade Building. As a result of twenty years of depression, war, and readjustment it had not changed until the opening of the Prudential Building just north of Grant Park in 1955. (Photograph by Charles W. Cushman; Indiana University Archives, P02219.)

he would need black support if he was going to get the prize of the mayoralty. Dawson agreed to support Daley because Daley knew enough to look the other way as far as the numbers went, and Kennelly's fate was sealed after his second term.[1]

The Central Committee of the Democratic Party of Cook County nominated Richard J. Daley for mayor in 1955, dropping Kennelly from the slate of party-sponsored candidates. A great cry went up from Kennelly's supporters, and the incumbent mayor decided to run as an independent candidate. All four Chicago newspapers stood against Daley, whom they thought would be controlled by corrupt aldermen. But Daley and an army of patronage "volunteers" took the campaign to the neighborhoods and won. That night, Alderman Paddy Bauler of Chicago's Old Town neighborhood celebrated and cried out, "Chicago ain't ready for reform!" The aldermen figured that they could

Figure 112. The Prudential Building ushered in a new era of Loop construction when it opened as Chicago's tallest building in 1955. (Photograph by Charles W. Cushman; Indiana University Archives, P10357.)

run Daley, and most of the Chicago newspapers and progressive politicians felt the same. But Daley was not to be controlled by anyone but himself. Much to the chagrin of Jake Arvey and the other Democrats, he announced that he would stay on as Democratic chairman, Eight years later, Arvey admitted that he had opposed this unprecedented move, but that it was good idea, at least for Daley. Daley said, "People told me that if you're a leader you can't be mayor. That's when I decided to lead my party and be mayor." And lead he did. Daley turned out to be a hands-on all-controlling boss who would centralize power in his office on City Hall's fifth floor. Not Bauler, not Arvey—no one—could match the new mayor. It all occurred so fast the party regulars hardly saw it coming, and they could not stop it. Daley was the new boss.[2]

The new mayor faced a city with immense problems, not the least being a lack of downtown investment. Scant new construction had occurred in the Loop since the Great Depression. The Prudential Building, begun during Kennelly's term, opened in 1955 and broke that cycle, but it would take much more for Chicago to maintain its position in the nation's economy. The forty-one story, $40 million Prudential Building opened in Daley's first year in office and ushered in a new round of downtown development. As the city's tallest and largest office structure, with more than 1 million square feet of rental space and 125 tenant firms, it stood 98 percent occupied by January 1959. The insurance company retained the first eight floors and employed 1,800 of the seven thousand people who made their living in the building. It took 345 people to manage and operate the huge edifice. A 924-foot antenna for WGN-TV topped off the building, and a large restaurant and observation deck gave the best views of the city. More than 1.5 million people visited the top of the Prudential Building from its opening late in 1955 to January 1959.[3]

Daley quickly went to work in his first term to make downtown more appealing for investors. Developers announced new buildings and drew up plans to make the Loop more attractive to businesses and visitors alike. In 1958, contractors added over 1 million square feet of office space to the Loop, the largest addition to office space in the Central Business District since the start of the Great Depression in 1930. By the end of the year, the downtown included 36,379,126 square feet of office space, at that time the most in Chicago's history.

As 1959 began, federal officials chose a new site for the U.S. Courthouse at Dearborn and Jackson. The agenda called for the razing of the old courthouse, the Northern Theater, and the Majestic Hotel. Planners also discussed various sites for the new University of Illinois campus to be located in the Chicago area. In 1959, no four-year public university existed in Chicago or Cook County. For years the University of Illinois offered courses at Navy Pier, but only for the first two years of college classes. The obvious need for a larger four-year facility presented both an opportunity and a problem for the Daley administration. The new institution needed a large site easily accessible to public and private transportation. University trustees discussed various near-Loop and suburban possibilities. The rail terminal site south of the Loop; Northerly Island, the home of Meigs Field on the lakefront; Garfield Park; and the Riverside Golf Club all seemed possible locations for the educational facility. Daley favored a city, and preferably downtown, location.[4] The choice of a site, however, was fraught with the class and racial politics of the day.

The mayor and businessmen who were interested in protecting a downtown that they saw as surrounded by blight, feared that black ghetto would scare off their wealthy white clientele. That customer base had many alternatives in the postwar world that had not been there before 1945. In addition the new administration faced increased suburbanization and white flight as well as the spread of blight and disinvestment in the city, particularly on the West and South Sides. This had much to do with racial and social class changes in these neighborhoods.

Building the Modern City: Public Housing and Expressways

Public housing dated back to the 1937 Federal Housing Act that gave birth to the Chicago Housing Authority (CHA), as New Deal Progressives sought to deal with the problems of Depression Era housing. During the Daley years, however, the CHA erected the massive high-rise public housing projects that later came to symbolize the program and its failures. From the CHA's inception, idealism infused the program, based on the belief that good planning, big government, and modern architecture could solve the problems of the city in a way the private real-estate market could not. In its first stage, public housing advocates saw their mission as a way of helping those families displaced or disadvantaged by the Great Depression and World War II.[5] Soon, however, the question of enduring poverty presented itself.

CHA began with two major design phases. The first prevailed in the late 1930s and early 1940s, when the Public Works Administration (PWA) built three- and four-story walkups and two-story row house projects such as the Jane Addams Homes, Julia C. Lathrop Homes, and Trumbull Park Homes on the West, North, and Far South Sides, all of which opened in 1938 and which the CHA managed. Architects designed these housing projects, massive by Depression era standards, on a walkable human scale and included courtyards, brick archways, sculptures, and other amenities. The Ida B. Wells Homes were the fourth and last of the prewar housing projects built by the federal government. Racial segregation remained the policy of the federal government as planners selected the site for this project (1934). The PWA built the Wells project exclusively for black residents. It proved to be the largest of the old PWA projects when it opened in 1941.[6]

The second phase witnessed the construction of large amounts of housing, usually in the form of townhouses primarily for war workers and returning veterans. Employment and wages increased during the war, as did the city's population. War workers arrived in large numbers and the Second Wave of the Great Migration in particular saw the African American population skyrocket. By federal mandate, all new public housing had to be built for war workers. These projects, already in the planning stage before the outbreak of hostilities, could be built if they were located in areas that had a dearth of affordable housing for workers. With this in mind, the CHA continued with four projects: Cabrini, Lawndale Gardens, Bridgeport, and Brooks. After the war, the CHA agreed that these would be switched to low-income housing. Rows and rows of houses constructed during this period seemed like army barracks. This "row house" era offered another reasonably successful attempt by the federal government to create attractive affordable housing for urban residents. The federal government built Altgeld and Wentworth Gardens during or just after the war. The CHA constructed another project, the West Chesterfield Homes, on the Far South Side that proved unique in the early history of the agency. The housing authority built these with the intention of selling them to tenants and therefore constructed them on substantial lots as freestanding single-family homes.

Temporary housing for returning veterans became an issue as the fighting came to an end in Europe and the Pacific. The imperative for the CHA quickly changed from providing shelter for war workers to providing dwellings for the former GIs and their new families. Temporary quarters for veterans appeared across the city on vacant property owned by the city, the Chicago Park District, the Chicago Board of Education, and the Cook County Forest Preserve District. This strategy allowed for the cheap and quick acquisition of land, although these sites tended to be on the outskirts of the city in middle-class areas. Housing for former military personnel consisted of everything from prefabricated factory-built houses to plywood homes and used Quonset huts. The later relocation of residents from these temporary quarters finally ended in 1955. Several racial confrontations of the postwar era resulted from the construction of this housing, as the CHA put aside the prewar rules regarding segregated housing. Airport Homes and Fernwood Park, both located on the Southwest Side, saw racial clashes. Mayor Kelly supported the CHA's integration policy, until he was replaced by Martin Kennelly.[7]

Various federal laws in the immediate postwar years paved the way for massive urban renewal. Many of these housing projects would be publicly funded, but private developers funded others, such as the South Side's Prairie Shores and Lake Meadows. Reformers and planners saw the Blighted Areas Redevelopment Act (1947) and the Urban Community Conservation Act (1953) as tools to rebuild the nation's cities. The New Deal and postwar housing acts also fueled the transformation of the American city. The Home Owners Loan Corporation and the Federal Housing Administration, both reactions to the economic downturn of the 1930s, transformed suburbia by redirecting investment from what were now seen as blighted inner cities to postwar suburban development. These federal programs, along with the long-term impact of automobile and highway building, created a new urban system already visible in outline in the late 1920s but put on hold by the financial collapse of the 1930s and war.[8]

Working-class white ethnics found themselves trapped between the suburbs and the expanding black ghetto. African Americans also felt frustrated and caught between an aggressive attempt to rebuild the central city and hostile white communities both in and outside the city that did not want black residents living near them. Meanwhile, the reality of black population growth presented itself daily on the streets of the city's South and West Sides, home to its largest and most overcrowded ghettoes.

In 1940, the U.S. Census counted 277,731 African Americans in Chicago, just over 8 percent of the city's population. Ten years later, their number had jumped to 492,265, and by 1960, 812,637 African Americans lived in Chicago, comprising just over 22 percent of the population. Chicago's blacks faced severe overcrowding both during and after the war. Meanwhile private developers saw the suburbs as presenting a great opportunity to build housing and make money. During the fifteen-year period after the war, they built nearly seven hundred thousand housing units in the suburbs and on the city's outskirts on the Northwest, Southwest, and Southeast Sides. Between 1950 and 1956 alone roughly 270,000 white Chicagoans left for the suburbs, while others moved to the city's edge. The postwar era saw almost a complete reversal of the population trends of the nineteenth century. In 1940, Chicago contained 74 percent of the area's population. Twenty years later, the city's percentage stood at just under 64 percent. This trend continued into the next century, with only about one out of three residents of Greater Chicago living in the city itself by 2008.

Daley faced this exodus of traditional white Democrats as he came into office in 1955. Racially motivated panic peddling meant big profits for real estate firms and loan companies. Clashes between white ethnics and blacks seemed inevitable and did break out across the city as frustrations mounted. In the 1950s, a series of small race riots over public spaces such as beaches and parks buffeted Chicago. The city government aimed massive redevelopment in the old Black Belt in part to relieve the housing pressure in the ghetto and promise a better future for the city's poor. But in many ways these developments further exacerbated conditions and caused more friction.

Figure 113. The St. Cyril Hotel at Thirty-sixth and Ellis (1949) stood in the decaying South Side near the lakefront and Michael Reese Hospital. (Photograph by Charles W. Cushman; Indiana University Archives, P04208.)

Figure 114. The Maxwell Street Market (1950) remained a bustling outdoor market in the immediate postwar era. Chicagoans from all over the city came to Maxwell Street to get a "bargain." (Photograph by Charles W. Cushman; Indiana University Archives, p04865.)

As World War II came to an end, Chicago's public housing leadership chose to follow New York's example and instituted a third stage of public housing construction and design—the high-rise era. In 1947, the Chicago Housing Authority decided to raise the height of the Dearborn Park Homes, the first elevator buildings built for the authority on South State Street. Both CHA Director Elizabeth Wood and Robert R. Taylor, chairman from 1943 to 1951, pushed for higher densities. The Public Housing Administration advised against highrises for families but in turn created policies that made anything but high-rise construction impossible. The Truman administration in Washington wanted to keep the cost of public housing down. Money thus became the overriding factor. Chicago might have kept costs down and high-rises to a minimum if land on the outskirts of the city had been available, but the opposition of white aldermen to black-occupied public housing in their wards made this impossible. By late 1951, Elizabeth Wood came out against high-rise construction, and in 1955 the CHA proposed low-rise construction for two housing projects, the Taylor Homes and the Green Homes next to the Cabrini Townhouse project on the Near North Side. Richard J. Daley twice went to Washington to argue with the Eisenhower administration for the four-story buildings that might have created more humane housing projects for families. Finally, in 1959, the city gave in and continued high-rise construction.[9]

By 1958, the Stateway Gardens Project had opened on Thirty-fifth and State Street, stretching south to Pershing Road. This massive project contained 1,168 units in two ten-story buildings adjacent to State Street and six seventeen-story high-rises along the Rock Island Railroad tracks to the west. Designed by Holabird, Root and Burgee, they were box frame reinforced concrete buildings, which covered only 13 percent of the thirty-three-acre site that stretched four blocks south on State Street, leaving windswept plazas between buildings, but no stores, factories, or other neighborhood institutions.[10]

Some residents moved into Stateway Gardens as early as 1957, when the first apartment building of the eight-building complex opened. The first tenants, Mr. and Mrs. Don P. Gibson, moved with their two children, into Apartment 303 of the 3542–44 South State Street Building. The Gibsons relocated from a two-story house that had been converted into small flats, where they paid $12.50 per week. The new two-bedroom apartment in the housing project cost the Gibsons $55.00 per month. Don Gibson, a twenty-five-year-old veteran, worked at the Electro-Motive Division of General Motors in La Grange, Illinois. African Americans, the Gibsons could not find housing anywhere near his job in the western suburbs.[11]

The city slated a second, even larger, housing project, the Robert Taylor Homes, to open south of Stateway Gardens. The site included ninety-five acres and was only a quarter-mile wide, stretching from Pershing Road south to Fifty-fourth Street. It included twenty-eight identical sixteen-story buildings mostly in U-shaped groups of three. The only thing that distinguished one group from another was the red or yellow brick veneers. The two housing developments eventually combined to create the longest housing project in the world, replacing the old Federal Street slum, which some called the longest slum in the world. Despite Daley's attempt to build the Taylor homes as a low-rise project, construction began on the high-rises in 1960, the biggest construction year in CHA history, as the authority started eight thousand units that year, including the 4,415 apartments in the Taylor Homes. Construction of the Taylor Homes took place in four stages and lasted two years. Two thousand workers poured concrete frames at the rate of seventeen floors per week. As building came to an end, CHA had more apartments than applicants screened for adequate income, criminal histories, and other factors. This resulted in relaxed rules and the final phase from Fifty-first to Fifty-fourth Streets saw a large number of unscreened tenants admitted. These buildings later had the most problem tenants.[12]

Figure 115. The Maxwell Street Market was a colorful amalgam of street vendors, entertainers, and preachers. Its reputation hardly fit into the image of a modern city that planners presented to the public in the postwar era. (Photograph by Charles W. Cushman; Indiana University Archives, P04907.)

Plans called for 75 percent of the apartments built in CHA projects between 1957 and 1968 to go to large families. All but 696 of these were situated in high-rises. This concentration of families on relatively small pieces of urban land caused extreme population densities. In the Taylor Homes seven thousand adults and twenty-one thousand children, almost all black, lived on ninety-five acres. The project itself only covered 7 percent of the land. The average family contained nearly six people. Many critics felt that these official numbers did not tell the real story, as indeed extended families lived in these apartments with their large spacious rooms. Many came and went as necessary. While public administrators publicized the high-rises as a way to modernize aging communities and to create new neighborhoods, these buildings had thousands of people living on top of each other. The old slums were horrific and overcrowded; soon so were the newly built housing projects.[13]

On March 5, 1962, Mayor Daley welcomed the first tenant, James Weston, to the Taylor Homes. Even as late as 1962, the high-rise projects seemed to hold the promise of a new city and a new start for the urban poor. CHA Executive Director Alvin E. Rose wrote a letter to the tenants personally thanking them for "making our communities the most beautiful in the whole city. I hope you are as proud as I am of your fine lawns and flower beds and the cleanliness of the buildings in which you reside."[14] Some saw these projects as the first step toward rebuilding the South Side. They based their hopes on the experiences of those who had lived in the low-rises and townhouses of the CHA. Those original pubic housing units, built on a much smaller scale and occupied by residents who had gone through a rigorous screening process, had been much more successful in fulfilling the hopes of housing reformers. Numerous former residents of the Ida B. Wells and Jane Addams homes have fond memories of life in these projects before 1960. But urban planners and architects under the influence of Corbusier and other members of the International School, and awash in dreams of the Bauhaus, saw both Stateway Gardens and the Taylor Homes as the future of the city. These towers standing high above the surrounding neighborhood and adjacent to the soon to be opened South Side Expressway fulfilled many of the principals advocated by Corbusier. Both mass and private transportation systems served these communities, which were close to both the Loop and large-scale industrial employers. The realities of high-rise life soon became apparent and smashed these utopian dreams. One resident complained in 1965: "The world looks on all of us as project rats, living on a reservation like untouchables."[15]

The location of these massive projects resulted from ten years of political and racial wrangling between the CHA and the city council. These public policy decisions resulted in the creation of a second black ghetto. White aldermen continued to oppose any public housing construction in their communities, while African American aldermen welcomed them theoretically as a source of better housing but also as a solid block of voters living securely in their wards. Both groups of aldermen feared integration as a way of eroding support for their political ambitions. White aldermen, of course, also largely represented their constituencies in opposing public housing and any black inroads into their communities. In the 1950s this would seem the natural way of life in the city and across the urban North; the following decade would question much of this arrangement as the black civil rights movement broke out of the American South.[16]

Neighborhood disruptions became an everyday experience as land clearance for highways, housing projects, and other developments took place. The 1950s and the early 1960s saw major changes to the cityscape as government took on the task of remaking Chicago and other cities. In 1959, the Chicago Land

Figure 116. This building at Fifty-first and Dearborn housed the Church of God in 1949. It was demolished for construction of the Robert Taylor Homes. (Photograph by Charles W. Cushman; Indiana University Archives, P04238.)

Clearance Commission had twenty-eight projects in progress. Executive Director Phil A. Doyle pointed out that the agency slated fifteen of the projects for housing. Planners intended a shopping center in one and light industry in four others. During 1958, the commission assisted in relocating 428 families and 253 individual householders. The agency appraised a total of 1,390 properties, acquired 375 properties, and demolished 107 buildings.[17]

The real wave of the future finally came into its own in the 1950s. Automobiles, perhaps more than any other consumer product, symbolized postwar America's success, optimism, and brash outlook. The automobile shaped the physical, economic, and social future of the city. The Congress Expressway (now the Eisenhower) was the first to cut across the city, and planners charted new roadways for the South and North Sides. The city and state unveiled a design for a new fourteen-lane superhighway to cut across the heart of the South Side. A "dual-dual" expressway design marked the five mile segment from Twenty-sixth to Sixty-seventh Streets at a projected cost of $110 million. Designers hoped to provide a national model with the new road. The new system tied the city and suburbs together and cut great holes in the cityscape bringing dramatic demographic changes in its wake.[18]

The highways were part of a larger national plan that had emerged with the Interstate Highway Act of 1956. In that act, Congress provided for the construction of forty-one thousand miles of toll-free highways and agreed to pick up 90 percent of the tab. Proponents expected the entire system to be in place by 1971 at an estimated cost of $27 billion. The scheme ended up costing about twice the estimate. Beyond the superhighways, a still greater and more expensive effort went into building and improving conventional roads so that every part of the United States could be accessible by motor vehicles. No one in 1956 comprehended the impact on the economy and on American travel of such work. Yet, by 1958, the consequences began to be felt. Schools, churches, shopping strips, and entire neighborhoods disappeared in Chicago and other metropolitan areas. Passengers abandoned the railroads, and trucks competed with freight trains for moving goods across the country. This naturally influenced Chicago as the major rail center in the United States.

While the new highway system quickly became a reality, Illinois completed its part of the older interstate tollway system. The state of Illinois officially opened the new tollway scheme in December 1958. The tollway extended 187 miles across the Chicago area and took twenty-seven months to complete. It joined the Eastern Toll Roads system, which dated from the pioneering efforts of the state of Pennsylvania. The completion of the Illinois section finished off the "main line"—composed of the New Jersey, Pennsylvania, and Ohio Turnpikes, along with the Indiana Toll Road—which stretched 837 miles from Chicago to New York. This older system planned and built largely before the federal largess provided an important link between the Midwest and the East Coast.[19]

Governor William G. Stratton pointed out late in 1958 that highway construction in Chicago and vicinity conferred the largest public works program in the history of the area and surpassed all other metropolitan road programs in the nation. The state, federal, and local governments slated $137,679,000 for highways in Cook County alone in 1959. Over the previous five years $346 million had been spent on streets and highways in Chicago, including $103 million for the purchase of rights-of-way and the rest for construction costs. The *Chicago Tribune* attested to the fact that the city would benefit from over $500 million in public works projects in the coming year. Highways provided a major proportion of this economic bounty. In 1958, the West Side Subway opened in the median strip of the Congress Expressway. The CTA slated a similar rapid transit line for the future Dan Ryan Expressway as Chicago planners, like urban experts all over the nation, feebly attempted to temper the American appetite for the private automobile with good public transportation.[20]

Highway construction cut across the cityscape, dislocating people, businesses, and institutions throughout the era. To the southwest, the Stevenson Expressway took people's homes and even threatened St. Bridget's, the first Irish church in Bridgeport, whose parishioners ironically erected a small shrine to Our Lady of the Highway. Supposedly Mayor Daley had personally intervened to save the edifice where he and his wife married in 1936. Certainly the mayor had already intervened to save Bridgeport from destruction when he

Figure 117. The Congress Expressway seen here from Marshfield Avenue in 1958 was the first highway to force the removal of residences in Chicago and to have a rapid transit line run down its median. Here the Douglas "L" enters the Congress median. (Photograph by Charles W. Cushman; Indiana University Archives, P10257.)

moved the Dan Ryan Expressway further east from its original planned location through the heart of the neighborhood along Normal Avenue. After a year in office Daley had the plans changed. His commissioner of public works, George De Ment, approved the new path and the city council quickly accepted it. Commentators have argued this was to maintain the "Great Divide" separating blacks and whites, but in the cases of Bridgeport and Canaryville located in Daley's Eleventh Ward, the expressway made little difference for the racial balance. Political power, white street gangs, railroad viaducts, rail yards, and even Comiskey Park provided a much greater obstacle to the expansion of African American neighborhoods. The expressway was routed through poor and working-class white and minority neighborhoods into the city in Chicago, just as they did across the country. Engineers spoke of slum removal as one of the positive results of highway construction. Racial concerns aside, Daley could hardly allow an expressway to destroy his political base.

Indeed the highway system had dissected both white and black neighborhoods in Chicago. The Kennedy Expressway resulted in the removal of some four hundred Polish American families in the parish of St. Stanislaus Kostka,

Figure 118. This view of the ramps connecting the Stevenson and Dan Ryan Expressways shows the amount of land turned over for highway development along Archer Avenue in Bridgeport. (Photograph by D. Pacyga.)

the first Polish parish organized in Chicago. Polish American politicians, led by Dan Rostenkowski, could not stop the expressway's construction, but they had it moved slightly to prevent the destruction of their beloved church on Noble Street. West Side Italians fared worse as Holy Guardian Angel Parish lay right in the path of the Dan Ryan Expressway. In 1959, parishioners celebrated the last mass in the church and built a new parish complex at 860 West Cabrini Street. Four years later the city again began demolition to make way for the new University of Illinois campus in Chicago, and the relocated Italian church was again bulldozed. Urban renewal and expressway development trumped the concerns of all kinds of communities in a city where clout mattered more than race.

The Dan Ryan Expressway opened on Saturday, December 15, 1962. Mayor Richard J. Daley and Ruby Ryan—the widow of the late Cook County Board president and expressway advocate, Dan—cut the ribbon at Eighteenth Street. Daley and his associates took the first ride on it south to Sixty-third Street then back north to the Loop for a celebration. Daley had recently expressed doubts about whether it was such a good idea to keep slicing up the city in such a manner. Several months after the Ryan's opening, roughly 130,000 vehicles flowed across its fourteen lanes every day. Trucks and other commercial vehicles made up 14 percent of the traffic. The words "Dan Ryan" and "traffic jams" became synonymous. Planners originally designed the Dan Ryan to handle 142,000 cars and 7,400 trucks daily, numbers that were soon vastly exceeded. Engineers estimated that a small truck did as much wear and tear on the expressway's

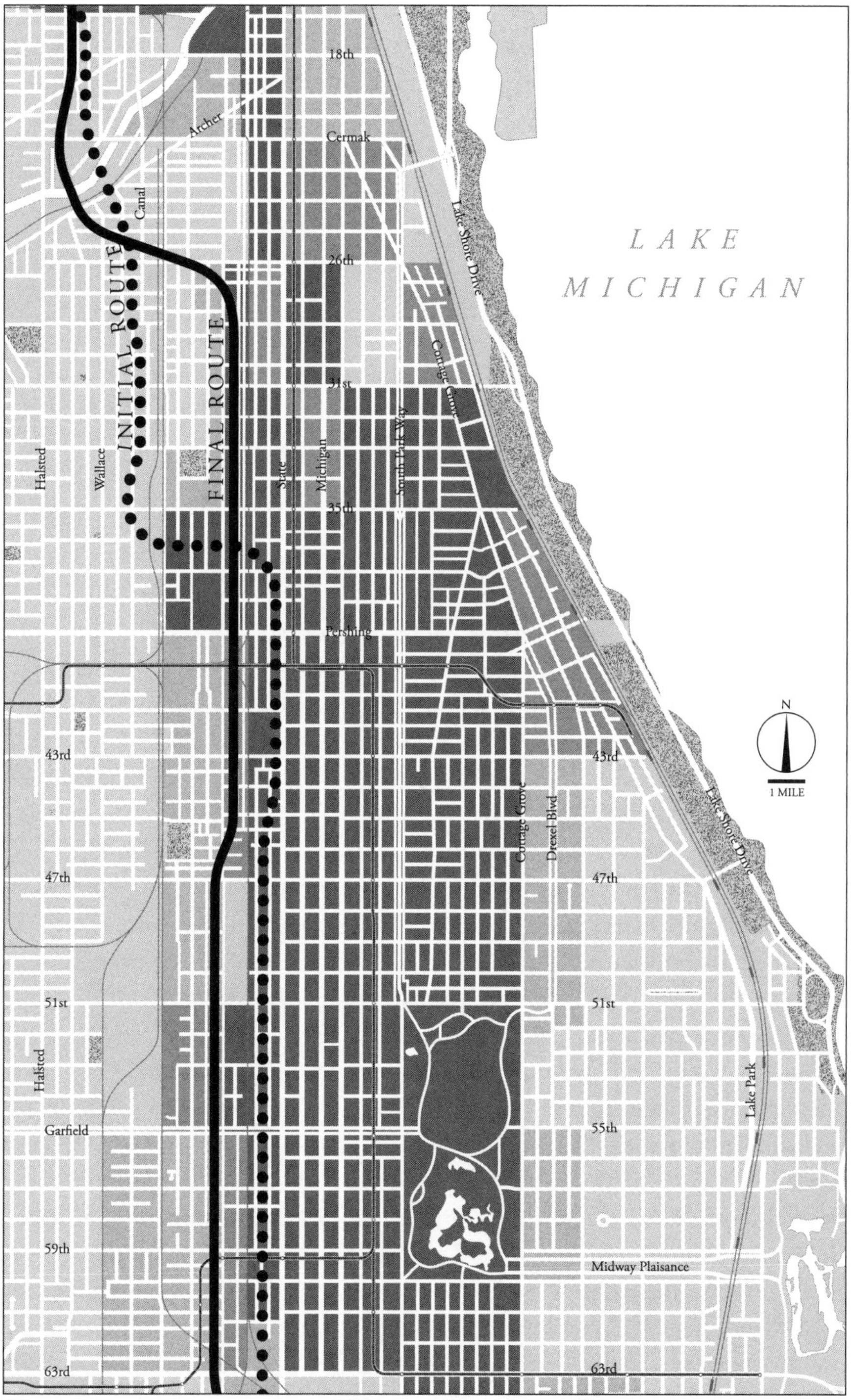
18th
Archer
Cermak
Canal
26th
LAKE
MICHIGAN
Lake Shore Drive
INITIAL ROUTE
FINAL ROUTE
Cottage Grove
31st
South Park Way
Halsted
Wallace
State
Michigan
35th
Pershing
N
43rd
43rd
1 MILE
Lake Shore Drive
Cottage Grove
Drexel Blvd
47th
47th
51st
51st
Halsted
Lake Park
Garfield
55th
59th
Midway Plaisance
63rd
63rd

10–50% black in 1950 | 50–90% black | more than 90% black

Map 6. This map shows the percentage of African Americans living on both sides of the expressway's original and eventual routes. The idea that the expressway was built to curtail the black population seems obviously wrong. (Dennis McClendon.)

pavement as three hundred cars, while a tractor-trailer impacted on the asphalt as much as 2,900 cars. The new road soon wore out. Between 1967 and 1974, the state paid $7.5 million for repairs. In 1974, a $22.5 million repair project was announced, and in 2006–7 the whole thing was rebuilt. Chicago traffic officer, Richard Wiser, simply summed up the road, "Its not at all well-designed." By that time the Dan Ryan had the unchallenged record of being the most dangerous highway in Chicago with 5,478 accidents in 1972, nearly five times the number on the Calumet (Bishop Ford) and 1,648 more than the Kennedy during the same time period. Despite the new expressways and gleaming high-rises, Daley's new modernist city obviously had its problems. Many of these resulted from bad planning or of unintended consequences from decisions made in city hall and Washington D.C. High-rises and massive highway construction would result in Chicago's neighborhoods organizing again to control change as they did in the 1930s.[21]

Daley's Prime

As the 1950s ended, much seemed right in Chicago and across the nation. Despite a deep recession, the economy bounced back in the final quarter of 1958, and most Americans could look with some sense of optimism toward the coming year. In Chicago, "Hog Butcher to the World," the smell of the "yards" still permeated the South Side and the explosive rush of steelmaking lit up the night sky from South Chicago to Gary. Located in the middle of the country, Chicago stood, if shaken, still unwavering as an industrial and transportation center with a large and diverse population. Yet, with the rise of a large class of office and service workers, more people seemed to be wearing white collars, or even "pink" collars, rather than blue collars. The city continued nonetheless as a bastion of organized labor. Over twelve thousand workers struck the huge West Side International Harvester plant in November, and the strike dragged on into the New Year. Despite the delicate balance between change and continuity and the image of stability, a hidden dynamism transformed Chicago and the nation at the decade's close.[22]

The old familiar Chicago of factories, churches, and neighborhood bars seemed intact along many streets lined with two-flats, bungalows, and storefronts. Despite the growth of suburbs during the postwar building boom, the "ritzy" neighborhoods such as the Gold Coast, Sauganash, Beverly, or South Shore continued to attract the well-to-do and those who wanted to be well-to-do. Precinct captains still rang doorbells and made promises as election time neared. The corner cop walked his beat, and certain "types" knew their place in a city and a nation of strict racial, social, and gender boundaries.

Despite the optimism, 1958 had been a long, somewhat trying year. Indeed the 1950s, with all their energy and self-assurance, had been an anxious decade because of the advent of nuclear weapons and as a result of social change largely

Figure 119. Richard J. Daley saw himself as a builder. Here he celebrates the construction of the new St. Mary of Nazareth Hospital Center as he turns over the ceremonial first shovel of dirt for the project with Sister Stella Louise Slomka, CFSN, on February 2, 1972. (Archives of St. Mary of Nazareth Hospital Center.)

brought about, or at least encouraged, by World War II. For a generation raised in times of Depression and war, tragedy never seemed too far beneath the face of optimism and progress. As 1958 came to a close, events quickly reminded Chicagoans of that reality; on December 1, the Our Lady of the Angels School fire tainted Chicago's holiday season with tragedy, as ninety-three children and nuns died in the fire. For months the city reeled from the disaster, which changed the city's approach to fire prevention forever—sprinkler systems soon appeared in schools and other buildings across the city, and fire inspection methods were updated.[23]

Richard J. Daley was in the last few months of his first term as mayor. In the November 1958 elections the Cook County Democratic Organization trounced the Republicans. The Democrats eagerly prepared for another mayoral election in the spring of 1959, and Republicans seemed less than eager for a fight with their local foes. The Chicago GOP looked far and wide for a candidate to stand against Daley, but most refused. One report had the nomination offered to popular disc jockey Howard Miller, who apparently also declined. At that point Herb Lyon of the *Chicago Tribune* wrote, "C'mon, somebody, anybody, be a candidate." Finally the GOP turned to feisty Republican stalwart Timothy P. Sheehan, who had lost a bid to return to Congress in the fall. Tim Sheehan was the first Roman Catholic Republican candidate for Chicago's mayoralty. Democrats routinely nominated Catholics in a city where they made up more than 50 percent of the population and probably even a greater percentage of regular voters. Sheehan called for an end to machine politics and the rule of "Boss" Daley as he accepted the nomination on Christmas Eve.[24]

As 1959 arrived, Daley prepared for his second mayoral campaign and announced various plans for a new city. A. Andrew Boemi, president of the Madison Bank and Trust Company and chairman of the new Gateway Committee, led a drive to revamp the Near West Side and do away with Madison Avenue's Skid Row. Boemi announced the city's new twenty-two-year $1.5 billion plan to create "wholesome suburban living conditions at the fringe of Chicago's busy Loop." The scheme called for the revitalization of the area from North Avenue south to Twenty-sixth Street and from Ashland Avenue east to Lake Michigan. Planners claimed that Chicago would join Paris, London, and New York among the great cities of the world having fine residential areas adjacent to their downtown business districts. Attracting middle-class families into the central city became one of the more popular answers to urban problems in the 1950s but was not accomplished until much later.

In January the city announced the start of a $120 million O'Hare Terminal Project in the spring. Approximately 603,000 passengers or 11 percent of the city's total air traffic arrived at O'Hare Airport in 1958. The new airport, to the northwest of the city, already claimed the title of the world's largest civilian airfield. Midway Airport on the Southwest Side remained as the "World's Busiest," but its days seemed numbered due to its location, hemmed in by housing and light industry. Airlines scheduled the first jet flights into O'Hare for early in 1959. William Downers, the Chicago commissioner of aviation, predicted that O'Hare would quickly surpass Midway Airport in volume once jets became common because the new jets needed the longer runways available at O'Hare to take off and land safely. The city estimated that 6.8 million passengers, or 75 percent of the city's total, would land at O'Hare by 1965.

While bulldozers plowed through neighborhoods and Chicago prepared for the jet age at O'Hare, Daley's national reputation and influence grew. The "Boss" of Chicago had certainly solidified his power during his first administration. He calmly but energetically approached the 1959 municipal election, as Republicans feared the worst. Daley kept a busy schedule during the campaign. During a rainstorm on Wednesday, April 1, he broke ground for a new terminal at O'Hare Airport, and on the Sunday before the election Daley made various public appearances including attendance at Mass at St. Peter's in the Loop. That evening he addressed Italian Americans at the Sherman Hotel, then Greek Americans at the Congress Hotel. He also had plans to drop by the Twelfth Ward Regular Democratic Organization Headquarters at the end of the night. Daley's hard work paid off; when the totals were in, he had racked up an impressive victory with a 465,000 vote plurality over GOP candidate Tim Sheehan. Seventy-one percent of the city's voters had pulled the Democratic lever. Daley carried every ward except the Forty-first on the city's Far Northwest Side. That night Daley promised to "embrace charity, love mercy, and walk humbly with my God," a statement that he would use many times in his victory speeches. The *Chicago Tribune* congratulated the newly reelected mayor but also reminded him of the city's problems. Its editorial page pointed out rising taxes and the deterioration of residential areas as the most important issue. The paper then went on to mention others, such as keeping public transportation affordable, the new location of the University of Illinois campus, the consolidation of railroad terminals, and the handling of the expansion of commerce on the Great Lakes with the opening of the St. Lawrence Seaway. Daley's in-box seemed full, and the mayor attacked the job with the usual energy that he had exhibited in his first administration.

Daley immediately outlined ambitious plans for the city. On the night of his second inauguration, Daley called for the federal government to pump hundreds of millions of dollars into the nation's cities. He told the audience of nine hundred jammed into the city council chambers: "No city alone has the financial resources to rebuild and conserve its central area, neighborhoods and communities."[25] Daley strongly felt that the government, local, state, and federal, must play a positive role in society. For the mayor, that meant that the federal government should spend, and spend big, to help America's cities, especially Chicago. The problem was that in 1959 the White House was occupied by Dwight D. Eisenhower, a Republican. Daley and the Democrats hoped to change that in November 1960.

The year 1959 proved to be a good one for the city. Not only did the St. Lawrence Seaway open, but the Chicago White Sox won the American league pennant, their first in forty years—bringing the first pennant to Chicago since 1945, when the Cubs won their last National League championship of the twentieth century. Despite mayoral predictions of victory, the go-go Sox lost the World Series to the Los Angeles Dodgers and would not see another World Series until 2005; for a moment though, Chicago fans had much to celebrate. The city also hosted the Pan American Games and feted Elizabeth II of England on her visit. Daley, ever the homebody, suggested that she return and next time "bring the kids."[26] Daley looked forward to the 1960s and the possibility of a Democrat in the White House but also warned presciently that the coming decade would present many trials to the country and Chicago.

The final years of the 1950s certainly presented political challenges to Daley, despite his power. Charges of corruption and scandal arose. In late 1958 and early 1959, the "Sin Corner" scandal spread in the Woodlawn community,

Figure 120. Over the years Daley met many dignitaries. He is pictured here in 1969 standing with Cardinal Karol Wojtyla (later Pope John Paul II) to his right and with John Cardinal Cody of Chicago to his left. (Archives of St. Mary of Nazareth Hospital Center.)

implicating police in a prostitution ring. The following year, the Summerdale scandal broke, as several Chicago police officers were found to be part of a ring of burglaries. This revelation proved to be a turning point for Daley's relationship with the police and the old aldermanic system of picking police commanders. Daley forced the resignation of Police Chief Timothy J. O'Connor. He appointed an outsider, University of California criminal justice professor Orlando W. Wilson, who then led a complete overhaul of the politically corrupt and often crooked police department. Even the color of police cars changed, and their flashing lights turned from red to blue as Wilson consolidated police districts and seized the power to name police commanders away from aldermen. Daley took control of the scandalous situation and cleaned up his image.[27]

By the end of 1959, Democratic presidential hopefuls began to make their appeals to party leaders. Adlai Stevenson had been the party's candidate in 1952 and again in 1956. Now, with the popular Eisenhower stepping down, many hoped that Stevenson would yet again lead the Democratic Party. Stevenson proved to be a reluctant candidate, and in the spring of 1960 Daley approached the former governor but came away without a commitment. For the mayor, a longtime Stevenson ally, the 1960 election presented both an opportunity and a challenge, and he would not wait for the indecisive former Illinois governor. Daley had the chance to present himself as a kingmaker. The challenge would be to deliver Illinois for the Democrats.

While Stevenson played the reluctant patrician, John F. Kennedy, who had announced his candidacy on January 2, entered and won Democratic primaries. In the 1950s the primary system was more of a popularity contest than a decisive factor at the convention, but Kennedy certainly proved his ability to attract Democratic voters. His victory in the West Virginia primary on May 10 demonstrated that, despite the fact that Kennedy was a Roman Catholic, he could draw support in an overwhelmingly Protestant state. Finally on July 13, while the Democrats met at the 1960 convention, Stevenson decided he wanted to be president. By that time it was too late, as Daley had made up his mind to support Kennedy. He bluntly told the two-time Democratic presidential candidate that he had no support among the Illinois delegation. The young senator from Massachusetts had moved to gather support from Daley early, along with other important Democratic leaders. Most importantly for the Chicago machine, the charismatic Kennedy could help the party win local elections. Daley had played a crucial role in organizing Kennedy's nomination, and Daley had to prove the importance of the Chicago machine by delivering Illinois and the election for JFK and the Democrats.[28]

As Kennedy began to campaign against Richard M. Nixon, Chicago again promised to influence national politics. Mayor Daley assured the Democratic nominee that Chicago would give him five hundred thousand votes, which would guarantee Kennedy winning Illinois. It was Daley's big chance to become the ultimate player in presidential politics as Illinois could prove to be a swing state in what promised to be a close election. Kennedy's Catholicism and his Boston Irish connection had been an issue even before he won the nomination. Now Democrats feared it might prove significant in various states especially in the South. Many feared that even in downstate Illinois the religious issue could sway voters who might fear a Catholic Irish American in the White House. The state tended to vote Republican, and in the 1956 Eisenhower landslide even Chicago voted for the GOP. Despite this political reality, Daley knew that his chance to become a kingmaker depended on a big turnout that left Cook County with enough votes to offset Republican votes in the suburbs and in the GOP strongholds in the southern part of the state.

Daley orchestrated the local media every time Senator Kennedy arrived in Chicago, getting extra coverage on the news. Kennedy, understanding how important Chicago and Illinois were to his hopes of gaining the White House, made his last appearance in the city on the Friday before the election. Daley pulled out all the stops in order to make Kennedy's appearance memorable. Despite a steady rain, Chicago's Democrats turned out for a massive torchlight parade. City workers lined the streets from the Loop out to the Chicago Stadium where twenty-eight thousand cheering Democrats greeted the nominee. Labor leaders promised the support of 650,000 union members. Daley wanted the whole event televised, and the Kennedys paid $125,000 for prime time coverage. The speech at the Chicago Stadium received national exposure, as Daley promised JFK that those supporters lining the streets would all turn out on Election Day.[29]

On Monday, Daley told reporters that Kennedy would carry the city by an unlikely six hundred thousand votes. The next day, November 8, 1960, an amazing 89.3 percent of Chicago's eligible voters turned out. Kennedy carried the city by a margin of 456,312 votes, not quite the figure Daley had publicly predicted, but enough to carry Illinois by 8,858 votes. Nixon captured only three of the city's fifty wards.[30] Daley called Kennedy at 3 a.m. on the morning of November 9 to tell him the results from Illinois. He was probably the first person to call Kennedy "Mr. President." Daley remained secluded in the Morrison Hotel, local Democratic Headquarters, until 1:15 p.m. when he told the press, "I am very happy over the election. It appears as though Senator Kennedy will win Illinois. This is a tremendous win for a great candidate." Daley had much to be happy about, as the mayor had also defeated scandal-loving Republican Ben Adamowski in his bid for another term as state's attorney. In Chicago, national elections are always subordinate to local ones. The Democrats nonetheless swept Illinois, electing Otto Kerner as governor and reelecting Paul Douglas to the senate.[31]

Almost immediately rumors spread claiming that Daley had stolen the election for Kennedy and that the corrupt Chicago machine had taken control of the White House. Nixon and his party cried voter fraud. In reality, the Illinois results did not have an impact on Kennedy winning the White House. Kennedy's victories in California and Texas would more than have offset a Nixon victory in Illinois, but the reputation of the Chicago Democratic machine attracted the focus of the national press. In the end, the state board of elections certified the results and Illinois' electoral votes stayed within the Kennedy column. Most commentators believed that the Democrats had stolen votes in Chicago, but that the GOP had stolen votes in the suburbs and downstate. In the end, the results stood.[32] National attention focused on Daley as he stood at the peak of his power. Local Republicans, including the hated Adamowski who repeatedly threatened Daley's organization with investigations, seemed vanquished, and nationally even the president listened to the council of "the boy from the stockyards." Daley's power seemed absolute.

Daley had new found influence in the White House with an administration that saw itself as an active force in American life. Urban renewal and new construction remained the mayor's highest priority. In April 1961, Daley unveiled a new five-year capital improvement plan that would cost $2.1 billion and included public housing, expressways, bridges, viaducts, street improvement, sewers, and other projects. Daley worked to build a coalition of local supporters to reach his goals. A Republican-controlled state senate stopped Chicago's plans to raise the sales tax, so he had to rely on property tax increases to pay for the local share of the projects. Nevertheless the compliant city council approved Daley's budget and his vision of the city's future by a 40–3 vote.[33]

In 1963, Daley prepared for another election. His opponent this time would be former state's attorney Adamowski. Many felt that the 1960 election had been more about defeating Adamowski than getting Kennedy elected. Just before the general election *Time* magazine ran Daley on its cover and proclaimed him the "Clouter with a Conscience." In the article Daley stated that "if something is in the public interest, then it is in the party's interest. Good government is good politics." The news magazine extolled the progress that Chicago had made during Daley's first two terms. It wrote of "a new rhythm as exciting as any in the city's lusty past." Still, *Time* did mention problems, such as the Summerdale scandal and growing racial conflict, as well as the fact that even the Catholic Church had opposed Daley on urban renewal issues. The Church believed that as Daley's projects displaced African Americans, they would flood predominantly Roman Catholic white ethnic neighborhoods. The controversial Hyde Park–Kenwood Project, which transformed the University of Chicago's neighborhood into a middle-class academic fortress on the racially shifting South Side, seemed to validate these fears.[34]

Despite national media acclaim, the 1963 mayoral election proved to be a difficult one for Daley. The citywide building campaign had many detractors as bulldozers cut down neighborhoods full of voters. On the West Side, the Italian community that was being displaced for the new University of Illinois at Chicago Circle campus protested Daley's tactics. On the Near North Side the building of the massive Sandburg Village, for upper-middle-class residents, caused the same reaction. In addition, gunmen killed two aldermen in an apparent gangland slaying in February. Finally the property tax rate angered homeowners. Chicago's large Polish American population came out for Adamowski, and several of the Southwest Side's white ethnic wards joined the Republican camp for the election: even many Southwest Side Irish voted against Daley as racial issues became paramount. Adamowski played the race card, and while Daley still won by a substantial margin, he learned his lesson. The Republican candidate had made great inroads in those wards where racial change threatened. Adamowski won 51 percent of the white vote, but black Democrats carried the day for Daley. For many white Chicagoans Daley was the black candidate. The 1960s had begun.[35]

No one knew in April 1963 how shocking a year it would be for America. On November 22, Lee Harvey Oswald assassinated John F. Kennedy in Dallas. Suddenly Daley's power seemed threatened as the tragedy captured the world's attention. Daley lunched with aides at the Democratic organization's headquarters in the Morrison Hotel when the news arrived of Kennedy's death, and the next day Daley led a memorial service in the city council chambers. Daley mourned that he had "lost a great friend," and one week later the council voted to rename the Northwest Expressway after the slain president.[36]

Two days after the assassination, Lyndon Johnson, the new president, called Daley, and thus began one of the truly remarkable relationships in Chicago's political history. Both men had grown up poor and raised themselves up through the political process. In many ways, despite their obvious differences—Texan versus South Side Chicagoan, Protestant versus Catholic, Washington politician versus big city mayor, southerner versus northerner—they were cut of the same cloth. Both Johnson and Daley understood power and how to use it. The president and the mayor could both be ruthless, but both also felt that government and politics should be positive forces in society. They both remembered Franklin Roosevelt and began their political careers during the New Deal. In those dark days after November 22, they embraced each other and in many ways tied their destinies together. Communication lines between the two men stayed open at all times. Johnson often seemed in awe of the Chicago mayor. Daley felt at home visiting the White House and had a closer relationship with Johnson than he had had with JFK. Daley continued to have "clout" in Washington, D.C., and in many ways Johnson's Great Society programs would deeply resonate with Daley and his vision of ameliorating Chicago's physical and social problems.

Their dedication to a common vision of the future should not be underestimated. Johnson and Daley were pragmatic politicians who worried about the decline of America's cities and favored an activist government. While they might disagree with or ignore many social liberals, they agreed that government should be used as a tool to make society fairer for everyone. They both embraced the basic tenets of Kennedy's New Frontier but in many ways had the vision and the power to take it further than the slain president. The passage of the 1964 Civil Rights Bill was fundamental to the development of Johnson's Great Society. Daley pushed hard for a Civil Rights Bill in the early 1960s, and Johnson concurred. For Daley, this bill seemed the logical outcome of years of expanding the American Dream. In practical terms, Daley knew that the number of African American voters in Chicago continued to grow at a phenomenal rate. More than a million blacks called Chicago and Cook County home by the mid-1960s. A new state law that streamlined voter registration increased

African American participation in both local and national races. These voters tended to vote Democratic and might ensure the party's control over the city for the foreseeable future. Neither Daley nor Johnson could afford to ignore such an important voting block. So in Daley's and Johnson's mind, the right thing to do was also the best thing to do for the Democrats.

As the 1964 election neared their relationship grew stronger. Johnson, always insecure, wanted a decisive victory against Barry Goldwater and the Republicans. For this he relied on established Democratic power brokers including Daley. The president came to Chicago for the traditional torchlight parade and called the mayor "the greatest politician in the country." Chicago Democrats did not let Johnson down, as LBJ's campaign left Chicago with a plurality of 675,000 votes that November. Chicago's African American community handsomely repaid the president and the Democrats for the Civil Rights Act, as Johnson received more than 90 percent of the black vote. Daley, who had seconded the nomination of LBJ at the Democratic Convention, basked in the glow of victory and of his power both in Chicago and in Washington, D.C.[37]

Daley was very interested in getting money from the Johnson administration. While Johnson guided a flood of new legislation through Congress to support his War on Poverty and Great Society initiatives, Daley gave constant support. LBJ planned to extend Roosevelt's New Deal to create a new and progressive America. In reality, Daley did not always agree with the architects of the Great Society, but he was more than willing to take advantage of the federal largesse for Chicago. Strategies such as the Community Action Program (CAP), which called for community control over public funds, did not warm Daley's heart. He was not a believer in welfare programs, but the mayor wheeled and dealed with his Johnson connections and soon embraced the various Great Society programs. Daley took the money but refused to let Chicago's CAP operate the way that Washington mandated as he planned to control CAP and any other federal program that arrived in Chicago. The mayor had learned well from Ed Kelly and his relationship with Roosevelt in the heyday of the New Deal that federal cash was important, but only if Daley and the local Democrats controlled it. The idea of letting the poor actually control CAP or any other federal program seemed absurd to Daley, who said, "It would be like telling the fellow who cleans up to be the city editor of a newspaper." Chicago's Boss knew that the laws required "maximum feasible participation" by local communities meant taking money, patronage, and ultimately power, away from city hall. Daley declared, "Local government has responsibilities it should not give up." He established the Chicago Committee on Urban Opportunity (CCUO) to oversee CAP, naming himself as chairman. The ninety-member CCUO board included only seven residents of poor Chicago neighborhoods, and this evasion of the intent of federal law quickly became known as the "Chicago Concept," as the program basically turned into an appendage of the Chicago machine.[38]

Johnson always sided with Daley. When the Elementary and Secondary Education Act passed in September 1965, with an appropriation of $1 billion for low-income areas, it was seen as a payoff by LBJ to southern and border-state school districts to comply with the Civil Rights Act and desegregate. But the first racial confrontation over the act came from Chicago, not from the South. The federal government had given the city a $32 million grant. Health, Education, and Welfare Secretary John Gardner understood that Johnson's goal was desegregation. Chicago civil rights activist Al Raby filed a complaint about the Chicago school system and its racial segregation, and the federal government suspended distribution of funds pending an investigation. On October 3, Daley, in New York to greet Pope Paul VI, exploded and complained bitterly to Johnson. The president seemed stunned and promised to look into the matter. When Johnson met the pope, who praised him for his work to help educate poor children, Johnson remarked, "That's the work I want to do, your Holiness . . . but they're trying to stop me. One of my own cabinet members wants to shut off funds for poor children in one of our largest cities, Chicago, run by a fine Catholic mayor." Johnson pushed for integration across his native South, but Richard Daley's political power came first.[39]

Black Chicago

In the early 1960s, race presented the greatest challenge to Daley and other big city mayors. Despite Daley's support of the Civil Rights Act and his full political support for Johnson's programs, Chicago's African American leadership began to see him as increasingly hostile to civil rights and the full integration of blacks in American society. Much of this attitude first arose over the issue of school integration, the very issue that had caused Daley to scold Johnson in New York. The 1963 mayoral election had taught Daley the lesson that he was losing support among the white ethnic communities out of which he came. His Eleventh Ward stayed loyal, but even there many wondered what the former president of the Hamburg Athletic Club was up to as he helped the African American community. Black Chicago had elected Daley in 1963, but he now looked to shore up his support among the white ethnic communities.

White neighborhoods felt under increasing pressure from Chicago's growing black population, particularly when it came to the public schools. Chicago's school superintendent, Benjamin Willis, became a symbol of everything that black Chicago felt had gone wrong with the schools and with the city. In July of 1963, a group of black and white hecklers jeered Daley as he addressed a rally of the National Association for the Advancement of Colored People (NAACP), the nation's oldest civil rights organization. Outrage over Chicago's overcrowded ghetto schools seethed throughout the black community. On July 10, the Chicago chapter of the Congress on Racial Equality staged a sit-in at the Chicago Board of Education. A few weeks later neighborhood protests reached their zenith. Protestors pointed to white schools not far from black schools that stood half empty while black children attended class in what protestors called "Willis Wagons," mobile classrooms constructed near overcrowded schools. Willis remained intransigent, causing black neighborhoods to protest even more. By 1963, the *Chicago Defender* referred to Willis as "the Governor Wallace of Chicago," linking him to the segregationist governor of Alabama. On October 22, black leaders called a school boycott to protest the school board's rejection of Willis's resignation. Northwest and Southwest Side whites rallied to the superintendent's defense while 225,000 African American students stayed home from class. Chicago organizers opened "Freedom Schools" in churches and neighborhood clubs. Many hoped that the boycott might initiate a mass movement in the city and inspire others throughout the country.

The school issue galvanized Chicago's black community. The Coordinating Council of Community Organizations (CCCO) became the leader of civil rights protests in Chicago. CCCO called another boycott in February, with the same basic result. As the months passed some foresaw the quick demise of the radical CCCO, but in late May 1965 the board of education renewed Willis's contract, and the usually cautious and conservative NAACP reacted by calling for another boycott. On June 10, despite a court injunction restraining both the NAACP and CCCO from leading the movement, over one hundred thousand black children stayed home from school. Al Raby led several hundred demonstrators in a sit-down strike next to City Hall, and Daley agreed to meet with the protestors, but no significant changes in school policy emerged from the meeting.

The struggle over the schools persisted. Civil rights leaders felt that Daley used Willis as a front man to blunt attacks against his political organization. Technically, the superintendent's office was independent of the mayor, but everyone knew that in Chicago Daley called all the shots. In 1965, some six thousand people marched in protest against the school board's policy. While this number might seem small, Raby claimed it showed overwhelming support and others agreed. Still the protests seemed more like hopeless cries of frustration as Willis and the school board refused to budge on policy, but eventually the situation attracted Martin Luther King's attention. The civil rights leader declared his intention to come to Chicago on July 7, 1965, and his three-day visit led King to decide to make Chicago the target of a northern civil rights movement that he hoped to lead.[40]

King found a worthy adversary in Daley. The decision to target Chicago, made against the counsel of some of King's closest advisors, led to a confrontation between these two giants of American politics. King came to Chicago in 1966 to give impetus to the Chicago Freedom Movement, which had grown out of the struggle with Willis and the school board. After his largely successful struggle for black rights across the Deep South, King looked north to reinvigorate his movement and make it more national in character. Northerners had often considered the "Negro Problem" a southern problem, but King knew that the struggle for minority rights was also an issue north of the Mason-Dixon

Figure 121. Martin Luther King, Jr., speaks during a press conference for the Illinois Rally for Civil Rights in Chicago in 1964. (Photograph by Larry Cameron; ICHi-24452, Chicago History Museum.)

Line, especially in cities like Chicago. With the Chicago Freedom Movement he hoped to bring his nonviolent crusade into the heart of the North and thus disarm the growing number of his black power critics. King made a mistake, however, in seeing Daley as a northern incarnation of Bull Connor, Birmingham's notoriously violent and bigoted police chief.

The 1965 Watts Riot in Los Angeles ushered in a new period of racial conflict in America's cities, and big city mayors held their breath in the summer of 1966 as the threat of more riots loomed. King frequently visited Chicago in the early part of the year, raising expectations as he presented his "Chicago Plan." He leased an apartment at 1550 South Hamlin in North Lawndale. On sweltering Freedom Sunday, July 10, 1966, King addressed a crowd at Soldier Field and then marched with about five thousand protestors to the Loop to post his demands on the City Hall door. Two days after the Soldier Field rally, a riot broke out on Chicago's West Side at the corner of Roosevelt Road and Throop Street over a conflict between police and black children about an open fire hydrant. In response Daley agreed to put sprinklers on fire hydrants and build swimming pools in black neighborhoods, but the deep-seated antagonisms between the races remained. King led open housing marches that summer and remarked, "I have never seen such hate, not in Mississippi or Alabama, as I see here in Chicago."[41] Often these marches attracted violent counterprotestors.

In the end King received little for his efforts in Chicago. Daley simply agreed to various reforms and then did little to implement them. In many ways he was caught in a bind: he needed both black and white voters to maintain power, but his actions alienated both groups. In May 1967, in light of the Leadership Council of Open Communities announcement of "Project: Good Neighbor," a massive fair housing educational campaign, King took the opportunity to announce that great progress had been made and left Chicago.[42] Race remained a very divisive issue in the city, and the agreements signed by Daley and others meant little to the black poor still stuck in their overcrowded ghettoes. Chicago, while it escaped the racial violence that swept the country in 1967, continued to anticipate riots. The year 1968 would see that violence return.

1968: The Whole World Is Watching

Nineteen hundred and sixty-eight began inconspicuously enough. On New Year's Eve, Chicagoans who chose not to brave the icy temperatures could stay home and watch TV as Lena Horne performed on Channel 7 with breakaways to the crowd gathering at Randolph and State, the traditional Loop location for Chicagoans to celebrate a New Year. Channel 2 televised "New Year's Eve with Guy Lombardo," while WBBM Radio 780 broadcast music from across the country on its New Year's Eve Dance Party. For those who made their way downtown there were always the movies: the Cinestage presented *Gone with The Wind, Camelot* played at the Bismarck, and *The Graduate* at the Loop, while *Cool Hand Luke* appeared at the Woods. In the *Chicago Tribune,* columnist Mary Merryfield, wondered about a future world of high-rise living as the Hancock Building rose above North Michigan Avenue. The one-hundred-story skyscraper, to be topped off in the spring, offered efficiency apartments for $175.00 per month, while families could rent a four-bedroom apartment for $750.00. Merryfield, reflecting on the recent past, told her readers to "Stay Loose—Big Changes are Coming!" She closed the column by prophetically proclaiming that the skyscraper "can herald a step forward on the radically changing world of 1968." The optimistic Merryfield could not have imagined how drastically things would change.[43]

The mostly young crowd at Randolph and State gathered to ring in the New Year as an official temperature of nine degrees below zero kept their numbers the lowest in years. Approximately fourteen thousand Chicagoans gathered beneath the Marshall Field's Clock and surged into the intersection at the stroke of midnight. The surge lasted fifteen minutes before one hundred police pushed the crowds back to the sidewalk. Near the clock one man kissed another on the cheek and proclaimed in a foreign accent, "Welcome to the new year in this new country."[44]

By the end of January, the news from Vietnam, where the United States had been actively engaged in fighting for several years, was not good. The son of one

of the mayor's closest friends died in Vietnam and brought the war home to
Daley. He could not understand the loss of life and the futility of the war, but
Daley also could not join the protestors or support them in any way. The Tet
Offensive shocked the nation and led to the decision of Lyndon B. Johnson not
to run for a second term. Tet began a hurricane of catastrophes that shook the
nation to its core. Mayor Daley had opposed the war in private while publicly
supporting Johnson's efforts in Southeast Asia. He remained faithful to Johnson and what he saw as a hierarchical system in which he played a vital role. The
mayor, always welcome in LBJ's White House, warned the president to cut his
losses and leave Vietnam behind, but to no avail. Loyalty remained paramount
in his moral universe.[45]

That moral universe would be severely shaken that April 4 as James Earl Ray
shot Dr. Martin Luther King, Jr., to death on the balcony of his hotel room in
Memphis. Chicago lay in stunned silence, but it would not last long. The next
day, riots broke out on Chicago's West Side, and the so-called King Riots shook
the city and the nation. Cities burned all across America that spring, as urban
African American communities erupted and King's message of nonviolent protest disappeared in the chaos of the streets. The riots shook Daley profoundly
and caused him to make one of the biggest political mistakes of his career. He
took the disturbances very personally, saying, "Why did they do this to me?"[46]
During the night of April 6 the Illinois National Guard placed 4,200 troops on
the streets of Chicago, and regular Army troops also arrived to quell the violence.

Heavy sniper fire pinned down police and firemen. On West Madison Avenue,
arsonists started fires up and down the street as Chicago firemen struggled in
vain to douse the flames. On Roosevelt Road between Kedzie and Homan
Avenues, fires consumed thirty buildings on the south side of the street and sixteen structures on the north.[47] On April 5, Daley ordered the Chicago police to
"shoot to kill" arsonists and to "shoot to maim" looters. Police Superintendent
James Conlisk ignored the order further infuriating Daley, but most probably
rescuing the mayor from more embarrassment, and—most importantly—saving
lives. The mayor publicly scolded Conlisk after the riot, bringing his order to
light and attracting national headlines and criticism. The stark violence of
the order shocked the nation, and just five years after being crowned the nation's most successful mayor the media painted Daley as a rampant reactionary willing to spill the blood of young black rioters to protect white property.[48]

The Tet Offensive and the April riots had set the stage for the rest of the ca-
lamitous year. For Daley the "shoot to kill" order had cast him as a hero among
his white working-class supporters but as a hasty violent reactionary to most
others. That April during the rioting antiwar protestors clashed with militia in
Chicago and promised more of the same for the coming Democratic Convention. The more than two hundred white protestors, members of the National
Mobilization Committee to End the War (Mobe), gathered at the Civic Center
Plaza (Daley Plaza) and marched to the Chicago Avenue Armory where about

two hundred guardsmen confronted them using tear gas and arresting twenty-five. The protestors carried signs urging the guard not to kill African Americans in order to protect property. One protest leader later said, "Our black neighbors might feel better when they hear that National Guard troops were used against white people demonstrating for a Negro cause."[49] It would not be the last protest or the last whiff of tear gas for Chicago in 1968.

Tuesday, August 20, brought news of the Soviet invasion of Czechoslovakia, as the Prague Spring movement to liberalize communism was crushed. Chicago area Czechs protested the attack in Daley Plaza and Vietnam War protestors gathering in Chicago for the coming Democratic Convention joined them. Two days later, Chicago policemen stopped two long-haired boys near Lincoln Park for curfew violations. One of the boys, Dean Johnson from South Dakota, drew a handgun. It misfired, and the two Chicago policemen shot him three times, killing him. Abbie Hoffman and other protest leaders were in the offices of the *Chicago Seed,* a counterculture newspaper, and the *Seed* people decided to hold a public funeral for the seventeen-year-old drifter, resulting in the first Democratic Convention protest. The next day, Jerry Rubin and a band of Youth International Party members, aka yippies, nominated Pigasus—an actual pig—for president at the Chicago Civic Center Plaza. The Chicago police arrested Pigasus and six yippies creating a mass media event.[50]

Chicago walked into the morass that became the 1968 Democratic Convention. Over five thousand National Guardsmen mobilized at local armories on August 23. The FBI and other intelligence agencies also descended on the city. A saloon, the Horn Palace, across the street from the International Amphitheater, the site of the Democratic Convention in the Union Stock Yards, became headquarters for local federal operations. Jets flew low over the city and took aerial photographs. The city resembled an armed camp. Federal agents seemed everywhere. To add to the impending chaos, a CTA strike soon followed during the convention, closing down the city's mass transit system. Meanwhile, Mobe attempted to organize further protests across Chicago. The government's intelligence services had completely, almost comically, infiltrated the group of protestors. Military intelligence later estimated that by midweek one out of every six protestors was really an undercover government agent. Meanwhile, the vast numbers of demonstrators expected in Chicago did not materialize. Many liberal middle-class groups had decided not to come to Chicago leaving mostly students and other young protestors to confront police and the politicians gathering in the city.

On Sunday, August 25, the first major confrontation of the convention took place in Lincoln Park. The night before, the police had peacefully cleared the park at the 11:00 p.m. closing time, but Sunday proved to be a different story as Mobe leaders had decided that a confrontation was necessary. A violent fight between the police and protestors broke out, lasting until 2 a.m. when law enforcement officials finally cleared the streets surrounding Lincoln Park.

Figure 122. The 1968 Democratic Convention in Chicago and the resulting televised demonstrations and the ensuing riots between police and demonstrators hurt Mayor Daley's national reputation. (ICHi-20688, Chicago History Museum.)

Another, even more violent, clash took place the next night, which was the first evening of the Democratic Convention. Yet again the following night another battle took place as police used tear gas to clear Lincoln Park.

Other demonstrators gathered in Grant Park where they were allowed to sleep that night. Many of these were supporters of presidential contender Eugene McCarthy. The National Guard relieved the Chicago police and had no intention of clearing the park. Most protestors moved on, but some spent the night. The next day, the returning Chicago police moved on a rally at the Grant Park band shell, and the violence again shook the city. That evening, yet another televised clash took place on Michigan Avenue as Chicago slipped into chaos. Neither the police nor the protestors were innocent as violence reigned in the Loop.

Daley had seemed to lose control of his city with the second round of riots in four months. Meanwhile, on the floor of the Amphitheater he seemed more and more the hardened reactionary. As television broadcasts of his police beating protestors and newsmen in Lincoln Park or at the corner of Balbo and Michigan flooded TV screens across the nation, so did images of Daley angrily lashing out at Senator Abraham Ribicoff on the convention floor. Daley attempted to save his reputation in an interview with Walter Cronkite on CBS-TV, but to little avail. Mobe leader, David Dellinger, called the convention a "tragic victory" for antiwar forces.[51]

The year 1968 proved to be a turning point for the Daley administration. Afterward he or his allies came under constant attack. Chicago too remained under siege and under the magnifying glass of the national media. The following year proved to be no better. The trial of the Chicago Eight (later reduced to the Chicago Seven) accused of causing the convention riots, the Days of Rage riots led by the Weather Faction of the Students for a Democratic Society, as well as the fateful police raid on Chicago's Black Panther Party headquarters that resulted in the death of state party chairman Fred Hampton and downstate organizer Mark Clark—all brought further infamy to Daley and the city. State's Attorney Edward Hanrahan's defense of the police raid on the Panthers further outraged Chicago's African American community. Hanrahan quickly emerged as a "law and order" hero among white working-class and conservative Chicagoans, thus positioning him as a possible political rival to Daley. Even Daley's attempt to win back Chicago's youth by presenting free rock concerts in Grant Park backfired when a riot occurred at a Sly and the Family Stone concert on July 27, 1970.[52]

Daley's stature as a national political figure also slipped badly. In 1972, Democratic reformers denied Daley and his allies delegate seats at the Democratic Convention, replacing them with a contingent led by Rev. Jesse Jackson and independent alderman Bill Singer. The man who could claim to have made John F. Kennedy president could now not even vote at his party's convention. He would return in 1976, but his power and influence had waned. Even as the embattled Daley Democrats continued to dominate city and Cook County politics, they saw their national power and influence shrink considerably.[53]

In 1972, maverick Democrat Dan Walker took the party's nomination and then won the governor's mansion. Once in Springfield, Walker remained an enemy of the Chicago machine. George McGovern's catastrophic presidential campaign impacted on the entire Illinois ticket that year with only Walker winning statewide office. Worse, with the overwhelming support of Chicago's black community, Bernard Carey defeated Hanrahan, and the GOP controlled the state's attorney's office. The Democratic machine never seemed more vulnerable. Only Daley's personal popularity seemed solid, as he had won reelection in both 1971 and 1975.

While Daley remained firmly in power, his allies began to fall to corrup-

Figure 123. The construction of St. Mary of Nazareth Hospital Center pictured here in 1974 in the Wicker Park/Ukrainian Village neighborhood meant much to the city as another institution agreed to stay and invest in the city. Mayor Daley saw these projects as vital to Chicago's future. (Archives of St. Mary of Nazareth Hospital Center.)

tion charges. Accusations of nepotism regarding city business and Daley's sons surfaced. Daley responded by saying that "if I can't help my sons then they can kiss my ass.... I make no apologies to anyone."[54] Meanwhile the ambitious U.S. attorney James R. Thompson indicted Daley allies Earl Bush, Paul Wigoda, Matthew Danaher, and Thomas Keane. The pressure mounted on the seventy-two-year-old mayor and on May 6, 1974, he suffered a mild stroke. Rumors ran through the city about possible successors, but Daley eventually returned to City Hall's fifth floor and to win yet another mayoral contest. Chicago and Richard J. Daley remained synonymous.[55]

11

Apocalypse "Now" or Regeneration?

When on December 20, 1976, at the age of seventy-four, Mayor Richard J. Daley died in his North Michigan Avenue doctor's office, he left no heir apparent to his mayoral throne. His oldest son Rich Daley was too young and too inexperienced to take over the reins at city hall. Besides that, such an immediate seizure of power by the dead mayor's son would have seemed too "fixed," too royal in its symbolism.

An African American, Alderman Wilson Frost of the Thirty-fourth Ward, president pro tem of the city council, claimed the mayoralty. Unlike many other aldermen, black and white, Frost was well educated; he had earned his bachelor's degree from Fisk University in 1950. Later he attended Chicago-Kent Law School and studied at DePaul University's Lawyer's Institute. In 1973, after working with several law firms, Frost formed the firm of Meyer and Frost, later Frost and Greenblatt. Frost had been active in the machine since 1967 when he first won election as an alderman, but most aldermen saw the position held by Frost as largely ceremonial, and they moved quickly to block his claims. While long lines of Chicagoans stood quietly to view Richard Daley's coffin in Bridgeport's Nativity of Our Lord Church, the aldermen met and chose a different candidate. The dead mayor's allies, both loyal and only nominally so, began to position themselves to get a larger piece of the political pie. The "Young Turks," Aldermen Ed Burke and Ed Vrdolyak, saw opportunity knocking and tried to increase their power. The mayoralty was not to be theirs; the Daley loyalists held sway, so they supported a compromise candidate in Michael Bilandic, the alderman from Daley's Eleventh Ward and a Croatian American like Vrdolyak. Bilandic seemed likely to be a caretaker until the young Daley could make his move, thus assuring continuity in the Democratic machine's hierarchy. The Northwest Side's Roman Pucinski and the Poles felt cut out once again by the South Side coalition but agreed to the compromise as Pucinski planned for the next election. At first Alderman Frost protested, but the victorious aldermen offered Frost the chairmanship of the powerful finance committee in the city council, and he later went on to serve as a commissioner of the Cook County Board of Tax Appeals.[1]

The Tragedy of Michael Bilandic

Michael J. Bilandic was a quiet man who, when Daley died, still lived at home with his mother in Bridgeport. He had joined the local Democratic Party and was picked by Daley to run for alderman of the Eleventh Ward in 1969, an election he easily won. The honest Bilandic rose in power in a city council badly tainted by corruption and served both as chairman of the finance committee and Daley's floor leader. He seemed a perfect caretaker candidate, and he pledged to serve out Daley's term and not run in the general election. The city council began to flex its muscles, as it had never been able to do under Boss Daley.[2]

Bilandic inherited a city with many problems. Those problems had been largely unaddressed for some time and now were boiling over. Chicagoans could hardly remember a mayor before Daley but had vivid memories of the years since that fateful day in April 1968 when Rev. Martin Luther King, Jr., died in Memphis. Racial strife haunted the city. Wilson Frost and the black aldermen had been denied their place in the political sun as Bridgeport's whites kept the traditional machine alliance together, but many African Americans felt their day would come. The black population continued to grow and spread across the South and West Sides knocking on the gates of the white ethnic Southwest and Southeast Sides as well as suburban Oak Park. Some felt that Chicago would go the way of Detroit, with its overwhelmingly black city core and a defensive white suburban ring. Racial violence remained a constant threat in Bilandic's city.

Another even more ominous problem confronted the city as its economy continued to stumble. Inflation caused by Vietnam War spending now was joined by the OPEC oil crises of the mid-1970s. Long lines at gas stations and high prices threatened to bring the local and national economy down, while soaring interest rates endangered the housing market. Chicago still remained an important industrial center, but the deterioration of the city's manufacturing base continued unabated as industries fled the inner city. Increased unemployment in Chicago's ghettoes did not bode well for the "city that works."

Bilandic won a six-way race in the special election in 1977 to finish out Richard J. Daley's term. Roman Pucinski provided the most serious challenge, as the Polish American politician had hoped to attract black support for his candidacy. Pucinski had been a congressman but had run an unsuccessful campaign for the U.S. Senate and then was elected a Chicago alderman in 1974. He had said that the late mayor had had too much power and blamed Daley for allowing the city to deteriorate and jobs to leave Chicago. Bilandic grew to like being mayor and he now planned to run again in 1979 after finishing out Daley's term. Mother Nature, however, was about to step in where Pucinski and others could not go.

Chicago in the late 1970s had endured several brutal winters, and the winter of 1978–79 proved to be Michael Bilandic's undoing. A blizzard began on Friday night January 12, 1979, and lasted until 2:00 a.m. on Sunday, January 14.

Over twenty inches of snow fell on top of a seven- to ten-inch snow base left over from a New Year's Eve blizzard, setting a record level for snow on the ground in Chicago. The city reeled from the storm: transportation came to a standstill; the electrical motors of CTA trains running down the center of expressways failed because of the excessive use of salt used to try to deice the roads; rapid transit as well as buses, cars, and planes came to a halt; garbage piled up, and cemeteries delayed burials.[3]

The snow kept falling that winter, and Bilandic could not seem to deal with it. His public statements were out of touch with reality to say the least. When he ordered CTA trains to bypass African American neighborhoods on their way to the Loop, he may have warmed white commuters, but he infuriated his black constituents who protested the machine's insensitivity to their needs. Those black voters who had already been staying home during the final elections of Daley's era now grew infuriated as they walked through the snow to their jobs, if they had jobs. Bilandic seemed remote, and city government seemed unable to respond.

Jane Byrne, whom Daley had appointed consumer sales commissioner but Bilandic had fired, emerged as the hapless Croatian's opponent in the 1979 Democratic primary. They had been feuding for some time and that feud involved Rich Daley, the late mayor's son. Byrne lashed out against the machine, calling Aldermen Ed Burke and Ed Vrdolyak "evil twins." On February 28, 1979, Byrne won the Democratic primary and many proclaimed the machine dead. Columnist Mike Royko said he was never prouder of his city. An era had seemed to end.

Beyond the catastrophic response to the snows of 1979, Bilandic was an intelligent, perceptive man, but out of his league as a politician sitting in Daley's old office on the fifth floor of City Hall. Neither stupid nor confused, Bilandic went on to have a very distinguished career as an Illinois Supreme Court justice.

Deindustrialization: Phase Two

The city's economic downturn continued into the 1980s. This time industries that had replaced meatpacking in the pecking order of Chicago manufacturers began to fade. In the late 1970s, the American steel industry endured a sudden collapse that hit the Chicago region hard. Old inefficient plants still produced much of America's steel, and they faltered in competition with modern foreign steelmakers that could easily undersell American producers. Much of this dynamic was a result of being the leading steelmaker for so many decades and having no competition after World War II while Europe and Japan attempted to lift themselves out of devastation. The American steel industry became flabby. New Japanese, German, and Scandinavian mills used modern, cost-effective technology, a transformation that did not occur in American mills. On top of the new competition, the market for steel declined during this time period, put-

Figure 124. This abandoned packinghouse in the old Union Stock Yards symbolized the de-industrialization Chicago witnessed in the last half of the twentieth century. Swift and Company shuttered this plant, pictured here in the 1990s, in the early 1960s. In 1971, the Union Stock Yards closed. (Photograph by D. Pacyga.)

ting the industry under further stress.[4] In the seven years after 1979, about sixteen thousand Chicago-area steelworkers lost their jobs. In 1980, Wisconsin Steel in Chicago's Southeast Side neighborhood of South Deering shuttered its doors. The mill had supplied much of the steel needed by its parent company, International Harvester Company (IHC) to produce its farm equipment and heavy trucks. But IHC began to purchase more and more of its steel overseas, even more cheaply than it could purchase from its own subsidiary. Wisconsin Steel and other mills attempted to introduce various labor-saving devices but were neither willing nor able to modernize the way the Japanese had. In 1976, International Harvester reportedly lost $20 million on steel production alone. The following year IHC sold off Wisconsin Steel to the engineering company Envirodyne, which also failed to make the plant profitable. In 1979 during a strike at IHC that closed off that market for Wisconsin Steel, the company defaulted on its loans from both IHC and the Chase Manhattan Bank. Chase froze the company's assets and padlocked the plant on March 30, 1980, leaving 3,500 workers without their final paychecks, benefits, or retirement.[5] Deindustrialization had come to Chicago's metal industry, and once again global economic changes had a direct impact on Chicago.

Other mills followed Wisconsin Steel's collapse. U.S. Steel's South Works, which had produced the structural steel used in building the Sears Tower, at one time employed nearly eighteen thousand laborers. Women found jobs in the mill in the 1940s and remained a major component of the mill work force right until the end. Eddie Sadlowski, the president of Local 65 of the United Steelworkers Union and then in 1974 head of District 31, the largest steelworkers district in the nation, worked in the plant. In 1977, the brash young labor leader led an all out, though unsuccessful, attempt to take control of the national union and reform it. After years of enduring terrible conditions and low pay steelworkers had reached a safe and secure place in the American economy. Local 65 built a huge hall and community center on South Chicago Avenue near the center of the neighborhood. Steelworkers enjoyed good wages and excellent benefits. The smoke and dust from the mills covered the city's Southeast Side, and if visitors found it difficult to breathe on the Southeast Side, it meant money in workers' pockets.[6]

The collapse of the industry hit the neighborhood and Commercial and Torrance Avenues hard. Stores began to shutdown. Taverns closed. Families moved away. The eventual closing of the South Works, LTV (Republic Steel), and Acme Steel shocked the surrounding neighborhoods' remaining white ethnic, African American, and Mexican American population. An entire way of life disappeared. Neighborhoods with names like Irondale, Slag Valley, Arizona, Millgate, East Side, and the Bush no longer saw their nighttime skies lit up by the huge open hearth and Bessemer steelmaking processes. Other plants outside Chicago also closed, including Inland Steel. U.S. Steel's Gary Works laid off thousands of workers. What had been a slow process for the Back of the Yards and the meatpacking industry was an avalanche of change on the steelmaking Southeast Side and the entire Chicago-Calumet Region.[7]

The industry survived but only after going through a huge transformation. By the end off the 1980s, several minimills in the area recycled scrap metal. Often nonunion operations had been built in so-called green field areas. Northwest Indiana mills continued to produce about 25 percent of the steel made in the United States, but the heyday of the industry had passed. The great mines of iron ore ranges of the upper Great Lakes sat vacant. The huge industrial expanses of Chicago's once flourishing industry left environmentally difficult to deal with vacant land. The neighborhoods of the Southeast Side from Pullman to the lake had to figure out how to survive without the industries that had created them in the nineteenth century and nurtured them through the first eighty years of the twentieth century.[8] Large Catholic Churches stood in the shadows of the mills. Many of these had seen their congregations change from one ethnicity to another and then dwindle altogether. St. Michael's Polish Catholic Church on Eighty-third and South Shore Drive still marked the entryway to the Bush neighborhood. First its high school and then grammar school were shuttered, but its parishioners, both past and present, remained dedicated to this huge cathedral for steelworkers and restored the magnificent structure. Today the parish offers masses in English, Spanish, and Polish, although most of the Poles have long left the neighborhood. The high steeples no longer have to compete with the South Works for the dominance of the South Chicago skyline as some eight hundred acres of former steel mill land lay empty on the lakefront just south of Chicago's Rainbow Beach. Russell Square Park sits across the street, waiting for what urban transformation will come next.

Other industries also felt the impact of deindustrialization. Cicero's huge Western Electric Hawthorne Plant, once home to over forty-five thousand workers hit hard times in the 1980s. In its day the Hawthorne plant had been on the cutting edge of technological innovation. It was the analog Silicon Valley of the first half of the twentieth century. The plant, along with the Bell Labs, pioneered all types of communication innovations for AT&T, the national telephone monopoly. It opened in 1906 as the nation's first "fireproof" manufacturing plant. Nearly one hundred buildings containing 5 million square feet stood at Cermak Road and Cicero Avenue, which provided the economic base for much of the Southwest Side of Chicago as well as the towns of Cicero and Berwyn. During World War II, Bell Labs developed an accurate radar system produced at Hawthorne. Talking movies also depended on the experts at Bell and Hawthorne. This plant and the Motorola and Zenith plants helped to make the Chicago area a technological innovator in communications. The quality inspection department alone at Hawthorne Works employed five thousand people. The American telephone system was the finest in the world, largely due to products pioneered in the Cicero plant. In the 1920s and 1930s the Hawthorne Works were also the site of various human behavior studies that examined modern production techniques and their impact on individual workers. Hawthorne even developed its own railroad.

In 1983, after years of rumors and a reduced work force, Western Electric closed the aging plant, moving its production to new sites around the nation. The main building was demolished, and the site became a shopping mall and industrial park. The next year the U.S. Department of Justice forced a breakup of the Bell phone monopoly, and after 112 years the Western Electric name disappeared. The company was at first absorbed into AT&T Technologies, which then became Lucent Technologies. The old Hawthorne Railroad survived as the Manufacturer's Junction Railway and served some of the new industries that made their home at the Hawthorne Works Business Center.[9] But despite some development, the manufacturing base of Cicero and of many Chicago neighborhoods was gone. The scene repeated itself over and over again in the 1980s as Chicago and the region continued to bleed jobs. Shuttered stores, bars, and restaurants followed the Hawthorne Works closing and its kind.

Gentrification meant further problems for Chicago's industrial base in the 1980s and later. As early as 1987, the *Chicago Tribune* reported that the Clybourn Industrial Corridor was under siege by the rush to convert inner-city factory buildings to loft apartments and retail spaces. The city attempted to halt the trend with a zoning law that would protect such industrial districts. By 1990, the Clybourn shopping district was a reality, along with six small strip shopping centers. Traffic congestion became a problem for the few remaining manufacturers, as did the appearance of upscale lofts along Clybourn. New residents found it unpleasant to live with the noise and pollution of the old plants. Factories found it hard to stay in such areas. The Haymarket District provided another example, as a growing middle-class residential and entertainment population drove out meat processors, jobbers, and others. As the old manufacturing city changed, many thought it was dying.[10]

Nationally the problem dated back to 1968, when inequality began to grow in the United States. A cycle began in which the rich got richer and the vast majority did not. The American economy grew at a slower rate, and Chicago was no exception. In fact with its large poor minority population it symbolized the changes. Between 1973 and 1993, the real wages of working women and men dropped 11 percent, while the top 20 percent of wage earners saw their incomes rise with the 29 percent increase in the gross national product. The mass employment of wives and overtime pay prevented a total collapse of the system. This shift in gender roles resulted in household incomes rising slowly until 1989. From 1989 to 1995, however, household incomes declined in real dollars by 7 percent. By the early 1990s the percentage of wealth owned by the top 1 percent of Americans more than doubled, back to the rates of the 1920s just before the Great Depression. Years of economic readjustment during the Nixon through Reagan administrations had returned America to a wide gap between the rich and the working middle class and an even wider gap between the rich and poor. Various explanations have been proposed for this shift, including increased foreign competition, the decline of unions, the move from a manufacturing to a service economy, and inflation. Both private and public policy changes, in taxation rates, in the welfare system, and in governmental labor policy, also have fueled this trend. The United States had the greatest social inequality of all industrial nations. Between 1973 and 1989, roughly four out of five American families saw a decline in their incomes. Chicago reeled from the results.[11]

Between 1967 and 1982, Chicago lost a quarter of a million jobs, or 46 percent of the city's former industrial might. While some of the manufacturing positions simply moved beyond the city limits, as they had earlier, a deeper restructuring also took place. Between 1972 and 1981, the city lost 10 percent of its private sector jobs while the suburban market grew by 25 percent. Much of this growth was racially selective. Inner-city African Americans and Hispanics were cut out of the job market. On both sides of the suburban/city divide, minority and racially mixed areas saw a decline in jobs while white areas saw all the increase. During the 1970s, 25 percent of all Chicago factories closed. Between the high point, in 1947, and 1981 the entire region lost 14 percent of its industrial jobs. The brutal trend continued. During the decade from 1982 to 1992, manufacturing employment dropped another 18 percent. In the year 1991–92, some twenty-five thousand industrial jobs disappeared from the Chicago region, nineteen thousand of these from the city.

This disruption of Chicago's and the Midwest's industrial strength had been going on for sometime. The federal government invested heavily in California and other Pacific Coast states after 1940. Since then, the United States had fought three Pacific wars, first against the Japanese and then in Korea and Vietnam. Federal money built bases and invested in the aerospace industry and in other military-oriented industries in this and in the Gulf Coast and southern Atlantic states. Washington left the old industrial heartland to fend for itself. Federal defense contracts were at the heart of economic problems in the center of the country. Illinois slipped down the ranks of industrial states getting U.S. defense contracts; by 1984 it ranked last among major industrial states receiving federal defense money. The so-called gunbelt on both coasts out performed the Midwest in general and Illinois in particular in attracting federal defense contracts. Small western cities blossomed into urban giants in the late twentieth century.[12]

Seeds of a New Loop

Mayor Bilandic attempted to spur the city's traditional growth machine by following the ideas of his predecessor and the business community, led by Thomas Ayers, president of Commonwealth Edison. Bilandic tried to reclaim the South Loop as it lost its industrial base. Once known for its printing companies and for the massive railroads that had dominated the southern approach to the business district, the area now had become abandoned and desolate. The Dearborn Street Station, once one of the city's railroad station gems, sat in the automobile and jet age like the carcass of a dying dinosaur. Vice, albeit on a smaller scale than at the turn of the century, still flourished among the remaining burlesque houses and adult peep shows on State Street south of Van Buren Street. Major retailers left South State Street for North Michigan Avenue or the suburbs. Executives in Chicago's office skyscrapers, such as Sears Tower, might soon be looking down at the rotted urban core of the former regional shopping and entertainment center. Loop movie houses fell on hard times as they played to increasingly small audiences. The Loop population, both during the day and night, seemed to be more African American, causing more white flight from the stores and theaters. Race, as always, shaped the city. Middle-class patrons no longer felt safe in the downtown at night. Competition with the suburbs or North Michigan Avenue also played a role. All of these factors had a negative impact on the traditional downtown. Few ventured to the Loop at night. The busiest place on South State Street at night seemed to be the Pacific Garden

Mission, which provided shelter for the Loop's homeless, those who could not afford a room in one of the area's countless single-room occupancy hotels.

In 1970, during the turbulent years following the riots of the West Side and the Weatherman's Days of Rage, Ayers called a meeting in his office in the new First National Bank Building to discuss the abandoned railroad yards just to the south of the Loop. Joining Ayers was Gordon M. Metcalf, CEO and chairman of the board of Sears, and Donald Graham, CEO and chairman of the board of Continental Illinois Bank. These men, respected leaders of Chicago business community and in the prime of their influence, could, with the city's help, mobilize the business community to develop the railroad yards and begin the turnaround of the Loop.

The new development called for a mixture of townhouses and mid-rises. In its first phase it covered the railroad land just to the east of State Street south of Polk Street. Future phases pushed the development further south to Fourteenth Street. The Bilandic administration showed vision in promoting this site for residential housing, and Dearborn Park would set the stage for further Loop residential development in the coming decades.[13]

The city also looked toward State Street. Once a congested six-lane street through the heart of the city, by the late 1970s it had turned into a desolate strip. In June 1978, the city began construction of the State Street Mall designed by Kiyoki Kikuchi. The new transit mall opened during the first months of the Byrne administration. The city called it a "transit-way" because, although most of the street space was given over to pedestrians, a road was set up for CTA buses cutting through the heart of it. Kikuchi used a simple style to interact with State Street's classic architecture. Granite curbs, planters, and kiosks decorated the street, and asphalt blocks made up the sidewalks. The U.S. Mass Transportation Authority funded the $17.2 million doomed project. Some pushcarts and outdoor cafes, previously outlawed in Chicago, appeared, but few people wanted to sit on what remained a dingy street with fleets of buses spewing their exhaust at helpless visitors. Cars could no longer drop patrons off in front of stores. After a few years, the State Street mall failed in its attempt to suburbanize Chicago's heart.

Bilandic also attempted to revive interest in Chicago's Loop by organizing special events that brought attention to the downtown. He organized the first ChicagoFest and, an avid runner himself, supported the Chicago Marathon. The mayor organized low-interest loans for middle-class families in an attempt to attract them back into the city, especially to Dearborn Park. Despite his reputation, Bilandic planted the seeds of initiatives that proved successful under his successors.

Figure 125. (*Facing*) Marina Towers, seen here from the Michigan Avenue Bridge in 1963, marked the return of large-scale residential units to the Loop, a trend that would escalate later in the century. (Photograph by Charles W. Cushman; Indiana University Archives, P12877.)

Jane Byrne and the Politics of Angst

For Chicago's reform community, the promising election of Jane Byrne soon became a disappointment. Many had worked to elect Chicago's first woman mayor. Her attack on the Bilandic administration as not only incompetent, but corrupt, warmed the hearts of lakefront liberals and helped rally an already angry African American community in February 1979. In the same year that saw Margaret Thatcher elected as Britain's first woman prime minister, Chicagoans had also elected a brash, tough-talking woman to lead the city. The new mayor soon received accolades from the liberal community, as the city seemed to refute Paddy Bauler's claim that Chicago was not ready for reform.

Byrne had grown up politically in Daley's machine. She first met the late mayor during the Kennedy presidential campaign in 1960. Her second meeting did not come until 1964, when Daley again met her at a party honoring Msgr. Francis J. Dolan of Queen of All Saints Parish in Byrne's Sauganash neighborhood. At his suggestion, she got involved in grassroots politics, and four years later Daley appointed her consumer affairs commissioner; she was the only woman in his cabinet. The mayor also gave her visibility by making her cochair of the Cook County Democratic Party and giving her a seat on the Democratic National Committee. Byrne was Daley's token woman. The mayor, under pressure to open the party to women and minorities, made the natural choice of an Irish American widow of an air force pilot. Byrne knew the game, she said, "In the Game of 'Who's on First,' I was on first, I was the token woman. I was wise to what he was doing . . . but to me it was 'I'll do the job'. . . . After awhile I was no longer a token to him."[14] Byrne knew how the machine worked. When Bilandic fired her as commissioner, she could point to the "deals" that made the machine. An insider turned reformer, she would be a dangerous opponent, especially after Michael Bilandic had shown such poor public judgment in dealing with the winter of 1978–79. Chicago's black community rallied to her, and Chicagoans dumped Bilandic.

Byrne's first statements and appointments as mayor also pleased reformers. Political scientist Louis H. Masotti of Northwestern University headed her transition team that included former independent alderman Bill Singer; and the voice of independent aldermen, Leon M. Despres; as well as neighborhood, ethnic, and labor leaders. Singer had led (along with Operation Push's head, Jesse Jackson) the unseating of Richard J. Daley and his machine delegates form the 1972 Democratic National Convention. It appeared that the liberal Democrats had taken over city hall. Machine aldermen felt shut out of Byrne's transition team, and future plans as the new mayor seemed to be following a path of reform-populism.

On the other hand, Byrne had stayed in contact with the Daleys during the Bilandic administration, especially Michael Daley. Parts of the Bridgeport team behind Bilandic tried to push the Daley boys out and establish themselves as the power behind Bilandic. Byrne never broke completely with the Democratic organization. She placed Ray Simon, former corporation counsel under Mayor Daley, on her transition team, which included several other familiar names from the old Daley organization. The new mayor reconciled with the machine. State Senator Richard M. Daley, the late mayor's son, approached Byrne, but most of the others seemed cautious and waited for Byrne to make the first move. Byrne soon made it clear that she was a product of the Democratic Party, and while she had run specifically against Michael Bilandic and the "evil cabal," to the disappointment of her liberal supporters, Byrne began to make peace with Vrdolyak and Burke.[15]

According to Jane Byrne, her political advisor Don Rose—a longtime critic of the Daley machine who had masterminded the campaign against Bilandic—encouraged her to work with the regular organization, telling her she needed party regulars to run the city. At the first meeting after the primary victory, Alderman Matt Bieszczat walked out, refusing to talk with Byrne. Dan Rostenkowski took charge, but Byrne was puzzled at their attitude and even at President Jimmy Carter's who supposedly had asked Rostenkowski what would happen to "poor Chicago now?" Byrne later wrote, "Are these people crazy? I worked in City Hall for over fifteen years, yet they are treating me like an invader from outer space." Others telephoned Byrne, including Rich Daley and Michael Madigan, then Democratic minority whip in the Illinois House. Many

offered support for the regular election. Daley set himself up as a broker. The warm relationship between Byrne and Daley would not last long. Madigan and other Democratic regulars wanted to make clear that the young Daley did not speak for them. After the regular election on April 3, 1979, when Byrne won 82 percent of the vote, the lobbying heated up. Ed Vrdolyak, who had become the most powerful alderman in the city council under Bilandic, contacted Byrne through Charles Swibel, the chairman of the Chicago Housing Authority (CHA).[16]

Byrne soon became the de facto machine candidate. Her fiery temper and often erratic behavior filled the columns of Chicago newspapers. Sexist rumors persisted that her husband, newspaperman Jay McMullen, actually called the shots. Byrne made various dubious political moves, such as retaining Charles Swibel as chairman of the CHA and appointing white women to the school board while ignoring black candidates, thus alienating her African American supporters. She also

Figure 126. Jane Byrne won the 1979 mayoral election. (ICHi-19708, Chicago History Museum.)

Figure 127. The Cabrini-Green Housing Project, in the center and left of this photograph, stood within the shadow of the expanding downtown. Jane Byrne moved into this project, which had become one of the most notorious housing projects in Chicago. (Photograph by Charles W. Cushman; Indiana University Archives, P10243.)

began a running feud with Richard M. Daley and, like Bilandic's supporters, moved to cut back the Daley family's influence. Her alliance with Aldermen Vrdolyak, Burke, the aging Vito Marzullo, and the mobbed-up alderman Fred B. Roti caused lakefront liberals to abandon her. Nevertheless, she looked unbeatable as she and her supporters reorganized the old machine. The "evil cabal" soon became her influential supporters and advisors.

Byrne's term in office proved to be spectacular theater. The lakefront liberal coalition that had done much to elect Jane Byrne soon returned to being an out of power loyal opposition in the city council. The Daley family also seemed to be in exile as a divided Bridgeport lost power. But underneath it all, Chicago kept changing, and while the city might celebrate its first woman mayor those forces of change continued to percolate. The African American community had supported Byrne, but as the administration developed it was obvious that once again blacks were out in the cold and resentment grew. Perhaps Byrne felt she could ignore the racial problem as long as she had solid white ethnic and middle-class support, but Richard M. Daley, the late mayor's oldest son, presented another problem that would not go away.

Byrne attempted to brighten Chicago's fading economic picture and even reached out to the residents of the notorious Cabrini-Green Housing Project by temporarily moving into an apartment in the complex. Critics pointed out that if all the residents of CHA housing had as many police standing in the hallway as Byrne and her husband had the projects would be very safe. This stunt by Byrne brought more attacks. To many Chicagoans, Jane Byrne seemed to be more show than substance.[17]

The city faced a budget shortfall. Its industries declined and its middle-class tax base dwindled. Basic city functions such as street cleaning, pothole repair, and garbage pickup seemed out of reach. Chicago's police and fire personnel made demands for better pay and benefits and threatened to unionize. Chicago looked like the city that didn't work. Dearborn Park's opening in 1979 promised new life in the Loop, as did the development of residential lofts first in the Transportation Building and then along Dearborn Street under the leadership of architects Harry Weese, Will Hasbrouck, and others, but the glory days of the Loop seemed far behind. The new State Street Mall did nothing to perk up the Loop.[18] Byrne, as Bilandic before her, realized that something else had to be done. One answer was to draw suburbanites, people with money, back into the Loop. Byrne's answer was ChicagoFest, the redevelopment of Navy Pier, and above all a new World's Fair slated for 1992. Administration officials hoped this would restore confidence in Chicago and act as a funnel for renewed investment.

1983: It's Harold!

Jane Byrne entered the 1983 election as the regular Democratic Party organization's choice. Over the previous four years, she had built a vast war chest, made peace with the Vrdolyak-Burke-Roti wing of the party, and moved to isolate the Daley family. She wanted to prove that her election was no fluke but had marked a paramount change in the city's history. For Byrne, the only possible obstacle in the way was Richard M. Daley. Byrne had spurned him in the early days of her administration, and many of the deceased mayor's supporters felt she had snubbed his mother, the family's beloved matriarch, Eleanor "Sis" Daley. Rich Daley, a rather lackluster state senator, accepted her challenge and took on the Byrne organization by running against it for state's attorney and winning. Daley's victory gave him a base from which to possibly launch a run for city hall. Many of his father's old supporters rallied around him, but others who remembered the concentration of power in the elder Daley's hands feared a return of the dynasty. They felt that the Byrne leadership would keep their interests in mind, while the Daleys might simply take over. For most Chicagoans, this struggle appeared to be the major political story of the year. Earlier Edward R. Vrdolyak, with Byrne's support, ousted George Dunne from his powerful position as chairman of the Central Committee of the Democratic Party of Cook County. Byrne doubted Dunne's loyalty and feared that he might lead a Daley revolt. Both the Daley and Byrne camps sniped at each other as the election neared.

Meanwhile in the African American community, a little-noticed political movement began to emerge. Some observers thought Jesse Jackson would run for mayor, especially after Byrne arrogantly replaced two black Chicago Housing Authority board members, giving control of the CHA to its white board members. In addition the mayor replaced the longtime and controversial director, Charlie Swibel, with another white, Andrew J. Mooney. Some insiders felt that Byrne goaded the African American community to put forward a black candidate that would take away from Rich Daley's support in the primary; if so, she made a drastic political mistake that would come back to haunt her in the Democratic primary.

Jesse Jackson organized a black boycott of ChicagoFest and began a major voter registration drive in the African American community as a response to Byrne's actions. The drive proved successful, and the African American electorate awoke to its own power. On November 2, 1982, the huge number of Chicago black voters almost stopped Illinois Governor Jim Thompson from winning his third election for the state's highest office. As a result, a tremendous amount of pressure was put on First District congressman and former mayoral candidate Harold Washington to run for mayor in the upcoming Democratic primary.

Two days after the November 1982 election Richard M. Daley announced that he would challenge Byrne in the February 22, 1983, primary; less than a week later, Harold Washington also threw his hat into the ring. Byrne officially announced her candidacy on November 22, the day before the Democratic committeemen would meet to make their choice on whom to support. George Dunne—who, while no longer chairman, remained a powerful committeeman—led the anti-Byrne forces. Daley's and Washington's backers held their ground, and a divided party put Byrne forward as the official candidate. As victory in the Democratic primary all but insured victory in the mayoral election, the struggle for control of city hall was going to be a hard-fought one.

On primary day, over 77 percent of eligible Chicago voters went to the polls. Harold Washington garnered considerable support from the black wards while Byrne and Daley fought it out for white support. As many predicted, the primary would be decided along the lakefront and in the Hispanic wards. Here Washington also did well, gaining votes among liberals and Latinos. He won a hotly contested primary with 36 percent of the vote compared to Byrne's 34 percent and Daley's 30 percent. The city reeled as another surprising primary election made national headlines.[19]

While Chicago's black community celebrated, the city's white ethnic wards looked for a scapegoat. Many blamed Daley for splitting the white vote and

Figure 128. Judge Charles E. Freeman swore in Harold Washington as mayor of Chicago on April 29, 1983. Looking on are Jane Byrne and her family as well as other Chicago dignitaries and Washington supporters. (Chicago Public Library, Special Collections and Preservation Division, HWAC 4–29–1983.)

assuring Washington's victory. He was even attacked while shopping in a local store in his neighborhood Bridgeport. But such simple answers did not suffice. Byrne had acted in a manner that had angered black wards. African Americans felt that they had elected her in 1979 and that she then betrayed them. Jackson's registration drive further stirred up the black electorate, and then Washington's brilliant campaign solidified his base support and expanded it. Still, Harold Washington was a minority candidate who had only attracted about one-third of the votes. Had the regular Democrats not been divided, his election would not have occurred.

Chicago's Republicans found themselves in a quandary. The big names such as former governor Richard Oglivie and state's attorney Jim Webb had refused to run on the Republican side, and in the primary, Bernard Epton, a little known candidate, was nominated to run for mayor. Epton was a former liberal Republican congressman from Hyde Park who now lived on the Gold Coast, and he seemed to have an especially good record on racial issues. Epton seemed like the typical Republican sacrificial lamb, and so he would have been against either Byrne or Daley. But now Bernie Epton represented the last Great White

Hope to Chicagoans who feared a minority takeover of city government. Epton became a plausible, and even formidable, candidate in a racially divided city.

Meanwhile, Jane Byrne threatened a write-in campaign, but this proved to be futile, and she chose not to run against the winner of the party's primary. She did not, however, endorse Harold Washington or anyone else. In turn, eight Democratic aldermen openly supported Bernie Epton as race became the overriding issue of the election. Once again it seemed that the lakefront would provide the crucial votes in the election as the rest of the city was racially polarized. Both Epton (Gold Coast) and Washington (Hyde Park) hailed from crucial lakefront wards. In the end, Harold Washington won the April election with 51.8 percent of the vote, despite Epton's "Before It's Too Late" campaign slogan, taking twenty-two of the city's fifty wards and squeaking past Epton by just under fifty thousand votes. Chicago had its first African American mayor.[20]

The euphoria of Harold Washington's election soon gave way to the political realities of Chicago. The new mayor had to deal with a city council controlled by white ethnic aldermen who had opposed both his nomination and election. Vrdolyak and Burke put together a coalition of twenty-nine white city council members that could block anything Washington proposed. Unlike Byrne, Washington was both unwilling and incapable of making peace with the "Two Eddies," and the city soon fell into a legislative stalemate called the Council Wars. Political fighting paralyzed the first three years of the Washington administration and gained Chicago the unflattering sobriquet of "Beirut on the Lake" as it seemed to politically resemble that war-torn city in the Middle East.[21]

Finally in 1986, the courts ordered the redistricting of the city's ward boundaries to allow for greater black and Hispanic representation in the council. A special election set for March 18, 1986, resulted in the Washington forces controlling twenty-four of fifty seats. A special runoff election for one undecided seat was won by Luis Gutierrez and gave the Washington forces a split with the mayor able to cast a tie-breaking vote. After three years, the political landscape of the city had changed in Washington's favor.[22]

Washington's administration broke with the traditional Chicago growth machine on various issues. Where his predecessors spoke of large downtown projects, Washington's advisors attempted to funnel money to neighborhoods and smaller projects in the outlying areas of the city. Robert Meir, the city's commissioner of economic development, eschewed the "monumental and grandiose" in favor of smaller projects. Not surprisingly, the administration killed plans to revitalize Navy Pier and for a World's Fair. Furthermore Washington's people pushed the idea of "linked" development that called for investors to divert some of their money to charitable and public purposes in the neighborhoods, as an answer to what progressives saw as "unequal" development that traditionally favored downtown. Many of Chicago's movers and shakers thus saw the Washington administration as antidevelopment.[23] This image was not to be accurate as city hall gave its support to the building of a new baseball stadium for the Chicago White Sox, the expansion of McCormick Place, and the Block 37 Plan in the heart of the Loop.[24]

Meanwhile the deindustrialization of Chicago continued apace as businesses across the metropolis shuttered their facilities. City hall attempted to stop and reverse this decline with the announcement of industrial corridors across the city in the hope of preserving its manufacturing base. Even as jobs disappeared, Harold Washington remained tremendously popular in the African American community. Most expected him to run and win again in 1987, as the old Democratic organization remained in disarray and Vrdolyak continued to attack the mayor. Race again would be the key in both the primary and the mayoral election in 1987. Vrdolyak was expected to play a part; as one political insider said, "no way anyone could 'outwhite' Eddie." The election would prove to be one of the most bizarre in the city's long and colorful political history.[25]

On July 16, 1985, more than a year before the mayoral primary, Jane Byrne announced she would run again for the Democratic nomination. She immediately attacked both Washington and her old ally Ed Vrdolyak. Byrne had little support from organization regulars who had never warmed to her and had only a small war chest, but she always proved to be a favorite of the media who followed her antics with glee. Her campaign basically followed the plan to "declare and accuse." Once she entered the race Byrne pointed out that any other white candidate would be a spoiler who would assure Washington's reelection. The city braced for another racially charged political campaign. Insiders looked to see what Rich Daley and Vrdolyak would do. Rumors had Washington skipping the Democratic primary and running as an independent in the general election. Earlier Daley and his supporters had pushed the idea of a nonpartisan election but had failed to replace the primary system. Rich Daley decided to stay out of the upcoming fray.

Washington did not announce his candidacy until August 13, 1986, more than a year after Byrne's announcement. The mayor made his move at a huge fund-raiser, and the campaign began in earnest. The names of other white candidates began to be floated including both Jeremiah Joyce and Tom Hynes of the Southwest Side's Nineteenth Ward. Observers saw their possible candidacies as stalking horses for Daley. Vrdolyak also had no qualms about entering the contest. Byrne of course continued to make it clear that any white candidate beside herself would ensure a Washington victory. In the end, both Hynes and Vrdolyak decided to avoid the Democratic primary and joined other parties to run against the primary winner in the mayoral election, leaving Byrne and Washington as the only primary opponents. Hynes headed up the Chicago First Party, and Vrdolyak the all but dead Solidarity Party. Vrdolyak was an odd figure: the head of the Cook County Democratic Party running against the choice of his own party as an independent. "Beirut on the Lake" seemed beyond ridiculous in the eyes of the nation.

On the Republican side, Bernie Epton announced his candidacy to once again take on any and all Democrats, but he soon withdrew as he obviously had little support for another run. Don Haider, a Northwestern University business professor and a former advisor to Jane Byrne, emerged as the favorite candidate as once again Republicans with a statewide reputation avoided Chicago. Haider, a decent man with sound ideas, never rallied voters beyond a small core of Republican stalwarts in the primary. The white ethnic community focused on Byrne, Vrdolyak, and Hynes.

A bizarre and racially charged campaign followed in which Byrne attempted to play the racial liberal portraying Washington as a single-race candidate. Most knew that the vast majority of voters would again mark their ballots along racial lines. Washington's African American support seemed solid. Byrne could count on the white vote, if not the support of many of their political leaders. The election again revolved around the lakefront liberal wards and the Hispanic districts of the city. Those six lakefront and four Latino wards would be crucial if Byrne hoped to defeat Washington in the primary. Washington's campaign almost gave Byrne the opening she wanted when Judge R. Eugene Pincham addressed a rally at Operation Push Headquarters on the South Side and stated that any man south of Madison Street who votes against Washington "ought to be hung." Pincham's remarks created a firestorm, and Byrne hoped it would sway lakefront voters toward supporting her over purported "reverse racists." She claimed that the Washington campaign was bigoted and that only she could represent all of Chicago. Byrne overplayed her hand, however, and the backlash against Washington along the lakefront did not occur.

On February 24, 1987, Chicagoans went to the polls and voted almost exclusively along racial lines. Washington captured twenty-six out of fifty wards with incredible numbers in the black wards. Still he enjoyed only a marginal improvement in the white ethnic districts. Chicago remained racially divided. Washington gained 54 percent of the total vote with a 78,158 vote spread between himself and Jane Byrne. Over 1 million Chicagoans had gone to the polls. Unlike in 1983, Byrne seemed gracious in defeat and endorsed Harold Washington in the mayoral election. Hynes and Vrdolyak quickly stated that Washington could be beat, but the 1987 mayoral election saw Harold Washington as the obvious favorite. Hynes and Vrdolyak tried to maneuver each other out of the race. Bill Daley, the late mayor's youngest son, said, in an obvious reference to Hynes and Vrdolyak, "It's the dismantling of the so-called Democratic Party and a replacement of it by solo operators." The machine had died and given its ghost up to a leadership in total disarray. Hynes and Vrdolyak seemed on the verge of destroying the party. Both refused to accept the results of their own party's primary. For Vrdolyak, this seemed especially strange as he continued as Democratic Party chairman. Most observers totally dismissed the Republican, Haider.

As a last minute attempt to get him out of the election Hynes accused Vrdolyak of being connected to the mob. The accusation did not stick, and Hynes decided to withdraw from the race on the Sunday before Election Day.

Most of Hynes's supporters gathered behind Vrdolyak, but the Washington movement would not be denied, and on April 7, 1987, Washington won his second term as mayor by 131,797 votes over Vrdolyak and Haider. The mayor made significant gains in the Latino wards that offset some of his losses to Haider along the lake. Washington-supported candidates also did well in the city council runoff elections, solidifying the mayor's hold on the legislative body. Harold Washington now seemed to have it all.[26]

Washington knew that he had done well only because of his African American support and his tenuous hold on the lakefront and Hispanic wards. He hoped to reach out to the Northwest and Southwest Sides of the city and incorporate the white ethnic vote into his coalition. Despite Byrne's endorsement, some 85 percent of her supporters in the primary voted for Vrdolyak in the general election. On November 18, 1987, Washington reached out to those communities and slated both Aurelia Pucinski, the daughter of one of his most strident opponents, and Rich Daley for countywide offices. The mayor stated that this slate "tells people we have gone too far with this acrimony, this negativism, this inability to get along." Further he told his core black supporters, "If you don't support this ticket, then you are no friend of mine." The statement made a simple point: his organization must back both Pucinski and Daley for election.[27]

A week later, on the day before Thanksgiving, Harold Washington died in his office at the age of sixty-five. The promise of the November 18 slating disappeared as political chaos again threatened the city. While Alderman David Orr filled in as interim mayor, various claimants to the mayor's office appeared, with Alderman Timothy Evans, the mayor's city council floor leader, and Alderman Eugene Sawyer, who served as council president pro tempore, at the head. Meanwhile, three white aldermen, including Ed Burke, also emerged as candidates to serve out Washington's term via a city council election. Vrdolyak had already left the Democratic Party and joined the Republicans. Again the lakefront and Hispanic wards had the swing votes to decide who would replace Harold Washington, but with the recent unpredictability of Chicago politics observers felt anything was possible. Most feared a return to the racial infighting that had damaged the city's reputation.[28]

To the press, Tim Evans seemed the obvious successor, but they understood little about the true nature of the Washington organization. Many African American politicians felt liberated once Washington was out of the picture. He had held them on a close leash, and they did not want to go back to that relationship with Evans. One black alderman referred to Evans as "Harold's hitman." As it turned out Evans could only count on fifteen of the Washington aldermen to vote for him. The white candidates were as stymied as Evans. They could muster twenty-four votes, but the next two would be close to impossible to get. In the end, the white aldermen and the black machine aldermen settled on compromise candidate Eugene Sawyer.

More than 2,500 pro-Evans demonstrators jammed city hall the night of December 1 and morning of December 2. They threatened aldermen and called Eugene Sawyer names, screaming "Oreo" and "Uncle Tom Sawyer." The alderman was obviously shocked, and on several occasions said he would not accept the position. All five local television channels covered the story live as the city council struggled to find a new mayor. Finally at 4:01 a.m. on the morning of December 2, the council voted twenty-nine to nineteen to make Eugene Sawyer acting mayor. The Evans people promised revenge, especially on those African American aldermen who voted against Evans. But in reality the movement that had solidified around Harold Washington dissolved after his death.[29]

Eugene Sawyer proved to be a decent caretaker mayor but could not muster the support from the African American community that Washington enjoyed. Furthermore the Evans people went on to create a new political party, the Harold Washington Party, in a futile attempt to win the 1989 special election. As some predicted, Richard M. Daley emerged over the next two years as the leading white candidate and one who built support across the city.

The Second Daley

The election of Richard M. Daley seemed like a royal restoration to many Chicagoans who yearned for political stability after Bilandic, Byrne, and Washington. Harold Washington had not lived long enough to build upon his victory over the "Vrdolyak 29." The promise of his much heralded diversity ticket supporting Aurelia Pucinski and Rich Daley would not be fulfilled now that he had died. Eugene Sawyer did his best to keep the city moving along, despite economically difficult times.

On December 5, 1988, when Richard M. Daley announced his candidacy, the city braced for more conflict, but while Sawyer ran a hesitant campaign and Evans attempted to resurrect the Washington Movement, Daley triumphed by putting together a coalition of white ethnics, lakefront liberals, and Hispanics. The new Daley proved to be a masterful politician who had easily beat out Terry Ganier, his Republican opponent in the November 8 election for state's attorney. Later that November, the Illinois Supreme Court ordered a special election for mayor in 1989, frustrating Evans's attempt to put the election off so he could organize. In contrast to 1983, the black community stood divided between Sawyer and Evans supporters. Neither of the two African American candidates could force the other out of the race, and Daley became mayor in a mirror image of the 1983 Democratic primary.

Daley, however, also reached out to the African American community, and while the vast majority of voting blacks voted for one of the two African American candidates, the young Daley had attracted some votes in black Chicago. Publicly, Daley distanced himself from his father's old machine; after all, many in it had tried to block his chance at the mayor's office first by supporting

Bilandic and then Byrne. Daley instead reached out to groups that his father would not have considered politically viable, especially gays and lesbians, a group that might swing several North Side wards his way. Daley understood the growing importance of the Hispanic vote and realized its importance to the Washington coalition. Like his father, Daley always kept friendly relations with Chicago's Latinos. As for white ethnics, where else could they turn? One of Daley's goals for future elections was to enlarge his support in the African American community. If he could do that, then no one could beat him. He did not have his father's old organization, but the remnants of it would soon reach out to him. Daley could have it all.

Young, energetic, and smart, Daley was not publicly referred to as the new Boss. Instead Daley portrayed himself as a good manager, someone who would get the city moving in a positive direction. He tried very hard to put on a new image that would insure his support along the lakefront. There would always be adversaries, but if he could get things done and control the rambunctious city council, Chicagoans of every color and sexual orientation would be grateful. The city, tired of being "Beirut on the Lake," wanted political peace. The protests and threats of violence outside City Hall the night that city council selected Eugene Sawyer as mayor stood out in stark contrast to Chicagoan's nostalgic memories of the elder Daley's Chicago. The period ushered in by the Kennedy assassination had ended, and the city yearned for calm.

Richard M. Daley became mayor in April 1989, after defeating Eugene Sawyer in the Democratic Primary and then both Evans and Vrdolyak in the mayoral election by a substantial margin.[30] In many ways, like his father, Daley would benefit from incredible political luck. Some of the programs initiated by Bilandic, Byrne, Washington, and Sawyer began to bear fruit. Slowly, the Loop came back to life—most importantly, so did the national economy and especially the economy of the Midwest. This upturn hardly would be the new mayor's accomplishment, but he certainly benefited from the turnaround. Daley quickly realized that the city again would shed its skin and take on a new identity. Above all else, Daley knew the importance of seizing opportunity as it unfolded. Before the end of his first term, the Democrats stood on the verge of retaking the White House for the first time in twelve years. In addition, they would control Congress. All of this portended well for big city Democrats. Daley's younger brother Bill became involved with the Clinton organization, and while Rich Daley could not be called a "kingmaker" in the 1992 election, he and his brother played an important role in Bill Clinton's victory in Illinois. Again Chicago's fortunes were connected to events across the country and the world. Chicagoans had a positive take on the future, but were the good old days of Daley's father really back?

Not really. Richard M. Daley would be the first to admit that Chicago faced difficult challenges. He moved to consolidate his power, took advantage of political opportunities, and captured the city council. As early as 1990, Daley

Figure 129. Richard M. Daley and his family at his 1989 inauguration. Eleanor "Sis" Daley, the family's matriarch, stands proudly next to her oldest son. Governor James R. Thompson, standing behind the podium, and other local officials look on. (ICHi-59596, Chicago History Museum.)

appointed three aldermen to fill vacancies. In 1991, the city council saw the biggest turnover in decades when twenty-one new aldermen took seats. Many of these had won with Daley's support. Appointments to fill vacant aldermanic positions directly by Daley continued, and the mayor enjoyed the support of the majority of the council. A good politician, he appointed only those who would be personally loyal to him.[31]

Like his father, Richard M. Daley had definite likes and dislikes when it came to the physical city. Unlike his father, Rich Daley would become a world traveler taking the good news of Chicago to many different parts of the globe, always looking for investors in the city's future. Foreign investment became a crucial factor in the growth of Chicago as it looked toward the twenty-first century. By 1990, Chicago, long America's Second City, had slipped to third in population behind both New York and Los Angeles, but it remained a critical factor in the American economy. The new Daley administration realized that the future depended on making Chicago a more attractive location for corporations that were not tied to large physical plants in the new footloose information-based economy. The city would have to shed its "Big Shoulders" image and become a hip place for modern corporations to locate.

Daley, influenced by his wife Maggie, appreciated that the city's physical look needed a makeover. The State Street Mall stood as a shabby reminder of a failed urban modernism, as did the vast public housing high-rises that marked the second ghetto. The streets and boulevards looked worn out not only in the Loop but across the city. Chicago's minority groups needed job training and employment. U.S. Secretary of Education William Bennett called the school system the worst in the nation. This all would have to change if Chicago was to be a truly global city in the new emerging economy. It would have to hold on to its corporate and industrial base as well as it could and expand that base by attracting other companies. To put it simply, Chicago needed a facelift.

The year 1996 proved to be crucial for the city. After years of debate, the State Street Mall was remade, and the city allowed traffic to once again move down the fabled road. The project cost $30 million, as planners not only returned cars and taxis to the street, but also various other improvements including narrower sidewalks that brought pedestrians in closer contact with both Chicago's architectural gems and store windows, making it a livelier pedestrian street than it had been as a mall. Attractive 1920s-style light fixtures and handsome subway entrances proved that beauty and utility were not incompatible. Raised granite planters sprung to life with ornamental flowers. The "de-malling" of State Street brought life back to a street that quickly changed as old warehouse buildings to the west became home to a new generation of urban loft-condominium dwellers. Colleges and universities turned the South Loop into the biggest college town in Illinois with more than fifty thousand students entering or living in dormitories in the Loop during the academic year. Another major change also took place in 1996, as city planners moved South Lake Shore Drive west to create a museum campus along the lakefront. Motorists accustomed to the stark highways of the 1970s now drove past sculpted geometric designs and flower gardens.[32]

Daley's critics have made much fun of the street planters that began to appear on downtown streets and then out in the neighborhoods, but despite this early criticism Chicagoans and visitors alike began to appreciate them. They reflected a new energy and a new outlook. Daley's father had been responsible for massive building projects such as the University of Illinois at Chicago campus and O'Hare Airport, but at least initially the younger Daley focused on minor details. Street furniture, signage, lighting, all became important. Suddenly, at least in the Loop and on North Michigan Avenue, the shabbiness began to disappear. While the elder Daley appreciated sleek modern high-rises, the younger Daley wanted cast-iron fences, flowers, and even ethnic signage on neighborhood streets. His administration promoted neighborhood identification with street markers that proclaimed local names such as Andersonville,

Figure 130. The Richard M. Daley administration planted thousand of flowers and shrubs along Loop streets and in Grant Park in an attempt to beautify the city. (Photograph by David H. Krause.)

Greek Town, Lincoln Square, and North Halsted. Landmark preservation also mattered to Daley's approach although here the results were more mixed. Safeguarding landmarks was fine, but not if it got in the way of growth. The city's large preservationist community clashed often with the administration. The architecturally postmodern mayor agreed with his father the modernist mayor that development was good and downtown development essential for the life of Chicago.[33]

Unlike Harold Washington, who looked to direct development to the neighborhoods that elected him, Daley, like his father, saw the Loop as the city's front door. In the global economy he knew how important an impressive front door could be and knew Chicago's had to shine. The Daley administration reasoned that development would flow in waves out from its central core. In that manner Richard M. Daley was a traditionalist among big city mayors.[34]

The results were pretty clear, and Chicago became a more attractive place for corporate investment. In 1999, on the eve of the twenty-first century, Daley celebrated his first decade in power. Chicago seemed to have taken on a new vitality. Adele Simmons, the head of the prestigious MacArthur Foundation,

Figure 131. Daley's plans for beautification touched local communities. Here street markers on North Halsted celebrate Chicago's gay and lesbian community. (Photograph by David H. Krause.)

wrote that Chicago had been transformed, lauding the changes of Rich Daley's years as mayor. These included reform of the Chicago Housing Authority, and the Chicago Public Schools, and the Chicago Park District, but the physical beauty of the city seemed to be the most impressive.[35]

Shifts in the Economy and Immigration

Foreign corporations invested heavily in Chicago and Illinois, and the state became the number 1 destination for foreign-directed investment in the Midwest. Since the early 1990s the value of exports from the Chicago region has steadily increased and has had a positive effect on both employment and local economic development. During the period 1993–99, Chicago stood in sixth place in the nation with export sales with over $21 billion in 1999 alone. A new downtown, now home to many who made their money in the new economy, became a prime goal of the Daley administration.[36] Many corporations also found Chicago attractive. In March 2001, Boeing Corporation announced that it would move its headquarters to the city from its longtime Seattle home, reversing a bit the national economic shift to the West Coast. Some $56 billion in public subsidies brought only about 450 jobs to the Chicago area, but more importantly it reemphasized the city's attractiveness to corporations—this despite the fact that the city had lost a huge share of its corporate base over the previous two decades. This move, coupled with the fact that several months earlier the Brach's Candy Company had announced its closing by the end of 2003, seemed to underline the transformation of the city from a manufacturing town to one involved in a corporate global future. The loss of Brach's meant the loss of one thousand jobs, just one more milestone on the city's long road toward deindustrialization that began with the postwar shuttering of Chicago's packinghouses. Still, even with the closing of Brach's and the disappearance of the stockyards, Chicago remained an important manufacturer and the capital of candy making and food processing in the United States. Critics complained of the huge subsidy to Boeing, while working-class Chicagoans continued to fear the future. Indeed, they had much to fear, not only from plant closings but also from stagnant and often declining wages. Between 1979 and 2000, real manufacturing wages fell 17 percent in Illinois as compared to a 10 percent decline nationally. This downturn resulted from various factors, including the decline in the power of labor unions, but the fact remained a reality for working Chicago. Growing economic insecurity and inequality proved to be a national problem.[37]

Of course Chicago's geographic location and its dominance of the nation's transportation system also helped it to maintain its economic base. In 2006, Chicago ranked as the nation's tenth largest international freight gateway. Among the top twenty-five freight gateways, which together accounted for 65 percent of U.S. international trade, Chicago is the only one not situated along an international border or waterway. The larger Chicago region plays a dynamic role in both national and international trade. The greater Chicagoland area, including Northwest Indiana, contains over 3,200 miles of national highways, 2,000 miles of active Class I railway lines, 142 intermodal facilities, 163 cargo ports, and four major airports. Chicago's importance as an air transportation center is almost unrivaled. It ranks third among all American airports in value of international air freight and fifth in volume. As the twenty-first century began, Chicago led the nation in intermodal terminal capacity. Goods could be packed in containers and shipped anywhere in the world via boat, train, and truck. In fact it was listed as the third largest intermodal container port in the world. Chicago's hold on the nation's freight lines remained central for the city's recovery from a quickly deindustrializing economy to one that had become an active partner in the new global economy.

Despite this success, Chicago area transportation faces some very serious problems. Like much of the country's transportation infrastructure, Chicago's suffers from neglect; its airports need to be expanded despite opposition from local communities, the intermodal system has little space to grow, and many of the rail and barge freight yards were built over one hundred years ago and

Figure 132. A shipping container is being lifted onto a trailer in the massive Yards Container Pool facility. These operations occupy the site of the old Hammond Packing Company just north of Forty-seventh Street. (Photograph by D. Pacyga.)

are in need of upgrades. The only answer is for Chicago to continue its outward expansion as it enters this new era of growth. In 2002, the Burlington Northern Santa Fe Railroad (BNSF) opened a state-of-the-art intermodal facility south of the city in Will County that covers some six hundred acres. In response, ProLogis acquired 184 acres in Wilmington for a new distribution park to serve the BNSF facility. The ProLogis Park Arsenal stands on the site of the former federal Joliet Arsenal that closed in the 1990s. The Union Pacific Railroad opened its Global III Intermodal Facility in 2003, an even larger facility in Ogle County eighty miles west of Chicago.[38]

The problem of space remains an issue for maintaining Chicago's preeminence as a manufacturing center. Even with the success of the industrial corridors program initiated by Mayor Harold Washington and supported by Richard M. Daley, plants find it difficult to expand in the city. Despite attempts to curtail the market-led drive to turn old industrial neighborhoods into residential-only areas, many manufacturing concerns still feel the pressure to move. In 2006 on the South Side just beyond the boundaries of the old Union Stock Yards, the Chiappetti Lamb and Veal Company felt pressure to move from its sixty-year home. Located in an area once filled with the sounds and smells of meatpacking, new housing is being developed in the district between the gentrifying Bridgeport and Canaryville neighborhoods. Empty lots are a hot commodity, as developers realize their potential: some north of Pershing Road selling for over $300,000. The meatpacker, Chicago's last veal and lamb slaughterhouse, employs 125 mostly Hispanic employees in its two plants. The

Figure 133. Chiappetti Lamb and Veal Company is one of Chicago's last slaughterhouses. It is quickly being encroached upon by residential development along West Pershing Road. (Photograph by D. Pacyga.)

city says it will do what it can to keep Chiappetti in Chicago, as the packer's owners have expressed a desire to move into the old stockyards that are now one of the city's most successful planned manufacturing districts, or PMDs. In 2007, the city contained fourteen PMDs covering over ten thousand acres.

On the North Side, A. Finkl and Sons Company, a steelmaker located in the Clybourn Industrial District since 1902 and a Chicago manufacturer for 127 years, announced that it had been acquired by a German company and would move from its longtime base in the city's Clybourn PMD. Finkl's new owners hope to stay in Chicago and move to the Southeast Side, site of the city's now nearly defunct steel district, and are asking for a government subsidy to stay in Chicago. The question of what will become of Finkl's old site remains; the steel manufacturer wants to sell it for residential development, while the city hopes to attract industry to the site. Central to the PMD concept is that manufacturers cannot turn their old sites into residential projects, the future of the PMD program still remains to be seen.[39]

Chicago's manufacturing base has kept eroding. While not as harsh as during the period from 1970 to 1992, industrial jobs continue to decline. In the earlier period, many of the city's top manufacturers closed their plants, including U.S. Steel Corporation, Beatrice Foods, Campbell Soup, and General Mills. Manufacturing capital fled the region. Chicago's manufacturing base has been slow to recover, but its diversity has proven to be a saving grace. After 1985, the region settled into a slow but steady decline with an average manufacturing job loss of 1.6 percent; however, between 2000 and 2003, 103,000 industrial jobs disappeared from the Chicago area, or about 18 percent of total industrial employment. Not surprisingly, these shifts in job opportunities hurt minority communities the most.[40]

Still the City of Immigrants

As the twenty-first century dawned, Chicago remained an immigration magnet. Despite the loss of manufacturing jobs and uneven growth in its various economic sectors, people from all over the world continued to flock to the city. While Europeans dominated the pre-1950 immigration, both Hispanics and Asians would come to dominate the post-1965 immigrant numbers. Also, a significant number of African and Caribbean immigrants made their way to the city adding to the intense ethnic diversity of the area.[41]

Polish immigrants presented a significant exception to these demographic trends. Poles had long been a presence in Chicago and its suburbs, but after the influx of displaced persons after World War II their migration numbers went down. With the Solidarity labor movement in Poland and both the political and economic turmoil caused by the end of the Soviet system in East Europe, immigrant numbers again began to grow. Many of these newer Polish immigrants were better educated and had held managerial and professional positions in Poland. Also, many decided to settle in nonethnic suburbs as opposed to the older Polish American neighborhoods in Chicago proper.[42] Chicago's Polish settlement had maintained its long connection with the homeland, and for many Poles, Chicago was seen as a friendly, even a "Polish" city.

In 2000, 133,797 Polish immigrants lived in metropolitan Chicago, joining an estimated nine hundred thousand Polish Americans. Besides those Poles

Figure 134. The Claretian Fathers organized Our Lady of Guadalupe Catholic Church in South Chicago as the first Mexican parish in the city in the 1920s. The St. Jude Shrine located in the church draws a wide following including the annual meeting of the St. Jude Police League. (Postcard, Author's Collection.)

entering the country legally as refugees or with the requisite permission there were large numbers of "vacationers" from Poland who often disappeared into the Polish American underground economy for various periods of time. From 1986 to 1996, Poles provided the largest total number of legal immigrants to Chicago proper. During the 1990s, two out of every five Polish immigrants to the U.S. settled in the Chicago area. Only Mexican immigrants outnumbered them in the metropolitan region.[43]

Mexicans also had a long history in Chicago. As early as 1884, the Mexican government established a consulate in Chicago to deal with the needs of the growing Mexican immigrant population. By 1920, Chicago held the twelfth largest concentration of Mexicans in the United States—1,224 according to the census. Newcomers came from all over Mexico, but those from Guanajuato, Jalisco, Michoacán, and Zacatecas predominated. Many had come to work on the railroads or in the steel mills and packinghouses. By 1930, the census counted 19,516 Mexican immigrants in Chicago, many on the West Side near Roosevelt Road and Halsted, with others in South Chicago and Back of the Yards. But during the decade-long Great Depression, Mexicans faced the so-called repatriation movement. Unlike other immigrant groups Mexicans were sent home to Mexico in large numbers, reducing by as much as 75 percent Chicago's Mexican population. Only about seven thousand Mexican immigrants remained in Chicago in 1940. Then the need for war workers resulted in the International Bracero Labor Agreements (1942) between the United States and Mexico. Over the next two years, 15,000 Mexicans came to Chicago. By 1950 roughly 24,000 Mexican immigrants called Chicago home. After the 1965 immigration reforms, Mexican numbers began to increase. In the period 1986 to 1996, Mexico sent some 54,000 immigrants to the Chicago area. By 2004, Mexicans accounted for 1,271,710 residents of the Chicago metropolitan area with more Mexicans living in the suburbs (725,561) than in the city (546,149). More than 40 percent of all foreign-born people in the Chicago area came from Mexico, ranking them far ahead of the second-place Poles. In 2004, Chicago ranked second only to Los Angeles in the number of Mexican-born residents.[44]

Besides Mexicans and Poles, Chicago continued to attract immigrants from other parts of eastern Europe and Latin America. Large numbers of Puerto

Figure 135. Twenty-sixth Street is the heart of Chicago's Mexican American Little Village neighborhood, formerly known as Czech California. The gate pictured here stands near the old site of Pilsen Park. This strip is the busiest shopping strip in the city next to North Michigan Avenue. (Photograph by D. Pacyga.)

Ricans, Cubans, Guatemalans, Salvadorans, Colombians, and others came to Chicago's neighborhoods. Many of these left their homeland because of political strife, others for the usual economic reasons. One barometer of the growth of the Latino population is the increased activity of Hispanic politicians in the local Democratic organization. By the early years of the twenty-first century, some twenty-five Latino politicians had been elected in Cook County, and the Hispanic Democratic Organization was a force in the Daley organization.[45]

The Asian population of the city also began to take off as the century turned. Over the last thirty years, Asians have become the fastest growing immigrant group in the United States after Latinos. Historically Chinese, Japanese, and Filipinos dominated the Asian migration to Chicago. Since 1970, they have been joined by large numbers of Asian Indians, Koreans, and Vietnamese; these six groups make-up about 90 percent of all Asian immigrants to Chicago. Pakistanis have also grown in numbers since the 1990s.

In 2000, Indians made up the largest Asian group in the Chicago area, with 121,753 foreign born. Filipinos ranked second in numbers (96,632) with the

Figure 136. Vietnamese immigrants Zung and Kim Dao arrive at Chicago's O'Hare Airport in 1980. Like many others who left South Vietnam the Dao family had moved around the country before settling on Chicago's North Side. Zung Dao (center, with child) was a veteran of the South Vietnamese Army's Special Forces and escaped from Saigon the day that city fell to the Communists in 1975. (Courtesy of Zung and Kim Dao.)

Chinese in third place (75,305) and Koreans (48,467) in fourth place. The Japanese (23,267) and Vietnamese (17,326) numbers, while growing, remained far behind. While traditional Asian enclaves still exist in the city and some suburbs, the Asian population is spread throughout much of the metropolitan area. DuPage County may be the fastest growing Asian Indian community in the United States.[46]

A City Transformed? Race and Class in the Global City

During the last twenty years, even the casual observer has seen Chicago go through tremendous changes. Perhaps nowhere is this more evident than in the neighborhoods that circle the Loop. The very skyline of these communities and their residential makeup has been altered. In the 1950s and 1960s, the city moved to "protect" the Loop with various urban renewal projects such as Prairie Shores and Lake Meadows as well as the Illinois Institute of Technology campus and the Hyde Park/Kenwood conservation plan on the South Side; Sandburg Village and the Lincoln Park conservation plan to the north; and the campus of the University of Illinois at Chicago on the Near West Side. These various projects surrounded the downtown and provided a sort of middle-class barrier against the slum. Ideas circulating around the original 1957 Central Area Plan continued to develop and change over time, as city planners hoped to attract middle- and high-income residents back to the central city and shore up both the Loop and the city's tax base. At the same time, public housing transformed the skyline of much of Chicago's poor and mostly minority communities. The opening of Cabrini-Green just northwest of the Loop and of Stateway Gardens and then the Robert Taylor Homes on the South Side seemed to be a permanent fixture of the city's geography and skyline.

For various structural, architectural, and economic reasons, along with the racist attitudes that placed public housing only in certain neighborhoods, the Chicago Housing Authority's projects, especially those built after 1950, failed dismally. During the last year of the Harold Washington administration, the mayor appointed Vince Lane as the head of the CHA in an attempt to give the program new leadership and ideas. Lane's vision included a transformation of public housing into economically mixed neighborhoods, his Mixed Income New Communities Strategy (MINCS). Lane hoped to reincorporate the projects and their residents into the fabric of the city. The CHA petitioned for and received approval from Congress to lease up to half the units in selected housing projects to moderate income residents in the hope of solving some of the CHA's most pressing problems. As Lane began his tenure, the CHA had begun the renovation of the Victor Olander Homes in the South Side's Oakland neighborhood. These six sixteen-story high-rises faced Lake Michigan and provided an opportunity to try out the new MINCS idea.

The buildings had been vacated in 1985, and the CHA promised that tenants could eventually return. The CHA decided to focus on two of the structures, and Lane petitioned the Department of Housing and Urban Development to grant waivers to its modest design standards and let CHA renovation include features not normally allowed in public housing. Lane dubbed the project Lake Parc Place, and the CHA completed remodeling of the two buildings in 1991. By the end of 1992, the agency filled all of the renovated apartments, half of which moderate-income families occupied. Most of the former Olander Homes residents did not return to Lake Parc Place. Lane proved that moderate-income families could be attracted to Chicago's public housing, something that New York officials knew as a result of a very different history concerning the building of federal projects. Lake Parc Place convinced Chicago officials that they should pursue income mixing on a much larger scale.

In 1992, Congress passed the Housing Opportunities for People Everywhere Act, commonly known as HOPE VI. While it initially seemed to be a traditional federal housing initiative, it changed within a few years from simply a housing plan to a complete reform of public housing. It would be the most highly funded program in over two decades. HOPE VI would also reflect some fundamental changes in federal policy. The 1990s trend of governmental privatization shaped programs associated with HOPE VI, as government policies hoped to reduce budgets and refocus funds to subsidize market-based policies. By 1996, as the Clinton administration attempted to outmaneuver a right-wing dominated Congress, Chicago's program as it played out at Lake Parc Place, became a national model and with it the fate of the CHA was sealed.

Despite the general attitude that mixed-income public housing was bound to fail, Chicago's public housing officials realized that many public housing projects lay near gentrifying neighborhoods or near those that would soon be prime targets for gentrification. CHA planners understood the urban landscape well, and plans had already begun to transform the outlying areas of what was a newly expanding Loop. While Vince Lane was forced out of the CHA as the federal government temporarily took over the agency, when the Daley administration took full responsibility for public housing the mixed income idea began to fully flourish and quickly expand. After 1995, when Congress eliminated the requirement that new developments provide a one-to-one replacement for demolished public housing units, the wrecking balls were set to go. Most Chicagoans had little love for the CHA high-rises and saw them as a blight on the urban landscape, so there would be little opposition or demolition. Occupants, however, feared the destruction of their homes and their placement in other neighborhoods. Many of these CHA tenants protested the program, but they lost. By 1999, the CHA received nearly $160 million in six HOPE VI grants, and the program moved from renovation toward destruction, as the CHA demolished over twelve thousand units.

Chicago witnessed the massive displacement of CHA residents, as significant delays in revitalization and new construction occurred. The Section 8 Program, which provided rent vouchers for former public housing residents, was mismanaged, and former residents have found it difficult even to be placed on the waiting list for either housing or vouchers. Given the long history of bureaucratic inefficiency and overt racism, former residents did not trust the CHA. Some neighborhoods, such as South Shore and Englewood, felt that they were being overwhelmed with Section 8 "refugees." Residents attributed an increase in gang crimes and violence in Chicago neighborhoods to an influx of gang members from the demolished Taylor Homes. Some residents fought the CHA, but with little success. Former Seventh Ward Alderman William Beavers said he would try to "condo" as many buildings as possible in order to stop the movement of gangs into his ward. The south suburbs also experienced the impact of the dispersal program, as many former CHA residents looked for communities where they would feel comfortable.[47]

As Chicago's inner-city began to change and see increased investment, social class took to the forefront of issues that confronted older poorer residents.

Figure 137. A restored Holy Family Church and its neighbor St. Ignatius College Preparatory School stand above the gentrifying Near West Side as they stood over a poor immigrant neighborhood during the fire of 1871 and over an even poorer minority and public hosing community in the last half of the twentieth century. (Photograph by D. Pacyga.)

Nowhere has this been more true than in the Oakland/North Kenwood Community Area, home to Lake Parc Place. This community, originally a wealthy suburb, and then a neighborhood after the 1889 annexation of Hyde Park, was settled by some of Chicago's best families. It lost much of its prestige early in the twentieth century and became a lower-middle-class and working-class district. After World War II, racial change occurred rapidly, and the Hyde Park–Kenwood Conservation plan drew its northern border at East Forty-seventh Street. Old time residents referred to Forty-seventh Street as "the dividing line," "the invisible line," and "the Mason-Dixon Line." South of Forty-seventh Street, the neighborhoods increasingly dominated by the University of Chicago flourished, while north of the street they fell deeper and deeper into poverty. In 1990, Oakland bore the dubious distinction of being the poorest community area in Chicago, just as Lake Parc Place underwent transformation.[48]

Once Lake Parc Place attracted attention to Oakland/North Kenwood, investors became interested in its old housing stock and even its empty city lots. By the mid-1990s more and more newcomers appeared on the sidewalks north of East Forty-seventh Street. Most, but not all, of these strangers were African Americans with money. The story of gentrification in Oakland/North Kenwood became an intraracial one. Unlike on the North Side, where the impact of HOPE VI on Cabrini-Green would see a largely white group of urbanites moving into replacement housing, Oakland/North Kenwood remained a largely African American community. Longtime black residents felt that they would be pushed out by the new residents willing to pay higher prices for housing in the area. The growth of the African American middle and upper classes has accelerated; between 1990 and 2000, the proportion of black households with an annual income of over $50,000 doubled from 14 percent to 28 percent, and those earning over $100,000 rose even more dramatically from 1 percent to 6 percent. As one longtime resident remarked, "It's getting more expensive to live around here. So a lot of people tend to move away. Because it's our neighborhood but they're remodeling so much and doing some condos and our local income can't afford it." The pressure of class and gentrification had hit home north of Forty-seventh Street. Some felt that racial change would come on the heels of the class shift in Oakland/North Kenwood. Certainly more whites moved to the area, and the University of Chicago encouraged faculty and staff to buy in the area as they had south of East Forty-seventh Street. While the racial future of the community remained in question, the class basis of the transformation was without doubt.[49]

Whether gentrification takes place within or outside of the boundaries of race, there are various social problems that develop. Pilsen, a largely Mexican American community of the Lower West Side, is currently also going through gentrification. White artists have long occupied studios to the east of Halsted Street south of Sixteenth Street. Now developers are building condominiums and townhouses in the area. The struggle for affordable housing goes on, despite the expansion of University Village just to the north and the expanded presence of the University of Illinois at Chicago, which resulted in the relocation of the old Maxwell Street Market. The same can be seen in the old white working-class enclave of Bridgeport just to the south of Pilsen, where new townhouses and even mini-mansions are being erected. Here the real estate market energized by gentrifiers is putting pressure on industries such as Chiappetti Lamb and Veal Packing. McKinley Park, to the west of Bridgeport, is already being touted as yet another gentrifying district. Meanwhile, poorer Mexicans and blacks are being pushed to outlying neighborhoods, which continue to be abandoned by whites moving to the suburbs or into lofts in neighborhoods their parents and grandparents abandoned years ago. At times it seems as if everyone in Chicago is on the move, including the city's newest immigrant groups.[50]

The impact of HOPE VI on public housing in Chicago has been tremendous. Stateway Gardens, which opened in 1958, and the Taylor Homes, which opened four years later, no longer stand along the Dan Ryan Expressway. The

Figure 138. In 2007, Stateway Gardens was being replaced by the condominiums, townhouses, and single-family homes of Park Boulevard. The high-rise is part of the Illinois Institute of Technology campus just north of Thirty-fifth and State Streets. (Photograph by D. Pacyga.)

last of Stateway's high-rises came down in 2007. A new neighborhood designed to reweave itself into the urban fabric is rising down South State Street. At this point it seems that this South Side community area, known as Douglas, will go the way of Oakland/North Kenwood. In 1980, Chicago contained ten of the nation's sixteen poorest neighborhoods, including these CHA sites. In mid-1999, the federal government returned the CHA to local control. Mayor Daley took personal responsibility for public housing and soon won Washington's approval for the Plan of Transformation, which envisioned a very different CHA. The city estimated that some six thousand families would be displaced during this program.[51]

As Chicago entered the twenty-first century, it witnessed yet another transformation of its place in the American and world economy. Nearly one hundred years had passed since Daniel Burnham presented his 1909 Plan for the new Chicago that could be built out of the Industrial Revolution. The 1893 Columbian Exposition placed Burnham on the road of urban planner and originator of one of the most important movements in the planning of cities, the City Beautiful Movement. There is some doubt that Burnham ever spoke or wrote the words often attributed to him: "Make no small plans. They have no magic to stir humanity's blood and probably themselves will not be realized."

Figure 139. The Jane Addams Homes were built as one of the first public housing developments in the city. They were also one of the last to be demolished in 2007. The Driehaus Foundation is leading a project to save one of the Addams Homes as a public housing museum. (Photograph by D. Pacyga.)

But he certainly believed in large and extensive plans. The first Mayor Daley did too, and now his son Richard M. Daley places his mark on the city.

During his first year as mayor Richard M. Daley's administration hoped to solve the airport problem with the construction of a new facility on the Southeast Side, but that was soon defeated in part because of tremendous opposition by the residents of Hegewisch, a neighborhood that would have been plowed under. The proposed airport would have displaced 8,500 homes and forty-seven local businesses employing nine thousand workers, all in Ed Vrdolyak's Tenth Ward. Daley also called for the closing of Gary's airport. The city of Chicago said the proposed airport would create two hundred thousand permanent jobs, but Hegewisch residents did not trust it or the city's plans for their future.[52] In turn, Daley used funds originally established to build the Southeast Side facility to make Midway Airport a modern facility and to expand O'Hare Airport. The O'Hare expansion goes forward despite suburban opposition. In 2008, in an effort to raise revenue the city moved to privatize Midway Airport, Daley had plans also for Meigs Field on Northerly Island, which served an elite cliental of private and corporate pilots. After years of arguing with Springfield over the small airport's future, Daley struck in the dark of early morning on March 30, 2003. City crews closed the airfield, marking huge X's across the runways to

Figure 140. Crown Fountain at the southwest corner of Millennium Park has proven to be a major attraction for Chicagoans and visitors alike. Despite the incredible cost Millennium Park has had a very positive impact on the city and its reputation. (Photograph by David H. Krause.)

Figure 141. A new lakefront residential high-rise frames the General Logan statue in Grant Park. The statue and its mound received national attention during the Democratic National Convention in 1968 when protestors raised a Vietcong flag on it. Today the South Loop is the hottest neighborhood in Chicago. At least seven cranes can be seen from Logan's mound as residential development explodes as far south as Cermak Road. (Photograph by David H. Krause.)

prevent planes from landing or taking off. Daley wanted to turn the island into a ninety-one-acre park, as Burnham had originally planned.

This gesture fit well with Daley's interest in the environment. He likes his reputation as a "green" mayor, but it also redeemed a part of the original 1909 Burnham Plan and fit into a renewed City Beautiful Movement. The renovation of Soldier Field certainly has not followed City Beautiful guidelines, but some have called it a successful reuse of the old complex. In turn, the cost of construction of Millennium Park caused a good deal of criticism, but the park itself has proven to be a wonderful success and caused real estate values in its immediate North Loop area to soar. Also Block 37 is finally under construction after nearly twenty years of lying empty except as an ice rink and an occasional venue for local artists. Daley's plans have certainly been ambitious, and his administration has carried a good deal of them out.[53]

Like his father, Richard M. Daley has had a tremendous impact on Chicago. They both benefited from good national economies and activist Democratic administrations in Washington, D.C. Both have seen themselves as builders. But unfortunately, both have the cloud of scandal hanging over their later administrations. The Hired Truck Scandal and then the indictment and conviction of Richard Sorich, the mayor's former patronage chief, has cast a cloud over the son as the indictment and prosecution of various of his father's close advisors did over his father's administration. Investigations into torture by Chicago police during Daley's term as state's attorney also has proven to be an ongoing embarrassment. Where all the investigations will lead is anyone's guess.

Chicago stands at the beginning of the twenty-first century as it did in 1837 on the edge of a new frontier. It has entered the league of global cities. Chicagoans are struggling to capture new technologies and trying to take advantage of their long-standing position as a transportation network. No longer "hog butcher to the world," the city is still a "player with railroads." It stands in an envious place next to the largest fresh water lakes in the world and close to the Mississippi River. In a world where that may not seem as important as it did in the nineteenth century it is still the city's trump card. The snake that is Chicago, with its enormous intellectual and financial resources, is trying on a new skin in the new century.

Figure 142. Unveiled on November 16, 2006, "Agora" by Magdalena Abakanowicz stands at the southwest corner of Grant Park. The $3.5 million work is a gift from the artist and the Polish Ministry of Culture. The 106 figures were created at the Srem Foundry in Poland. (Photograph by David H. Krause.)

Figure 143. The renovation of Soldier Field proved to be most controversial. The new "bowl" was placed directly within the old structure by Holabird and Root's firm. This caused the revocation of national landmark status from the stadium. (Photograph by David H. Krause.)

Transforming Chicago and America

In the introduction, I explained my use of the biographical method for the history of a city. I have highlighted those people, places, events, and relationships that capture Chicago's spirit, but the city is a complex place, one of contradictions, of both continuity and change. In some aspects it has been a global city from its origins; in others it remains a small town where people are connected and know, if not each other, then a friend or a relative of most everyone they meet. From the very time that Marquette and Jolliet made their way up the South Branch of the Chicago River until today, Chicago has been intimately tied to the Atlantic and then the world economy. The first load of furs shipped east and then to Europe forged a connection that remains firm. Today, Chicago traders ship grain around the world and trade goods across international date lines.

In the beginning the arrival of the French heralded racial diversity. A kind of ethnic diversity already prevailed as Native Americans of various nations made their way to the Chicago River. Europeans soon flooded the area, bringing with them myriad languages and customs that first challenged and then replaced those of the Ojibwa, Miami, and Pottawatomie who knew the rivers and plains of northeastern Illinois well. Soon men and women from Africa, the Caribbean, Asia, and Latin America joined this ethnic and racial mélange as Chicago's true global roots set. Fittingly, Jean Baptiste Point de Sable, a fur trader of French and African descent, probably born in Haiti and married to a Pottawatomie woman, was the first person to settle more or less permanently on the shores of the Chicago River. This strange mixing bowl of cultures soon reflected the larger American ethnic experience. Neighborhood change appeared early in the city. The retreating Native Americans mourned the Chicago they had lost as they moved across the Mississippi River in 1837. Other Chicagoans have been following their retreat from the center city ever since, while grieving the loss of their Chicago. In turn they have been replaced by others attracted to the opportunities and excitement of living in the "Windy City."

Of all the constants in Chicago's history several stand out. First is of course ethnic diversity. At different times the city has been the largest Polish city out-

Figure 144. The Danza Azteka folk group performs a traditional Aztec ceremony in Harrison Park in the Pilsen neighborhood in August 2008. Chicago's rich ethnic traditions still mark the diversity of the city's culture as it enters the twenty-first century. (Photograph by D. Pacyga.)

side of Warsaw, the largest Czech city outside of Prague, the largest Swedish city outside of Stockholm, and on and on. By 1968, more African Americans called Chicago and Cook County home than Mississippi. Today, Mexicans and Asians are among the most populous of the region's ethnic groups, spilling across the city and suburbs. Another constant has been a diverse and dynamic economy. Chicago's wealth originally depended on its hinterland, whether for furs or later cattle and grain. Those who came here were quick to tap into the region's natural resources and created such institutions as the Board of Trade and the Union Stock Yards to do just that. At one point, Chicago's Potato Market, located near Ashland Avenue, was the largest in the world. Industry also made the city, heralded by the McCormick Reaper Works. Now in the twenty-first century, although diminished, the Chicago area is still the nation's largest industrial center, which was and remains possible because of the city's location. The river and the lake created Chicago. The railroads ensured its dominance of the West. Today the city's airports are overcrowded, and Chicago's railroads and trucks dominate the container business. Much of what made Chicago the fastest growing city of the nineteenth century remains intact. The legacy of the nineteenth and twentieth centuries gave Chicago its edge as it moves to the position of a major player in the twenty-first century's now truly global economy.

The third tradition that marks Chicago's history is politics. Here Chicago reigns supreme. In many ways politics is Chicago's favorite sport and the one the city is best at, even if it sometimes ignores or bends the rules. The Daley family has largely dominated the nation's view of Chicago over the last fifty years, but the city has a long tradition of political machinations. Businessmen dominated early politics, making up most of the mayors before the Great Fire in 1871. While, since 1931, government in Chicago has basically been a Democratic Party concern, politics actually comes in various flavors. The two most popular are machine politics and Progressive politics. These too have various shades and levels of acceptability to the larger public. Generally speaking, the Republicans also share a machine/Progressive tradition but have been most successful in the suburbs and "downstate," that great stretch of Illinois between the southern suburbs and St. Louis. Occasionally, as when Bernie Epton appeared as the "Great White Hope" in 1983, the GOP makes a splash in local politics, but generally in the city proper Democrats call the shots for both machine and Progressive politicians alike. This situation seems likely to continue well into the twenty-first century.

Nevertheless, Chicago's political culture is one with deep roots that transcend party affiliation and have grown in response to the economic development of the city. When nonprofessional politicians dominated the mayoralty, one early mayor was a blacksmith, another a candle maker; politics was "no big potatoes." As politics moved away from a sense of noblesse oblige and became seen as a way to make money for both politicians and their various sponsors, it entered a new era. The arrival of mass transit generally ushered in this new age as the city had to grant franchises to builders of mass transit, gas lines, and providers of telephone service. Especially just before and after the 1871 fire, professional politicians begin to enter the scene. Investors were quite willing to pay aldermen to vote to give them long-lasting and valuable franchises to serve the emerging industrial city. Others soon came to understand the "Chicago way" and paid to have the city support various moneymaking projects, adjusting zoning laws along the way. Still others were not above searching for political help to protect their illegal businesses in the bars, brothels, gambling parlors, and dope dens of the city's vice districts. Ethnic groups hoped to elect their own representatives in order to get a piece of the Chicago pie. Perhaps, as in so many other things, Chicagoans looked to New York City and its powerful Tammany Hall machine to learn how to deal with the new urban realities of the last half of the nineteenth century.

The names of Chicago's more famous politicians are legion, from Mike Mc-Donald, Hinky Dink Kenna, Bathhouse John Coughlin, and Big Bill Thompson to more recent mayors from Anton "Pushcart Tony" Cermak and the Daleys, both father and son. Many represented well Nelson Algren's view of the

Chicago spirit as one of a "City on the Make." The city's reformers are also numerous, starting with the elite women who opposed their husbands' views concerning the role of charity both before and after the Great Conflagration and including Jane Addams and the women and men of Hull-House. Such reformers, while often being tinged with a sort of middle-class elitism as compared to such colorful aldermen as Paddy Bauler—who upon the election of Richard J. Daley in 1955 proclaimed Chicago not ready for reform—have also won local and national office from the Progressive era to the present age. This struggle over politics and the role of government in Chicago has proven to be one of the enduring features of the city. It would be foolish to claim that the political fight today is the same as it was in Bauler's time or at the end of the nineteenth century, and yet certain issues persist, including patronage and various abuses of power. The present is not without both, although modern Chicago politicians are not as out in the open about these things as their precursors were. The political game is definitely a symbol of the city.

Yet another key to Chicago is that it remains a city with distinct and often fiercely competitive neighborhoods. While the Bureau of the Census and other governmental agencies, such as the post office, the police department, and the legislative map have their own idea about how Chicago is divided, it is the citizens that ultimately decide neighborhood boundaries. Such boundaries result from a mixture of influences, including race, ethnicity, and social class. It also includes factors such as age, sexual orientation, and cultural interests, as any trip to Wrigleyville will prove. If you try to find Wrigleyville on the official community area map of Chicago, you will be disappointed, as you will if you search out such legendary neighborhoods as Back of the Yards, Canaryville, or Hamburg on the South Side: but ask a local resident and they will point you in the right direction. Ask that same resident what their community's boundaries are they may be less clear, but they know when they are no longer in the "'hood." Chicago's neighborhood borders and even their names may change, but fierce local identification remains intact. In the 1950s, nobody would have said they live in Village East or River North, but most now know where those newly named neighborhoods are. The day when most Chicagoans identified with a local Catholic parish has long passed, but it still remains in some ethnic enclaves.

This of course also points back to the image of Chicago as a "City on the Make." Who names neighborhoods? Often developers looking for a quick buck name them. Who would want to live in West Town, sometimes called either Polish or Puerto Rican Downtown, when they could purchase a luxury condo or townhouse in Wicker Park, a name that today covers a much larger area then it once did? The South Loop did not exist before the late 1970s on anybody's mental map; it was a rundown portion of the downtown area. Now, as Chicagoans have embraced the unofficial sobriquet, that gritty name has held against the attempt by real estate developers to rechristen the area Burnham Park. Some things change, some don't.

Technological change has been one of the constants in the history of transforming Chicago. The city grew quickly in the nineteenth century because it embraced technological advances. Chicago was in many ways a child of the marriage between eastern capital and the technology that created the Transportation Revolution. Without first the Erie Canal opening the West to New York City and then the Illinois and Michigan Canal helping Chicago reach the Mississippi River and beyond, the city would never have been able to boom as it did in the 1830s and 1840s. Chicago quickly developed into a major port, and its harbor brought the natural resources of the expanding frontier together with the new capitalist market system. The long forty-one-mile protected harbor along the banks of the Chicago River also provided a natural place for the Industrial Revolution to put down roots. By the end of the 1840s the telegraph, the factory system, and the railroad arrived in the city, and Chicago's phenomenal growth soon followed. During the Civil War, Chicago boomed as both a transportation center and an industrial nexus for the North in its struggle against the secessionists.

In turn the localized transportation system, in the form first of the omnibus and then the horse drawn streetcar, allowed Chicago to grow beyond the boundaries of the walking city. The arrival of the cable car and the electric trolley further expanded the city's limits, as did the early development of commuter railroads and suburbs based again on eastern models. Finally the roar of the "L" concluded the nineteenth-century phase of the Transportation Revolution. The twentieth century with its airliners and jets, as well as with the ubiquitous automobile, further fashioned the cityscape.

Until the last third of the twentieth century, Chicago had always been on the cutting edge of technological change. It then faltered, seeming to depend on its prior predominance in the Industrial Revolution. As World War II ended, Chicago's business and political leadership sensed that the city had suffered from twenty years of neglect due largely to the Great Depression and war but seemed optimistic about the future. Plans for highways, housing developments, and downtown renewal sprouted up. Mayor Richard J. Daley imagined a modernist city with a strong industrial base. The mayor also seemed to have the vitality to pursue these dreams. But when he died, the city faced political chaos as well as deindustrialization and increased racial tensions as Chicago and the nation emerged from the Vietnam era.

The decades since the passing of Richard J. Daley have seen Chicago change once again as a new city has emerged out of the chaos of the 1960s and 1970s. First, under the leadership of various mayors from Bilandic through Washington to the younger Daley, the city began to cope with some of the issues of deindustrialization and turned itself into a global city. A renaissance has occurred along many of the city's streets both in the Loop and neighborhoods. While this is most likely seen on the streets of North Side neighborhoods such as Lincoln Park, where the new rich live and play, it can also be seen on the streets of the redeveloping South and West Sides. Thirty years ago no one would have predicted the resurrection of Oakland/North Kenwood or for that matter the appearance of million dollar homes in once thoroughly blue-collar Bridgeport. In working-class Mount Greenwood, bungalows and raised ranches are being demolished for bigger homes, the Southwest Side's equivalent of "McMansions." Obviously, as always, something again is changing in Chicago.

Thirty years ago, the city was seen as a vestige of America's industrial past. Pittsburgh, Cleveland, Detroit, and Newark seemed to be the equivalent of giant mastodons no longer relevant to a suburbanized America. Some referred to Chicago as a suburb of DuPage County. Chicago and other major American cities continued to lose population. Certainly Chicago's political clout seemed to disappear as the suburbs exerted more influence in both the state and federal legislatures. Many observers began to write Chicago off as a bit player in what some were beginning to call the global economy. New York and Los Angeles might continue to play an important role, but Chicago's days of glory had disappeared, along with the smell of the stockyards and the glare from its once mighty blast furnaces. Chicago without Richard J. Daley seemed hollow, a mere empty shell on its way to becoming a vast slum.

Change came back, but, as it often does, it arrived in an unexpected way. The attempts by the city to shore up the Loop and the manufacturing sector in the Bilandic, Byrne, Washington, and Sawyer years began to pay off in the 1990s under the leadership of Richard M. Daley. Like his father, Daley benefited from a growing economy in the 1990s and a friendly administration in Washington, D.C.—the Bill Clinton years proved beneficial for the leading Democratic city on Lake Michigan. Once again the importance of an activist federal government had an impact on Chicago. From the very beginning, Chicagoans have relied on Washington's largesse to expand the city's economy, from the early nineteenth century with the creation of the Chicago harbor and the Illinois and Michigan Canal or the expansion of the railroads to the building of expressways and public housing in the post–World War II period. By the end of the 1980s, federal attempts to reform public housing have also shaped the city. Once again Chicago became transformed and entered a new era.

Even Chicago's political demise seemed exaggerated, a result largely of Council Wars during the Washington years and the growth of suburban power. In reality Chicago has been resurrected as a political powerhouse. While it is true that the city no longer has as many state and federal representatives as it once boasted, it still has plenty of clout. The Daley family has reemerged on the national political scene. Both Richard M. and his brother Bill Daley became major players in national politics in the 1990s, and it remains difficult to ignore the city during either state or national elections. In 2008, the governor of the state hails from Chicago, and the newly elected Democratic president, Senator Barack Obama, is a South Sider and a White Sox fan. No U.S. president since Theodore Roosevelt has been so closely identified with a city as Obama, who

Figure 145. Dr. Cynthia Henderson and her spouse Prentiss Jackson greet Barack Obama at a fund-raiser in 2004, just before his successful run for the U.S. Senate from Illinois. Prentiss Jackson is the son of Angeline and George Jackson, who came to Chicago in 1952 and whose story is told in chapter 9. (Courtesy of Dr. Cynthia Henderson and Prentiss Jackson.)

cut his political teeth as a community organizer in the tough steel mill neighborhoods of South Chicago. While some have criticized President Obama's political background and his close connection to the Daley family, these proved especially important for him as he waged his historic campaign to be not only the first African American president but the first Chicagoan to occupy the White House.

Most importantly the public's attitude toward Chicago and American cities has changed yet again. Americans have always had a love/hate relationship with cities. After the repulsion that Americans felt for cities in the racially divided 1960s and their aftermath, cities began to become attractive again in the 1990s. Chicago became one of the leading cities of this transformation. While scholars might still debate whether or not Chicago is truly a global city, the public has made up its mind, and both resources and people seem to be flowing once again into the central city. Chicago is making an Olympic bid. The city's future, with its abundance of water and its location close to the agricultural heart of the nation, may once again depend on its location. How Chicago takes advantage of its "natural" position is crucial for the city's future. The South Loop and other neighborhoods are booming. Chicago is again, as it has so many times in its history, changed its skin. It is now both a global and a presidential city. Hopefully this book has touched on, and explained in part, those transformations.

Acknowledgments

While I wrote most of *Chicago: A Biography* in my Loop office at Columbia College and in my South Side home, I have also worked on this book while in Krakow, Paris, Ho Chi Minh City, and Italy. A large section of the manuscript came to light while I was a visiting fellow at Campion Hall, Oxford University. The support and friendship of the then master, Dr. Gerry Hughes, SJ, is warmly remembered and appreciated. Other members of that prestigious Jesuit community, especially Dr. Peter Edmunds, SJ, who attempted to explain the game of cricket to me while taking long walks in Oxford; Dr. Clarence Gallagher, SJ; Fr. Richard Randolph, SJ; and Dr. Michael Suarez, SJ, also gave freely their friendship and support. My colleague Dr. Brian Klug, senior research fellow and tutor in philosophy at St. Benet's Hall at Oxford arranged for my visit to the university. He provided a connection to the larger academic community and has long been a friend, advisor, and confidant.

My colleagues at Columbia College/Chicago, especially the former dean of liberal arts and sciences, Cheryl Johnson-Odim, now provost at Dominican University, and Provost Steven Kapelke generously provided me with a sabbatical and an extended leave that enabled me to complete this manuscript. Deborah Holdstein, the current dean of liberal arts and sciences, has been an unflinching supporter of this project and funded the maps. The chair of the Liberal Education Department, Lisa Brock, has been supportive and helpful. Oscar Valdez, the department administrative assistant and office manager, constantly helped with those small but nagging problems that anyone writing a book encounters. Krista Macewko Rogers, the department's administrative assistant, made sure that many bureaucratic problems disappeared.

This manuscript benefited from the close reading and advice of many friends and colleagues, especially Perry Duis, Ann Durkin Keating, Arnold Hirsch, Sue Ellen Hoy, Ted Karamanski, Eileen McMahon, Walter Nugent, Mark Rose, and Ellen Skerrett. Others gave advice, friendly criticism, and information, including Roger Biles, Peter McLennon, Janice Reiff, and Dorota Praszalowicz. I would like to thank Leo Schelbert, my longtime advisor and friend, who personifies all that is meant by the term *Doktorvater* and who continues to be an inspiration to me and countless others. Richard Rosenthal, John Rosenthal, Lawrence Trickle, Ted Swigon, Zung and Kim Dao, Neal Pagano, the Adlar family, David H. Krause, and Prentis Jackson and the Jackson family provided me with photographs, interviews, and a neighborhood perspective. I owe them much. I am very thankful to Jo Cates, the associate vice-president of academic research and dean of the Columbia College Library and her staff who supplied essential research help. The staffs of the Chicago Public Library, Special Collections Division and Preservation Department; the Spertus Institute of Jewish Studies; and the Chicago History Museum were most helpful. Joseph Zurawski of the Archives of the St. Mary of Nazareth Hospital Center also provided illustrations and information. Sister Joella Cunnane, RSM, archivist of the Sisters of Mercy, Regional Community of Chicago, provided rare photographs. Robert Devens has been an outstanding friend and editor. It is rare for one person to encompass both the obligations of friendship and editorship. He has done both, and with great patience. I would like to thank Bill Savage, who toiled over my prose and made suggestions that greatly improved the final product, and finally the unnamed readers, Laura Anderson, Anne Summers Goldberg, Mark Reschke, Emilie Sandoz, and the wonderful and gracious staff of the University of Chicago Press, for without them there would be no book.

None of this would have been possible without encouragement from my wife, the historian Kathleen Alaimo. She has been my partner in this and all of my various struggles. I could ask for no better friend and collaborator on life's pleasant and sometimes not so pleasant voyage. It is to her this book is dedicated. My two children Johanna and Beatrice have put up with this manuscript through thick and thin. Now as they embrace their own academic journeys they hopefully understand what a book really means.

Finally I owe much to the Richard H. Driehaus Foundation and to its dynamic executive director, Sunny Fischer. The Driehaus Foundation generously provided the funds for the illustrations in this book. They have over the years been generous in their support of those who would remember and preserve Chicago's history and architecture.

As part of the usual disclaimer let me say that while I received much advice, I sometimes ignored it and followed my own path. Therefore what is good in this book comes from the kind of collaboration that an urban academic world happily provides and any mistakes are naturally my own.

Notes

Introduction

1. At least five major books exist that focus solely on one neighborhood, the Back of the Yards! This book is based largely on these secondary sources. Even as I wrote this manuscript almost monthly more books appeared. I turned toward the city's long journalistic tradition to fill in where I found the secondary sources lacking. While many historians see the *Chicago Tribune* as the city's newspaper of record, Chicago benefited from many fine newspapers, such as the *Chicago Daily News,* the *Daily Inter Ocean,* the *Herald-American,* and the *Sun-Times* and many ethnic and neighborhood journals. I have used these sparingly, but encourage anyone interested in the city's history to look into the newspaper collections of the Chicago History Museum, the Chicago Public Library, and the Midwest Center for Research Libraries. The Chicago Foreign Language Press Survey, which provides translations taken from the city's ethnic press, is invaluable.

Chapter One

1. The account of Marquette and Jolliet's journey is taken largely from Jacques Marquette, *Voyages of Marquette in the Jesuit Relations,* ed. Reuben Gold Thwaites (Ann Arbor, Mich., 1966), 59.
2. Donald L. Miller, *City of the Century: The Epic of Chicago and the Making of America* (New York, 1996), 45–47.
3. Anka Muhlstein, *La Salle: Explorer of the North American Frontier,* trans. Willard Wood (New York, 1994), 87–88.
4. Bessie Louise Pierce, *A History of Chicago: The Beginning of the City, 1673–1848* (New York, 1937), 8–11. This is volume 1 of a three-volume study that ends at the turn of the century. In subsequent footnotes they will be referred to by their individual titles.
5. W. J. Eccles, *France in America* (New York, 1972), 233–35. For an excellent overview of French settlement in Illinois, see Roger Biles, *Illinois* (DeKalb, Ill., 2004).
6. De Sable may have been born in Santo Domingo although some sources point to St. Marc, Haiti, or even near Montreal or Peoria.
7. Frontier records are obscure and, while he is often portrayed as arriving in Chicago in 1775 or 1780, there is little evidence of his arrival before the end of the Revolutionary War.
8. Jean Baptiste Pointe de Sable's name is spelled in various ways. This book follows the most current research on early Chicago. Pierce, *History of Chicago,* 1:11, 12, and Milo Milton Quaife, *Chicago and the Old Northwest, 1673–1835* (reprint, Urbana, Ill., 2001), 138–42. The latest work exploring de Sable's impact on Chicago is Christopher Robert Reed, *Black Chicago's First Century, 1833–1900* (Columbia, Mo., 2005), 27–34; perhaps the most extensive look at de Sable's

life is John F. Swenson, "Jean Baptiste Point de Sable: The Founder of Modern Chicago," in *A Compendium of the Early History of Chicago to the Year 1835 When the Indians Left,* ed. Ulrich Danckers and Jane Meredith (River Forest, Ill., 2004), 388–94.

9. Pierce, *History of Chicago,* 1:12–13.

10. Reed, *Black Chicago's First Century,* 29–30; Swenson, "Jean Baptiste de Sable."

11. William H. Keating, Narrative of an Expedition to the Source of St. Peter's River: Lake Winnepeek, Lake of the Woods, &c., &c. Performed in the year 1823 (Philadelphia, 1824). See the excerpt in Pierce, As Others See Chicago: Impressions of Visitors, 1673–1933 (Chicago, 1933 [2004]), 31–39.

12. Pierce, *History of Chicago,* 1:16–37, 46; Dankers and Meredith, *Early Chicago,* 23–24; William Cronon, *Nature's Metropolis: Chicago and the Great West* (New York, 1991), 28. Cronon's is the best study of Chicago's role as a market and its impact on the environment.

13. Samuel A. Mitchell, *An Accompaniment to Mitchell's Reference and Distance Map of the United States* (Philadelphia, 1834), 315; Pierce, *As Others See Chicago,* 83.

14. Dionysius Lardner, *Railway Economy: A Treatise on the New Art of Transport* (New York, 1850), 325.

15. Robin L. Einhorn, *Property Rules: Political Economy in Chicago, 1833–1872* (Chicago, 1991); Pierce, *History of Chicago,* 1:47.

16. Miller, *City of the Century,* 70–71.

17. *Chicago American,* June 13, 1835.

18. *Chicago American,* July 27, 1835.

19. Stewart H. Holbrook, *The Yankee Exodus* (Seattle, 1968), 68–70.

20. Miller, *City of the Century,* 50.

21. Jacqueline Peterson, "The Founding Fathers: The Absorption of French-Indian Chicago," in *Ethnic Chicago: A Multicultural Portrait,* ed. Melvin G. Holli and Peter d'A Jones (Grand Rapids, Mich., 1995).

22. Ann Durkin Keating, *Building Chicago: Suburban Developers and the Creation of a Divided Metropolis* (Columbus, Ohio, 1988), 12–13; Ann Durkin Keating, *Chicagoland: City and Suburbs in the Railroad Age* (Chicago, 2005), 39–43.

23. *Chicago Tribune,* January 24, 1876.

24. *Daily Democrat,* September 16, 1852.

25. Einhorn, *Property Rules,* 31–33; Keating, *Chicagoland,* 37–38.

26. *Daily Democrat,* September 18, 1852.

27. *Chicago Tribune,* December 28, 1850; "Our City" (quoted from the *Cleveland Herald*), *Chicago Tribune,* June 9, 1854; *Chicago Tribune,* May 20, 1856, June 26, 1858, January 25, 1856 (originally printed in *New York Tribune*).

28. *Chicago Tribune,* June 4, 1853, June 26, 1858; for a history of schooners on Lake Michigan, see Theodore J. Karamanski, *Schooner Passage: Sailing Ships and the Lake Michigan Frontier* (Detroit, 2001); for shipwrecks, see chapter 5.

29. W. Williams, *Appleton's Railroad and Steamboat Companion* (New York, 1848), 299–301.

30. Michael P. Conzen, "1848: The Birth of Modern Chicago," in *1848: Turning Point for Chicago, Turning Point for the Region,* ed. Michael P. Conzen, Douglas Knox, and Dennis H. Cremin (Chicago, 1998), 12–13; *Chicago Tribune,* December 28, 1850; *Daily Democrat,* September 22, 1852.

31. Keating, *Chicagoland,* 52–61; "Points of the Great Triangle," *Chicago Tribune,* January 25, 1856.

32. Quote from William Cronon, *Nature's Metropolis,* 155. Much of the discussion on the lumber trade is taken from chapter 4.

33. *Chicago Tribune,* December 28, 1850, March 9, 1857; *Daily Democrat,* September 20, 1852.

34. Cronon, *Nature's Metropolis,* chapter 3.

35. *Chicago Tribune,* March 8, 1856.

36. Michael P. Funchion, "Irish Chicago: Church, Homeland, Politics, and Class—the Shaping of an Ethnic Group, 1870–1900," in Holli and Jones, *Ethnic Chicago,* 15.

37. Ellen Skerrett, "The Catholic Dimension," in *The Irish in Chicago* ed. Lawrence J. McCaffrey, Ellen Skerrett, Michael F. Funchion, and Charles Fanning (Urbana, Ill., 1987), 23. This book is the classic study of the Irish in the city.

38. Michael F. Funchion, "Political and Nationalist Dimensions," in McCaffrey et al., *The Irish in Chicago,* 61–62.

39. *Chicago Tribune,* April 21, 1852, March 18, 1856.

40. Christiane Harzig, "Germans," in *The Encyclopedia of Chicago,* ed. James R. Grossman, Ann Durkin Keating, Janice L. Reiff (Chicago, 2004), 333–36.

41. Anita Olson Gustafson, "Swedes," in Grossman et al., *Encyclopedia of Chicago,* 805–6; Ulf Beijbom, *Swedes in Chicago: A Demographic and Social Study of the 1846–1880 Immigration* (Stockholm, 1971).

42. "From the Voss Correspondence Society of Chicago to Friends in the Fatherland," in *Land of Their Choice: The Immigrants Write Home,* ed. Theodore C. Blegen (Minneapolis, 1955), 201–2.

43. For various activities of the St. George Society, see *Chicago Tribune,* May 2, 1861, September 24, 1861, March 26, 1864, March 27, 1864, May 25, 1866, June 5, 1866, October 4, 1870, July 26, 1871.

44. Ann Kelly Knowles, "Welsh," in Grossman et al., *Encyclopedia of Chicago,* 868–69; *Chicago Tribune,* December 12, 1872, August 2, 1875, October 19, 1876, March 3, 1854.

45. June Skinner Sawyers, "Scots," in Grossman et al., *Encyclopedia of Chicago,* 743; *Chicago Tribune,* December 2, 1852, December 3, 1852, December 2, 1857.

46. *Chicago Tribune,* April 9, 1856.

47. *Daily Democrat,* September 28, 1852.

48. *Chicago Tribune,* June 18, 1853, November 18, 1853, December 2, 1853, January 1, 1856. A perusal of advertisements in Chicago newspapers will speak to the variety of stores and services on Lake Street in the 1850s.

49. *Chicago Tribune,* July 11, 1857.

Chapter Two

1. *Chicago Tribune,* June 12, 1855.

2. Robert Ozanne, *A Century of Labor-Management Relations at McCormick and International Harvester* (Madison, Wisc., 1967), xv–xvi, 3–4.

3. *Chicago Tribune,* April 6, 1859.

4. *Chicago Tribune,* January 2, 1854.

5. For examples, see advertisements in *Chicago Tribune,* April 23, 1849, February 5, 1859.

6. *Chicago Tribune,* January 29, 1857.

7. *Chicago Tribune,* May 11, 1859.

8. *Chicago Tribune,* July 2, 1858.

9. Robin L. Einhorn, *Property Rules: Political Economy in Chicago, 1833–1872* (Chicago, 1991), 68–75.

10. *Chicago Tribune,* December 28, 1850.

11. Harold L. Platt, *Shock Cities: The Environmental Transformation and Reform of Manchester and Chicago* (Chicago, 2005), 78–80. For the 1857 flood, see *Chicago Tribune,* February 9 and 10, 1857.

12. Einhorn, *Property Rules,* 133–37; Platt, *Shock Cities,* 109–13.

13. Platt, *Shock Cities,* 148.

14. For the detailed discussion of these issues, see Platt, *Shock Cities,* 135–57.

15. Arnie Bernstein, *The Hoofs and Guns of the Storm: Chicago's Civil War Connections* (Chicago, 2003), 28–30.

16. Theodore J. Karamanski, *Rally 'Round the Flag: Chicago and the Civil War* (Chicago, 1993), 34–35. This is the best summary of Chicago's role in the election of Lincoln and the Civil War.

17. Bernstein, *Hoofs and Guns of the Storm*, 31–33.

18. Bessie Louis Pierce, *History of Chicago: From Town to City, 1848–1871* (New York, 1940), 2:246–47.

19. Karamanski, *Rally 'Round the Flag*, 19–31, 36.

20. *Chicago Tribune,* June 2, 1860, November 8, 1860, November 15, 1860, November 27, 1860, April 26, 1862, November 14, 1869.

21. Pierce, *History of Chicago*, 2:246–50; Karamanski, *Rally 'Round the Flag*, 60–65.

22. Bernstein, *Hoofs and Guns of the Storm*, 110–15.

23. Pierce, *History of Chicago*, 2:255–62; Karamanski, *Rally 'Round the Flag*, 66–92.

24. Karamanski, *Rally 'Round the Flag*, chapter 4.

25. Karamanski, *Rally 'Round the Flag*, chapter 5; Bernstein, *Hoofs and Guns of the Storm*, 202–6.

26. Karamnaski explains in detail the machinations of the various actors in *Rally 'Round the Flag*, chapter 5.

27. Karamanski, *Rally 'Round the Flag*, 189–97.

28. *Chicago Tribune,* May 15, 1861.

29. Karamanski, *Rally 'Round the Flag*, 160–63.

30. *Chicago Tribune,* January 30, 1862.

31. *Chicago Tribune,* January 12, 1861, January 16, 1861, March 30, 1861, October 17, 1861.

32. *Chicago Tribune,* July 27, 1863.

33. *Chicago Tribune,* December 3, 1864.

34. *Chicago Tribune,* August 5, 1863, August 23, 1865; "Manufacturers of Chicago," *Chicago Tribune,* September 29, 1865.

35. *Chicago Tribune,* January 17, 1865.

36. *Chicago Tribune,* January 13, 1865, January 15, 1865, January 24, 1865; *Act of Incorporation and By-Laws of the Union Stock Yard and Transit Co.* (Chicago, 1865).

37. Louise Carroll Wade, *Chicago's Pride: The Stockyards, Packingtown, and Environs in the Nineteenth Century* (Urbana, Ill., 1987), 11–15. This is the best history of the early years of Chicago's development as a meatpacking center.

38. Wade, *Chicago's Pride*, 47–54; Chicago Commission on Historical Landmarks, *Report on the Union Stock Yard Gate* (Chicago, 1971), 4; *Chicago Tribune*, January 1, 2, 1866; William Parkhurst, *History of the Yards, 1865–1953* (Chicago, 1953), 12.

39. "First Stock at New Union Yard" (typescript), Stock Yard Collection, Special Collections, University of Illinois at Chicago; Charles R. Koch, "A Country Fair Everyday," *Farm Quarterly* (Spring 1965), 80–83, 157–158; Union Stock Yard and Transit Co., *81st Annual Livestock Report, 1946* (Chicago, 1946); *Drover's Journal Yearbook of Figures, 1939* (Chicago, 1939), 195; Chicago Commission on Historical Landmarks, *Report on the Union Stock Yard Gate*, 5.

40. Wade, *Chicago's Pride*, 65–66.

41. Bertram B. Fowler, *Men, Meat and Miracles* (New York, 1952), 53; Louis F. Swift, in collaboration with Arthur Van Vlissingen, Jr., *The Yankee of the Yards* (Chicago, 1927), 185–92.

42. Phyllis Bate, "The Development of the Iron and Steel Industry of the Chicago Area," (Ph.D. diss., University of Chicago, 1949), 10–13; Victor Windett, " The South Works of the Illinois Steel Industry," *Journal of the Western Society of Engineers* 3 (Chicago, 1898): 789–93, 808; John B. Appleton, "The Iron and Steel Industry of the Calumet Region—a Study in Economic Geography," (Ph.D. diss., University of Chicago, 1925), iii–iv; William H. Rowan, "History of South Chicago" (typescript), Stephen Stanley Bubacz Collection, University of Illinois at Chicago, Urban Archives, folder 161, p. 9.; Gladys Priddy, "South Chicago" in Rev. Alfred

Abramowicz, *Diamond Jubilee, Immaculate Conception, B.V.M. Parish, 1882–1957* (Chicago, 1957), 23.

43. Harold M. Mayer and Richard C. Wade, *Chicago: Growth of a Metropolis* (Chicago, 1969), 184–86.

44. Joseph L. Arnold, "Riverside," in James R. Grossman, Ann Durkin Keating, and Janice L. Reiff, *The Encyclopedia of Chicago History* (Chicago, 2004), 712.

45. Ann Durkin Keating, *Chicagoland: City and Suburbs in the Railroad Age* (Chicago, 2005), 148–50.

46. Mabel NcIlvaine, ed., *Reminiscences of Chicago during the Forties and Fifties,* (Chicago, 1913), 76.

Chapter Three

1. *Chicago Daily News,* July 7, 1877.

2. Jevne's letter is reprinted in Bessie Louis Pierce, *As Others See Chicago: Impressions of Visitors, 1673–1933* (Chicago, 1933 [2004]), 176–79. Odd S. Lovoll, *A Century of Urban Life: The Norwegians in Chicago before 1930* (Chicago, 1988), 80–82.

3. Stewart H. Holbrook, *The Yankee Exodus* (Seattle, 1968), 71; Bessie Louis Pierce, *Chicago* (Chicago, 1940), 2:150–55; Lovoll, *A Century of Urban Life,* 24.

4. Harold M. Mayer and Richard C. Wade, *Chicago: Growth of a Metropolis* (Chicago, 1969), 54.

5. Mabel NcIlvaine, ed., *Reminiscences of Chicago during the Forties and Fifties,* (Chicago, 1913), 59–66.

6. "Chicago Surface Lines—History," *http://hometown.aol.com/chictafan/ctabhist.html* (June 21, 2004).

7. Dominic A. Pacyga and Ellen Skerrett, *Chicago: City of Neighborhoods* (Chicago, 1986), 165–69.

8. A communard's justification for the burning of Paris: Lissagray, *Les Huit Journées de mai,* 102–4, quoted in Stewart Edwards, ed., *The Communards of Paris, 1871* (Ithaca, N.Y., 1973), 168.

9. Carl Smith, *Urban Disorder and the Shape of Belief: The Great Chicago Fire, The Haymarket Bomb, and the Model Town of Pullman* (Chicago, 1995), 19.

10. Donald Miller, *City of the Century: The Epic of Chicago and the Making of America* (New York, 1996), 161–62.

11. Karen Sawislak, *Smoldering City: Chicagoans and the Great Fire, 1871–1874* (Chicago, 1995), 46–48, 29; Carl Smith, *Urban Disorder and the Shape of Belief,* 22, 47.

12. Sawislak, *Smoldering City,* 69; Maureen A. Flanagan, *Seeing with Their Hearts: Chicago Women and the Vision of the Good City, 1871–1933* (Princeton, N.J., 2002), 20–30.

13. Perry Duis, *Chicago: Creating New Traditions* (Chicago, 1976), 17.

14. Bessie Louis Pierce, *Chicago* (Chicago, 1957), 3:7.

15. *Illinois Staats-Zeitung,* May 2 and 3, 1867, translated and reprinted in Hartmut Keil and John B. Jentz, eds., *German Workers in Chicago: A Documentary History of Working-Class Culture from 1850 to World War I* (Urbana, Ill., 1988), 254–57; Pierce, *Chicago,* 2:171–79; Richard Schneirov, *Labor and Urban Politics: Class Conflict and the Origins of Modern Liberalism in Chicago, 1864–1897* (Urbana, Ill., 1998), 18, 35; Carl Smith, *Urban Disorder and the Shape of Belief,* 103; Sawislak, *Smoldering City,* 174–90, 207–10.

16. Jonathan J. Keyes, "The Forgotten Fire," *Chicago History,* Fall 1997, 52–65; Schneirov, *Labor and Urban Politics,* 56–57.

17. *Chicago Daily News,* July 24, 1877.

18. Carl Smith, *Urban Disorder and the Shape of Belief,* 107–9; Paul Avrich, *The Haymarket Tragedy* (Princeton, N.J., 1984), 26–34. For an almost hour-by-hour account of the strike, see *Chicago Daily News,* various editions, from July 20 to July 27, 1877.

19. *Chicago Daily News,* July 27, 1877.

20. Quoted in Avrich, *Haymarket,* 60.

21. Quoted in Avrich, *Haymarket,* 167.

22. Carl Smith, *Urban Disorder and the Shape of Belief,* 111–15; Avrich, *Haymarket,* 144–49.

23. *Chicago Tribune,* July 1, 1885, July 2, 1885.

24. Schneirov, Labor and Urban Politics, 168–73.

25. Quoted in Avrich, *Haymarket,* 185.

26. Quoted in Avrich, *Haymarket,* 194.

27. All quotations from Avrich, *Haymarket,* 197–209.

28. For a complete description of events, see Avrich, *Haymarket,* especially chapters 16 and 17.

29. See Carl Condit, *The Chicago School of Architecture: A History of Commercial and Public Building in the City Area, 1875–1925* (Chicago, 1964), 80–81.

30. Daniel Bluestone, *Constructing Chicago* (New Haven, Conn., and London, 1991), 108–15.

31. All quotes from Pierce, *As Others See Chicago,* 230, 252, 289. The best investigation of the European reaction to Chicago is Arnold Lewis, *An Early Encounter with Tomorrow: Europeans, Chicago's Loop, and the World's Columbian Exposition* (Urbana, Ill., 1997); for Chicagoans views on speed, see p. 57.

32. David M. Solzman, *The Chicago River: An Illustrated History and Guide to the River and Its Waterways* (Chicago, 1998), : 30–33; Lewis, *An Early Encounter,* 25–29; Pierce, *As Others See Chicago,* 252; Miller, *City of the Century,* 426.

33. Lewis, *An Early Encounter,* 30–31.

34. William T. Stead, *If Christ Came to Chicago* (Chicago, 1894), 247–52; Herbert Asbury, *Gem of the Prairie* (Garden City, N.Y., 1942), 135–41, 171–76; Norman Mark, *Mayors, Madams, and Madmen* (Chicago, 1979), 14; Gilian M. Wolf, "Everleigh, Ada and Everleigh, Minna," in *Women Building Chicago, 1790–1990: A Biographical Dictionary,* ed. Rima Lunin Schultz and Adele Hast (Bloomington, Ind., 2001), : 253–55. The classic study of the Levee is Lloyd Wendt and Herman Kogan, *Bosses of Lusty Chicago* (Bloomington, Ind., 1971) published in 1943 under the title *Lords of the Levee.* A recent work, Karen Abbott, *Sin and the Second City: Madams, Ministers, Playboys, and the Battle for America's Soul* (New York, 2007), is an interesting journalistic account of the Everleigh sisters and the Levee.

Chapter Four

1. Daniel Rodgers, *Atlantic Crossings: Social Politics in a Progressive Age* (Cambridge, Mass., 1998); Dominic A. Pacyga, *Polish Immigrants and Industrial Chicago: Workers on the South Side, 1880–1922* (Chicago, 2003); Carl Condit, *The Chicago School of Architecture: A History of Commercial and Public Building in the Chicago Area, 1875–1925* (Chicago, 1964).

2. I owe much of this interpretation of the West Side to my many conversations with Ellen Skerrett, who has pointed me to sources and shared freely her knowledge of the West Side Irish and Jane Addams.

3. *Chicago Tribune,* February 13, 1898.

4. *Chicago Tribune,* February 24, 1889.

5. For the story of Goose Island, see Perry R. Duis, *Challenging Chicago: Coping with Everyday Life, 1837–1920* (Urbana, Ill., 1998), chapter 4; Schaack quotation on p. 104.

6. Rev. Harry C. Koenig, ed., *A History of the Parishes of the Archdiocese of Chicago* (Chicago, 1980) 1:751–54; Ellen Skerrett, "Creating Sacred Space in an Early Chicago Neighborhood," in Ellen Skerrett, *At the Crossroads: Old Saint Patrick's and the Chicago Irish* (Chicago, 1997), 21–38.

7. Ellen Skerrett, "The Irish of Chicago's Hull-House Neighborhood," *Chicago History,* 30, no. 1 (Summer 2001): 22–63; see also the photograph essay by Michael A. Marcotte, "Holy Family Church," *Chicago History,* 22, no. 3, (November 1993): 38–51.

8. *Lakeside Annual Directory of the City of Chicago, 1874–1875* (Chicago, 1874), 70–71, 79.

9. Robert P. Swierenga, *Dutch Chicago: A History of the Hollanders in the Windy City* (Grand Rapids, Mich., 2002), 7–30.

10. Jan Habenicht, *Dějiny Čechův Amerických* (St. Louis, 1910), 566–67; Alice G. Masaryk, "The Bohemians in Chicago," *Charities,* December 3, 1904, 206; Joseph Slabey Roucek, "The Passing of American Czechoslovaks," *American Journal of Sociology,* March 1934, 612; *Lakeside Annual Directory, 1874–1875,* 70–71; *The Lakeside Annual Directory of the City of Chicago, 1886* (Chicago, 1886), 45, 55, 60.

11. Irving Cutler, *The Jews of Chicago: From Shtetle to Suburb* (Urbana, Ill., 1996), 72–91.

12. Koenig, A History of the Parishes of the Archdiocese of Chicago, 1:80–85, 724; *Chicago Tribune,* September 23, 1895, 8.

13. *Chicago Tribune,* February 13, 1898.

14. Stanley Buder, *Pullman: An Experiment in Industrial Order and Community Planning, 1880–1930* (New York, 1967), chapters 1 and 2. For statistics, see "The Development of the Sleeping Car," *Manufacturer and Builder* 25, no. 8 (August 1894): 176–77.

15. Carl Smith, *Urban Disorder and the Shape of Belief: The Great Chicago Fire, the Haymarket Bomb, and the Model Town of Pullman* (Chicago, 1995), 193–200, quote on p. 195.

16. Richard T. Ely, "Pullman: A Social Study," *Harper's New Monthly Magazine,* 70, no. 417 (February 1885): 452–66.

17. Janice L. Reiff, "A Modern Lear and His Daughters: Gender in the Model Town of Pullman," in *The Pullman Strike and the Crises of the 1890s: Essays on Labor and Politics,* ed. Richard Schneirov, Shelton Stromquist, and Nick Salvatore (Urbana, Ill., 1999), 65–86.

18. Ely, "Pullman," 464–65.

19. Victoria Bissell Brown, *The Education of Jane Addams* (Philadelphia, 2004), is the best study of Jane Addams's early years.

20. See Maureen A. Flanagan, *Seeing with their Hearts: Chicago Women and the Vision of the Good City, 1871–1933* (Princeton, N.J., 2002), especially chapter 2.

21. [Rev.] David Swing, "A New Social Movement," *Chicago Evening Journal,* June 8, 1889, 4.

22. *Chicago Tribune,* April 28, 1895, 47

23. The University of Illinois at Chicago has created an excellent Web site dedicated to Hull-House and its residents: Urban Experience in Chicago: Hull House and Its Neighborhoods, 1889–1963, http://www.uic.edu/jaddams/hull/urbanexp/. Perry R. Duis provides one of the best and most concise interpretations of the urban reform movement in his *Chicago: Creating New Traditions* (Chicago, 1976), 57–81.

24. Jane Addams, "Outgrowths of Toynbee Hall," address delivered to the Chicago Women's Club, December 3, 1891, http://www.uic.edu/jaddams/hull/urbanexp/.

25. An excellent study of Jane Addams's role in the founding of modern sociology is Mary Jo Deegan, *Jane Addams and the Men of the Chicago School, 1892–1918* (New Brunswick, N.J., 1990); see especially chapter 2 for the gendered approach to the social settlement.

26. See timeline on the Urban Experience in Chicago Web site; see also Allen F. Davis and Mary Lyn McCree, eds., *Eighty Years at Hull House* (Chicago, 1969), 22.

27. Rivka Shpak Lissak, *Pluralism & Progressivism: Hull House and the New Immigrants, 1880–1919* (Chicago, 1989), 22, presents a well argued criticism of Jane Addams and Hull-House.

28. Lissak, *Pluralism & Progressivism;* see especially chapter 3.

29. *Zgoda,* April 15, 1897; *Dziennik Chicagoski,* October 19, 1894.

30. Jane Addams, "Why the Ward Boss Rules," *Outlook* 58, no. 15 (April 2, 1898): 879–82.

31. Gerald R. Larson, "The Iron Skeleton Frame: Interactions between Europe and the United States," in *Chicago Architecture, 1872–1922: Birth of a Metropolis,* ed. John Zukowsky (Munich, 2000), 39–55.

32. Carl Condit, *The Chicago School of Architecture: A History of Commercial and Public Building in the City Area, 1875–1925* (Chicago, 1964), 28–30, 79–94.

33. Condit, *The Chicago School,* 31–34.

34. Lewis, *An Early Encounter,* 61–62. Pierce, *As Others See Chicago,* 291–94.

35. Joseph M. Siry, *The Chicago Auditorium Building: Adler and Sullivan's Architecture and the City* (Chicago, 2002), 9–11, 15, 29, 99–101.

36. Siry, *Chicago Auditorium Building,* 123–27, 151; Duis, *Creating New Traditions,* 23–24.

37. Condit, *The Chicago School,* 43–47.

38. Commission on Chicago Historical and Architectural Landmarks, *The Rookery* (Chicago, 1972); Condit, *The Chicago School,* 22, 65–69.

39. George A. Lane, *Chicago Churches and Synagogues: An Architectural Pilgrimage* (Chicago, 1981), 52–53

40. Louis P. Cain, "Annexation," in *The Encyclopedia of Chicago History,* ed. James R. Grossman, Ann Durkin Keating, and Janice L. Reiff (Chicago, 2004), 21–23.

41. Charles Moore, *Daniel H. Burnham: Architect, Planner of Cities* (New York, 1968 [reprint of 1921 version]), 31–44.

42. James Gilbert, *Perfect Cities: Chicago's Utopias of 1893* (Chicago, 1991), chapter 4.

43. *Chicago Tribune,* October 29, 1893.

44. Gilbert, *Perfect Cities,* 162–63.

45. Buder, *Pullman,* chapter 12 and pp. 168–69; Almont Lindsey, *The Pullman Strike: The Story of a Unique Experiment and of a Great Labor Upheaval* (Chicago, 1967), 122–26.

46. Buder, *Pullman,* chapters 13–16.

47. Gilbert, *Perfect Cities,* 193–99; Anita Olson Gustafson, "North Park: Building a Swedish Community in Chicago," *Journal of American Ethnic Studies* 22, no. 2 (Winter 2003): 31–49.

Chapter Five

1. David Brody, *Steelworkers in America: The Non-Union Era* (New York, 1969); Raymond A. Mohl and Neil Beitten, *Steel City: Urban and Ethnic Patterns in Gary, Indiana, 1906–1950* (New York, 1986).

2. Andrew Wender Cohen, *The Racketeer's Progress: Chicago and the Struggle for the Modern American Economy, 1900–1940* (Cambridge, 2004), 108–19.

3. Daniel T. Rodgers, *Atlantic Crossings: Social Politics in a Progressive Age* (Cambridge, 1998), 74–75.

4. See James R. Barrett, *Work and Community in the Jungle: Chicago's Packinghouse Workers, 1894–1922* (Urbana, Ill., 1987), 131–37, 165–82; David Brody, *The Butcher Workmen: A Study in Unionization* (Cambridge, 1964), 42; Dominic A. Pacyga, *The Polish Worker and Industrial Chicago: Workers on the South Side* (Chicago, 2003), 169–80.

5. Allan Spear, *Black Chicago: The Making of a Negro Ghetto, 1890–1920* (Chicago, 1967), 36–39.

6. Dominic A. Pacyga, "Chicago's Ethnic Neighborhoods: The Myth of Stability and the Reality of Change," in *Ethnic Chicago,* 3rd ed., ed. Melvin G. Holli and Peter d'A. Jones (Grand Rapids, Mich., 1995), 604–17.

7. For a discussion of the saloon, see Perry R. Duis, *The Saloon: Public Drinking in Chicago and Boston, 1880–1920* (Urbana, Ill., 1983). For the saloon and juvenile delinquency, see Albert Ellis Webster, "The Relation of the Saloon to Juvenile Delinquency" (B.A. thesis, University of Chicago, 1912).

8. Kenneth Finegold, *Experts and Politicians: Reform Challenges in New York, Cleveland, and Chicago* (Princeton, N.J., 1995), 20–25, 127; Melvin G. Holli, *Reform in Detroit: Hazen S. Pingree and Urban Politics* (New York, 1969), provides an important model for looking at Progressive Era reformers calling them structural and social reformers.

9. Edward R. Kantowicz, "Carter H. Harrison II: The Politics of Balance," in *The Mayors: The Chicago Political Tradition,* ed. Paul M. Green and Melvin G. Holli (Carbondale, Ill., and Edwardsville, Ill., 1987), 16–21.

10. James L. Merriner, *Grafters and Goo Goos: Corruption and Reform in Chicago, 1833–2003* (Carbondale, Ill., 2004), 61–88.

11. Richard Allen Morton, *Justice and Humanity: Edward F. Dunne, Illinois Progressive* (Carbondale, Ill., 1997), 9–10; Paul Barrett, *The Automobile and Urban Transit: The Formation of Public Policy in Chicago, 1900–1930* (Philadelphia, 1983), 21.

12. Barrett, *The Automobile and Urban Transit*, 20–23.

13. Morton, *Justice and Humanity*, 1–4; John D. Buenker, "Edward F. Dunne: The Limits of Political Reform," in Green and Holli, eds., *The Mayors*, 33–37.

14. Andrew Wender Cohen, *The Racketeer's Progress: Chicago and the Struggle for the Modern American Economy, 1900–1940* (Cambridge, 2004), 111–19; Steven L. Piott, "The Chicago Teamsters' Strike of 1902: A Community Confronts the Beef Trust," *Labor History* 26, no. 2 (Spring 1985): 250–67.

15. Morton, *Justice and Humanity*, 17–18.

16. Morton, *Justice and Humanity*, 35; Buenker, "Edward F. Dunne," 40–41.

17. Buenker, "Edward F. Dunne," 42–49.

18. Maureen Flanagan, "Fred A. Busse: A Silent Mayor in Turbulent Times," in Green and Holli, eds., *The Mayors*, 50–60.

19. Howard E. Wilson, *Mary McDowell: Neighbor* (Chicago, 1928), chapter 7.

20. For an overview of the development of children's rights, see Kathleen Alaimo, "Historical Roots of Children's Rights in Europe and the United States," in *Children as Equals: Exploring the Rights of the Child,* ed. Kathleen Alaimo and Brian Klug (Lanham, Md., New York, and Oxford, 2002), 1–24.

21. Florence Kelley, "The Illinois Child Labor Law," *American Journal of Sociology* 3 (January 1898): 492–95; *Eight Annual Report of the Factory Inspectors of Illinois for the Year Ending December 15, 1900* (Springfield, Ill., 1901), 21–26; John R. Commons, "Labor Conditions in Meat Packing and the Recent Strike," *Quarterly Journal of Economics* 19 (November 1904): 24; Florence Kelley, "The Working Boy," *American Journal of Sociology* 2 (November 1896): 363.

22. Kathryn Kish Sklar, *Florence Kelley and the Nation's Work* (New Haven, Conn., 1995), 237–42.

23. Anthony M. Platt, *The Child Savers: The Invention of Delinquency* (Chicago, 1969), 3–10, 33–38.

24. David Spinoza Tanenhous, "Policing the Child: Criminal Justice in Chicago, 1870–1925," 2 vols. (Ph.D. diss., University of Chicago, 1997), 1:1–9, 136–39, 153–64.

25. Victoria Getis, *The Juvenile Court and the Progressives* (Urbana, Ill., 2000), details the creation of the court and its role in Progressive thought.

26. This discussion of the municipal courts is based largely on Michael Willrich, *City of Courts: Socializing Justice in Progressive Era Chicago* (Cambridge, 2003).

27. Maureen A. Flanagan, *Charter Reform in Chicago* (Carbondale, Ill., 1987) is the best discussion of charter reform.

28. Charles Zueblin, "Municipal Playgrounds in Chicago" *American Journal of Sociology* (September 1898): 146–48.

29. *Chicago Record-Herald*, June 1, 1902, Chicago Park District (CPD) Clippings, Vol. 2.

30. Galen Cranz, *The Politics of Park Design: A History of Urban Parks in America* (Cambridge, 1984), 63.

31. *Chicago Tribune*, February 5, 1904, CPD Clippings, Vol. 3.; Cranz, *Politics of Park Design*, 87.

32. Untitled, undated ms., Page B, CPD Clippings, Vol. 3.

33. *The West Parks and Boulevards of Chicago* (Chicago, 1913).

34. Daniel Burnham and Edward Bennett, *Plan of Chicago* (Chicago, 1909), 4–6.

35. Robin F. Bachin, *Building the South Side: Urban Space and Civic Culture in Chicago, 1890–1919* (Chicago, 2003), 171–92.

36. Perry R. Duis, *Chicago: Creating New Traditions* (Chicago, 1976), 52–53.

37. Burnham and Bennett, *Plan of Chicago*, 32–42.

38. Bachin, *Building the South Side*, 197–99.

39. Duis, *Chicago: Creating New Traditions*, 53–55; Ellen Skerrett, "It's More than a Bungalow: Portage Park and the Making of the Bungalow Belt," in *The Chicago Bungalow,* ed. Dominic A. Pacyga and Charles Shanabruch (Chicago, 2001), 99.

40. Sophonisba Breckinridge and Edith Abbott, "Chicago Housing Conditions IV: The West Side," *American Journal of Sociology,* 17, no. 1 (July 1911): 1–34. While most of the argument for this section was taken from this article, Breckenridge and Abbott published a series of articles in the *Journal of American Sociology* from 1910 to 1915.

41. Lloyd Wendt and Herman Kogan, *Big Bill of Chicago* (Indianapolis, 1953), 13–33.

42. Douglas Bukowski, *Big Bill Thompson, Chicago, and the Politics of Image* (Urbana, Ill., 1998), 18–30. This is the best biography of William Hale Thompson. See also Douglas Bukowski, "Big Bill Thompson: The 'Model Politician,'" in Green and Holli, eds., *The Mayors,* 61–81.

43. Bukowski, *Big Bill Thompson,* 45–48.

44. Wendt and Kogan, *Big Bill of Chicago,* 141–43.

45. Bukowski, *Big Bill Thompson,* 25, 38–40, 52, 67.

Chapter Six

1. Glen E. Holt and Dominic A. Pacyga, *Chicago: A Historical Guide to the Neighborhoods; The Loop and South Side* (Chicago, 1979), 143; James L. Reidy, *Chicago Sculpture* (Urbana, Ill., 1981), 221–22.

2. Mary Jo Deegan, *Jane Addams and the Men of the Chicago School, 1892–1918* (New Brunswick, N.J., 1990), 82; *Chicago Tribune,* March 3, 1908. For the police version of the Averbach affair, see Richard C. Lindberg, *To Serve and Collect: Chicago Politics and Police Corruption from the Lager Beer Riot to the Summerdale Scandal* (New York, 1991), 104. See also Rivka Shpak Lissak, *Pluralism and Progressives: Hull House and the New Immigrants, 1890–1919* (Chicago, 1989), 91–92; Walter Roth and Joe Kraus, *An Accidental Anarchist* (San Francisco, 1998).

3. For a discussion of this, see Dominic A. Pacyga, "To Live amongst Others: Poles and Their Neighbors in Industrial Chicago, 1865–1930," *Journal of American Ethnic History* (Fall 1996): 55–74.

4. Thomas J. Jablonsky, *Pride in the Jungle: Community and Everyday Life in Back of the Yards Chicago* (Baltimore, 1993), 103–5.

5. For the best account of the saloon in Chicago, see Perry R. Duis, *The Saloon: Public Drinking in Chicago and Boston, 1880–1920* (Urbana, Ill., 1983).

6. For the history of Pilsen Park and events in the Czech community during World War I, see Dominic A. Pacyga, "Chicago's Pilsen Park and the Struggle for Czechoslovak Independence," in *Essays in Russian and East European History: A Festschrift for Edward C. Thaden,* ed. Leo Schelbert and Nick Ceh (Boulder, Colo., 1995), 117–29.

7. Lloyd Wendt and Herman Kogan, *Big Bill of Chicago* (Indianapolis, 1954), 149–50.

8. *Chicago Tribune,* February 27, 1916.

9. This discussion of World War I is largely based on Melvin G. Holli, "The Great War Sinks Chicago's German *Kultur*" in *Ethnic Chicago,* ed. Melvin G. Holli and Peter d'A. Jones (Grand Rapids, Mich., 1984), 460.

10. Edward R. Kantowicz, *Corporation Sole: Cardinal Mundelein and Chicago Catholicism* (Notre Dame, Ind., 1983), 10–11.

11. *Chicago Tribune,* February 11, 1916, February 13, 1916.

12. *Chicago Tribune,* February 13, 1916.

13. *Chicago Tribune,* for the following dates: February 14–21 and 26, 1916; March 17, 1916; May 16, 1916.

14. Rev. Msgr. Harry C. Koenig, S.T.D., ed., *A History of the Parishes of the Archdiocese of Chicago* (Chicago, 1980), 2:968–71.

15. *Chicago Tribune,* March 2, 1916.

16. Koenig., ed., *A History of the Parishes of the Archdiocese of Chicago,* 1:353–56.

17. *Chicago Tribune,* March 3, 1916, March4, 1916.

18. Wendt and Kogan, *Big Bill of Chicago,* 149–60, 161–71; Bukowski, *Big Bill Thompson,* 66–67.

19. Holli, "The Great War, " 490–511.

20. James S. Pula, "A Branch Cut Off from Its Trunk—the Affects of Immigration Restriction on American Polonia, *Polish American Studies,* 61, no. 1 (Spring 2004): 40.

21. William Z. Foster, *American Trade Unionism* (New York, 1970), 21–23; James R. Barrett, *Work and Community in the Jungle: Chicago's Packinghouse Workers, 1894–1922* (Urbana, Ill., 1987), 142.

22. Dominic A. Pacyga, *Polish Immigrants and Industrial Chicago: Workers on the South Side, 1880–1922* (Chicago, 2003), 183.

23. David Brody, *Labor in Crisis: The Steel Strike of 1919* (New York, 1965), 54, 66–76; William Z. Foster, *The Great Steel Strike and Its Lessons* (New York, 1920), 29; Pacyga *Polish Workers and Industrial Chicago,* 195–97.

24. James R. Grossman, *Land of Hope: Chicago Black Southerners and the Great Migration* (Chicago, 1989), 74–79. This is the best look at Chicago's role in the Great Migration.

25. Allan H. Spear, *Black Chicago: The Making of a Negro Ghetto, 1890–1922* (Chicago, 1967), 44–46.

26. Grossman, *Land of Hope,* 123–28.

27. Spear, *Black Chicago,* 11, 14–20, 130; St. Clair Drake and Horace C. Clayton, *Black Metropolis,* 2 vols. (New York, 1970), 1:61–62; Alzada P. Comstock, "Chicago Housing Conditions VI: The Problem of the Negro," *American Journal of Sociology* 28 (September 1912): 253–254.

28. Grossman, *Land of Hope,* 129–30.

29. Robin F. Bachin, *Building the South Side: Urban Space and Civic Culture, 1890–1919* (Chicago, 2004), 247–83.

30. Grossman, *Land of Hope,* 143–53; William M. Tuttle, *Race Riot: Chicago in the Red Summer of 1919* (New York, 1972), 96–97, 159.

31. Quoted in Tuttle, *Race Riot,* 131.

32. Tuttle, *Race Riot,* 132–42; *Chicago Tribune,* June 6, 1919.

33. Tuttle's book *Race Riot* is the classic account of the riot. For the immediate investigation and a collection of interviews and other evidence, see Chicago Commission on Race Relations, *The Negro in Chicago: A Study of Race Relations and a Race Riot* (Chicago, 1922). For the ethnic identity of the rioters, see Dominic A. Pacyga, "Chicago's 1919 Race Riot: Ethnicity, Class, and Urban Violence," in *The Making of Urban America,* ed. Raymond A. Mohl (Wilmington, Del., 1987), 187–207.

34. For both the 1919 steel strike and the 1921–22 packinghouse strike, see Pacyga, *Polish Immigrants and Industrial Chicago,* chapter 6.

Chapter Seven

1. James S. Pula, "American Immigration and the Dillingham Commission," *Polish American Studies* 38, no. 1 (Spring 1980): 5–31; James S. Pula, "The Progressives, the Immigrant, and the Workplace: Defining Public Perceptions," *Polish American Studies* 52, no. 2 (Autumn 1995): 57–69; Dale T. Knobel, *America for Americans: The Nativist Movement in the United States* (New York, 1996), 258–61.

2. John J. Bukowczyk, *And My Children Did Not Know Me: A History of Polish Americans* (Bloomington, Ind., 1987), 67.

3. David M. Young, *Chicago Transit: An Illustrated History* (DeKalb, Ill., 1998), 77–79; Bruce G. Moffat, *The "L": The Development of Chicago's Rapid Transit System, 1888–1932, Bulletin 131 of*

the Central Electric Railfan's Association (Chicago, 1995), 202–15; Alan R. Lind, *Chicago Surface Lines: An Illustrated History* (Park Forest, Ill., 1979), 221–347. An excellently illustrated account of Chicago's "L" is Greg Borzo, *The Chicago "L"* (Charleston, S.C., and Chicago, 2007).

4. Joseph Bigott, "Bungalows and the Complex Origin of the Modern House" in *The Chicago Bungalow,* ed. Dominic Pacyga and Charles Shanabruch (Chicago, 2001), 31–52. See also Joseph C. Bigott, *From Cottage to Bungalow: Houses and the Working Class in Metropolitan Chicago, 1869–1929* (Chicago, 2001).

5. Scott Sonoc, "Defining the Chicago Bungalow," in Pacyga and Shanabruch, eds., *The Chicago Bungalow,* 7–30.

6. Charles Shanabruch, "Building and Selling Chicago's Bungalow Belt"; Ellen Skerrett, "It's More than a Bungalow: Portage Park and the Making of the Bungalow Belt"; and Dominic A. Pacyga, "Moving on Up: Chicago's Bungalows and the American Dream," all in Pacyga and Shanabruch, eds., *The Chicago Bungalow;* Evelyn M. Kitagawa and Karl E. Tauber, eds., *Local Community Fact Book, Chicago Metropolitan Area, 1960* (Chicago, 1963), 172–73, 178–79.

7. Tauber and Kitagawa, *Local Community Fact Book, Chicago Metropolitan Area, 1960,* 172–73, 178–79; www.berwyn.net/Berwyn/history.asp (accessed February 23, 2005).

8. John J. Reichman, *Czechoslovaks of Chicago: Contributions to a History of a National Group* (Chicago, 1937), 15–16, 17–19, 26–27, 35–37, 38–43.

9. For the development and imposition of zoning laws, see Andrew J. King, *Law and Land Use in Chicago: A Prehistory of Modern Zoning* (New York and London, 1986).

10. Pacyga, "Moving on Up," 130–34.

11. King, *Law and Land Use in Chicago,* 70; Thomas Lee Philpott, *The Slum and the Ghetto: Neighborhood Deterioration and Middle-Class Reform, Chicago, 1880–1930* (New York, 1978), 185–89.

12. Glen E. Holt and Dominic A. Pacyga, *Chicago: A Historical Guide to the Neighborhoods: The Loop and South Side* (Chicago, 1979), 88, 99.

13. Allan H. Spear, *Black Chicago: The Making of a Negro Ghetto, 1890–1920* (Chicago, 1967), chapter 5; James R. Grossman, *Land of Hope: Chicago, Black Southerners, and the Great Migration* (Chicago, 1989), 94.

14. William Howland Kenney, *Chicago Jazz: A Cultural History, 1904–1930* (New York and Oxford, 1993), xiii, 3–34, 37–41.

15. http://chicago.urban-history.org/sites/theaters/th_bo_00.htm (April 7, 2006).

16. http://www.scottchilders.com/timecapsule/TCWMAQ.htm (April 6, 2006); http://www.richsamuels.com/nbcmm/wmaq/contents.html (April 6, 2006)

17. www.internationalpolka.com/hallof fame/1986/Zielinski.html (April 22, 2005).

18. www.worldseries.com (April 6, 2006).

19. Keith R. Gill, "Chicago Times-Herald Race of 1895," in Young, *Chicago Transit,* 55–56.

20. *Chicago Tribune,* December 12, 1897.

21. Young, *Chicago Transit,* 55–56

22. *Chicago Tribune,* June 30, 1899, July 8, 1899, May 8, 1900, August 4, 1900, December 11, 1902, February 24, 1905, September 26, 1907, March 22, 1910, April 23, 1913, February 13, 1915, January 28, 1917.

23. *Chicago Tribune,* March 20, 1901, March 22, 1901, March 24, 1901.

24. *Chicago Tribune,* January 6, 1925, January 8, 1925.

25. *Chicago Tribune,* January 25, 1925, October 31, 1929, November 1, 1929.

26. *Chicago Tribune,* January 1, 1925.

27. *Chicago Tribune,* January 1, 1929, January 2, 1929, January 1, 1930.

28. *Chicago Tribune,* August 1, 1929.

29. See the excellent map by Dennis McClendon on page 420 of James R. Grossman, Anne Durkin Keating, and Janice L. Reiff, eds., *The Encyclopedia of Chicago* (Chicago, 2004).

30. *Chicago Tribune,* January 20, 1925, April 26, 1925, May 13, 1925, June 5, 1925, August 20, 1925, August 30, 1925, October 1, 1925, March 6, 1930; Max Grinnell, in *Encyclopedia of Chicago.*

31. *Chicago Tribune,* March 5, 1927.

32. *Chicago Tribune,* February 15, 1927.

33. See Lawrence Bergreen, *Capone: The Man and the Era* (New York, 1994). This is the best book on Capone and his place in history.

34. John Landesco, *Organized Crime in Chicago, Part III of the Illinois Crime Survey, 1929* (Chicago, 1979), chapter One; Bergreen, *Capone,* 162–96.

35. Bergreen, *Capone,* 207–16.

36. *Chicago Tribune,* December 21, 1927.

37. *Chicago Tribune,* April 8, 1927.

38. *Chicago Tribune,* February 23, 1927, April 5, 1927, April 13, 1927.

39. *Chicago Tribune,* November 23, 1927, November 29, 1927

40. *Chicago Tribune,* December 6, 1927, December 7, 1927, December 18, 1927.

41. Bergreen, *Capone,* 305–15.

Chapter Eight

1. *Chicago Tribune,* August 25, 1931, October 4, 1931.

2. *Chicago Tribune,* February 25, 1930.

3. *Chicago Tribune,* February 28, 1930.

4. *Chicago Tribune,* March 13, 1930, June 29, 1930.

5. *Chicago Defender* (National Edition), February 14, 1931, April 23, 1932; Randi Storch, *Red Chicago: American Communism at Its Grass Roots, 1928–1935* (Urbana, Ill., 2007), 46, 58–59.

6. *Chicago Tribune,* August 28, 1930, November 12, 1930; Storch, *Red Chicago,* 33–34, 38.

7. *Chicago Tribune,* October 11, 1931.

8. *Chicago Tribune,* August 25, 1931; *Chicago Defender* (National Edition), December 20, 1930, January 10, 1931, December 6, 1931, January 2, 1932.

9. *Chicago Tribune,* September 8, 1931, November 1, 1932; *Chicago Defender* (National Edition), November 5, 1932.

10. *Chicago Defender* (National Edition), January 16, 1932; *Chicago Tribune,* July 16, 1932.

11. *Chicago Tribune,* October 13, 1932, October 27, 1932.

12. Douglas Bukowski, *Big Bill Thompson, Chicago, and the Politics of Image* (Urbana, Ill., 1998), 231–32.

13. *Chicago Tribune,* January 16, 1931.

14. Bukowski, *Big Bill Thompson,* 232.

15. *Chicago Tribune,* February 22, 1931.

16. *Chicago Tribune,* February 25, 1931.

17. *Chicago Tribune,* March 24, 1931.

18. Alex Gottfried, *Boss Cermak of Chicago: A Study of Political Leadership* (Seattle, 1962), 48–61, 169–204; *Chicago Tribune,* April 1, 1910.

19. *Chicago Tribune,* March 27, 1931, April 2, 1931, April 5, 1931, April 8, 1931; Gottfried, *Boss Cermak,* 235–37; Bukowski, *Big Bill Thompson,* 236.

20. Gottfried, *Boss Cermak,* 238–43.

21. Mary J. Herrick, *The Chicago Schools: A Social and Political History* (Beverly Hills, Calif., 1971), 187–90; *Chicago Tribune,* July 16, 1931, July 22, 1931, August 18, 1931.

22. Herrick, *The Chicago Schools,* 193–208; *Chicago Daily News,* November 16, 1932, November 21, 1932.

23. *Chicago Tribune,* September 29, 1931, August 9, 1933, January 25, 1932; Michael W. Homel, *Down from Equality: Black Chicagoans and the Public Schools, 1920–1941* (Urbana, Ill., 1984), 50; Herrick, *The Chicago Schools,* 209–15; *Chicago Tribune,* January 25, 1932; Roger Biles, *Big City Boss in Depression and War: Mayor Edward J. Kelly of Chicago* (DeKalb, Ill., 1984), 23; Gottfried, *Boss Cermak,* 238–87.

24. Gottfried, *Boss Cermak,* 288–335.

25. Quoted in Milton Rakove, *We Don't Want Nobody Nobody Sent: An Oral History of the Daley Years* (Bloomington, Ind., 1979), 9.

26. Biles, *Big City Boss,* 6–11.

27. See Biles, *Big City Boss.*

28. See the Chicago History Museum's Web site at http://www.chicagohs.org/history/century .html for an overview of the fair (July 24, 2006). For a study of the fair's architecture, see Lisa D. Schrenk, *Building a Century of Progress: The Architecture of Chicago's 1933–34 World's Fair* (Minneapolis, 2007).

29. *Chicago Tribune,* February 24, 1938, March 9, 1938.

30. *Chicago Tribune,* July 10, 1938, July 23, 1938, July 25, 1938, August 13, 1938.

31. *Chicago Tribune,* October 17, 1938, June 19, 1939.

32. *Chicago Tribune,* March 15, 1939, March 16, 1939; *Chicago Daily News,* March 15, 1939, March 16, 1939; *Zprava Tajemnika kIV. Sjezdu Cesekeho Národního Sdružení V Americe, konanem 1.,2. a 3, zá 1945 'v Chicagu,* 1–3; Handbill announcing the Masaryk talk, in Czechoslovak Heritage Museum, Library, and Archives, North Riverside, Ill.

33. See Clifford R. Shaw, *The Jack-Roller* (Chicago, 1966; original edition 1930); Frederick M. Thrasher, *The Gang* (Chicago, 1927); John Bartlow Martin, "A New Attack on Delinquency: How the Chicago Area Project Works," *Harper's Magazine* (May 1944), 502–3.

34. See Steven Schlossman and Michael Sedlak, *The Chicago Area Project Revisited* (Santa Monica, Calif., 1983); and Dominic A. Pacyga, "The Russell Square Community Committee: An Ethnic Response to Urban Problems," *Journal of Urban History,* February 1989, 159–84.

35. The two classic studies of the early years of the Back of the Yards Neighborhood Council are Robert A. Slayton, *Back of the Yards: The Making of a Local Democracy* (Chicago, 1986), and Thomas J. Jablonsky, *Pride in the Jungle: Community and Everyday Life in Back of the Yards Chicago* (Baltimore, 1993).

36. Jack M. Stein, "A History of Unionization in the Steel Industry in the Chicago Area" (MA thesis, University of Chicago, 1948), 38–66.

37. Robert A. Slayton, "Labor and Urban Politics: District 31, Steel Workers Organizing Committee, and the Chicago Machine," *Journal of Urban History,* November 1996, 39–41.

38. For a series of interviews regarding these events, see Alice and Staughton Lynd, eds., *Rank and File: Personal Histories by Working-Class Organizers* (Princeton, N.J., 1973, 1981), 95–96.

39. Slayton, "Labor and Politics," 41–45.

40. *PWOC-CIO News,* October 1, 1938, November 5, 1938, December 5, 1938, December 12, 1938, February 20, 1939, March 20, 1939, April 17, 1939, July 26, 1939.

41. *Chicago Tribune,* October 5, 1939, October 7, 1939, October 10, 1939, October 17, 1939.

42. *Chicago Tribune,* October 21, 1939, January 18, 1940, February 10, 1940.

43. *Chicago Tribune,* February 29, 1940, February 26, 1940, March 11, 1940, April 4, 1940, September 15, 1940.

44. *Chicago Tribune,* March 6, 1941.

45. *Chicago Tribune,* October 2, 1941.

46. Perry Duis and Scott LaFrance, *We've Got a Job to Do: Chicagoans and World War II* (Chicago, 1992), 33–34. Surprisingly, there is little written about Chicago's role in World War II. This book, which served as a catalog for an exhibition at the Chicago History Museum, is the best overall look at the city's wartime experience.

47. *Chicago Tribune,* December 9, 1941.

48. Duis and LaFrance, *We've Got a Job to Do,* 67–70.

49. *Chicago Tribune,* December 11, 1942, January 8, 1942, January 11, 1942.

50. *Chicago Tribune,* January 14, 1942, March 12, 1942.

51. Duis and LaFrance, *We've Got a Job to Do*, 8–9, 14.

52. *Chicago Herald-American*, September 5, 1943, September 8, 1943, September 15, 1943, September 16, 1943, September 17, 1943; *Chicago Defender* (National Edition), April 1, 1944, June 24, 1944, February 6, 1943.

53. Duis and LaFrance, *We've Got a Job to Do*, 40–42, 48–57, 92–102.

54. *The Columbian* (a newsletter of the employees of Columbia Aircraft Production, Inc. Somerville, N.J.), July 14, 1944.

55. See Marilynn Johnson, *The Second Gold Rush: Oakland and the East Bay in World War II* (Berkeley, Calif., 1993).

56. The best look at western expansion is Carl Abbott, *The Metropolitan Frontier: Cities in the Modern West* (Tucson, Ariz., 1993).

57. Philip M. Hauser and Evelyn M. Kitagawa, eds., *Local Community Fact Book for Chicago, 1950* (Chicago, 1953).

58. *Chicago Defender*, January 23, 1943, June 26, 1943, September 25, 1943, February 5, 1944; Duis and LaFrance, *We've Got a Job to Do*, 84.

Chapter Nine

1. "Clouter with Conscience," *Time*, March 15, 1963. Retrieved from http://www.time.com /time/archive/preview/0,10987,870170,00.html (June 4, 2005).

2. Chicago folksinger Steve Goodman wrote a song "Daley's Dead" in which he remarked, "What if heaven was like the 11th Ward and you had to know someone to get your just reward?"

3. My discussion of Daley relies heavily on Roger Biles's outstanding biography, *Richard J. Daley: Politics, Race, and the Governing of Chicago* (DeKalb, Ill., 1995).

4. Fay Lee Robertson, "A Study of Some Aspects of Racial Succession in the Woodlawn Community Area of Chicago" (masters thesis, University of Chicago, 1955), 40–43. St. Clair Drake and Horace R. Cayton's classic study of Chicago's African American community, *Black Metropolis: A Study of Negro Life in an American City*, 2 vols. (revised and expanded edition, New York, 1970) remains a crucial source for the development of the black community.

5. For a brief history of Woodlawn, see Evelyn M. Kitagawa and Karl E. Taeber, eds., *Local Community Fact Book: Chicago Metropolitan Area, 1960* (Chicago, 1963), 98–99; Chicago Fact Book Consortium, ed., *Local Community Fact Book: Chicago Metropolitan Area, 1990* (Chicago, 1995), 138–39. For the period in the 1950s and early 1960s, see Irving A. Spergel and Richard E. Mundy, "A Community Study, East Woodlawn: Problems, Programs, Proposals" (report, School of Social Service Administration, University of Chicago, 1963). Jack Lait and Lee Mortimer, *Chicago Confidential* (New York, 1950), 291.

6. The classic study of this process, which also gave the name the "Second Ghetto," is Arnold Hirsch, *Making the Second Ghetto: Race and Housing in Chicago, 1940–1960* (Chicago, 1998).

7. Interview with Prentiss and George Jackson, January 16, 1998; interview with Angeline Jackson, January 6, 1997.

8. Interview with Prentiss and George Jackson.

9. Chicago Daily News, April 28, 1959.

10. Interview with Theodore J. Swigon, Jr., December 26, 1997.

11. Interview with John Rosenthal, January 7, 1997.

12. Interview with Swigon.

13. For a history of St. Xavier University, see Joy Clough, RSM, *First in Chicago: A History of Saint Xavier University* (Chicago, 1997).

14. *New World*, November 11, 1958, August 22, 1958, August 29, 1958.

15. Rev. John J. McMahon, *City of Chicago Catholic Map and Directory, 1954/1955* (Chicago, 1954). Rev. Msgr. Harry C. Koening, STD, ed., *A History of the Parishes of the Archdiocese of Chicago*, 2 vols. (Chicago, 1980).

16. The best discussion of the Hyde Park urban renewal program is Hirsch, *Making The Second Ghetto* (Chicago, 1998). See chapter 5. Letter quoted in *Chicago Defender* (City Edition), October 4, 1958.

17. *Chicago Daily News*, April 23, 1958; *Woodlawn Booster*, July 1, 1958, July 23, 1958.

18. "Special Bulletin—United Woodlawn Conference," July 29, 1958," WBCC Papers, Box 1, Folder 11. *Woodlawn Booster*, July 30, 1958, November 19, 1958, January 28, 1959; Letter to Julian Levi from Ruth C. Porter, April 28, 1958, in Despres Collection, Box 203, File 5.

19. Robert Slayton, *Back of the Yards: The Making of a Local Democracy*, 227–28; Thomas J. Jablonsky, *Pride in the Jungle: Community and Everyday Life in Back of the Yards Chicago* (Baltimore, 1993), 148.

20. John T. McGreevy, *Parish Boundaries: The Catholic Encounter with Race in the Twentieth-Century Urban North* (Chicago, 1996), 110–11.

21. New World, April 25, 1958. Also see Rudolph M. Unger, The Community of Fuller Park: Those Were the Days My Friend (self-published, 1997).

22. *New World,* May 16, 1958.

23. *New World,* June 20, 1958, September 26, 1958.

24. *Chicago Defender* (City Edition), March 16, 1957; *Chicago Daily Defender,* June 27, 1957.

25. *Chicago Defender* (City Edition), March 16, 1957.

26. *Chicago Defender* (City Edition), March 16, 1957; *Chicago Daily Tribune,* March 13, 1957, March 14, 1957.

27. *Chicago Daily Tribune,* March 13, 1957, March 14, 1957, March 18, 1957; *Chicago Defender* (City Edition), March 16, 1957.

28. *Chicago Daily Defender,* March 18, 1957.

29. *Chicago Daily Defender,* March 20, 1957, June 27, 1957; Interview with Brothers Michael Griffin and Basil Rothweiler, FSC.

30. While working-class white neighborhoods reacted to any African American presence as a threat, the black middle-class experience thrived on a part of the South Side and in such summer places as Idlewild, Michigan. For an excellent description of the African American middle-class experience, see Robert B. Stepto, *Blue as the Lake: A Personal Geography* (Boston, 1998).

31. Quoted in Richard Harris, "Chicago's Other Suburbs," *Geographical Review,* 84, no. 4 (1994). Retrieved from www.questia.com (June 3, 2005).

32. Austin Weber, "The Hawthorne Works," *Assembly Magazine,* August 14, 2002. Retrieved from http://www.assemblymag.com/CDA/ArticleInformation/coverstory/BNPCoverStoryItem/0,6490,98914,00.html (June 9, 2005).

33. Harris, "Chicago's Other Suburbs."

34. Pierre de Vise, *A Social Geography of Metropolitan Chicago: Trends and Characteristics of Municipalities in the Chicago Metropolitan Area* (Chicago, 1960).

35. See Arnold R. Hirsch, *The Making of the Second Ghetto,* chapter 1.

36. *New World,* January 24, 1958.

37. De Vise, *A Social Geography of Metropolitan Chicago,* 20–25.

38. Irving Cutler, *The Chicago-Milwaukee Corridor: A Geographic Study of Intermetropolitan Coalescence,* Northwestern University, Studies in Geography No. 9 Evanston, Ill., 1965), 163–73, 193–94, 228–29.

39. Chicago Plan Commission, Chicago Industrial Study, Summary Report (Chicago, 1952).

40. Todd J. Tobutis, "Park Forest," *Encyclopedia of Chicago*. Retrieved from http://www.encyclopedia.chicagohistory.org/pages/957.html (June 10, 2005). See also Gregory C. Randall, *Amer-*

ica's Original G.I. Town: Park Forest, Illinois (Baltimore, 2000). See the Park Forest Public Library Web site. Retrieved from http://www.pfpl.org/PARKFOR.html (June 10, 2005).

41. Interview Leona DeLue, http://www.eliillinois.org/30531_00/HTML/ohtranscriptsleona-delue.htm (June 10, 2005).

42. For an excellent look at the diversity of Chicago's railroad suburbs, see Ann Durkin Keating, *Chicagoland: City and Suburbs in the Age of the Railroad* (Chicago, 2005); de Vise, *A Social Geography of Metropolitan Chicago,* 20–25.

43. Glen Holt and Dominic A. Pacyga, *Chicago: An Historical Guide to the Neighborhoods* (Chicago, 1979), chapter 2.

44. "Prince in Armour," *Time,* September 16, 1957. Retrieved from http://www.time.com/time/archive/preview/0,10987,809926,00.html?internalid=related (June 1, 2005).

45. "Armour to Halt Slaughtering Operations at Chicago and Six Other Meat Plants," *National Provisioner,* June 13, 1959, 34; "Equipment at Three Closed Armour Plants to be Sold," *National Provisioner,* July 18, 1959, 54. "Armour's Star," *Time,* March 3, 1961. Retrieved from http://www.time.com/time/archive/preview/0,10987,897706,00.html?internalid=related (June 1, 2005). "Huge Cattle Feeding Program Gets Underway in Alabama," *Butchers' Advocate,* January 21, 1959, 6; *Swift & Company Year Book* (Chicago, 1956, 1959, 1960, 1961); *Butchers' Advocate,* April 1, 1959, 39.

46. "The Prince, the General, and the Greyhound," *Time,* May 9, 1969. Retrieved from http://www.time.com/time/archive/preview/0,10987,844837,00.html?internalid=related (June 1, 2005).

47. Zarko G. Bilbija and Ezra Solomon, *Metropolitan Chicago: An Economic Analysis* (Glencoe, 1959). Retrieved from www.questia.com (June 4, 2005). Chicago Plan Commission, Chicago Industrial Study, Summary Report (Chicago, 1952), 9. Joseph Russell, Jerome D. Fellman, and Howard G. Roepke, *The St. Lawrence Seaway: Its Impact, by 1965, upon Industry of Metropolitan Chicago and Illinois Waterway-Associated Areas,* 2 vols. (Chicago, 1959), 1:10–13; Ray Vicker, "From Sand Dunes to Steel," in *The Chicago Story,* ed. Alan Sturdy (Chicago, 1954), 3, 44–45, 312–16; Russell Freburg, "Candy Capital of the World," in Sturdy, ed., *Chicago Story,* 48, 331–32.

48. South Side Planning Board, An Opportunity to Rebuild Chicago through Industrial Development of the Central South Side (Chicago, 1953).

Chapter Ten

1. Roger Biles, *Richard J. Daley: Politics, Race, and the Governing of Chicago* (DeKalb, Ill., 1995), 32–35.

2. "Clouter with a Conscience," *Time,* March 15, 1963. Retrieved from http://www.time.com/time/archive/preview/0,10987,870170,00.html (June 4, 2005).

3. *Chicago Sunday Tribune,* January 4, 1959.

4. For downtown development, see Carl Condit, *Chicago, 1930–1970: Building, Planning, and Technology* (Chicago, 1974). See table 2 for statistics on Loop construction. For the struggle over the location of the University of Illinois at Chicago Circle, see George Rosen, *Decision-Making Chicago-Style: The Genesis of a University of Illinois Campus* (Urbana, Ill., 1980); *Chicago Daily News,* January 6, 1959.

5. Sudhir Alladi Venkatesh, *American Project: The Rise and Fall of a Modern Ghetto* (Cambridge, 2000), ix.

6. Devereux Bowly, Jr., *The Poorhouse: Subsidized Housing in Chicago, 1895–1976* (Carbondale, Ill., 1978), 18–33.

7. Bowly, *The Poorhouse,* 34–55.

8. For the impact of Home Owners Loan Corporation and the Federal Housing Administration,

see both Arnold Hirsch, *Making the Second Ghetto: Race and Housing in Chicago, 1940–1960* (Chicago, 1998), and Kenneth Jackson, *Crabgrass Frontier: The Suburbanization of the United States* (New York, 1985).

9. D. Bradford Hunt, "Understanding Chicago's High-Rise Public Housing Disaster," in *Chicago Architecture: Histories, Revisions, Alternatives,* ed. Charles Waldheim and Katerina Rüedi Ray (Chicago, 2005), 301–13.

10. Bowly, *The Poorhouse,* 115–16.

11. *Chicago Defender* (City Edition), June 19, 1957.

12. Bowly, *The Poorhouse,* 124–25.

13. Janet L. Smith, "Diminishing High-Rise Public Housing," in Waldheim and Ray, eds., *Chicago Architecture,* 292–300.

14. Quoted in Sudhir Alladi Venkatesh, *American Project,* 13–14.

15. See J. S. Fuerst, *When Public Housing Was Paradise* (Urbana, Ill., 2005). "Project rats" quote from Smith, "Diminishing High-Rise Public Housing," 298

16. Gregory D. Squires, Larry Bennett, Kathleen McCourt, and Philip Nyden, *Chicago: Race, Class, and the Response to Urban Decline* (Philadelphia, 1987), 102–9.

17. *Chicago Daily Tribune,* January 1, 1959. For the impact of the city government on the rapidly changing racial scene of Chicago's West Side, see Amanda Seligman, *Block by Block: Neighborhood and Public Policy on Chicago's West Side* (Chicago, 2005). For the reaction of a single ethnic group and a parish neighborhood to racial change, see the excellent study by Eileen M. McMahon, *What Parish Are You From? A Chicago Irish Community and Race Relations* (Lexington, Ky., 1995).

18. Chicago Daily News, January 2, 1959.

19. Ray, The *American Automobile,* 180–89; *NADA Magazine,* January 1958, 32–34; *Chicago Daily Tribune,* December 24, 1958.

20. *Chicago Daily Tribune,* December 18, 1958, December 26, 1958; Jon C. Teaford, *The Rough Road to Renaissance: Urban Revitalization in America, 1940–1985* (Baltimore: John Hopkins University Press, 1990), 103.

21. See Dominic A. Pacyga, "The Busiest, the Most Dangerous, the Dan Ryan," in Jay Wolke, *Along the Divide: Photographs of the Dan Ryan Expressway* (Chicago, 2004).

22. *Chicago Daily News,* December 26, 1958.

23. David Cowan and John Kuenster, *To Sleep with the Angels: The Story of a Fire* (Chicago, 1996).

24. *Chicago Daily Tribune*, December 15, 1958, December 25, 1958.

25. *Chicago Daily Tribune,* April 2, 1959, April 5, 1959, April 8, 1959, April 9, 1959, April 22, 1959.

26. Quoted in F. Richard Ciccone, *Daley: Power and Presidential Politics* (Chicago, 1996), 16. This is perhaps the best look at Daley as a presidential power broker.

27. Joe Smith, *Sin Corner and Joe Smith: A Story of Vice and Corruption in Chicago* (New York, 1963), is an autobiographical account by an African American involved in the scandal. For the Summerdale scandal, see Richard C. Lindberg, *To Serve and Collect: Chicago Politics and Police Corruption from the Lager Beer Riots to the Summerdale Scandal* (New York, 1991), chapter 11.

28. Ciccone, *Daley,* chapter 2.

29. Ciccone, *Daley,* 5–6.

30. Biles, *Daley,* 71–73.

31. Quoted in Ciccone, D*aley,* 135.

32. Biles, *Daley,* 73–74.

33. Adam Cohen and Elizabeth Taylor, *American Pharaoh: Mayor Richard J. Daley—His Battle for Chicago and the Nation* (Boston, New York, and London, 2000), 280–83.

34. "Clouter with a Conscience."

35. Biles, *Daley,* 77–83.

36. Quoted in Cohen and Taylor, *American Pharaoh,* 310.

37. See Ciccone, *Daley,* chapter 7. Quote from LBJ on p. 186.

38. All quotes from Cohen and Taylor, *American Pharaoh,* 318–19.

39. Quoted in Ciccone, *Daley,* 192–93.

40. James R. Ralph, Jr., *Northern Protest: Martin Luther King, Jr., Chicago, and the Civil Rights Movement* (Cambridge, 1993), chapter 1.

41. Quoted in Ciccone, 123.

42. Ralph, *Northern Protest,* 218–19.

43. *Chicago Tribune,* December 31, 1967.

44. *Chicago Tribune,* January 1, 1968.

45. Ciccone, *Daley,* 224–27.

46. Quoted in Biles, *Daley,* 144.

47. *Chicago Tribune,* April 7, 1968.

48. Biles, *Daley,* 146–47.

49. Quoted in *Chicago Tribune,* April 7, 1968.

50. David Farber, *Chicago '68* (Chicago, 1994), 165–67.

51. Farber, *Chicago '68,* chapter 7.

52. Biles, *Daley,* 168–82; *Chicago Tribune,* July 29, 1970.

53. Biles, *Daley,* 190–96.

54. Quoted in Biles, *Daley,* 197.

55. See Biles, *Daley,* chapter 9, for the mounting scandals.

Chapter Eleven

1. See Frost's biography on the History Makers Web site, www.thehistorymakers.com/biography/biography.asp?bioindex=530&category=politicalMakers (June 18, 2005).

2. See the St. Jerome Croatian Catholic Parish Web site, http://www.stjeromecroatian.org/eng/bilandic.html (June 20, 2005).

3. Retrieved from Chicago Public Library Web site on Chicago disasters, http://www.chipublib.org/004chicago/disasters/snowstorms.html (June 19, 2005).

4. See David Bensman and Roberta Lynch, *Rusted Dreams: Hard Times in a Steel Community* (New York, 1987).

5. Linda Pendelton, *Portrait of a Steelworker,* http://www.globalchicago.org/reports/arch/MedillReport/portrait%20f%20a%20steel%20worker.pdf (June 20, 2005, 2–3).

6. For a look at the early years of the steel industry, see Dominic Pacyga, *Polish Immigrants and Industrial Chicago: Workers on the South Side, 1880–1922* (Chicago, 2002).

7. I witnessed much of what is described in this section as the associate director of the Southeast Chicago Historical Project between 1980 and 1984.

8. David Bensman and Mark R. Wilson, "Iron and Steel," in *Encyclopedia of Chicago,* http://www.encyclopedia.chicagohistory.org/pages/653.html (June 20, 2005).

9. Austin Weber, "The Hawthorne Works," *Assembly Magazine* (August 14, 2002). Retrieved from http://www.assemblymag.com/CDA/ArticleInformation/coverstory/BNPCoverStoryItem 0,6490,98914,00.html (June 10, 2005). For the MJ Railway, see Manufacturer's Junction Railway, http://www.omnitrax.com/mj.shtml retrieved (June 20, 2005).

10. *Chicago Tribune,* June 28, 1987; Connie Lauerman, "The Clybourn Experiment—the Fit May Not Be Perfect, but the Goal Is to Gentrify an Urban-Wasteland without Losing Its Industrial Muscle," *Chicago Tribune Sunday Magazine,* February 18, 1990.

11. Lester Thurow, "Why Their World Might Crumble: How Much Inequality Can a Democracy Take?" *New York Times Magazine,* November 19, 1995. Janet L. Abu-Lughod, *New York, Chicago, and Los Angeles: America's Global Cities* (Minneapolis, 1999), 274–78.

12. Abu-Lughod, *America's Global Cities,* 322–27. For the growth of Western cities as a result of the war, see Carl Abbott, *Metropolitan Frontier: Cities in the Modern American West* (Tucson, Ariz., 1993); Ann Markusen, Peter Hall, Sabina Dietrich, and Scott Campbell, *The Rise of the Gunbelt: The Military Remapping of Industrial America* (New York, 1991).

13. For a fascinating account of the development of Dearborn Park and how Chicago's business community worked together, see Lois Wille, *At Home in the Loop: How Clout and Community Built Chicago's Dearborn Park* (Carbondale, Ill., 1997).

14. Quoted in Ellen Warren, "Jane Byrne Reconsidered: No Apologies, No Regrets" *Chicago Tribune Magazine,* December 5, 2004, 14.

15. Samuel K. Gove and Louis H. Masotti, *After Daley: Chicago Politics in Transition* (Urbana, Ill., 1982), xi.

16. Jane Byrne, *My Chicago* (Evanston, Ill., 2003), 271–75.

17. For an interesting early psychological look at Jane Byrne, see Kathleen Whalen Fitzgerald, *Brass: Jane Byrne and the Pursuit of Power* (Chicago, 1981).

18. Wille, *At Home in the Loop,* 106–21.

19. Paul M. Green, "The 1983 Democratic Mayoral Primary: Some New Players—Same Old Rules," in *The Making of the Mayor: Chicago 1983,* ed. Melvin G. Holli and Paul M. Green (Grand Rapids, Mich., 1984), 17–38. Also see Paul Kleppner, *Chicago Divided: The Making of a Black Mayor* (DeKalb, Ill., 1985).

20. Don Rose, "How the 1983 Election Was Won," in Holli and Green, eds., *Making of the Mayor,* 101–24.

21. William J. Grimshaw, *Bitter Fruit: Black Politics and the Chicago Machine, 1931–1991* (Chicago, 1992), 185–86.

22. Melvin G. Holli and Paul M. Green, *Bashing Chicago's Traditions: Harold Washington's Last Campaign* (Grand Rapids, Mich., 1989), 27–33.

23. For a discussion of Washington's economic policies, see Pierre Clavel and Wim Wiewel, eds., *Harold Washington and the Neighborhoods: Progressive City Government in Chicago, 1983–1987* (New Brunswick, N.J., 1991).

24. Ross Miller, *Here's the Deal: The Buying and Selling of a Great American City* (New York, 1996), 182.

25. Quoted in Holli and Jones, *Bashing Chicago Traditions,* 50.

26. Most of this discussion of the 1987 election was taken from Holli and Jones, *Bashing Chicago Traditions; Chicago Tribune,* April 8, 1987.

27. Quoted in Holli and Jones, *Bashing Chicago Traditions,* 188.

28. *Chicago Tribune,* November 26, 1987.

29. *Chicago Sun-Times,* December 2, 1987; *Chicago Tribune,* December 7, 1987; Gary Rivlin, *Fire on the Prairie: Chicago's Harold Washington and the Politics of Race* (New York, 1992), 413–20.

30. For a discussion of the 1989 campaign and election, see Paul M. Green and Melvin G. Holli, eds., *Restoration 1989: Chicago Elects a New Daley* (Chicago, 1991).

31. *Chicago Sun-Times,* December 6, 1990, April 7, 1991; Dick Simpson, *Rogues, Rebels, and Rubber Stamps: The Politics of the Chicago City Council from 1863 to the Present* (Boulder, Colo., 2001), 253–62.

32. *Chicago Tribune,* November 25, 1996, December 1, 1996; *Chicago Sun-Times,* January 24, 1996, November 15, 1996.

33. *Chicago Sun-Times,* April 23, 2003.

34. For a discussion of Daley's approach and possible alternatives, see Joel Rast, *Remaking Chicago: The Political Origins of Industrial Change* (DeKalb, Ill., 1999).

35. *Chicago Tribune,* January 4, 2000.

36. Fassil Demissie, "Globalization and the Remaking of Chicago," in *The New Chicago: A Social and Cultural Analysis,* ed. James B. Koval, Larry Bennett, Michael I. J. Bennett, Fassil Demissie, Roberta Garner, and Kijong Kim (Philadelphia, 2006), 24–27.

37. David Moberg, "Economic Restructuring: Chicago's Precarious Balance," in Koval et al., eds., *The New Chicago*, 32–43.

38. Andrew J. Krmenec, "Chicago: Transportation and Trade Gateway to the Midwest," in *Chicago's Geographies: Metropolis of the 21st Century,* ed. Richard P. Greene, Mark J. Bouman and Dennis Grammenos (Washington, D.C., 2006), 87–102; "ProLogis Acquires Illinois Land for Logistics Park," *Reuters,* June 11, 2007. Retrieved from www.reuters.com/article /companyNewsAndPR/idUSN1146469520070611 (August 28, 2007). "Exurbia on Board with Railport; Union Pacific Finds a Welcome Site," *Crain's Chicago Business*, March 26, 2001.

39. *Chicago Tribune,* October 21, 2006, December 8, 2006, January 12, 2007.

40. Marc Doussard and Nik Theodore, "From Job Loss to Jobless Recovery: Chicago's 30 Years of Uneven Growth," in Greene et al., eds., *Chicago's Geographies*, 103–12.

41. Koval et al., eds., *The New Chicago,* contains various articles on Chicago's newest immigrant groups.

42. The best discussion of this post-Solidarity immigration and their reception by the older Polish American community in Chicago is Mary Patrice Erdmans, *Opposite Poles: Immigrants and Ethnics in Polish Chicago, 1976–1990* (University Park, Pa., 1998).

43. Mary Patrice Erdmans, "New Chicago Polonia: Urban and Suburban," in Koval et al., eds., *The New Chicago*, 115–27; *Chicago Sun-Times,* December 8, 1996.

44. Dennis Grammenos, "Latino Chicago" in Greene et al., eds., *Chicago's Geographies*, 205–16. For the early history of Mexican immigration to Chicago, see Gabriela F. Arrendondo, *Mexican Chicago: Race, Identity, and Nation, 1916–1939* (Urbana, Ill., 2008).

45. For a look at the impact of Latino immigration on Chicago, see Wilfredo Cruz, *City of Dreams: Latino Immigration to Chicago* (Lanham, Md., 2007). Two excellent studies of Puerto Rican Chicago are Ana Y. Ramos-Zayas, *National Performances: The Politics of Class, Race, and Space in Puerto Rican Chicago* (Chicago, 2003), and Gina M. Perez, *The Near Northwest Side Story: Migration, Displacement, and Puerto Rican Families* (Berkeley, Calif., 2004).

46. Siyoung Park, Su-Yeul Chung, and Jongnam Choi, "Asians in Chicago" in Greene et al., eds., *Chicago's Geographies*, 217–31. For an excellent study of the city's Indian community, see Padma Rangaswamy, *Namaste America: Indian Immigrants in an American Metropolis* (University Park, Pa., 2000).

47. Much of this discussion comes from Daniel J. Hammel, "Public Housing Chicago Style: Transformation or Elimination?" in Greene et al., eds., *Chicago's Geographies*, 172–88. See also Larry Bennett, "Transforming Public Housing," in Koval et al., eds., *The New Chicago*, 269–76.

48. Mary Pattillo, *Black on the Block: The Politics of Race and Class in Chicago* (Chicago, 2007), 7. This is the best study of black on black gentrification in Chicago.

49. Quoted in Pattillo, *Black on the Block*, 85. For figures on African American income and the role of the University of Chicago, see 10–11.

50. For a recent look at the impact of racial and ethnic groups on Chicago's neighborhoods, see William Julius Wilson and Richard P. Taub, *There Goes the Neighborhood: Racial, Ethnic, and Class Tensions in Four Chicago Neighborhoods and Their Meaning for America* (New York, 2006).

51. Gregory D. Squires, Larry Bennett, Kathleen McCourt, and Philip Nyden, *Chicago: Race, Class and the Response to Urban Decline* (Philadelphia, 1987), 24; Larry Bennett, "Transforming Public Housing," in Koval et al., *The New Chicago,* 269–76.

52. *Chicago Tribune,* February 21, 1990, February 22, 1990.

53. For Millennium Park, see Timothy J. Gilfoyle, *Millennium Park: Creating a Chicago Landmark* (Chicago, 2006); for sports stadiums including Soldier Field, see Costas Spirou and Larry Bennett, *It's Hardly Sportin': Stadiums, Neighborhoods, and the New Chicago* (DeKalb, Ill., 2003).

Index